War Crimes and Just War

War crimes are international crimes committed during armed conflict. Larry May argues that the best way to understand war crimes is as crimes against humaneness rather than as violations of justice. He shows that in a deeply pluralistic world, we need to understand the rules of war as the collective responsibility of states that send their citizens into harm's way, as the embodiment of humanity, and as the chief way for soldiers to retain a sense of honor on the battlefield. Humanitarian considerations of mercy and compassion count morally in war, even if soldiers fight with just cause and their opponents have committed atrocities. Throughout, May demonstrates that the principle of humaneness is the cornerstone of international humanitarian law and is itself the basis of the traditional principles of discrimination, necessity, and proportionality. He draws extensively on the older Just War tradition to assess recent cases from the International Criminal Tribunal for Yugoslavia as well as examples of atrocities from the archives of the International Committee of the Red Cross.

LARRY MAY is professor of philosophy at Washington University in St. Louis. He is the author of several books, including *The Morality of Groups, Sharing Responsibility*, and *Crimes Against Humanity*, the first book in a trilogy of volumes on the normative foundations of international criminal law. *War Crimes and Just War*, the second volume in the trilogy, received the Frank Chapman Sharp Prize from the American Philosophical Association.

War Crimes and Just War

LARRY MAY
Washington University, St. Louis

CAMBRIDGE
UNIVERSITY PRESS

CAMBRIDGE UNIVERSITY PRESS
Cambridge, New York, Melbourne, Madrid, Cape Town, Singapore, São Paulo, Delhi

Cambridge University Press
32 Avenue of the Americas, New York, NY 10013-2473, USA

www.cambridge.org
Information on this title: www.cambridge.org/9780521691536

© Larry May 2007

First published 2007
Reprinted 2008

Printed in the United States of America

A catalog record for this publication is available from the British Library.

Library of Congress Cataloging in Publication Data
May, Larry
War crimes and just war / Larry May
p. cm.
Includes bibliographical references and index.
ISBN 0-521-87114-X (hardback) – ISBN 0-521-69153-2 (pbk.)
1. War (Philosophy) I. Title.

B105.W3M39   2006
172'.4'5–dc22   2006014489

ISBN 978-0-521-87114-3 hardback
ISBN 978-0-521-69153-6 paperback

Contents

Acknowledgments

The subject of war crimes is one that I first explored as a college senior at Georgetown University's School of Foreign Service in the early 1970s. I was then motivated by the revelations of the My Lai massacre. A few years later, while completing my Ph.D. in philosophy at the New School for Social Research, I had several discussions about the Nuremberg trials with Hannah Arendt, whom I was then assisting, that caused me to think hard about how 17th-century thinkers might have set the stage for such trials. Many years later, just after the Rome Treaty was signed in the late 1990s, I came back to this topic while attending a class on international criminal law taught by Leila Sadat at Washington University's School of Law. And most recently, I felt inspired to try to write about war crimes by developments since September 11, 2001. My work defending convicted murderers on appeal has also inspired my work on war crimes. At various points in my philosophical and legal careers, I have been intrigued by the fascinating literature in Just War theory. The idea behind the current volume is to try to provide a normative bridge between the classical Just War theory, especially of the 17th century, and prosecutions that occur in contemporary international humanitarian law.

I have been very lucky that several people have generously agreed to read and comment on drafts of this manuscript over the last two years. My greatest debt is to Marilyn Friedman, who read various versions of the manuscript chapters and gave meticulous comments. Many of her helpful ideas are now contained as my own in the text. Special thanks also go to Mark Drumbl, who came along near the end of the drafting process and gave me excellent suggestions about the whole manuscript, forcing me to engage better with international lawyers. Jeff McMahan has been quite generous with his time, and his comments on several chapters forced me to rethink what I say about the relationship between *jus ad bellum* and *jus in bello*. I would also like to thank Clare Palmer, who commented on a very early draft of the first half of the manuscript. Mark Rollins, my department chair, is to be thanked for finding me both time and financial support for this project.

In addition, I would like to thank the following people who commented on one or another of the chapters: Andy Altman, Jovan Babic, Jim Bohman, Eric Brown, Claudia Card, Angelo Corlett, Michael Davis, Leslie Francis, Gerald Gaus, Carol Gould, Thomas Hurka, Aleksandar Jokic, Ken Kipnis, Jack Knight, Bruce Landesman, Stephen Lee, David Luban, Alistair McLeod, Colin McLeod, Mark Murphy, Christian Nadeau, Linda Nicholson, Mark Osiel, Carol Prager, Andrew Rehfeld, Leila Sadat, Eric Schliesser, Nancy Sherman, Peter Weidenbeck, Carl Wellman, Kit Wellman, and Burleigh Wilkins.

I would also like to thank my students who sat through several graduate seminars in which I rehearsed some of these arguments. Steve Viner, Eric Rovie, Jeff Brown, and Emily Crookston were especially helpful here. I am grateful to Jeff Brown for research help on some of the international case law. Kimberly Mount was also very helpful in retrieving and updating recent cases for me. Mindy Danner helped sort out various technical problems with the production of the manuscript. Zach Hoskins did an excellent job constructing the Index. I am also grateful to my undergraduate students who took several courses on these topics and who also invited me to give various lectures on campus and to present, in a series of articles, some very preliminary views on these topics in their campus newspaper, *Student Life*.

Earlier versions of parts of this book appeared in journals or as book chapters. Chapter 2 appeared as the lead essay in an issue of the *Journal of Social Philosophy*. Chapter 5 appeared in *Ethics and International Affairs*. Chapter 10 appeared as the lead essay in an issue of the *International Journal of Applied Ethics*. Chapter 12 appeared in *Metaphilosophy*. Chapter 7 will be published in a volume of essays titled *Reconsidering Just War Theory*, published by Springer Verlag. And I presented versions of these chapters at conferences in Chicago, Granada (Spain), Jacksonville, Lund, Montreal, Oslo, Palo Alto, Pomona, San Francisco, Santa Barbara, and Washington, DC.

A first draft of this book won the American Philosophical Association's Frank Chapman Sharp Prize for the best unpublished work on the ethics of war and peace. This is the second volume of a projected multivolume work on the moral foundations of international criminal law. The first volume was published in 2005 as *Crimes Against Humanity: A Normative Account*. The third volume is tentatively called *Aggression and Crimes Against Peace*. Somewhere down the road, there will undoubtedly also be a volume on genocide, as I try to grapple philosophically with the most important crimes in this emerging field of law and normative jurisprudence.

Lastly, I am grateful to my daughter Elizabeth, who kept reminding me of the human side of these crimes. Even as I defend the "defendants" in international criminal law, I remain committed to the idea that there should be prosecutions for the horrendous crimes that will fill the pages of what follows.

War Crimes and Just War

1

Introduction

Justifying war but restricting tactics

A sense of honor may be said to forbid what the law permits.
Hugo Grotius, *De Jure Belli ac Pacis*, 1625, p. 716

This is a book about the normative foundations of international criminal law, specifically international humanitarian law, concerning the
violations of the rules and customs of war. The philosophy of international criminal law is both very old and very new. Debates about the
rules of war have been ongoing for several thousand years, culminating
in truly impressive and original work by Just War theorists in the 17th
century, especially Hugo Grotius and Samuel Pufendorf. But it is also
true that debates about the theoretical foundations of international
criminal law are only in their infancy in that relatively few articles and
books have been written about this subject since the Nuremberg trials,
an event that caused a sea change in the way international law addressed
war crimes. At Nuremberg, individuals rather than States were the
subject of prosecution for war crimes, and the defense of superior
orders was greatly curtailed. It is my hope to draw extensively on the
older, Just War, tradition, in ways that will make these older ideas
relevant for practitioners and theorists today, as well as to make political
philosophers working in the Just War tradition aware of recent cases
and legal theories that will enrich their philosophizing.

War crimes are crimes committed during armed conflict. In this book,
I argue that the best way to understand war crimes is as crimes against
humaneness. By this I mean that war crimes are not best understood as
crimes against the whole of humanity or as crimes of aggression or
even primarily as crimes against justice, but that they are violations of

1

the principle requiring that soldiers act humanely, that is with mercy and compassion, even as these same soldiers are allowed to kill enemy soldiers. The apparent paradox of this remark illustrates the conceptual problems of understanding, and normatively grounding, the idea of war crimes and of international prosecutions for such crimes.

The book tries to make sense of one of the ideas embedded in contemporary international law, namely that there are severe restrictions on how soldiers can fight in war, even if they fight with just cause and their opponents have committed atrocities. Humanitarian considerations of mercy and compassion count morally in war, and often these considerations are not reducible to considerations of justice. There are two reasons for thinking this. First, sometimes humanitarian considerations become duties because one has rendered another person completely dependent on one, by taking that person prisoner for instance, and that then create fiduciary or stewardship duties toward the one rendered dependent and vulnerable. Second, even if humanitarian considerations are not duties of soldiers, they must be adhered to if soldiers are to fight with honor. This is because soldiers, to be more than mere killers, must restrain themselves according to higher than normal standards of behavior. Honor is the key component in the way the military academies have trained soldiers for hundreds of years.

In this book, I explore whether a minimalist natural law theory can ground humanitarian restraints during war. This theory could help support many of the wide-ranging practices normally condemned by the rules of war and prosecutable as war crimes in international tribunals. The Just War tradition about *jus in bello*, the moral justification of using certain tactics in war, is confronted by very recent developments in international criminal law, especially concerning the law of war crimes. Ultimately, I develop a new understanding of the central principles that govern the rules of war. Drawing on literature in both moral philosophy and international law, this book attempts to reset the debate about war crimes in the 21st century.

I argue that the idea of war crimes can be made sense of and that prosecutions for war crimes can also be justified, but in a more restricted way than is normally thought. Specifically, major changes need to occur in how we distinguish combatants from civilians, in the way that we distinguish so-called conventional from unconventional weapons, and in the way in which we think we are entitled to act toward prisoners of war, even those who are illegal combatants. In making these changes, we will need to reconceptualize the main normative principles that have governed our understanding of what counts as a war crime: the traditional principles of discrimination (or "distinction" as it is called in legal circles), necessity, and proportionality, in light of what I regard as the cornerstone of the rules of war, the principle of humane treatment. Such a rethinking will also require, at the most fundamental level, a change in how we understand the universal moral or natural law basis of international law, the main subject of the early chapters of this book.

This book is the second volume of a projected multivolume set on the philosophical foundations of international criminal law. The volumes argue for a defendant-, rather than a victim-, oriented approach to international criminal law. Following the division of criminal law set out at the Nuremberg trials, the first volume dealt with crimes against humanity, this second volume deals with war crimes, and a third volume is projected to deal with crimes against peace. All three volumes proceed from a minimalist moral position indebted to 17th-century thinkers not normally linked: Thomas Hobbes, Hugo Grotius, and Samuel Pufendorf. The books draw on a rich historical tradition as a way to shed light on very recent conceptual and normative issues in international criminal law.

In the first section of this introductory chapter, I set out some of the main reasoning that has shaped the Just War tradition, specifically why some wartime tactics are justified and others are not. In the second section, I begin to explain what is involved in the principle of humane treatment, going back to the Roman philosopher Seneca for guidance. In the third section, I discuss the general idea that rules of war can be justified, even in just wars, and that these rules proscribe certain forms of treatment, regardless of whether the soldiers fight with just cause or not and even though the intentional killing of soldiers is itself justified. In the fourth section, I describe the differences between crimes against humanity and war crimes and discuss the difficulty of trying to categorize the very disparate provisions of the rules of war. And in the final section, I present a brief summary of the arguments of the four main parts of the book.

I. THE JUST WAR TRADITION AND WAR CRIMES

In the Just War tradition, a tradition that goes back at least two thousand years, the best-known theorist is Hugo Grotius, who wrote in the early 17th century. I will draw heavily on Grotius, and indeed the view that I espouse in this book could easily be called Grotian. Grotius is the most obvious bridge between contemporary war crimes law and the old Just War tradition because he is one of the few non-contemporary theorists to be included in a small group of experts in international law whose views are actually sources of international law.[1] But there are many other theorists in the Just War tradition who are regularly referred to by international legal scholars and even by courts today.

The close relation between Just War theory and the international law of war crimes is accepted by many scholars but not well explained. One explanation for this close relation is simply that the major categories of both Just War theory and international criminal law overlap. In Just War theory, there are two important questions: Was the decision to wage war morally justified (*jus ad bellum*), and were the tactics employed in war morally justified (*jus in bello*)? This Just War division is reflected in international criminal law's distinction between crimes against peace and war crimes. The decision to wage war in an aggressive manner is subject to prosecution as a crime against peace. The use of inhumane tactics during war is subject to prosecution as a war crime. Indeed, it is sometimes said in international law that crimes against peace are *jus ad bellum* violations and war crimes are *jus in bello* violations.[2]

Traditionally, *jus ad bellum* considerations were thought to be unrelated to *jus in bello* considerations. Similarly, there is generally no conceptual connection between crimes against peace and war crimes. I take up this point in greater detail in Chapter 2, arguing that war crimes should be conceptualized independently of considerations of whether those fighting in a war are fighting for a just cause or not. Contrary to what some theorists and politicians currently believe, the

---

[1] The Statute of the International Court of Justice, T.S. No. 993, 59 Stat. 1055 (June 26, 1945), article 38, identifies the sources of law that this international tribunal may refer to. These sources include "the teachings of the most highly qualified publicists of the various nations." Grotius is one of the only noncontemporary "publicists" recognized as falling under this category. There are also other sources that will be discussed subsequently.

[2] See *The Handbook of Humanitarian Law in Armed Conflicts*, edited by Dieter Fleck, Oxford: Oxford University Press, 1995, p. 1. "Although the subject of this Manual is the law applicable to the conduct of hostilities once a state has resorted to the use of force (the *ius in bello*) that law cannot be properly understood without some examination of the separate body of rules which determine when resort to force is permissible (the *ius ad bellum*)."

same tactical restraints should apply to all combatants, even those who are sometimes called "terrorists." This is at least as much due to what is important for "victim" soldiers as for the "victimizers," who must maintain a sense of honor even as they engage in intentional acts of killing that would – outside of war, with its unique code of moral conduct – be considered monstrous.

While I largely follow the Just War tradition in this book and hence take an explicitly moral approach to international relations and law, many of the positions I advance are equally at home with other approaches to international theory. For instance, my approach is not inconsistent with that of Hedley Bull and Benedict Kingsbury. Both of these theorists, like me, are influenced heavily by the work of Grotius. Hedley Bull supports a view he sometimes calls "solidarism," which seeks solutions to international problems by looking to the common good of a world where States are recognized as actors and which is strongly influenced by the success that consensual international organizations have achieved, most especially the United Nations, in solving global problems. In general, Bull supports the idea, which he associates with Grotius, that "States and rulers of states are bound by rules and form a society or community with one another, of however rudimentary a kind."[3] I also do not presume that there is more than a rudimentary global society or community and seek after principles that would reasonably guide States in that world.

Similarly, I think that my approach is also consistent with that of Benedict Kingsbury, who argues in favor of an "internationalized public law approach." This approach, he says,

cuts across the inside/outside distinction that has structured traditional public international law analysis and in doing so moves outside the standard parameters of pluralism and solidarism – but it does not correspond with approaches that locate the impetus for law in transnational interactions of global civil society.[4]

Kingsbury says that his approach differs from pluralist, or realist, approaches in that it does not depend on agreement among States, but

[3] Hedley Bull, "The Importance of Grotius in the Study of International Relations," in *Hugo Grotius and International Relations*, edited by Hedley Bull, Benedict Kingsbury, and Adam Roberts, Oxford: Oxford University Press, 1990, p. 71; also see his classic study *The Anarchical Society: A Study of Order in World Politics*, London: Macmillan, 1977.

[4] Benedict Kingsbury, "People and Boundaries: An 'Internationalized Public Law' Approach," in *States, Nations, and Borders*, edited by Allen Buchanan and Margaret Moore, Cambridge: Cambridge University Press, 2003, p. 303.

instead looks to extrapolate principles from how States actually have resolved disputes, especially within their own borders, as when one part of a federated State has a dispute with another part. This approach is also similar to my own, especially in Chapter 2, where I explain why it is in a State's interest to adopt rules of war that will restrain its soldiers who fight in foreign wars. Such reasons do not depend on there being a global civil society or generally a cosmopolitan moral theory, as was also true for 17th-century Just War theorists like Grotius.

Indeed, as will become clear, one of the central claims of this book is that the rules of war are grounded in concepts of honor and mercy, not necessarily in global justice. Honor is best understood within a particular population group, such as a group of soldiers of a particular nationality. Codes of honor can be grounded in a sense of integrity, where soldiers see themselves not as hired assassins but as members of a profession with rules restricting their behavior in often quite limiting ways. These rules and codes can also be grounded in universal moral principles, as I argue in Chapter 3, but they need not be. Codes of honor can be justified as dispute resolution mechanisms that operate especially well within given societies and that then form a model for how interstate disputes about the conduct of soldiers might be resolved as well. Generally, international criminal law can often find good guidance in domestic law.

Throughout this book, my focus is on war crimes and therefore on the *jus in bello* branch of Just War theory. In a future volume, I will address crimes against peace and the *jus ad bellum* branch of Just War theory.[5] "War crimes" is thus being used in its technical sense to mean only certain international crimes committed during war. There is a more popular use of the term "war crimes" that effectively equates all international crime with war crime. This is even seen in legal circles where the ad hoc international criminal tribunals at The Hague and Arusha, which involve prosecutions for genocide and crimes against humanity as well as for war crimes proper, are referred to as war crimes tribunals. I will be interested in the conceptual link and obvious parallels between war crimes understood narrowly and the *jus in bello* branch of Just War theory.

There is also a normative reason for why the Just War theory and the international law of war crimes are connected, as they will be in this

---

[5] That volume, now in draft, is tentatively called "Aggression and Crimes Against Peace."

book. International law generally, and international criminal law in particular, of which the international law of war crimes is one part, is in an early developmental stage today. As judges and legal scholars try to establish a normative jurisprudence of international criminal law, they are drawn to work in many fields. And as one might imagine, when looking for grounding principles, moral and political theorists are often referred to. It is as if international criminal law were being built from the ground up, often out of moral sources. As has been well recognized, law and morality merge at the point where law is first founded. I will not defend the mixing of law and morality, and I am certainly aware of the pitfalls to be avoided here. My point is only that emerging law often draws on moral sources, and the international criminal law is no exception.

The Just War tradition is a good starting point, primarily because of the way it forces us back to a moral ground that is more easily accessible. To answer the question of whether or not one State might be justified to go to war against another State, a question that initially seems daunting, we ask, for instance, about what we would consider justifiable if you, as an individual, were interacting with a stranger who has threatened you, challenging you to a duel for a perceived offense. While this strategy is not without its own difficulties, it seems intuitively plausible to many people who do not know how else to get started in thinking about war. In what follows, I will say something about what sort of moral questions seem apt when considering war, especially in the way that Just War theorists traditionally did, although there are significant criticisms of this approach that must be assessed as well.

It is normally assumed, based largely on the Just War tradition, that engaging in some wars can be justified. The difficulty is to explain why killing, even massive killing that is characteristic of war, can be considered justified while the use of certain tactics, such as the use of fragmentation bombs, or even tactics that fall short of killing, such as the destruction of cultural artifacts, are not considered justified in war. The intentional taking of life in combat is not condemned, but nonetheless restrictions are placed on how much suffering can be caused during such combat. The idea that during war certain acts of soldiers are morally and legally wrong seems initially to strain credulity. There has been a very healthy debate about such matters over the centuries. The founder of the Just War tradition, Augustine of Hippo, argued against the Early Church Fathers, who were largely pacifists.[6] Early Just War theorists argued that wars, especially wars to stop the slaughter of the innocent or wars to protect helpless States, could be justified, as could the killing that war involves, but that there were moral rules that had to be adhered to nonetheless.

The idea that needs normative support is that even in war there are moral or legal rules that require not that intentional killing be stopped, but that killing and its ancillary activities be conducted with moral restraint nonetheless. Just War theory was intimately connected to natural law theory, with its central idea that there were universally binding moral obligations that transcended culture, historical epoch, and circumstance. While many versions of both Just War theory and natural law theory have been proposed, it seems to me that Grotius was right that the most plausible approach admits the least number of principles or, put differently, that has a minimum of moral principles that are proposed. There is a secular natural law tradition, extending at least from the works of Grotius and Pufendorf, that is important for my theoretical arguments.[7]

The rules of war constitute a system of norms for regulating the behavior of States and their agents during war in the absence of a World State. And the system of norms is meant to apply to what is probably the most stressful of times, when war has broken out and both sides to a dispute not only call the other "enemy" but also can find no other way to resolve the dispute but to attempt physically to coerce or even annihilate each other. In such times, to have any agreement about what the rules of the game are must be seen as a good thing. Every time it is possible to get people who have sworn themselves to be enemies to stop and think before they assault or kill each other, surely much more good than harm has been achieved, even if the rules that produce the "stop-and-think" are themselves not as clear-cut as we might otherwise have hoped for.

II.   HUMANITARIAN CONCERNS

The area of law that is closest today to the *jus in bello* rules of war is sometimes called "international humanitarian law." Throughout this

---

[6] Augustine, *The City of God* (c. 420), translated by Henry Bettenson, New York: Penguin Books, 1984, Book 19, pp. 843, 861–862, 866–867.

[7] On this topic, see Richard Tuck, *The Rights of War and Peace*, Oxford: Oxford University Press, 1999; and J. B. Schneewind, *The Invention of Autonomy*, Cambridge: Cambridge University Press, 1998.

book, I will argue for a conception of humanitarian law that is a combination of morality and legality. It is for this reason that I, and others, have sought the roots of these principles in what has been called natural law theory, albeit a secular and minimalist version. Natural law theorists have traditionally not been as bothered by a porous border between law and morality as have other theorists. Indeed, natural law theorists have championed the view that this is the correct way to understand that border. The codes of honor and chivalry have also been based on moral principles, especially as they have connected their rules with natural human feelings of compassion and mercy. Such codes were premised on the idea that legal rules of conduct should reflect the moral virtues. As I will argue, in wartime the chief value that legal codes should be modeled on is the principle of humane treatment as more important than the principles of discrimination, necessity, or proportionality.

I will defend a Grotian approach to international humanitarian law in the next three chapters. To give a sense of the origins of this view, I wish to rehearse some of Seneca's ideas, advanced more than a thousand years before Grotius' time and upon which Grotius clearly built. In his great work, *De Jure Belli ac Pacis*, Grotius refers to Seneca many times, regarding him as one of the main authorities on the idea that soldiers should avoid cruelty, which Grotius believed to be central to how soldiers should conduct themselves.[8] After rehearsing some of Seneca's views, I will then provide a preliminary sense of how I will adapt these ideas in later chapters as I develop a normative grounding for international humanitarian law.

Seneca is one of the first philosophers seriously to consider the rules of war.[9] Writing at the end of the Roman Empire, Seneca wrote *De Clementia*, which explicitly talks about the restraints of war in terms of humanity and mercy. Seneca first proposes that we think of mercy as "leniency on the part of a superior towards an inferior in imposing punishment." After considering several other possible definitions of mercy, Seneca finally settles on defining it as something that "stops short of what could deservedly be imposed."[10] Seneca says of mercy that it has cruelty as its opposite. And cruelty is best understood, says

---

[8] Hugo Grotius, *De Jure Belli Ac Pacis* (On the Law of War and Peace) (1625), translated by Francis W. Kelsey, Oxford: Clarendon Press, 1925, p. 722.

[9] See Nancy Sherman, *Stoic Warriors*, Oxford: Oxford University Press, 2005.

[10] Seneca, *On Mercy*, Book 2, para. 3, in *Seneca: Moral and Political Essays*, edited by John M. Cooper and J. F. Procope, Cambridge: Cambridge University Press, 1995, p. 160.

Introduction

Seneca, as going "beyond the limit of anything humane or justifi-able."[11] Sternness is compatible with mercy, but cruelty is not. So, the obvious question is what more is involved in humane treatment than merely not being cruel. Seneca says that mercy may involve forgiveness but not pity. Indeed, he makes the telling statement that there are some people, "senile or silly, so affected by the tears of the nastiest criminal that, if they could, they would break open the prison. Pity looks at the plight, not at the cause of it. Mercy joins in with reason."[12]

So, for Seneca mercy is not merely a knee-jerk reaction to the misery of others. Rather, it is a rational consideration of what it is appropriate to do, grounded in one's feelings of common humanity. But the rea-sonable course is not necessarily that which is consistent with retribu-tion. Seneca goes on to say that some have understood Stoicism to be a doctrine that should eschew both pity and mercy. But Seneca again invokes the idea of humanity, saying: "[W]hat on earth is this science which tells us to unlearn our humanity."[13] And he then explains this idea by saying:

A wise man then will not feel pity. But he will be of help and service, born as he is to assist the community and promote the common good. Of this help he will give his part. Even unfortunates who deserve reproach and correction will be allowed a due measure of his kindness.[14]

Seneca eventually comes back to the Aristotelian position that the wise man judges "not by legal formula, but by what is equitable and good."[15] And this is not to do what is opposed to justice, but that which is in the fullest sense just, even though it is contrary to what is properly deserved as a matter of retribution. Here, Seneca, like Aristotle, looks to a broader conception of justice, one that involves more than mere retribution, although one that still seeks to give people what is their due. The idea is that even when a person has done wrong he may be "due a measure of kindness."[16] For there are several reasons why one has done wrong, many of which involve fortune or luck, and the wise man will struggle against this. "Whenever he can, he will intervene against fortune."[17] Concerning prisoners of war, Seneca says that they should be released "unharmed, sometimes even commended, if they had an honorable reason – loyalty, a treaty, their freedom – to drive them to war."[18]

[11] Ibid., para. 4, p. 161.   [12] Ibid., para. 5(1), p. 161.   [13] Ibid. para. 5(2), p. 162.
[14] Ibid., para. 6, p. 163.   [15] Ibid., para. 7, p. 164.   [16] Ibid., para. 6, p. 163.
[17] Ibid.   [18] Ibid., para. 7, p. 164.

Quite interestingly, Seneca says that mercy can sometimes take on the status of a duty, especially for rulers. Indeed, the duty is so strong that Seneca talked of rulers as being in a kind of slavery in that mercy was such a powerful burden of their office, one not felt by private individuals.[19] The ruler is often bound by duties that are not binding on normal people. For rulers are especially well placed to see when fortune is a factor and how best to counteract the effects of fortune while still giving to each what is his due, at least understood in a larger context than mere retribution. One way to interpret this is that it is the status of ruler and ruled that changes things morally, and indeed it is status rather than past conduct that drives Seneca to advocate for humaneness and mercy, especially in times of war. For this reason, I see Seneca as one of the first to begin to articulate the moral grounding for the rules of war in a way that is consistent with Grotius' and my own view of placing humane treatment rather than justice at the center of humanitarian law.

The situations of war and the institutions created during war, such as prisoner-of-war camps, change the normal moral situation. This is mainly because the circumstances of war make all of us into different people than we would be otherwise. Especially in the case of soldiers, these men and women become trained killers, when in their previous lives such behavior would have been anathema. In addition, there is the instilled hatred and anger that cloud our judgment about the actions of others and what is their due for so acting, as well as the seeming need to respond right away lest our own safety be jeopardized.

When the world is a blur of emotions and violence, the best thing is to get people to stop and think, to shake them out of their normal ways of reacting. And one of the best methods here is to get people to stop reacting to each other as evil enemies and instead see each other as just fellow humans. Torture and other forms of physical coercion are to be condemned, even in most situations of emergency. Military necessity will rarely, if ever, be sufficient to justify these most inhumane ways of treating prisoners of war. Grotius followed Seneca in thinking that prisoners of war were like slaves. We can do to them what we want, and nearly with impunity, because they are controlled by us. But for war to be something other than morally repugnant forms of slaughter and slavery, prisoners of war should be treated with restraint.

[19] Ibid., Book I, para. 8, p. 136.

Because prisoners of war are dependent on their captors, I will argue that there is a kind of fiduciary or stewardship relationship between prisoners of war and those who detain them. In addition, the captors often see prisoners of war as deserving of vengeance for what these prisoners did to the detaining soldiers' comrades, making abuse even more likely and therefore needing even more restraint. And then there is also the prudential argument that one should not abuse prisoners of war lest one's own soldiers who become prisoners of war will themselves be abused. And finally, there is the consideration of humanity, that to be humane one must display mercy in certain circumstances. There are thus several reasons for treating prisoners of war with restraint, especially when we are considering the use of torture and other forms of physical violence against those who cannot defend themselves.

The rules of war are often grounded in three principles: discrimination, necessity, and proportionality. These principles mean that normally only soldiers, not civilians, should be targeted for attack, and the tactics used should only be those that are necessary to achieve a military objective that provides more benefit than the tactics cost. But these principles are not often connected to each other or morally grounded. In this book, I will argue that discrimination, necessity, and proportionality must themselves be grounded in, and remain secondary to, the principle of humane treatment. I will argue that the best way to understand humane treatment is in terms of compassion and mercy, not in terms of (retributive) justice. Grounding international humanitarian law is about just this attempt to reconfigure the way people think, so that it is possible that peace might be restored and that in the meantime suffering is reduced. It is in this way that we can understand why the rules of war are said to derive from the "laws of humanity and the dictates of public conscience."[20]

III. JUSTIFICATORY HURDLES

War crimes are distinguished from other international crimes having to do with tactics, such as crimes against humanity, in that war crimes

---

[20] The so-called Martens Clause of the Preamble of Hague Convention (IV) Respecting the Laws and Customs of War on Land, 1907, declares: "Until a more complete code of the laws of war has been issued . . . the inhabitants and the belligerents remain under the protection and the rule of the principles of the law of nations, as they result from the usages established among civilized people, from the laws of humanity, and the dictates of the public conscience."

are committed during armed conflict, whether international or internal. By contrast, crimes against humanity could or could not be committed during war, but are committed by members of one State against a population, often the State's own citizens, and, at least for persecution-type crimes, normally involve some sort of discriminatory animus.[21] The increasing number of prosecutions for war crimes during civil wars has made the distinction between war crimes and crimes against humanity not as neat as it once was. Nonetheless, the paradigm examples of a war crime – the torture of a prisoner of war or the killing of an innocent noncombatant – have been recognized as international crimes for at least five hundred years, whereas the concepts of crimes against humanity and crimes against peace are of more recent vintage. There are difficult, yet different, justificatory hurdles that are posed for international prosecutions for these crimes.

International prosecutions for *crimes against humanity* face the first and most important justificatory hurdle concerning sovereignty. Crimes against humanity involve such practices as ethnic cleansing of a minority population by a majority within the same State or the systematic rape of members of one subgroup by the representatives of a State. A sovereign State is presumed to have exclusive jurisdiction over the criminal activities of its citizens. Because crimes against humanity are often crimes committed by the State or its agents against its own citizens, international prosecutions of crimes against humanity must overcome the presumption that a sovereign State is the appropriate determiner of jurisdiction for such crimes. Of course, there is a problem in that the State is often an interested party. Thus, State sovereignty poses the most serious hurdle to prosecutions for crimes against humanity.

In a previous work, I began with a discussion of the minimal moral principles necessary to overcome the presumption of exclusive State sovereignty over crimes committed within a State's territories by such practices as ethnic-cleansing campaigns. I proposed two principles: one

---

[21] For a good discussion of the difference between war crimes and crimes against humanity in contemporary international law, see *Prosecutor v. Erdemovic*, International Criminal Tribunal for Yugoslavia, Judgment of the Appeals Chamber, October 7, 1997, para. 24: "War crimes are acts and omissions in violation of the laws and customs of war. By their very nature they can affect only nationals of belligerents and cannot be committed in time of peace. The crime against humanity . . . may occur during peace or in war. The animus of criminal intent is directed against the rights of all men, not merely the right of persons within a war zone."

stressing that when a State will not or cannot provide for the security of its citizens, it loses the presumption of exclusive jurisdiction over criminal matters, and the other stressing that international bodies could intervene into the otherwise sovereign affairs of States to prosecute crimes against humanity if the crime in question harmed humanity because of its widespreadness or its systematicity and ideally when both conditions are satisfied. When crimes are widespread by being group-based or systematic by being orchestrated by a State, the world community has an interest in seeing that the perpetrators are brought to justice internationally.[22]

International prosecutions for *war crimes* do not face the same initial hurdle as crimes against humanity; or if they do, it is not the most important conceptual hurdle. For war crimes have typically concerned assaults by members of one sovereign State against the members of another, "enemy" State or where there has already been a de facto division of a State during a civil war. In war crimes, borders have normally already been crossed; and because both offending and defending States are sovereign, there is no presumption that priority should be given to the exclusive jurisdiction of one State over another. A third-party adjudicator is often necessary in such cases. This is one reason why the consensus about the justifiability of prosecutions for war crimes goes back quite far historically, whereas the idea that there should be prosecutions for crimes against humanity is relatively recent.

The first and most important justificatory hurdle for international prosecutions for war crimes has to do with the nature of war itself. If one State has sent its troops across another State's borders to kill its soldiers, it is unclear why a justifiably defending State has any duties at all in terms of the treatment of the soldiers of the offending State. And it is not clear why the defending State's troops should restrain themselves in terms of tactics. In war, where both sides seem to be justified in killing the soldiers of the other side, why should prosecutions of soldiers, let alone international prosecutions for so-called war crimes, ever be justified? This is the first conceptual question that defenders of prosecutions for war crimes must address, and it is the main issue I will take up in the first part of this book.

A moral defense of international prosecutions for *war crimes* is not alone justified by the idea, crucial for justifying prosecutions for *crimes*

---

[22] See my *Crimes Against Humanity: A Normative Account*, New York: Cambridge University Press, 2005.

against humanity, that a State must protect the security interests of its citizenry and that if it fails to do so it gives up its exclusive jurisdiction over criminal matters. This idea might be included in a full defense of prosecutions for war crimes, especially of war crimes committed by a State against its own citizens in an internal conflict, such as a civil war, but the moral minimalist will also need to offer a conceptual justification of one State, or its members, having obligations to another State, or its members, even if the other State has attacked it. This task will be made much more difficult than normal because of the common assumption that in wartime States do not owe to other States a duty not to kill or injure the soldiers of that other State, for this would render unjustified the very idea of defensive war itself. Instead, what is needed is some justificatory scheme that shows why the world community, or humanity, should care when inhumane treatment occurs in the course of certain treatment of persons during war, but not necessarily the killing of soldiers. I will argue that prohibitions on the abuse of prisoners and other soldiers, as well as on the killing of civilians, will have to be grounded in an idea such as that of humane treatment. And yet, seemingly paradoxically, for war crimes prosecutions to make sense, the moral duties of humane treatment cannot include the prohibition on all killing during war.

Because I wish to argue that it is the duty of humane treatment of soldiers and civilians during war, rather than the duty of a sovereign State to protect its citizens that is key to justifying prosecutions for war crimes, I draw on a discussion of Grotius rather than Hobbes.[23] Both Hobbes and Grotius are moral minimalists, in that they start from the least number of morally intuitive assumptions. But Grotius worries more about humane treatment than sovereignty, whereas Hobbes is focused on sovereignty and not on humane treatment. I will also discuss the debates between Grotius and some other 17th-century philosophers in the Just War tradition, especially Samuel Pufendorf. For international law, at least as initially conceived, concerned the way that States should interact with each other, especially in wartime, rather than whether it is appropriate to interfere with the internal affairs of a sovereign State. In the first major part of the book, I will defend a Grotian idea of natural law – minimalist natural law to be sure – as a basis for the duty of humane treatment of persons during war and the

---

[23] I began my book on crimes against humanity by defending a Hobbesian minimalist moral position.

justification of international prosecutions for war crimes when inhumane treatment occurs. I will also engage in an examination of an important idea from Pufendorf having to do with how collective responsibility also plays a grounding role for the rules of war.

Throughout this book, I will take a soldier-oriented approach, which often translates into a defendant-oriented approach to war crimes prosecutions. It is certainly true that war needs to be restricted so that it is restrained, as much as it can be, by humane considerations. But soldiers are often caught in the middle: ordered to do what is necessary for promoting their State's military objectives and yet to do so in a way that does not offend the conscience of the society from which they came, as well as the conscience of humanity. Added to this importantly is that soldiers are often also defending their own lives, placed by their military and political leaders into the position of being attacked by other soldiers. In part, this book attempts to shift the discussion of responsibility from the shoulders of these soldiers to those individuals who do not risk their lives, namely the leadership of the army and the State, as well as the society as a whole. Restraint on the conduct of soldiers is still morally important, but restraint on their leaders is also important in making war more humane.

I will critically engage recent writers who claim to be working within the Just War tradition, as well as certain pacifists. Speaking in defense of the current conception of war crimes, especially "the moral equality of soldiers," Michael Walzer argues that "soldiers have an equal right to kill."[24] I ask whether there is any consistent basis for saying that soldiers should not kill civilians or prisoners of war but have a moral right to kill other soldiers, or that soldiers should not use poisons or so-called weapons of mass destruction but have a moral right to use bullets and bombs. The upshot of these deliberations, elaborated over many chapters, is that the idea of war crimes, at least as currently conceived and applied to soldiers, lacks an adequate normative foundation. I attempt to supply this foundation, but such a foundation, in many situations, does not support soldiers having a right to kill other soldiers or to use many so-called conventional weapons. The most important practical implication of my main thesis is that war crimes prosecutions brought against soldiers need to be thoroughly rethought, especially in light of some traditional Just War arguments that have seemingly been forgotten today. At certain points in the argument, I suggest that the

---

[24] Michael Walzer, *Just and Unjust Wars*, New York: Basic Books, 1977, 2000.

difficulty of normatively distinguishing among banned and accepted tactics might even support a "contingent pacifism."[25]

IV. CLASSIFYING WAR CRIMES

One of the difficulties in defining war crimes is that there have been so many candidates for war crimes over the centuries that they seem not to form a coherent set. Indeed, it sometimes appears that what counts as a war crime is simply what one side developed as a new strategy of war and the other side had not yet developed. For example, catapults, poisoned arrows, and even arrows with feathers were once condemned as violating the rules of war.[26] Nonetheless, there have been various attempts to categorize and codify the rules of war over the years, including one attempt as early as 1400 BC in Egypt.[27] The best-known categorization of war crimes historically is probably the rules of chivalry, which governed how knights were to comport themselves in battle against other knights. Because knights considered themselves equals, they thought they owed one another humane treatment during battle.[28] The modern rules of war are also based on the idea of the equality of soldiers.

We can pare down the long list of actions that have historically been considered war crimes into four large categories:

1. assaults, including killing, of civilians;
2. assaults, including killing, of confined soldiers (that is, soldiers who have surrendered, who have been captured, or who are held as prisoners of war);
3. assaults, including killing, of nonconfined soldiers that are not directly necessary for winning battles (including the use of poisons and certain weapons that produce more suffering than is militarily necessary); and
4. assaults against property or the environment (including attacks on cultural artifacts and monuments, as well as other targets not directly necessary for winning battles).

[25] See my paper "Grotius and Contingent Pacifism," *Studies in the History of Ethics*, an online journal (http://www.historyofethics.org/022006/022006May.html or http://www.historyofethics.org/022006/MayContingentPacifism.pdf), February 2006, pp. 1–22.

[26] See Ingrid Deter, *The Law of War*, 2nd ed., Cambridge: Cambridge University Press, 2000, Chapter 5.

[27] Ibid., p. 151.

[28] Ibid., p. 152. I discuss this point in more detail in Chapter 2.

These categories will be examined in the second and third parts of this book. I will spend most of my time discussing the first three categories and only a bit of time on the fourth. This is not because I do not think that the destruction of cultural artifacts or oil fields, for instance, is important, but I wish to focus on assaults on persons, the paradigmatic form of harm in war and the controversial question of why there are generally few restraints on the killing of soldiers but many restraints on assaults short of killing.

The first category of war crimes – assaults, including killing, of civilians – seems to be the easiest to conceptualize and then to justify, but recent philosophical discussions have rendered this category quite problematical. One way to see the difficulty is by trying to distinguish between a reluctant conscripted soldier and a war-mongering munitions manufacturer. Is the latter someone who should never be killed and the former someone who can always be killed? As I ask in Chapter 5, what about soldiers who are not a threat and not wearing a uniform, such as soldiers naked in the bath? Another example of conceptual difficulty can be seen in the way that guerrilla war is often waged by using old men or women as suicide bombers. Are these people civilians or combatants? And what do we make of the claim by Averroes in the 12th century, and repeated sometimes today, that all able-bodied adult males could be killed because they are likely to take up arms at any moment for a jihad?[29] I attempt to rework the principle of discrimination in Chapter 8.

The second category of war crimes – assaults, including killing, of confined soldiers – has been seen as problematical for many hundreds of years. This is at least in part because of three facts. First, confined soldiers can escape confinement; and because they are typically housed deep behind fighting lines, they can wreak havoc in ways they could not if they were at the front. Second, confined soldiers often know militarily important information that could significantly shorten the war and diminish casualties on both sides, but that might take torture to cause these confined soldiers to divulge. Third, confined soldiers require resources, both material and personnel, in order to be maintained, which can significantly displace funds needed at the front to

---

[29] Averroes (Ibn Rushd), "Jihad" (from Al-Bidaya) (c. 1167), para. 3, in *Jihad in Classical and Modern Islam*, translated and edited by Rudolph Peters, Princeton, NJ: Markus Weiner, 1996, pp. 29–33. There was a similar argument used to justify the slaughter of 7,000 Muslim boys and men in Srebrenica in 1995.

fight opposing forces. Because of a worry about such considerations, it has become common to ask whether a prohibition on assaulting, or even killing, confined soldiers might not be justified on straightforward consequentialist terms, especially when winning a Just War is at stake.[30] As I ask in Chapter 7, can torture of prisoners of war to extract needed information be justified? Later in the text, I will address the relationship between consequentialist considerations and those of natural law, most importantly when I take up the principle of proportionality in Chapter 10.

Since the Middle Ages, questions have been raised about the third category – assaults, including killing, of nonconfined soldiers not directly necessary for victory in battle. The key question is whether assaults not directly necessary for achieving a military objective can be justified when, for instance, troops are assaulted as a means to demoralize or punish them for waging aggressive war, a question I address in Chapter 9's reformulation of the principle of necessity. Indeed, until quite recently it was thought justified to wage war and even assault civilians in order to punish a State for its aggressive acts of war. If one State has clearly acted wrongly, such as by invading another State, should that other State have to restrain its retaliatory assaults? Is it inhumane to engage in assaults not directly necessary for winning battles, given that the defending State has a significant interest in punishing the aggressor State that is not closely connected to winning battles at all? As I ask in Chapter 6, is it not permissible for poisons or weapons of mass destruction to be used by an attacked State to stop an aggressive State?

The fourth category of war crimes – assaults against property or the environment – may not seem as important as the others because it does not concern attacks on persons, and for this reason I will not address it systematically in this book. But wars must end eventually, and significant hardship can be had on both sides of a war if the cities and countryside have been ravaged by rampaging troops. And morale, as well as culture itself, can be significantly damaged if significant cultural and artistic creations have been wantonly destroyed. Indeed, civilization itself can be adversely affected by these crimes against property. But a conceptual difficulty arises in attempts to compare these crimes to the other three categories of war crimes, especially in those

---

[30] For a discussion of this issue, see Richard Brandt, "Utilitarianism and the Rules of War," *Philosophy and Public Affairs*, vol. 1, no. 2 (1972), pp. 145–164.

situations where it seems unavoidable that one choose either loss of life or loss of property.

I will propose principles of humane treatment and mercy that are based on the minimal natural law principle that even when it may be "necessary" to kill, there are still moral rules that apply. Take for example the possibly justified use of capital punishment. Even if intentionally taking the life of a serial killer could be morally justified, it would not be morally justified to torture him to death or to kill him in a way that risks killing his nonguilty neighbors. The means used matter, even when the circumstances are such that one of the most important moral restraints, the prohibition against intentional killing does not apply. I will also argue, in Chapter 4, that there is a moral principle of humanity, or humane treatment, that has an even more important role in justifying the rules of war than does justice.

V.   SUMMARY OF THE ARGUMENTS OF THE BOOK

Finally, let me summarize the main arguments that will be advanced in this book. In Part A: Philosophical Groundings (Chapters 2, 3, and 4), I set out the main philosophical ideas upon which a defense of international war crimes can be based. In Chapter 2, I build on a Pufendorfian consensus-based, or positive law, basis for the rules of war, focusing on the idea that a society has a collective responsibility to provide and enforce the rules of war. This is partly because soldiers are doing the bidding of the society, and the society needs to make sure that soldiers act in ways the society approves. But more importantly, the rules of war protect soldiers as well as restrict them, and such protection is morally required of a society that makes its young men and women vulnerable by sending them off to war. Then, in Chapter 3, I defend a Grotian idea of minimalist natural law as a ground for the duty of humane treatment of persons during war and the justification of international prosecutions for war crimes when inhumane treatment occurs. I focus on the connection between honor and the principle of natural humanity. In Chapter 4, I bring together both positive and natural law considerations to develop a concept of humane treatment, which is typically understood to mean that unnecessary suffering is to be eliminated and mercy is to be shown in wars – that is the normative centerpiece of international humanitarian law.

In Part B: Problems in Identifying War Crimes (Chapters 5, 6, and 7), I examine three types of case that are often covered by the rules of war. I will focus on the most important prohibitions, the violations of which give rise to war crimes prosecutions: the prohibition on the killing of the innocent, such as those who are unarmed; the prohibition on the use of certain "unconventional" weapons, such as poisons and chemical, biological, and nuclear devices; and the prohibition on the punishment or torture of confined combatants, such as captured combatants and prisoners of war. In each case, I will explore possible positive and natural law bases for the rules that have been proposed to cover these cases. And in all three cases, I will uncover significant conceptual problems in being able to proscribe these practices and yet leave many similar cases not proscribed. In this second part of the book, I will begin to discuss the particular types of humane treatment that a minimalist natural law theory requires during war.

In Part C: Normative Principles (Chapters 8, 9, and 10), I reconceptualize the most important principles in *jus in bello* Just War theory as well as in war crimes prosecutions: discrimination (or distinction), necessity, and proportionality. I will reconceptualize these principles in light of our earlier discussion of the principle of humane treatment. The principle of discrimination is typically understood to mean that tactics must clearly distinguish between combatants and non-combatants, sparing the latter as much as is possible. The principle of necessity is understood to mean that only that use of force that can accomplish the military objective is justified; and the principle of proportionality is typically understood to mean that the cost of the use of various tactics must be commensurate with the benefit of the military objectives pursued. I will explore what is required by these principles, ultimately wondering whether it is ever possible to wage war in an honorable way. I reach the conclusion that it *is* possible to attain honor in war, but only if the traditional principles underlying the rules of war – the principles of discrimination, necessity, and proportionality – are significantly reformulated. Specifically, I argue that these principles need to be understood as intimately linked with the principle of humane treatment.

In Part D: Prosecuting War Crimes (Chapters 11, 12, and 13), I discuss who should be prosecuted for war crimes and what sorts of defenses should be allowed in such prosecutions, and I argue that it is the military and political leaders, rather than normal soldiers, who should typically be prosecuted for war crimes, because the leaders best represent the State and often are more instrumental in effectuating the policies and decisions of the State and are more clearly responsible for

any harms that are perpetrated by soldiers than are the soldiers
themselves. But if soldiers are not merely carrying out orders, by acting
ultra vires, or by intentionally seeking to cause harm by their inhumane
treatment, then it is they who should be prosecuted. I also explore two
defenses often employed in war crimes trials. I argue that both those
who follow commands and those who issue them have defenses readily
available, although the defense of superior orders and the defense of
duress are a stronger basis of defense for normal soldiers than for
leaders.

   In the final section (Chapter 14), I discuss how terrorism affects the
arguments in this book, ultimately concluding that even terrorists are
owed humane treatment. I then use the discussion of the difficult case
of terrorism to draw out various conclusions that have been argued for
in the book. One of the main conclusions is that even when we find
people who are seemingly "evil" or "enemies of humanity," and
especially in those cases, there is a need to restrain our normal emotional responses. I end with a few more thoughts on what it means to
engage in a Grotian project in international humanitarian law, pulling
threads together in an attempt to set the stage for further work by
philosophers and international lawyers.

   Throughout the book, I bring very recent cases in international
criminal law into conversation with quite old discussions of *jus in bello*
considerations in the Just War tradition. For example, I will consider
very recent cases from the International Tribunals for Yugoslavia and
for Rwanda as well as examples of atrocities from the archives of the
International Committee of the Red Cross. I will examine all of these
cases in light of the ideas first expressed by Alberico Gentili, Hugo
Grotius, and Samuel Pufendorf.[31] The combination of contemporary
international criminal practice and Just War theory produces a very
rich basis for rethinking the idea of war crimes and provides a timely
basis for assessing the new prosecutions that are being undertaken by
the permanent International Criminal Court seated at The Hague. In
this way, I hope to begin to bring theoretical concerns to the forefront
of the fast-moving changes in international war crimes (or as it is often
called, international "humanitarian") law today.

---

[31] This combination also suits my own personal interests because I am a scholar of 17th-
century thought, a political philosopher, and a part-time practicing criminal lawyer.

PART A

PHILOSOPHICAL GROUNDINGS

that war, so as to minimize the harms to these soldiers. In the end, I discuss a specific case of the application of these rules of war drawn from the ad hoc war crimes tribunal sitting at The Hague.

I will argue that the positive actions of States, in sending some of their citizens into harm's way, create an obligation to set rules of war that will provide at least minimal protection for those subjects. In the next chapter, I develop another ground for the rules of war that provides more than mere minimal protection for those affected by war. The rules of war function to protect those who are fighting, and the bindingness of the rules comes from the fact that all soldiers are so protected. The obligations of the rules of war are especially binding because they aim to protect soldiers and civilians regardless of whether a State might otherwise wish to violate these rules or whether it actually turns out that a given State is in the wrong for having waged war.[1]

A State that sends its soldiers into harm's way has a responsibility to do what it can to protect those soldiers even if protecting them might somewhat limit the effectiveness of the State's military campaigns. Adhering to the rules of war is a major way of discharging this responsibility because the rules of war cut both ways, protecting both the soldiers of a State and enemy soldiers. The protection mainly comes, as we will see, from the mutual following of these rules by multiple States, but there is also a sense that a State's soldiers are less vulnerable if poisoned weapons are not being used by its own side, for there is a significant danger of poisoned gases, in particular, adversely affecting one's own as well as enemy soldiers. The way in which a State's responsibility is discharged varies widely according to time and context. At some times protecting them from arrows with feathers is key, and at other times protecting them from tactical nuclear weapons is key. Throughout, I shall try to develop an understanding of a State's collective responsibility that grounds such highly variable rules of war and corresponding notions of war crimes, independent of the justice of the war itself.

In the first section, I discuss the Just War tradition's definition of war and the idea that all soldiers are to be similarly restrained in war. In the second section, I elaborate on Hugo Grotius' idea that honor is

---

[1] See Jeff McMahan, "The Ethics of Killing in War," *Ethics* vol. 114, Summer (2004), pp. 693–733, who argues that there are different obligations that soldiers have if they are fighting a Just War versus an unjust war. I offer an alternative view, based on a relatively new argument, but that is in keeping with two thousand years of tradition on this topic.

crucial for soldiers and that equal restraints on all soldiers is intimately linked to a soldier's honor – that is, to the honor of soldiers as soldiers. In the third section, I develop a relatively new argument for thinking that a State has a collective responsibility to establish and enforce the rules of war among its soldiers. In the fourth section, I explain why violations of the rules of war should be prosecuted as international war crimes. And in the final section, I take up the case of protected persons, such as prisoners of war and other noncombatants, during war, explaining why such protection is crucial for a soldier's honor and for a State's collective responsibilities.

I. THE MORAL EQUALITY OF SOLDIERS

Alberico Gentili, writing at the end of the 16th century, said, "War is a just and public contest of arms." He explained that war is nothing but a contest where one side attempts to subjugate the other. For Gentili, the most important part of this definition concerns the fact that war must be public, not merely "a broil, a fight, [or] the hostility of individuals." Gentili claimed that the earliest use of the term "war" was for battles between two persons (a duel). Even so, war proper is not merely a private two-person battle, but a public contest in which the parties are (roughly) equal.[2] According to Gentili, wars are by definition matters that are importantly connected to justice. Gentili built justice into his definition of war, but others did not follow his lead.

Francisco Suarez, the Jesuit follower of Thomas Aquinas, writing at the beginning of the 17th century, gave a somewhat more subtle definition of war. He said that war is "an external contest of arms, which is incompatible with external peace." He then distinguished among three types of contest: contests of arms waged by "two sovereign princes or between two states," which is properly called war; contests of arms "between a prince and his own people;" which is called sedition; and contests "between private individuals," which is a duel or quarrel.[3] He then declared that the difference among these

---

[2] Alberico Gentili, *De Jure Belli* (On the Law of War) (1598), translated by John C. Rolfe, Oxford: Clarendon Press, 1933, p. 12. Gentili was an international lawyer and professor at Oxford University.

[3] Francisco Suarez, "On War," in *Selections from Three Works*, (Disputation XIII, *De Triplici Virtute Theologica: Charitate*) (c. 1610), translated by Gwladys L. Williams, Ammi Brown, and John Waldron, Oxford: Clarendon Press, 1944, p. 800. Suarez was a theologian and philosopher who taught at the University of Salamanca in Spain.

contests is not in form but in matter – that is, that the duel is very much like war except that the material components, such as the number of participants, are different. Unlike Gentili, Suarez did not define war to be just, but nonetheless he said that it is wrong to think that war is intrinsically evil instead of something that can be just.

Hugo Grotius, also writing in the early 17th century and often said to be the founder of modern international law, said that war is merely "the condition of those who are contending by force," which includes a duel as much as a public war. Indeed, Grotius said that private and public wars have the same nature and "should be designated by the same term."[4] Probably reacting to Gentili's definition, Grotius said,

> I do not include justice in my definition because this very question forms a part of our investigation, whether there can be a just war, and what kind of war is just; and a subject that is under investigation ought to be distinguished from the object toward which the investigation is directed.[5]

Grotius then went on to distinguish two very different issues: "whether any war can be just, and then, what is just in war."[6] As I said above, the first of these issues is today referred to under its Latin name "*jus ad bellum*," and the second is referred to as "*jus in bello*."

Grotius thus made the important point that we need to leave open whether wars can indeed be just, and this needs to be divided into two further questions: Can the waging of war be just, and what tactics of war can be just? Grotius added even more subtlety to these debates by then distinguishing three distinct ways in which something like war can be just, grounded respectively in natural law (universal principles), the laws of nations (reached by consensus), and what is honorable (found in the individual conscience). In this way, Grotius, surely the most important figure to write on war in the last five hundred years, sought to carve up inquiry about the morality of war into a number of distinct questions, rather than to presume that war either must *always* be just, as his fellow international lawyers insisted, or cannot *ever* be seen as just, as pacifists and many religious leaders had urged.[7]

---

[4] Hugo Grotius, *De Jure Belli ac Pacis* (On the Law of War and Peace) (1625), translated by Francis W. Kelsey, Oxford: Clarendon Press, 1925, p. 33. Grotius was an international lawyer and taught at the University of Leiden, The Netherlands.

[5] Ibid., p. 34.   [6] Ibid.

[7] There is a good treatment of this subject by Martin Wight, a member of the "English School" of international relations. See his essay on Grotius in the collection of his papers titled *Four Seminal Thinkers in International Theory*, Oxford: Oxford University Press, 2005, pp. 28–61.

So, early modern Just War theorists not only shed quite a bit of light on what counts as war and whether war should include, or be modeled on, duels, but also on the nature of morality itself. I will draw on this very rich literature, primarily from the late 16th and early 17th centuries in my own investigation into the normative underpinnings of prosecutions for war crimes, the supposed violations of the rules of war, in particular, of the *jus in bello* part of the Just War tradition. It is, I think, highly interesting that debates in contemporary political philosophy and international law mirror rather directly the much earlier discussions that we will rehearse among such thinkers as Grotius and his follower Pufendorf.

Most significant for our purposes is the idea often accepted, then and now, that regardless of whether one wages a war for a just cause there are nonetheless severe restraints on the type of tactics that can be used by both sides in a war. The general idea here is that even though some wars can be just, or justified, the moral story does not end there. This idea is often discussed under the label "the moral equality of soldiers." Those who fight a Just War nonetheless can act unjustly in their choice of tactics. This is strange, indeed, for what is being said is that it might be justified to kill intentionally but not to harm in a less severe way, such as by torturing. And even more counterintuitively, the idea is that the very same moral restrictions on tactics apply regardless of whether one wages war for a just cause or for an unjust one.

One of the main practical reasons for the "moral equality of soldiers" is that it is very hard for theorists, writing after the fact, to determine whether a war was waged for a just cause or not. Primarily, this is due to the fact that intentions matter, and it is very hard to figure out what were the intentions of the parties to a war. When two people engage in a fistfight or a duel, it is also often difficult to determine what their intentions were. Was one the aggressor and the other exercising self-defense? Or was the "aggressor" actually provoked by the seemingly innocent party? And it is here that the parallel between war and a duel might also break down, because public wars are fought for many different reasons and a group of a State's decision makers may have quite different intentions for fighting the war. Hence, there is often no clear single intention on the part of a State that embarks on war or seeks to "defend" itself or a third party.[8]

---

[8] For a good discussion of the relationship between duels and wars, and generally whether individual self-defense can ground State self-defense, see David Rodin, *War and Self-Defense*, Oxford: Oxford University Press, 2002.

If it is difficult for theorists, many years after the fact, to determine whether a State had just cause to wage war, we cannot reasonably expect soldiers during wartime to make such a determination. In any event, soldiers are required to follow orders and generally have few choices but to do so. When soldiers on both sides are similarly commanded to station themselves opposite each other on a battlefield, it is not reasonable after the fact to treat these soldiers differently based on whether we now think that one side was in the right and the other was in the wrong. Rather, at least concerning soldiers (if not also military leaders), it makes sense to use the same moral rules for both sides to determine if soldiers are acting rightly on the battlefield. I will say much more about this doctrine in later sections. Here, it suffices to give a sense of the historical debates about the idea that rules of war apply equally to all soldiers in order to show that this idea is not as implausible as it might at first seem.

II. THE HONOR OF SOLDIERS

The general idea behind the rules of war, and corresponding war crimes prosecutions, is that soldiers, qua soldiers, have various duties (as well as rights). The best way to restrain soldiers who have been given a license to kill is to require the same restraints from each of them at a given time regardless of whether they fight on the just or unjust side in a war. For soldiers not to be merely simple killers, they need to be men and women of honor, that is, people who kill but only under heavily restrained conditions and only on behalf of their States, not for their own interests or pleasure. The idea of a "soldier's honor" is as old as war chronicles going back at least as far as the *Iliad*.[9] Socializing soldiers to view their honor as of paramount importance is the chief way that soldiers are motivated to restrain themselves according to the rules of war. If such restraints varied based on whether one was, or was perceived to be, on the just side of a war, it would be much harder to restrain warriors, which has been recognized for millennia, for all soldiers are trained to assume that their own side wages war justly.

Jeremy Bentham's writings are almost always a good place to start when investigating concepts in moral psychology. He first discusses

---

[9] See Shannon E. French, *The Code of the Warrior: Exploring Values Past and Present*, Lanham, MD: Rowman and Littlefield, 2003.

honor in his *Introduction to the Principles of Morals and Legislation*, where he says:

A man's moral sensibility may be said to be strong, when the pains and pleasures of the moral sanction show greater in his eyes . . . (and consequently exert a stronger influence) than in the eyes of the person he is compared with; in other words, when he is acted upon with more than ordinary efficacy by the sense of honor: it may be said to be weak when the contrary is the case.[10]

Honor here seems to be an enhancement of the ordinary efficacy of moral prohibitions. Those who act from a sense of honor have an enhanced desire to do what is right and seem to need fewer incentives to do what is right. Consider the soldier again. If he or she is motivated to act humanely even when not required to do so, and sometimes even when it is not in his or her interest to do so, such enhancement comes most easily from a concern for behaving scrupulously.

From David Hume's perspective, one could describe the scrupulousness of the soldier in conforming to rules of war as a form of heightened sympathy. On Hume's view, these would be people who are more sensitive to the needs and interests of others than to even their own needs and interests. However, in many ways this doesn't ring true. Soldiers are not typically sensitive and sympathetic in that sense. Rather than acting out of a concern for the other person, they act out of a concern for themselves. They hold themselves, or think that they do, to a higher standard than the rest of us. This is due, in part, to the fact that they need to think of themselves as acting in a way that is morally superior to the rest of us, even as they are engaged in killing, which in other contexts would be strongly morally condemned. I think that Bentham is right to think of honor as an enhanced scrupulousness to moral prohibitions, rather than as a form of Humean sympathy, like that held by a parent for a child.

When Bentham first investigates the causes of action, he distinguishes motive from intention. Honor seems to be a kind of motive that then has a causal influence on our intentions. This fits with the general account of motive that Bentham gives:

The motives with which alone we have any concern, are such as are of a nature to act upon the will. By a motive then, in this sense of the word, is to be understood any thing whatsoever, which by influencing the will of a sensitive

---

[10] Jeremy Bentham, *Introduction to the Principles of Morals and Legislation* (1789), edited by J. H. Burns and H. L. A. Hart, Oxford: Oxford University Press, 1970, p. 57.

being, is supposed to serve as a means of determining him to act, or voluntarily to forbear to act, upon any occasion.[11]

Intentions are the immediate aims of actions, whereas motives are the broad psychological factors, such as fear and malice, that cause us to have intentions.

Honor is a motive in that it influences the will in a certain way – namely, to follow certain moral rules scrupulously. This is quite different from the Humean idea of sympathy as a sensitivity to the particular plight of a given person. Soldiers don't necessarily care about fellow soldiers fighting on the other side, but they do care about their own honor, their sense of being morally superior to others as scrupulous followers of moral rules. Honor is the motive to follow the rules as enhanced beyond what is true of the normal person. Here there are two forms of enhancement: first, that some of us are to follow rules more scrupulously than the rest of us follow these rules, and second, that there are certain rules to be followed by some of us that the rest of us do not follow at all. In the end, from a Benthamite perspective, it is their sense of self, not, as it seemingly was for Hume, their sympathy for the other person, which is key.

Honor is the combination of enhanced respect for normal moral rules plus the respect for special rules that require conscientious reflection and socialized motivation crucial for humanitarian law's requirement that soldiers act with restraint even when their lives are jeopardized on the battlefield. On my account, the primary motivation for humane treatment comes from a sense of self-worth of the person who acts humanely. Honor generally calls for acting in ways that we would not only approve of, but that we would seek to emulate and use as a basis for educating others. In fighting a war with restraint, we seek to do that which we would heartily approve of if it were aimed not at others but at ourselves. Yet, the behavior in question is not aimed at us but at the other, and so there is still a need for some socialized motivation. Having a socialized sense of honor instilled in the form of respect for the rules of war is one of the main motivations for humane treatment.

Let us consider the code of chivalry in the Middle Ages. Knights who acted contrary to the code apparently experienced shame because they had not lived up to their own conception of the minimal standards of behavior for knights. They were also subject to sanctions for violating

[11] Ibid., p. 97.

the code. Mean-spiritedness, for instance, was condemned and sanctioned. And although this was clearly still in the purely moral domain, it was also written into the code of chivalry in various ways. One might object that a code of chivalry was extrajudicial and thus not a good model for understanding how honor can play a role in law properly conceived. It is important to point out, though, that there was no alternative system of international law at the time. Indeed, chivalry codes were more lawlike than any other set of rules. For example, the multilateral treaty of Westphalia wasn't signed until the mid-17th century.

The honor-based enforcement mechanism for the rules of war is either effected through informal means, or somewhat more formal domestic means, such as socialization through internal tribunals, such as courts martial, or through international mechanisms, such as international criminal tribunals. Localized ways of instilling and enforcing the rules of war can be highly effective. Even today, some have argued that informal mechanisms of socialization might be better than the highly formalized mechanisms of international and domestic criminal tribunals.[12] I do not necessarily disagree that informal mechanisms can be highly effective in some circumstances. But for there to be widespread compliance, and for this compliance to result in the adherence to roughly the same code of behavior across States, some sort of international tribunal also makes a great deal of sense. Indeed, international criminal law could be seen as merely a complement to the more informal, localized mechanisms of effecting compliance with the rules of war, as is seen in the principle of complementarity in the ICC Statute.

Grotius was one of the first to discuss international law in terms of international humanitarian restraints. In the famous discussion in Chapter 11 of Book III of *De Jure Belli ac Pacis*, Grotius says,

> From humanitarian instincts, or on other worthy grounds, [the victorious soldiers] will either completely pardon, or free from the penalty of death those [enemy soldiers] who have deserved such punishment.[13]

Grotius also spends much time discussing honor in the context of the humanitarian laws of war. In Chapter 10 of Book III, Grotius says that

---

[12] See Mark Drumbl, "Collective Violence and Individual Punishment: The Criminality of Mass Atrocity," *Northwestern University Law Journal*, Winter 2005, pp. 101–179.

[13] Hugo Grotius. *De Jure Belli ac Pacis*, (On the Law of War and Peace), p. 733.

"you may often see justice associated with the sense of honor." Indeed, "a sense of honor may be said to forbid what the law permits."[14]

Grotius talks of honor as providing a higher sense of what is owed than is provided by justice narrowly conceived. Justice is mainly determined by two considerations: what is strictly permitted or forbidden by black-letter law, and what is owed to one another by virtue of what is deserved on the basis of our past behavior. It may be that a creditor is owed some money by a debtor. There will be a strict legal obligation here that the creditor is within his rights to act on against the debtor. But there is a higher duty that the creditor owes to the debtor, in which the creditor is obligated first to try to give the debtor, who is now dependent upon him, the benefit of the doubt, before seeking action against him.[15]

The soldier's duty is grounded in a sense of honor for Grotius, which goes beyond a strict legal duty that is itself based on formal justice. Such considerations lead Grotius to say that even in an unlawful war, there are various restraints that should be placed on how soldiers whose State is in the right are to behave toward those soldiers whose State is in the wrong. This is the model for what is today called "the equality of soldiers," that is, that soldiers have the same duties (and rights) in humanitarian law regardless of which side they are fighting on. And for Grotius, all of this is captured in talk of honor, as well as in the *jus in bello* rules of war.

A sense of honor offsets other emotions, especially anger, that can run so high in war. In "On Anger," Seneca rails against the sort of anger that he defines as "a burning desire to avenge a wrong."[16] If States only instill a strict sense of justice – at least that form of justice that is based on what is owed to another because of what he or she has done – the violence of war can spiral out of control as we move from one angry episode of revenge taking to another. If soldiers see their own honor as requiring restraint toward their enemies, now seen as merely fellow soldiers, such a spiral can be broken. Both sides in a war should lead their soldiers to feel honor-bound to restrain themselves,

---

[14] Ibid., p. 716.

[15] Ibid. Grotius does not employ the term "fiduciary duty" per se, but I think that this idea is at the heart of his account nonetheless, as a careful consideration of his text will bear out.

[16] Seneca, *Moral and Political Essays*, edited by John M. Cooper and J. F. Procope, Cambridge: Cambridge University Press, 1995, p. 19.

and instilling a code of honor for all soldiers enforced by rules of war is one of the best ways to do this.

I am investigating what normative principle(s) could initially ground the idea of rules of war, the violations of which are called war crimes, and set the stage for the justification of international criminal prosecutions. The problem with grounding the *jus in bello* rules of war that give rise to prosecutions for war crimes is that there are so many things prohibited and there has been considerable variation in what prohibitions have applied at any given point in time. Today, no one would seriously propose that the use of arrows with feathers, catapults, or submarines constitutes a war crime, but in earlier ages this was seriously proposed. For justificatory purposes, we will need quite a nuanced normative principle, or set of principles, to account for the prohibitions expressed by the rules of war. Universal normative principles, those that could hold for all people at all times, would have to be so general that they would not be well suited to this enterprise.

III.   COLLECTIVE RESPONSIBILITY FOR INCREASED VULNERABILITY

I will now propose a relatively new way initially to ground the *jus in bello* rules of war and the prosecutions for war crimes that are based on violations of these rules. The proposal takes the chief challenge to be to find an initial normative grounding for the rules of war that does not differentiate between soldiers based on which side they are on and that is adaptable to highly variable circumstances that render soldiers and civilians vulnerable. As we will see, the key is to see why a State should feel compelled to instill and enforce rules of war that minimize the vulnerability of its soldiers at a given time or in a given war. And in the next chapter, a broader but less specific principle, the principle of humanity, is also defended. Together, the principle of collective responsibility that I am about to discuss, and the principle of humanity, ground war crimes prosecutions for violations of the rules of war.

Samuel Pufendorf, writing at the end of the 17th century, said that soldiers are in the unenviable position of being commanded to do things by others.[17] As a result, they are not the "principal cause" of

---

[17] Samuel Pufendorf, *De Jure Naturae et Gentium* (*On the Law of Nature and Nations*) (1688), translated by C. H. Oldfather and W. A. Oldfather, Oxford: Clarendon Press, 1934, p. 75.

their own actions.[18] He then held that "an action is ours the execution of which we have laid upon another." The effects of the soldier's actions can be "imputed" to the collectivity that is the actual principal actor.[19] Indeed, Pufendorf argued that the individual soldier who is commanded and often coerced to act is the mere agent of the collectivity that so directs him. As a result, the collectivity, not the soldier, is primarily responsible for his actions, even though it is the soldier who perpetrates the actions.[20]

It is but a short step from this position to the claim that the State is collectively responsible for what soldiers are ordered to do. And because the collectivity is to be imputed to the effects of the soldiers' actions, the collectivity should take a special interest in what soldiers do and try to make sure that they do not act in ways that the collectivity does not approve of. Of course, if soldiers act in ways that they have not been ordered to act and are not being coerced into doing, the connection between the principal and the agent is weakened. But when soldiers do act according to orders and are sufficiently coerced to follow those orders, as is usually the case, the effects of their actions are properly the responsibility of the collectivity that those soldiers represent. And soldiers need to act with honor where that means that they are not mere indiscriminate killers if they are to retain a sense of self-respect and easily return to society after they have fought their States' wars. The society, the State, is collectively responsible for what it has directed these soldiers to do.

There are two forms of collective responsibility: distributive and nondistributive.[21] The imputation to the society of responsibility for the effects of the soldier's actions is a form of nondistributive collective responsibility. That is to say, the society is collectively responsible, but this does not necessarily mean that any member of the society is personally responsible for these effects. If all of us were to issue an order – for example, by all simultaneously shouting it – then this might be a

---

Pufendorf was a philosopher who was the first in Europe to hold a chair in international law, at the University of Lund, Sweden.

[18] Ibid., p. 81.   [19] On this point, see ibid., p. 66.

[20] I would not follow Pufendorf in thinking that soldiers are relieved of responsibility, but only in thinking that the State is also responsible. Saying that the State is responsible does not necessarily relieve the soldier of responsibility. Responsibility is not like a pie, with only a limited number of slices.

[21] Here I draw on some of my previous work on this subject. See Larry May, *The Morality of Groups*, Notre Dame, IN: University of Notre Dame Press, 1987; and Larry May, *Sharing Responsibility*, Chicago: University of Chicago Press, 1992.

form of distributive collective imputation and responsibility. But in societies and States, typically we do not all issue orders together; rather, there is someone who has been delegated to issue orders for the group, and that person, acting in his or her office, is the one who links the group to the effects of the soldier's actions. But in a highly organized group, it is not immediately evident who is personally responsible for these effects. Indeed, it may be that no one is personally responsible for them and yet the group is nonetheless collectively responsible, in a nondistributive way, for what occurs.

This gives us a ground for saying that the society, or the State, is responsible for what the soldiers bring about. If the society is collectively responsible for the effects of its soldiers' actions, then the society has a strong interest in trying to minimize the likelihood that soldiers will act in ways that the society disapproves of and that will bring them dishonor. Giving soldiers a license to perpetrate mayhem is not conducive to this goal. Rather, it seems more reasonable for the collectivity to try to put the representative of the collectivity on a short leash, as it were. For the society would have an interest in making sure that its soldiers did in fact carry out the society's orders and not go beyond those orders, seemingly still acting in behalf of the society. Even when clearly acting *ultra vires*, the actions of soldiers wearing the uniform of a given country still partially implicate the society in what they do, for they could not accomplish what they do if it were not for the initial backing that the society gave to these soldiers.[22]

Because soldiers are acting on behalf of the society, or the State, the society should also take a special interest in trying to protect them from the worst effects of being a soldier, for harm to soldiers is also the collective responsibility of that society. The society is responsible for what the soldiers suffer because it has ordered them to put themselves in harm's way and has coerced them to remain there, steadfastly defending us from our perceived enemies. The soldiers represent their society, or State, on the battlefield; but when they are harmed, it is a personal not a collective harm – they bleed and lose limbs for us,

---

[22] The doctrine called "apparent authority" holds that even if one is not, strictly speaking, authorized to act for a principal, if the principal has not clearly and publicly marked off the extent of the agent's authority, the agent may still be said to be acting on behalf of the principal even when acting contrary to the principal's instructions. See my essay on this issue: "Professional Action and Liability of Professional Associations: ASME v. Hydrolevel," *Business and Professional Ethics Journal*, vol. 2, no. 1 (1982), pp. 1–14.

and we are responsible for these wounds and lost limbs because
it is we, collectively, who have commanded them to be put in harm's
way.

The rules of war accomplish the two goals mentioned above. First,
they restrict what soldiers can do as a way of restraining them in
situations where they might be tempted to engage in mayhem against
anyone perceived to be the enemy. Second, the rules of war also
protect soldiers when any restraints placed on one side's soldiers are
reciprocally placed on the soldiers who fight against them. The rules of
war, adopted by States at a particular time, are restraints that protect
soldiers whom a society or State has placed into harm's way and thus is
responsible for. The rules of war add motivational force to the code of
honor that protects all soldiers and also leads soldiers to act to protect
themselves from many of the ravages of war.

When ordered into battle, soldiers are placed in harm's way and
thereby their vulnerability to harm is increased. Their vulnerable
position is the responsibility of the society which conscripted these
solders, or which now commands them. So, even if there is no absolute
moral principle grounding the rules of war, there is a very strong
hypothetical grounding for providing the rules of war a home in the
positive laws of each State that maintains an army. If a person's vulnerability is increased by the society, then it is the society that has the
responsibility either to remove the vulnerability or to help minimize its
harmful effects. For just as a volunteer soldier – a mercenary, for
instance – is responsible for his own increased vulnerability, we can
impute responsibility to a society, or a State for the increased vulnerability of soldiers who do not voluntarily go into the military. Even
those who voluntarily join the military, but who are then coerced into
the most dangerous of positions, can have their increased vulnerability
imputed to the society, or the State.

It does matter how a soldier came to acquire the role of soldier, but
not as much as one might initially think. If one is conscripted, then the
State or society has a very strong responsibility to do all it can to
protect him or her. If the soldier volunteers, it might seem that there is
less responsibility on the part of the State for the soldier's plight
because the soldier has seemingly chosen it. But the volunteer soldier
does not necessarily choose to do everything that he or she is commanded to do as a member of a military unit. Soldiers do not generally
volunteer for military service thinking that they will be asked to act
cruelly, for instance, or realizing that others might act cruelly toward

them. States still have a responsibility to minimize cruelty even for those of its soldiers that volunteer.

I would make a similar argument even for mercenaries and privatized contract soldiers, although as we proceed to this level the responsibility of a State for contract soldiers probably gets somewhat weaker than for conscripted soldiers.[23] Private contract soldiers could be seen as merely free agents or independent contractors who are owed little if anything by those who hire them. But this seems wrongheaded for two reasons. First, these soldiers still represent the State, and the State thus has an interest in having them act with the restraints it approves of. Second, privatized contract soldiers are still soldiers and in order to make sure that they do not see themselves merely as paid assassins the same, or nearly the same, restraints should be part of their code of honor. For these reasons, it remains true that the best way to protect both the interests of the State and the honor of soldiers is to instill and enforce the rules of war for all soldiers, even those privatized contract soldiers.

The society, or State, owes a minimally safe environment to those whom the society sends off to do its bidding.[24] In wartime, it might seem that nothing is safe and all such restraining considerations are off the table. But there are, indeed, safer and less safe ways for war to be waged. In particular, a war that is fought with respect given to every soldier who has fallen in battle is a considerably safer one than a war, like most ancient wars, where soldiers simply die of their wounds on the battlefield, often in agony. In addition, as Henry Shue has argued so effectively, it is a much better environment for soldiers not to face torture, even though they already face death, than to have soldiers feel that they are unrestrained to torture the enemy because they can also kill them. Indeed, there are several things worse than death itself, especially a death that is relatively painless.[25]

The rules of war can be grounded as a way to help societies and States meet their responsibilities toward those who have had their vulnerability increased by that same society, or State. The rules of war

---

[23] See Peter W. Singer, *Corporate Warriors: The Rise of the Privatized Military Industry*, Ithaca, NY: Cornell University Press, 2003.

[24] In another context, I would urge that we seriously think about whether this principle commits us to a form of contingent pacifism when it is not possible to protect soldiers during war. This is taken up in my book manuscript "Aggression and Crimes Against Peace."

[25] Henry Shue, "Torture," *Philosophy and Public Affairs*, vol. 7, no. 2 (1978), pp. 124–143.

are premised on the idea that a State promotes its own soldiers' obedience to *jus in bello* rules and also promotes other States in doing
likewise toward their soldiers. Thus, the rules of war not only protect a
State's soldiers but also protect other soldiers in the international
community. Collective responsibility will give us a grounding of particular types of minimal forms of restraint on soldiers. When societies,
or States, create increased vulnerabilities, they have a responsibility to
create rules that reduce the harm likely to be caused by these increased
vulnerabilities.

IV.   HARMING HUMANITY AND WAR CRIMES PROSECUTIONS

If prosecutions are to take place in international tribunals for violations
of the laws of war, then there must be some ground for these trials that
goes beyond the mere accidental agreement of States concerning their
positive laws. Indeed, it seems that if a custom develops that is
necessary for the security of the people, then that custom is binding
across States. And this is just how many States understand the rules of
war. But why do the violations of the rules of war constitute an international crime? At least until recently, most war crimes involved the
crossing of State borders by an enemy State's soldiers. But these acts
are most clearly prosecuted as crimes against peace rather than war
crimes. In order for there to be prosecutions for war crimes, in most
cases the violations of the rules of war must be so significant that the
international community would have an interest in them. It is to this
topic that I now turn.

The general idea that there can be "crimes" committed during war
needs a bit of explanation. The most obvious war crime would be one
that violates a multilateral international treaty. There have been many
such treaties over the last two centuries, most famously The Hague and
Geneva Conventions.[26] Those conventions made it wrong for one State
to employ certain tactics against another State during war. Various
other treaties, such as the multilateral Rome Statute of 1998 establishing the International Criminal Court (ICC), transform the wrongs
of States of The Hague and Geneva Conventions into crimes that
individuals can be punished for committing. There have also been
long-standing customs condemning other tactics during war, customs
that have come to constitute a kind of common law of war crimes, much

---

[26] See the 13 Hague Conventions of 1907 and the four Geneva Conventions of 1949.

like Anglo-American common law. Certain practices, such as torture and terrorism, are morally condemned so universally that they become international crimes.[27] One of the main questions taken up in this chapter is what sort of normative principles would initially ground the rules against international war crimes.

Aside from the question of what makes something an international crime, there is also the question of what entity has jurisdiction to prosecute such crimes. There are two main answers: Prosecution for international crimes can be conducted by a particular State's courts or by an international tribunal. When States prosecute international crimes, it is typically either because the crime was committed within its borders, directed against one of its nationals, or committed by one of its nationals.[28] But there is also an emerging doctrine of "universal jurisdiction," according to which any State may be said properly to prosecute an international crime as long as the State does so in good faith and follows international law, not merely its own domestic law.[29] Most recently, the new International Criminal Court was established to be a free-standing international tribunal with authority derived from two sources: the multilateral treaty that established it and the principle of universal jurisdiction. The United States challenged the legitimacy of this court because, among other reasons, it usurped the traditional prerogative of the United States to have exclusive jurisdiction over the crimes committed by, or against, its own nationals. This chapter will offer a partial response to this challenge.

War crimes affect the interests of the international community chiefly in the way that soldiers responsible for war crimes represent a State. Crimes against humanity involve sheer terror inflicted on a civilian population in one geographical region that also has strongly felt effects in other geographical regions. In most cases, war crimes are not prosecuted internationally unless they have occurred on a mass scale. But there is a more subtle reason than the sheer size of the harm that implicates the international community in war crimes, namely that

---

[27] For a good discussion of the customary law status of torture and terrorism in international criminal law, see Antonio Cassese, *International Criminal Law*, Oxford: Oxford University Press, 2003, pp. 117–135.

[28] For an excellent discussion of international jurisdiction, see Mark Janis, *An Introduction to International Law*, New York: Aspen Law and Business, 1993.

[29] For a recent statement, see, "The Princeton Principles on Universal Jurisdiction," edited by Stephen Macedo, Princeton, NJ: Program in Law and Public Affairs, 2001. Also see the critical treatment of this type of jurisdiction by Luc Reydams, *Universal Jurisdiction*, Oxford: Oxford University Press, 2003.

war crimes are often organized, or at least facilitated, by a State, and then the *systematic* nature of the war crimes affects an interest of the international community in deterring those crimes. For when a State is involved, then the domestic legal apparatus of that State will not be likely to deter its actions.

The international community has an interest in enforcing these rules by instituting international prosecutions of the soldiers or State leaders because impunity is likely to result otherwise. This is similar to those cases where there is a failed State and the international community must step into the gap to make sure that enforcement occurs. It is also like those cases where a group of individuals act as a rogue State – that is, a State that has demonstrated a will to disregard the legitimate interests of other States. In both cases, the international community has an interest in intervening in order to maintain some semblance of order among soldiers.

War crimes are crimes against *humaneness*, not really crimes against all of humanity. War crimes affect an interest of the international community to minimize suffering by preventing inhumane treatment. The international community's interest in preventing inhumaneness is perhaps not as strong as its interest in preventing harms against the whole of humanity, so it may be justifiable to allow for more defenses against war crimes than against the more egregious crimes against humanity. This is seen in the way the ICC Statute is structured so that superior-orders defenses may be allowed in some cases of war crimes but not in cases of genocide or crimes against humanity.[30]

Nonetheless, the international community has a strong incentive to prosecute war crimes: to rein in the leaders of States that perpetrate or facilitate war crimes. When a State is involved in the perpetration of war crimes, then the leaders of that State normally should be prosecuted internationally, if any individuals are to be prosecuted at all. I will discuss this topic in much greater detail in later sections of this book, especially Section D. Suffice it here to note that soldiers who are ordered to disobey or who are facilitated in disobeying the rules of war by lack of State enforcement are clearly not the main ones responsible for these violations, because the soldiers did not place themselves in harm's way.

After soldiers have been protected by the reciprocal adoption and enforcement of the rules of war, it would then seem odd to hold them

---

[30] Statute of the International Criminal Court, Art. 33(2).

responsible for violating those rules if the same State that promulgated the rules also urged that they be violated. Rather, the military leaders of these soldiers most represent the State's intentions if not its actions, and the leaders are the ones who are best placed to stop any war crimes from occurring. Thus, as we will see in greater detail in Chapter 12, it is the leaders who are most deserving of being prosecuted for war crimes. When collective responsibility is distributed out to individuals, it is the leaders – who most clearly represent the group – who should stand trial.

As we will see in the next chapter, there is also something universally immoral about inhumane treatment that calls out for some kind of sanction. And while the sanction need not be a criminal one, there are obvious advantages to the use of criminal prosecutions to deter crimes against humaneness. I mentioned above that one thing to be aimed at is a mechanism that results in uniform humane treatment by all parties to wars regardless of whether the States fight for a just or unjust cause. Such uniformity can best be achieved by *international* norms and sanctions, rather than by those that vary from State to State. In addition, I would argue that one of the best mechanisms for creating this uniformity is to threaten criminal sanctions against military leaders, and to a lesser extent individual soldiers, rather than merely against the States themselves.

So why hold individuals criminally liable when the laws of war are violated? This is surely one of the hardest questions for my account. A turn was made in the history of how we think about war crimes when tribunals started prosecuting individuals rather than States for violations of international law in times of war. In many ways, this turn was an inevitable one if war crimes are to be deterred, for after all it is individuals who commit war crimes, individuals who give orders to the soldiers in the first place. So while the State, or the society, is collectively responsible for providing and enforcing rules of war to minimize the vulnerability of soldiers, when soldiers violate these rules it is the soldiers, or those who commanded them to break the rules of war, who should be prosecuted and, if convicted, punished for these violations. Those who do the proscribed actions are the ones who can most easily be deterred, rather than the States, which lack a soul to damn or pants to kick, to paraphrase an old saying about corporations. It is by punishing individual persons that enforcement of the rules of war can best be achieved.

V. PROTECTED PERSONS DURING WAR

In this last section, I will briefly consider an example of war crimes. In 1949, the International Committee of the Red Cross, the leading humanitarian organization in the world, held a convention to update its charter. What emerged are the modern Geneva Conventions. Michael Ignatieff claims that unlike the specific reference to natural law in the Geneva Convention at the end of the American Civil War, the 1949 Geneva Conventions "make no ringing claims about human brotherhood. Instead, they accept war as a normal anthropological ritual – the only way that certain human disputes can be resolved. They seek only to [ensure] that warriors conform to certain basic principles of humanity, the chief principle being to spare civilians and medical personnel."[31]

Consider the Geneva Convention's prohibition on soldiers harming certain protected civilians in time of war. To get a sense of how this prohibition is understood, consider the debates about how to understand the fourth of the 1949 Geneva Conventions.[32] The obligations of the Convention are explicitly grounded in a multilateral treaty signed in 1949 and ratified by most States over the ensuing decades. The obligations apply only to the High Contracting Parties, that is, to those States that have ratified this Geneva Convention. The obligations continue to hold as long as the terms of the Convention apply. "Nationals of a State which is not bound by the Convention are not protected by it."[33] But today, many of the provisions of the Geneva Conventions are considered part of customary international law and are said to apply even to those States that did not sign the original Conventions.[34] In the 1997 Tadic Case, the Trial Chamber of the International Criminal Tribunal for the Former Yugoslavia (ICTY) considered whether civilians who were "placed into camps run by the authorities of the Republika Srpska"[35] were "protected persons,"[36] as

---

[31] Michael Ignatieff, *The Warrior's Honor: Ethnic War and the Modern Conscience*, New York: Henry Holt, 1997, pp. 119–120.

[32] The Geneva Convention Relative to the Protection of Civilian Persons in Time of War of August 12, 1949.

[33] Ibid., Article 4.

[34] I am critical of this use of the idea of custom in international criminal law. See my treatment of this topic in Chapter 3 of *Crimes Against Humanity*, Cambridge: Cambridge University Press, 2005.

[35] *Prosecutor v. Tadic*, International Criminal Tribunal for the Former Yugoslavia, Judgment of the Trial Chamber, Case no. IT-94-1-T, May 7, 1997, para. 575.

[36] Ibid., para. 578.

understood by the Fourth Geneva Convention, and thus whether there was a special obligation on the part of the former Yugoslavia to prevent its soldiers from harming these civilians.

The status of protected persons is crucial for determining whether the harming of a civilian constitutes a violation of the Fourth Geneva Convention and thereby today constitutes a war crime subject to prosecution by an international tribunal. Perhaps surprisingly, not all harming of civilians in time of war is proscribed as a war crime. Think specifically of the harm that occurs when people are not provided food, water, and medical supplies. Arguably, there is no obligation to provide such things to everyone in the world, for if there were such an obligation then all the States in the world would quite likely violate that obligation. But if a person is "in the hands of a party to the conflict or Occupying Power of which they are not nationals," then not providing food, water, and medical supplies would constitute a war crime on the basis of the Fourth Geneva Convention.[37] The crucial considerations are whether a civilian is indeed "in the hands of a party" and whether that party is bound by the Geneva Convention.

I do not want to get bogged down here in the details of the Tadic case, but it is interesting to note that there were several serious problems that led the ICTY to drop the charge against Tadic of having violated the Fourth Geneva Convention. One of the main problems was that those who set up the camps did not have effective control of a given geographic area and thus were operating as irregular forces, not the kind of armed forces of a State contemplated by the Geneva Conventions.[38] The rules of war generally only bind soldiers, for it is they who represent a State and are honor bound to abide by the rules of war. I discuss this complex issue in the final chapter of this book, where I argue that even irregular combatants, such as terrorists, are owed humane treatment.

While there is no universal obligation to provide food, water, and medical supplies to everyone in the world, there is such an obligation if a State, acting through its soldiers, acts to confine a person and take that person away from the normal protection of his or her State. By

[37] Ibid., para. 578, quoting Geneva Convention IV, Article 4.
[38] Tadic Case, paras. 579–583. The narrow interpretation of the requirement that war crimes only occur in such cases if civilians are "protected persons" was recently reaffirmed in the case of *Prosecutor v. Naletilić and Martinović*, International Criminal Tribunal for the Former Yugoslavia, Judgment of the Trial Chamber, Case no. IT-98-34-T, March 31, 2003, para. 176.

confining a civilian of another State, the confining State makes it impossible for the civilian to secure food, water, and shelter on his or her own. Hence, the confining State assumes obligations to provide for these necessities that it did not have before confinement. Certain expectations may be created by the conduct of States at certain times, such as that people will not be subject to certain kinds of harm and do not need to protect themselves against those harms, which might not be true at other times. For example, there might once have been an expectation that soldiers will be in uniform and not in plain clothes. In such a time, it might have been a war crime for soldiers to take off their uniforms and attack other soldiers.

Having created expectations and the ensuing vulnerability when they are thwarted, a moral rule is violated. It might be thought that the Tadic Trial Chamber came to the wrong result by focusing only on whether the forces that captured and confined civilians within the Opština Prijedor camps were soldiers of a State and that the court had too narrow a view of how to understand the obligations arising from the principle of humane treatment. After all, anyone who confined these civilians and then deprived them of food and medical supplies certainly did something morally abhorrent. But the rules of war seem to require only soldiers, not civilians, to display humane treatment, which is enforced by the code of honor and by war crimes tribunals.

The rules of war governing the appropriate tactics to be used in fighting will often be quite historically specific, such as prohibitions on specific types of bullet or bomb. The specific restraints will largely be based on the need to reduce vulnerability of soldiers and civilians. Indeed, there are three types of rule aimed at reducing vulnerability that collective responsibility grounds:

1. rules to reduce vulnerabilities created when citizens are turned into soldiers
2. rules to reduce vulnerabilities created when specific institutions are created during wartime
3. rules to reduce vulnerabilities created when surprise occurs because soldiers do not fight in expected ways.

For example, if the use of certain tactics creates unfair surprise in war, rules will need to be tailored to try to reduce the vulnerability by temporarily banning these tactics.

The case we have been examining is a good one to illustrate how the rules of war can be supported by collective responsibility to create a firm basis for war crimes prosecutions. Some obligations, such as to protect medical personnel, kick in when a State decides to go to war, and other obligations kick in only when, in addition, that State transforms the citizens of the enemy State into "protected persons." Various international conventions then proscribe certain forms of behavior. In such situations, States have a collective responsibility to protect those who have been rendered increasingly vulnerable by the decision to go to war or the creation of certain institutions and expectations during war. Such an obligation attaches to all States, those that go to war supposedly for a just cause and those that do not, for the collective responsibility is one that attaches to States that send their soldiers into harm's way, regardless of whether they do so for a just or unjust cause. The best way to protect soldiers and civilians who are rendered increasingly vulnerable is to instill a code of honor among all soldiers that is enforced by the sanctions of the rules of war during war crimes prosecutions.

In the next chapter, we will turn from a consensual account of the rules of war to a minimalist natural law account. States commit themselves to protect citizens who are rendered vulnerable when the States go to war. And because so many things about war change over time, quite different restraints will be needed at different times for a State to meet its collective responsibility to its vulnerable citizens. But there also seems to be a core to the rules of war over time, often expressed in terms of the principle of humane treatment and mercy, which seems to be grounded in universal moral norms. In Chapter 3, I will provide this additional grounding for the rules of war by a discussion of what I call a "minimalist natural law theory," specifically the Grotian principle of humanity.

3

Jus gentium and minimal natural law

In the previous chapter, I argued that the rules of war can be supported by the largely consensual ideas of honor and collective responsibility. In this chapter, I will explain how some of these rules of war can also be supported by minimal natural law considerations, especially those having to do with the protection of the vulnerable. The general idea that there should be restraints on the behavior of soldiers during war was supported in the previous chapter. Now I begin the task of explaining why certain behaviors of soldiers in nearly every wartime situation have been and should be proscribed by the rules of war. Perhaps surprisingly, this discussion does not lead me into considerations of justice, although there is surely a place for justice in the rules of war. Instead, I will be investigating the role of humaneness or mercy in the rules of war, an idea that we will see in Chapter 4 is the cornerstone of the main international legal documents that treat the rules of war.

The idea that there is a *jus gentium*, a law of nations or a law of peoples, is longstanding.[1] Some have argued that such a law can only be understood as a set of agreements among nations that shift over time, but that may have a common core of consensus. Indeed, contemporary courts have equated the law of nations with customary international law. In the previous chapter, I suggested that collective responsibility might ground such a consensus. Other theorists,

---

[1] The Latin term *"gens"* (or *"gentis"*) can mean a clan, tribe, people, or nation. And the Latin term *"jus"* can mean either a law or a right. "Nation" does not normally mean a country or a state but rather a collection of families bound together by common descent. See Cassell's *New Latin Dictionary*, 1968, pp. 263–264.

extending back at least as far as Cicero and Augustine, have argued that there is a universal moral law governing how nations and soldiers should conduct themselves during wartime. In the late Middle Ages and the beginning of the Modern Age, this idea gained strong adherents. By the time of the late Middle Ages, it became clear that if *jus gentium* was to have a natural law grounding it would have to be found in those minimalist principles that were connected to the protection of the innocent or vulnerable that seemed to have universal appeal and that were deeply embedded in individual conscience. Even Augustine argued that war is justified primarily on grounds of the defense of the innocent and then secondarily on self-defense, only extending to the punishment of the wicked as a tertiary concern.[2] Gentili, writing at the end of the 16th century, summarized the overall sentiment by arguing that even if one did not like particular men "he should at least have had regard for humanity."[3]

In this chapter, I wish to construct a plausible, minimalist natural law view that would indeed ground certain basic principles of international humanitarian law, such as are often found in the law of war crimes. I will focus on the principle of humanity and its related notions of humane treatment and mercy. I will generally draw on Grotius, as someone who clearly sits squarely in the humanist or secular natural law tradition. I offer a ground for the rules of war that is consistent with the major documents on the rules of war, especially the Geneva Conventions, and that sees humane treatment as the cornerstone of the rules of war.

In the first section, I will rehearse some of Grotius' arguments concerning the law of nations, focusing on universal principles and agreements among States, as well as how these are related to each other. In the second section, I focus on two universal principles: the principle of natural justice and the principle of humanity. I work out a Grotian understanding of the rules of war based mainly on the principle of humanity. In the third section, I leave Grotius and formulate a principle of humane treatment grounded in a minimalist natural law theory, which will establish a basis for contemporary rules of war, and I explain in what sense there are duties to act humanely. And in the

---

[2] Augustine, *De Civitas Dei* (*The City of God*) (c. 420), Book 19, translated by Henry Bettenson, New York: Penguin Books, 1984.

[3] Amberico Gentili, *De Jure Belli* (*The Law of War*) (1598), translated by John C. Rolfe, Oxford: Clarendon Press, 1933, p. 69. I have changed Rolfe's translation from "mankind" to "humanity."

fourth section, I connect the ideas of collective responsibility and honor from the previous chapter with the minimal natural law considerations of the current chapter. Then I indicate why it is appropriate to prosecute individuals for inhumane acts especially in times of war. Throughout, I provide minimalist natural law grounds for holding that soldiers, whether they fight for a just or an unjust cause, should act humanely.

I.   GROTIUS ON THE SOURCES OF *JUS GENTIUM*

Hugo Grotius, writing at the beginning of the 17th century, gives us a good place to start in our investigation of the relationship between *jus gentium* and *jus naturale*. Grotius distinguishes between a primary and secondary law of nations: *jus gentium primarium*, the moral precepts discovered by universal right reason; and *jus gentium secondarium*, the largely consensual precepts based on "agreements concerning the international good."[4] Grotius says that the primary law of nations is closely related to natural law.[5] What Grotius is trying to indicate is that the law of nations, generally the principles that nations have governed themselves by over the centuries, has two different sources. The most obvious source is the treaties and other agreements that States have made with each other – largely contingent sources of law. But more important, at least for Grotius, are the laws of nations that exist independently of such agreements but that are felt to be binding by nations over the centuries nonetheless.

Grotius was struggling to distinguish consensual norms from what today, in contemporary international legal theory, is called *jus cogens* norms, international norms that cannot be derogated even by explicit agreement, and that are binding on all (*erga omnes*), independent of any such agreements. In his later work,[6] Grotius dropped this distinction in favor of the simpler distinction between the law of nature and the law of nations. But I believe that the earlier distinction between primary and secondary laws of nations is much more informative, largely because it keeps separate two senses of the law of nations that have been commonly confused.

[4] Hugo Grotius, *De Jure Praedae* (*On the Law of Prize and Booty*) (1605), translated by Gwladys L. Williams, Oxford: Clarendon Press, 1950, pp. 12, 26.
[5] Ibid., p. 12.
[6] Hugo Grotius, *De Jure Belli ac Pacis* (*The Law of War and Peace*) (1625), translated by Francis W. Kelsey, Oxford: Clarendon Press, 1925.

For Grotius, the two forms of *jus gentium* (the consensual and the universal) are related to each other in that even when people reach international moral norms by explicit agreement they normally reach such agreements because they have in mind moral principles that appear to them to be universally binding as well. Grotius claims that international norms grounded in agreements are related to those grounded in universal principles. The reason why people feel bound by their agreements is, at least in part, because they see the substance of those agreements as independently binding. In any event, people adhere to a universally binding obligation to keep their promises, of which treaties are merely one subspecies.

So, following Grotius, the laws of nations derive from different, and often confused, sources: universal right reason, on the one hand, and explicit agreement or long-standing custom, on the other. In international law, universal morality is not normally recognized as one of the main sources of the law of nations, but such a source is recognized nonetheless when the International Court of Justice (ICJ) Statute talks of "the general power of the court to "decide cases *ex aequo et bono*."[7] International courts often refer to what they regard as moral sources in deciding cases, although the main source is Article 38(1) of the ICJ Statute: treaties, customs, general principles of law, and judicial decisions.[8] What I am interested in is which particular moral principles that could help ground the rules of war are also supported by explicit conventions as well as by custom.

In many cases, the laws governing how States should behave toward each other derive from a combination of these sources. But what is crucial is to try to disentangle the sources so that we can ascertain what are the truly universal sources, if any, that should govern international relations. Of course, for philosophers the most interesting category concerns these possible universal sources. For it is in untangling such sources that we can uncover possible natural law or universal sources of the law of nations – the subject of this chapter.

Grotius offers a good definition of natural law, especially as it bears on the law of nations: "The law of nature is a dictate of right reason which points out that an act, according as it is or is not in conformity with rational nature, has in it a quality of baseness or moral necessity;

---

[7] Statute of the International Court of Justice, T.S. no. 993, 59 Stat. 1055 (June 26, 1945), Art. 38(2). That is, judges can consider matters of equity and public good.
[8] Ibid., Art. 38(1).

and that, in consequence, such an act is either forbidden or enjoined by the author of nature, God."[9] And to prove that his is a secular version of natural law, Grotius then says that not even God can change the laws of nature.[10] The laws of nature would continue to bind "even if we should concede that which cannot be conceded without the utmost wickedness, that there is no God, or that the affairs of men are of no concern to him."[11]

What Grotius seems to intend by speaking of the laws of nature is to carve out a set of moral norms that apply to all people at all times. Such moral norms could then ground principles of international law. To say that international legal norms can be grounded in natural law principles is not to say that there is a straightforward derivation from morality to legality. Indeed, Grotius does not say that there is; nor does he say what else is needed to make this move. The connection between morality and legality is, unfortunately, a neglected topic in natural law theory and the Just War tradition.

Grotius begins this search for universal moral norms, as did many others in the 17th century, by turning to the universal desire for security and happiness.[12] The first principle of human affairs gives a person the liberty and the duty both "to defend [one's own] life and to shun that which threatens to prove injurious" and "to acquire for oneself, and to retain, those things which are useful for life."[13] Grotius refers to these precepts as the first and second laws of nature. The second law of nature – which gives a person the liberty to get and retain things useful for living – requires the assistance of others – what he calls "the attachment of one body to another." Grotius argues that all are thus linked in "mutual harmony" by the need to help each other achieve security and happiness so that, quoting Seneca, "You must needs live for others, if you would live for yourself."[14]

Grotius refers to this extension of self-interest to encompass the interests of those who can aid us as the principle of "friendliness,"[15] or "sociableness."[16] He later extends the application of this principle from relations among individual persons to relations among States: "[L]aw is not founded on expediency alone, [for] there is no State so powerful that it may not some time need the help of others outside itself . . . [so] even the most powerful peoples and sovereigns seek

---

[9] Ibid., pp. 38–39. [10] Ibid., p. 40. [11] Hugo Grotius, *De Jure Praedae*, p. 13.
[12] Ibid., p. 9. [13] Ibid., p. 10. [14] Ibid., p. 11. [15] Ibid.
[16] Hugo Grotius, *De Jure Belli ac Pacis*, p. 11.

alliances."[17] Those alliances are important for security, but even more important if people have any hope of attaining a type of life that is marked by happiness. For both security and happiness, restraints are needed on human behavior, and our natural desire for allies and friends moves us to rein in our otherwise selfish interests so as to be able to achieve long-term security and happiness, especially by the creation of legal institutions, both domestic and international.

Indeed, for Grotius, "no association of men can be maintained without law," and he illustrates this with the idea that "shameful deeds ought not to be committed even for the sake of one's country."[18] Grotius then draws the conclusion for which he is justly famous:

Least of all should that be admitted which some people imagine, that in war all laws are in abeyance. On the contrary, war ought not to be undertaken except for the enforcement of rights; when once undertaken it should be carried on only within the bounds of law and good faith . . . *in order that wars may be justified, they must be carried on with not less scrupulousness than judicial processes are wont to be.*"[19]

Grotius then maintains that even in war "unwritten laws are in force, that is laws that nature prescribes, or the agreement of nations has established."[20]

In the next chapter, I wish to dig a bit deeper into the Grotian construal of natural law as applied to nations. I will take up the question of how one can move from a very general natural law principle, such as that of "sociableness" or "friendliness," to a very specific principle, such as that soldiers should not inflict unnecessary suffering. As we will see, the intermediate step is to set out and defend a broad principle of humanity, a universally binding and minimalist grounding for the laws of war and war crimes prosecutions.

II.   GROTIAN NATURAL LAW THEORY AND THE RULES OF WAR

Grotius was the first to set out systematic laws of nature concerning how States should conduct themselves during war (*jus in bello*). He separates these considerations into two groups: those concerning natural justice and those concerning humanity understood in terms of humane treatment and mercy.[21] Grotius attempts to derive quite specific rules

[17] Ibid., p. 17.   [18] Ibid.   [19] Ibid., p. 18 (italics mine).   [20] Ibid., p. 19.
[21] My interpretation of Grotius is nonstandard, although an increasing number of scholars are interpreting him in ways similar to the way I will set out. The most

of war from the general principles of the laws of nature. He begins with a discussion of what is strictly speaking permissible, but later moves to considerations of broader permissibility and eventually to moral considerations beyond mere permissibility. Justice is the natural law grounding of what is strictly permissible; the laws of nations grounded in agreements and treaties offer a broader construal than justice does of what is permissible. However, permissibility is not the only moral consideration that derives from natural law. Grotius quotes Cicero as saying, "For there is something which is not right, even if it is permitted."[22]

Grotius identifies another set of natural law concerns, those arising not out of natural justice but out of humanity, and he grounds such concerns in what he calls our "humanitarian instincts."[23] Specifically, Grotius argues that it

is the bidding of mercy, if not of justice, that, except for reasons that are weighty and will affect the safety of many, no action should be attempted whereby innocent persons may be threatened with destruction.[24]

Grotius defends such claims on the basis of what he calls the "duty of . . . humanity."[25] Thus, for Grotius, we have two natural law sources of the law of nations: natural justice and natural humanity.

Grotius says that if a person fights with a just cause, "he is permitted to harm an enemy; both in his person and in his property."[26] But this does not seem to be the morally best way to treat people – that is, a virtuous way that takes into account all moral considerations. All of this

important scholar to agree with my general interpretive line was Hersch Lauterpacht in his essay "The Grotian Tradition in International Law," *British Year Book on International Law*, vol. 23 (1946), pp. 1–53. More recently, G. I. A. D. Draper discusses Grotius in a way similar to mine, but he sees what I call "humanitarian concerns" as merely hortatory rather than obligatory. See his essay "Grotius' Place in the Development of Legal Ideas About War," in *Hugo Grotius and International Relations*, edited by Hedley Bull, Benedict Kingsbury, and Adam Roberts, Oxford: Oxford University Press, 1990, especially pp. 198–199. Richard Tuck agrees with some of my interpretations of Grotius, but he disagrees about how to assess the overall project, believing that Grotius set the stage for the "modern liberal rights theories" but also allowing for "the often brutal implications of his ideas." See Richard Tuck, *The Rights of War and Peace: Political Thought and the International Order from Grotius to Kant*, Cambridge: Cambridge University Press, 1999, especially pp. 107–108.

[22] Ibid., p. 643.
[23] Ibid., p. 733. Grotius also discusses these issues under the category of the moderation, *temperamenta belli*, that should be displayed by honorable soldiers. See G. I. A. D. Draper, "Grotius' Place in the Development of Legal Ideas About War," p. 197.
[24] Ibid., pp. 733–734.　　[25] Ibid., p. 744.　　[26] Ibid., p. 643.

indicates that while natural justice requires some restraint, the truly virtuous person is more greatly restrained in attempting to act in a fully humane manner, even sometimes pardoning those who have taken up arms against him. The emphasis on virtues like honor places Grotius' natural law theory squarely in the Aristotelian camp. And it is here that Grotius, although only in a rudimentary way, provides us with an extremely important and lasting insight into the normative foundations of international law. Grotius supplies us with the idea of the minimal natural law grounding for what is today called "humanitarian law," that is, the rules placing severe restraints on conduct in war, even if one is in the right in waging war.

For Grotius, acting honorably is going beyond what is required by the laws of nations and even beyond what is required by justice. In this sense, we see a basis for thinking that honor can bridge the considerations of the previous chapter and those of the current one. Grotian honor is instilled in soldiers by particular societies, but what is instilled is a higher standard than that which ordinary people hold themselves to. Codes of honor are consensual in that these codes are based on the consent of soldiers and their leaders. In addition, some of the substantive requirements of honor track minimal natural law ideas such as acting mercifully toward those whom one has rendered vulnerable.

Grotian natural law has to do not only with what conduces to our own preservation and interest directly, but also to what conduces to the good of others. The sociableness and friendliness that are so crucial for a Grotian understanding of natural law lead to rules of engagement in war that are not merely based on what is necessary for the survival of a State or a given soldier, even one fighting for a just cause. It is concern for humanity that is, on my reading, linked to honor that causes Grotius to "deprive those who wage war of nearly all the privileges which I seemed to grant, yet did not grant to them" on the basis of what is merely "'lawful' or 'permissible.'" Going beyond what is just to encompass a sense of honor is necessary for the establishment of the "bonds of friendship."[27]

Grotius thinks that the domain where such considerations are most relevant concerns who can justifiably be killed. In a just war (*jus ad bellum*), as also in the situation of slavery, there is a sense in which any action done to advance military objectives is justifiable. In Grotius'

[27] Ibid., p. 717.

time, a soldier is not legally prohibited from harming an enemy soldier if the enemy does not fight with just cause. And this might even be seen to be true from the standpoint of natural justice, on the assumption that wars can be justifiably fought when there is a just cause; and when one side fights without just cause, the other side owes them nothing. The honorable person restrains himself or herself and takes into consideration the universal principle of humanity, thereby leading a life that goes beyond merely what is permissible. Acting honorably, not merely permissibly, is motivated by the desire for friendship and social bonds. Later, we will see that mere sociability is not enough. There is something specific to the circumstances of, for example, slavery and prisoners of war, namely that confinement has occurred, and this changes what is now required, not as a matter of justice, but as a matter of humane treatment and mercy.

According to Grotius, natural law considerations require that "[O]ne must take care, so far as it is possible, to prevent the death of innocent persons, even by accident."[28] Indeed, Grotius goes so far as to say that natural law requires one "even to spare those who are guilty for the sake of the innocent."[29] This position derives not from justice but from humanity. The Grotian position, and still the position three hundred years later in international law, is that there should be a prohibition on even the accidental killing of the innocent and a corresponding principle of discrimination that one should not employ tactics that fail to differentiate between combatants and civilians. The principle of discrimination is not merely about doing one's duty according to natural justice, but going beyond this to act in a way that is fully in line with acting virtuously, even in war against one's enemies. Such a consideration is one of the cornerstones of humanitarian law.[30]

For Grotius, the principle of natural humanity is the natural law moral principle that requires restraint even when dealing with one's enemies. This principle of humanity is minimalist in the sense that it is supposed to represent what any person would accept and that "no one

[28] Ibid., p. 733.   [29] Ibid., p. 734.
[30] Michael Ignatieff comments: "The protection afforded by chivalric code applied only to Christians. Toward infidels, a warrior could behave without restraint. The unique feature of the European natural law tradition, which began to take shape in the sixteenth century, as jurists struggled to reconcile the laws and customs of competing and often warring religions and states, was its universal ambition. Natural law, upon which the Geneva Convention was based, attempted, for the first time, to imagine rules that would apply to everyone." *The Warrior's Honor*, New York: Henry Holt, 1997, pp. 117–118.

can deny them without doing violence to himself." Grotius says that these are principles that one can deny only at the risk of "absurdity."[31] If we think of war in terms of law and justice, as Grotius tried to show, we could justify nearly any tactic in a war, assuming that the enemy was in the wrong. But truly honorable behavior during war cannot be so construed, even when one is in the right and one's enemy is in the wrong. For without the principle of humanity, we are still lost in a sea of individuals asserting their rights but with little hope of sustaining lasting relationships. The honorable soldier realizes that the enemy soldier is a fellow human upon whom he might need to rely – in any event, someone whom he will have to live with in peace after the war is over.

On this Grotian account, we owe people more than natural justice would dictate. We should go beyond what is permissible, especially in those circumstances where our actions have instituted something that ultimately increases the vulnerability of our fellow humans. The principle of justice will require that we be sure not to harm the innocent, for otherwise this would not be giving the innocent their due. But the further requirement that one be willing to spare the guilty so as to protect the innocent, or even sometimes to pardon the guilty, needs to be supported by a different principle than natural justice, because pardoning the guilty is not what is their due. Even though Grotius does not have a fully formed defense of the principle of humanity, he does stand as one of the first thinkers to give this principle as much respect as the principle of natural justice. And by doing so, Grotius was truly the founder of modern humanitarian law, with its severe restraints on what soldiers can do to enemy soldiers, even when the enemy is fighting an unjust war.

III.   REFINING THE PRINCIPLE OF HUMANITY

In this section, I will refine the principle of humanity as a basis for the rules of war and defend it from several obvious contemporary objections. I begin with a somewhat modified account of what constitutes a minimalist account of natural law. Minimalism is meant to be deflationary in two respects: It is supposed to minimize the number of assumptions that one begins with and then minimize the likely objections to the place where one starts. Indeed, my account aims to be

---

[31] Hugo Grotius, *De Jure Praedae*, p. 12.

explicitly minimalist in the latter sense, for I seek minimal starting assumptions that are the least controversial that I can find. Toward this end, I start from principles of peace and security.

The laws of nature are really not laws, properly called, as Hobbes taught us,[32] but norms – that is, considerations that provide reasons for action. Historically, natural laws, or universal norms, are reasons for action that are grounded in human reason or desire or some other aspect of human nature. The term "law" was employed largely to indicate that the norms in question are binding, as if lawgivers were issuing commands that humans ought to obey. Minimalist natural law theory derives norms from features of human nature that are the least controversial. So, unlike traditional natural law theory,[33] minimalist natural law theory does not proceed from a robust listing of all the features that might ground basic goods for humans. Rather, there is a very short list (two or three features) of human nature that set the ground for a very small set of norms.

In this respect, Thomas Hobbes is a minimal natural law theorist who proceeds to construct norms on the basis of human desires for self-preservation and for peace; and Hugo Grotius is a minimal natural law theorist who constructs norms, as we saw, grounded in the human desire for a peaceful and happy life in a community. For Hobbes, the laws of nature are better seen as theorems about what will advance our natural desires.[34] For Grotius, the "laws" of nature are requirements that connect to a "characteristic of humankind."[35] So, to call something a natural law, for 17th-century philosophers, was to use the term "law" as a kind of metaphor for what is obligatory. I will follow this tradition in moral and legal philosophy in thinking of the laws of nature as laws of humanity – that is, norms governing humans wherever and whenever humans act.[36]

---

[32] See Thomas Hobbes, *Leviathan*, Chapter 15.

[33] See John Finnis, *Natural Law and Natural Rights*, Oxford: Clarendon Press, 1980; or Mark Murphy, *Natural Law and Practical Rationality*, Cambridge: Cambridge University Press, 2001.

[34] See the end of Chapter 15 of Hobbes's *Leviathan*.

[35] Hugo Grotius, *De Jure Praedae*, p. 13.

[36] One could advance a challenge to any natural law framework, wondering why it is that natural states of desire or reason, which are facts of human nature, can ground laws or obligations, which are norms of human behavior. One way out of this conceptual difficulty is provided by contemporary natural law theorists, as well as in my interpretation of 17th-century natural law theory, namely by discussing what is reasonable, rather than what is grounded in reason, where reasonableness is already a normative idea. Richard Tuck has provided a good treatment of such issues in his

It may seem odd to say that a minimalist natural law theory would embrace something that seems to be controversial, such as the principle of humanity. The difficulty is that in war it seems especially dangerous to treat the enemy according to this principle – that is, humanely. If there are to be restraints in war, it seems less controversial to restrict ourselves only by narrowly drawn justice considerations. And because we owe very little if anything to people who are attacking us, or who have tried to attack us, the laws of war will provide very minimal restraints. But there are good reasons to think that most enemy soldiers have not done anything wrong in attacking us, because most soldiers act merely because they have been ordered to act. Therefore, even enemy soldiers do not deserve a lethal response on our part. Indeed, for many centuries philosophers have accepted the moral equality of soldiers, that whether they serve on the aggressing or defending side, soldiers, as soldiers, have duties of humane treatment and mercy toward each other.

One can imagine a Hatfield-and-McCoy situation where people are completely governed by the principle of (retributive) justice, but where society between warring families is nearly impossible. The reasonable strategy for the maintenance of relationships is that people give each other the benefit of the doubt, so that a cycle of vengeance does not arise. The principle of humanity is a key consideration in the maintenance of societies because it posits the kind of attitude that makes for friendly or sociable relationships. If one does not consider the interests of others in deciding whether to restrain oneself, especially if one is about to engage in violent action, it is hard to see why others will engage in restraint either. Yet, it is mutual restraint that is the cornerstone of sociable relationships.

Now, when it is an "enemy" that one confronts, it might seem odd to think that restraint should even be considered. After all, what is the point of worrying about friendly relations? The answer is relatively simple: The world is small enough that after wars end people need to be able to live with each other, unless a cycle of vengeance taking is desired. Hopefully, enemies do not stay enemies. In any event, peace is normally premised on the idea that people will come to see that they have more in common, than not, with those whom they previously saw as mortal enemies. The principle of humanity is aimed at getting even

book *Natural Rights Theory: Their Origin and Development*, Cambridge: Cambridge University Press, 1979.

enemies not to see each other as demons or madmen. It might be necessary for one's own survival to harm or even kill a fellow human, but surely this should only be in the most extreme cases and under the most stringent constraints. And, at least in part, it is the lack of the acceptance of such a principle that has created the endless cycle of wars between Indians and Pakistanis, Serbs and Croats, Israelis and Palestinians, Hutus and Tutsis, Greeks and Turks, Kurds and Arabs, and Irish Catholics and Protestants.

The principle of humanity is best seen as a natural law principle because it provides minimalist reasons for action based on the natural reasons and desires of humans, or what is reasonable behavior, consistent with peace and happiness. The principle calls merely for restraint when one's own preservation or comparable interests are not jeopardized by such restraint and where restraint provides a positive good for other humans. It is humane treatment and mercy that are more important than even justice in providing restraints. Indeed, as the debates about reconciliation have made clear, justice sometimes gets in the way of lasting peace among peoples.[37] Of course, one does not want peace at the cost of freedom or other important values. But in order to have a chance at lasting peace, one must not treat even one's enemies in an unrestrained way.

I want to consider one more problem with the principle of humanity: namely, why this principle should be a basis for duties rather than merely supererogatory acts, as mercy generally is understood. Grotius presented us with a kind of puzzle. He distinguished between two viewpoints, "the one external, the other internal."[38] The internal viewpoint is that which "is right from every point of view and is free from reproach," and "might be more honorably done."[39] Within the law, both of nature and of nations, it is permissible to contract marriage, says Grotius, but "the chastity of celibacy is more worthy of praise."[40] Grotius drew an important distinction between what is permitted from the narrow perspective of what is owed or deserved

---

[37] See the essays in *Truth v. Justice*, edited by Robert I. Rotberg and Dennis Thompson, Princeton: Princeton University Press, 2000; as well as the essays in *Looking Backward, Reaching Forward: Reflections on the Truth and Reconciliation Commission in South Africa*, edited by Charles Villa-Vicencio and Wilhelm Verwoerd, Cape Town: University of Cape Town Press, 2000. Also see *Dilemmas of Reconciliation*, edited by Carol Pranger, Kingston, ON, Canada: Queens University Press, 2001.

[38] Hugo Grotius, *De Jure Belli ac Pacis*, p. 717.   [39] Ibid., p. 641.   [40] Ibid., p. 642.

and what is permitted from every point of view,[41] where considerations of justice and legality are consigned to the internal point of view.[42]

Rulers and other leaders are seemingly permitted to act whenever their actions are not illegal or violations of natural justice, which has to do with what is deserved by others. Yet when people have been utterly subjugated by a ruler, then other constraints on rulers enter in – external constraints having to do with what is honorable. Those constraints, argued Grotius, arise from humanitarian concerns, where, in a sense, we are not permitted to do, on grounds of legality and retributive justice, what we would otherwise be permitted to do.[43] Grotius spoke of only two clear cases where the subjugators have a *duty* to treat people humanely: slaves and prisoners of war.

The slave can be subjugated according to justice, if that is indeed the form of the slavery contract. An enemy soldier, even a prisoner of war, can be justly punished for what he did on the battlefield. Both the laws of nations and of natural justice can support this conclusion. But there is nonetheless a more honorable way to behave, where the slave and the prisoner of war must be treated humanely. For Grotius, all slaves and prisoners of war are to be treated humanely. In many cases, what this means is that they are to be pardoned or released, no matter what they otherwise deserve, even if that is "the penalty of death."[44] Because they have been subjugated, their status is more important than their behavior is.

Humanitarian concerns involve disregarding what people have done in the past, as well as how the institutions of the world might optimally be rearranged. Humanitarian concerns are deeply individual – something about this person and his or her current predicament requires lenient treatment. My initial thought here is that it is the status of being dependent on another person, despite what one has done to warrant that dependency, that seems to count. If, for whatever reason, you are rendered dependent on another, the person who keeps you in that state has special duties toward you. I might otherwise have no duty to feed you; but if I am confining you, I violate a duty to you if I do not feed you. The normative grounding of such a view has to do with treating people not on the basis of what they have done but on the basis of who they are, on their status. In the case of prisoners of war, humanitarian concerns become duties insofar as these prisoners have been rendered vulnerable by our voluntary acts.

[41] Ibid., p. 643.   [42] Ibid.   [43] Ibid., p. 733.   [44] Ibid.

The most appropriate way to look at it is to think that there is a fiduciary or stewardship relationship between prisoner and jailer/warden due to the fact that the prisoner is utterly dependent on the jailer/warden. Fiduciary or stewardship relationships do not arise very often because they are based on one party having been entrusted with the care of another. For this reason, humane treatment or mercy that should be displayed toward the prisoner is not outweighed by what the prisoner might deserve as a matter of retribution. It is the consideration of special circumstances or relationships that makes it the case that humanity can be but is not always of overriding concern. If there are not special considerations that trigger a fiduciary or stewardship relationship, such as confinement, it may turn out that retributive justice is the most appropriate way to treat a particular class of case.

IV. CONNECTING CONSENSUAL AND UNIVERSAL SOURCES OF THE RULES OF WAR

In the current and previous chapters, two grounds for the laws of war have been discussed. In this section, I wish to bring these two sources together into a coherent account. Some of the rules of war can be justified on grounds of the protection of the vulnerable. Other rules of war can be grounded in the idea that soldiers should reciprocally hold themselves to greater restraint than justice might require in order to indicate that they are engaged in an honorable activity, even though it involves the intentional killing of fellow humans. One of the most significant attempts to link these two ideas was proposed by Grotius' follower, Samuel Pufendorf. I will begin with a brief discussion of his ideas and then build on them in the final pages of this chapter.

Pufendorf, writing in the second half of the 17th century, made a good start at linking these two normative sources of the rules of war when he said,

Positive law is that which is by no means derived from the general condition of human nature, but proceeds entirely from the pleasure of the legislator, although it should not lack reason and usefulness, at least for the particular society of men for which it is passed. . . . [T]he reasons for it are not sought in the universal condition of mankind, but in the special and sometimes temporary advantage of distinct social groups.[45]

[45] Samuel Pufendorf, *De Jure Naturae et Gentium* (*On the Law of Nature and Nations*) (1672), translated by C. H. Oldfather and W. A. Oldfather, Oxford: Clarendon Press, 1934, p. 112.

I have somewhat similarly argued that some of the rules of war are just the sort of advantage to a distinct group – namely, soldiers as representing the State – that States commit themselves to supporting when they send their soldiers into harm's way.

Pufendorf also believed that some moral rules could be grounded in universal morality, or what he called natural law considerations. Natural law sets out what is required for peace given our natures, whereas the law of nations deals with the conditions for peace given the contextual contingencies faced in each society at the time when peace is sought. Our natures may not demand more than that rules restrain certain natural passions that would get in the way of the pursuit of peace. But for lasting peace to be accomplished in a given region of the world at a given period of time, more than these relatively abstract rules might be needed.

Of course, it may turn out that there are good reasons for nearly any State to endorse the rules of war, based on considerations of prudence. As long as there are wars and those wars put one's soldiers into harm's way, these prudential reasons will apply. And it may appear that these rules are grounded in something universal, for few if any States would reject the prudential grounds of these rules. Such reasons do not rise to the level of universal natural reasons because they are not based on human nature but rather on the contingent features of the lives of humans.

Pufendorf offered a good analysis of the way that contingent events connect to principles of universal morality. In his view, natural laws are imposed on humans by God and concern what it is necessary for humans to do in order to be good at all times. Positive laws are rules imposed on humans by sovereigns and other kinds of superiors. Morality aims "primarily to direct and temper the freedom of the voluntary acts of man, and thereby to secure a certain orderliness and decorum in civilized life."[46] As soon as humans proceed to form societies, they also differentiate themselves into special roles and functions. The majority of laws are positive laws, "superadded later at the pleasure of men themselves, according as they felt that the introduction of them would help to develop the life of man and reduce it to order."[47]

One of the crucial ways that positive or consensual norms operate is to impose obligations on those who assume certain social roles. It is of

[46] Ibid., p. 5.   [47] Ibid.

course not necessary that anyone would assume such a role; but once it is assumed, humans then are assigned different obligations. "On the basis of a difference in their status or functions," obligations "are either public or private, as their function is directly for the use of a civil group, or for the advantage of individuals as such."[48] Pufendorf was explicitly concerned with public roles in war, especially "common soldiers who . . . may be considered public persons, because they are authorized, directly or indirectly, by the highest civil power, to bear arms in behalf of the state."[49] Common soldiers thus come to have both obligations and rights posited due to their contingent public status. These obligations and rights are no less certain even if they are not grounded on anything that is, strictly speaking, naturally or morally universal.

In a significant set of passages for the development of the law of war, Pufendorf connected his earlier account of how obligation can be imposed by civil authorities, based on the roles that people come to serve, to the universal moral restraints that exist naturally as well. Toward the end of his treatise *De Jure Naturae et Gentium*, Pufendorf took up the topic of what might be legitimately done to a certain kind of hostage in war. He generally argued that positive law obligations and rights are due to the public assumption of roles. And so the question is whether the hostage has assumed his role voluntarily or not and then whether the hostage agreed to lose his liberty and also his life. It would be clearly wrong to punish "an innocent hostage who did not himself consent to the violation of the pacts" that now risk his destruction.[50]

Pufendorf could not have been aware of how important this argument would be for the development of the rules of war. Indeed, Pufendorf qualified his position on hostages when he said that they might indeed be placed in jeopardy if it was for the common good, just as a State might justifiably "assign any of its citizens in war a post, in the defense of which, they must perish or be captured."[51] In this admission, Pufendorf seemed to fail to see the import of his remarks about the much more vulnerable position of hostages as opposed to soldiers, although perhaps he was not unaware of this because he spoke of a very special case where soldiers have no other option but to be killed or captured. Yet even in such situations, soldiers are provided

[48] Ibid., p. 11.   [49] Ibid.   [50] Ibid., p. 1156.   [51] Ibid.

with weapons to defend themselves, even against overwhelming odds, whereas hostages are "miserable" in that they are utterly defenseless.

While the positive law is not founded on the laws of nature, it should be nonetheless consistent with it. As Pufendorf said, "All civil laws, indeed, presuppose or incorporate the general principles at least of natural law, whereby the safety of the human race is maintained; and these latter are by no means done away with by the former, which are merely added to them as the distinct advantage of each state has required."[52] The positive law of each State, also called the civil law, is consistent with the natural law in that both are primarily aimed at peace. But what the positive laws add concerns the specific features of a particular society that need to be changed in order to achieve a just peace. This is what Pufendorf seems to mean by talking about positive, consensual norms serving the specific advantage of each State.

In wartime situations, not only when a State is fighting a just war, Pufendorf contended that some advanced States saw it as important to "prevent great warriors from unduly exposing their skills to envy when they exercised the full license of war."[53] The rules concerning warriors' behavior became customs over time. Indeed, they seemed to arise out of some kind of tacit consent. But because these customs are only added onto natural law, they do not have the universal bindingness that is normally thought to attach to natural law precepts. Nonetheless, because they are consistent with the natural law's motivation toward peace, "it seemed best to many peoples to restrain the excesses of war by a form of humanity and magnanimity."[54]

One last insight can be gained from Pufendorf's rich treatment of those who are governed by positive law on the basis of the roles they have undertaken, or at least not refused to assume. For Pufendorf, positive law is not founded on human nature but is grounded in the pleasure of sovereigns. And in war, a "large number of nations have set no limit or measure on the license, against an enemy, allowed us . . . by the law of nature."[55] Indeed, Pufendorf does not seem to recognize a ground for the law of nations based on what is "common to all of mankind" except that which comes to us through the law of nature. For whatever else is part of the law of nations belongs "to the civil laws of different nations," which only is "accidentally" agreed to due to the sovereigns' pleasure.[56]

---

[52] Ibid., p. 199.   [53] Ibid., p. 227.   [54] Ibid.   [55] Ibid., p. 1307.   [56] Ibid., p. 226.

Without a common sovereign over all of the States of the world, there is no ground for a law of nations other than such mutual agreements and the natural law provision that States should restrain themselves by "universal reason that is common to all mankind."[57] Pufendorf has supplied us with a valuable insight into the reasons why it would be prudent for States to acknowledge certain rules of war that would restrain themselves – namely, a concern for the miserably vulnerable position that soldiers have been placed into by their States. This will also be true of the vulnerable positions of civilians, prisoners of war, and medical personnel, as we will see. Pufendorf also helps us see that such consensual or positive grounds are also supported by general humanitarian considerations more broadly grounded in universal principles of minimal natural law. In the next chapter, I will pull various threads together from Chapters 1–3 to set out what I regard to be the normative cornerstone of international humanitarian law as epitomized in the Geneva Conventions.

[57] Ibid.

4

Humane treatment as the cornerstone of the rules of war

The least discussed, and yet arguably the most important, principle of international humanitarian law and the corresponding war crimes law is humane treatment. The other main principles – discrimination, necessity, and proportionality – have been extensively written about, although not, as we will see in subsequent chapters, always clearly explained and justified. But the idea of humane treatment, which is mentioned many times in The Hague and Geneva Conventions, the main sources of war crimes law, has not been subject to the same scrutiny and defense. At least one reason for this apparent lacuna is that humane treatment may simply be thought of as shorthand for that treatment which satisfies the other principles of *jus in bello* regulations. I will dispute this simple explanation in this chapter and then set out a clear account of the principle of humane treatment. I will also connect the Grotian principle of humanity to the contemporary idea of humane treatment.

The principle of humane treatment is a principle that calls both for the minimizing of suffering and for merciful treatment, as a way of displaying honor. At its core, humane treatment is related to the principle of humanity that involves treating another person as a fellow human, as a member of the same group, the human race, rather than in any number of other ways that take account of his or her otherness. What it means in any particular situation to treat another person as a fellow human is not always easy to see. Restraint is crucial because there are so many competing interests that people have that they will often not see themselves as primarily fellow humans, instead of as oppressors or victims, for instance.

When we conform to the Grotian principle of humanity, we disregard many of the particularities and differences of our lives and give to others the benefit of the doubt, as if we were all pretty much the same. But humane treatment also calls for sensitivity to context, not so that we can disregard our common humanity, but rather so that we can identify how a fellow human should be treated in a situation of vulnerability, rather than seeing the person as stripped of any particularity or as an enemy rather than a fellow human. Humanitarian considerations, as Grotius acknowledged over three hundred years ago, call for discounting what it is alleged that a soldier did on the battlefield, but not disregarding the fact that the soldier was a prisoner completely under the care of the capturing army. Humane treatment in accordance with the Geneva Conventions views a person as a prisoner, for instance, and treats him or her as much like a fellow human as one can. In this sense, the contemporary principle of humane treatment combines consensual and universal moral considerations that we discussed in the previous two chapters.

In this chapter, I begin with a discussion of how the principle of humane treatment grounds the Geneva Conventions. I then explain why the principle of humane treatment should be seen as the cornerstone of humanitarian law generally, not merely a combination of the principles of discrimination, necessity, and proportionality, and thus why it is a distinct requirement of the *jus in bello* part of Just War theory. I then divide up the components of humane treatment into two, compassion and minimizing suffering on the one hand and mercy and equity on the other hand, devoting Sections 3 and 4 to each of these. In the final section, I assess the recent debate about whether humanitarian law and human rights law have the same grounding. Throughout this chapter and subsequent chapters, I argue that *jus in bello* restraints cannot be fully conceptualized without a proper understanding of the principle of humane treatment.

I. THE GENEVA CONVENTIONS AND INTERNATIONAL HUMANITARIAN LAW

In a 1999 article, two U.S. Army lawyers said, "The seemingly vague and ambiguous standard of humane treatment is actually the crux of the Geneva Convention."[1] It is clear to most scholars who examine the

---

[1] Geoffrey S. Corn and Michael L. Smidt, "'To Be or Not to Be, That is the Question': Contemporary Military Operations and the Status of Captured Personnel," *Army Lawyer*, vol. 1, June 1999, p. 10.

Geneva Conventions and related documents on the rules of war, that "humane treatment is a fundamental guarantee" of the Geneva Conventions, which provide that all persons who have ceased to take part in hostilities "shall in all circumstances be treated humanely, without any adverse distinction. . . ."[2] If enemy soldiers are to be treated as fellow humans, rather than as enemies, how can war itself be justified? Is the principle of humane treatment the key to all of the laws of war or only those concerning noncombatants?

In the Common Article III to the Geneva Conventions, there is a relatively clear indication of what inhumane treatment involves:

Persons taking no active part in the hostilities . . . shall in all circumstances be treated humanely. . . . To this end, the following acts are and shall remain prohibited at any time and in any place. . . .

a) violence to life and person, in particular murder of all kinds, mutilation, cruel treatment and torture;
b) taking of hostages;
c) outrages upon personal dignity, in particular, humiliating and degrading treatment;
d) the passing of sentences and the carrying out of executions without previous judgment. . . .[3]

From this list, we can get a clear model of what counts as inhumane treatment. But it is the first provision that causes the most trouble when we move to those who are taking part in active hostilities. For these hostilities are premised on the idea of inflicting "violence to life and person," seemingly a prerequisite to fighting a war at all.

Yet, if we look at the whole of the first subcategory, we see a possible way to understand how this model of humane treatment might be applied even to those who are actively engaged in hostilities. For what is ruled out primarily is murder, which is normally defined as the unjustified intentional taking of life. In war, it is thought that both sides can lay claim to something like the principle of self-defense in order to show that they are not engaged in simple murder. In addition, the rest of the first subcategory could be perfectly at home on the battlefield as well as off. For war does not require mutilation, cruel

---

[2] Suzanne M. Bernard, "An Eye for an Eye: The Current Status of International Law on the Humane Treatment of Prisoners," *Rutgers Law Journal*, vol. 25, Spring 1994, p. 765.

[3] Geneva Convention IV, August 12, 1949, 75 U.N.T.S. 287, 6 U.T.S. 3516, T.I.A.S. No. 3365, Article III.

treatment, or torture. So, if most killing is not considered murder on the battlefield, then there is no obvious incompatibility between the principle of humane treatment as understood in Common Article III of the Geneva Conventions and the fighting of war. Indeed, we have what the laws of war have always aspired to provide: a restrained and morally acceptable way for war to be conducted.

Protocol II of the Geneva Conventions, which somewhat amends Common Article III, is no worse off either. For this protocol adds: collective punishment, acts of terrorism, slavery and slave trade in all its forms, and pillage, to the list of things proscribed.[4] It is true, of course, that wars will be harder to wage if they do not use terrorizing tactics, but they will not be rendered impossible. Indeed, this may be one of the main reasons why the United States has not ratified this Protocol. But subscribing to the principle of humane treatment, as so understood, certainly does not rule out all wars and can make the wars that conform to this standard considerably more likely to be regarded as morally acceptable wars by all but pacifists.

There are restraints on tactics in war that affect both combatants and noncombatants and do not necessarily render all war immoral. As noncombatants, medical personnel are obviously vulnerable in war in ways that combatants are not. Here is an example described quite graphically by Michael Ignatieff:

On December 17, 1996, six Red Cross personnel were asleep in their beds in an I.C.R.C. hospital at Novye Atagi, near Grozny, in Chechnya. The hospital, which provided medical care for all factions in the conflict, had been officially accepted by both Russian and Chechen authorities. The hospital compound was guarded by unarmed Chechen staff. At around 4 A.M., an unknown number of armed and masked men scaled the wall of the compound. They all had pistols fitted with silencers. They knocked one guard unconscious, pumped several shots into the hospital computers, and then made their way to the dormitory block where the Red Cross staff were sleeping. The killers were questioned by a Chechen nurse, and she was told to get out of the way. The six sleepers – from Canada, Norway, New Zealand, The Netherlands, and Spain – were shot at such close range that powder burns were found on them. . . . The incident was the worst massacre of Red Cross personnel in history."[5]

The next day, a field delegate sent the following message: "All our endeavor is based on the belief that, even in the middle of the worst

[4] Protocol Additional to the Geneva Conventions of 12 August 1949, and Relating to the Protection of Victims of Non-International Armed Conflicts, 1977.
[5] Michael Ignatieff, *The Warrior's Honor*, pp. 161–162.

depravities of war, man retains a fundamental minimum of humanity."[6] No one claimed responsibility for these killings. Because of their vulnerability, their status rather than their behavior, medical personnel are in desperate need of protection, and this is the basis of the restraints of the principle of humanity. This is undoubtedly why the first Geneva Convention, created during the Civil War, started laying out the rules of war by focusing on the immunity from attack of medical personnel. The principle of humane treatment is the cornerstone for humanitarian law, including the protection of medical personnel, especially during wartime.

II. THE CONCEPT OF HUMANE TREATMENT

Crimes against humanity are best understood as violations of absolute moral requirements concerning group-based torture or murder of the innocent. Crimes such as ethnic cleansing are condemned everywhere and in all circumstances. These crimes are "against humanity" in the very broad sense of assaulting all of humanity whenever they occur. Most *war crimes* are not best understood as violations of absolute moral requirements, at least not ones of universal binding force, because the rules of war, the violation of which count as war crimes, have changed dramatically over the years, often due to changes in circumstances. In a sense, war crimes are crimes against humaneness rather than against humanity, and humaneness is highly context-specific.

Humaneness is itself not even a duty, but simply a matter of charity, in most situations. It is considered inhumane today not to release prisoners of war after a war has ended. But of course, outside of the context of a war ending, it is not considered inhumane to fail to release prisoners. In the latter case, it would be morally good, in the sense of displaying mercy, to release prisoners, but hardly anyone would say that it is morally wrong not to do so. Similarly, it would merely be morally good for me to feed your children; but if I had captured your children, it would be morally wrong not to feed them. As an indication of the difference between crimes against humanity and war crimes, note that the Rome Statute of the International Criminal Court has a very short list of crimes against humanity and a very long list of war

---

[6] Ibid., pp. 162–163.

crimes. The Rome Statute lists only 11 crimes against humanity, but over 50 war crimes.[7]

What counts as humaneness also varies from one historical time to another. The most obvious case to think about is war. It is said to be inhumane to use poisons rather than bullets in battle. But this is only a relatively recent proscription. It was also once considered to be inhumane to use arrows with feathers, but it is not considered so today. It was once considered to be a war crime to use a catapult, or a submarine, or a helicopter, yet today the use of none of these weapons is proscribed as a war crime. At least in part, the changes in what counts as a war crime are based on the development of new types of weapons, where each new weapon is banned until the technology is available to both sides. But there is more to it than this, for our conception of what is humane has evolved over time as well, and tactics in war once thought to be normal and acceptable, such as raping the women of a town taken by assault, is now strongly condemned.[8]

In this section, I develop a minimalist conception of the principle of humane treatment. Minimalism is meant to be deflationary in two respects. As I indicated in Chapter 3, minimalism is supposed to minimize the number of assumptions that one begins with. And this is then also supposed to minimize the likely objections to the place where one starts. A minimalist principle of humane treatment provides the least controversial way to understand the norms governing appropriate behavior during war. When we speak of humane treatment, we refer to greater restraint than that which is called for due to considerations of justice and what we strictly owe to each other. While still operating within the domain of minimalist principles, a soldier's sense of honor dictates that she or he do more than provide what is due. In following the principle of charity, she or he is quick to forgive or pardon rather than to punish.

The difficulty is that in war it seems especially dangerous to give to the enemy the benefit of the doubt. If there are to be restraints in war, it seems less controversial only to restrict ourselves by the principle of justice rather than the principle of humaneness. And because we owe very little if anything to people who are attacking us, or who have tried to attack us, the laws of war will provide very minimal restraints indeed. But there are good reasons to think that most enemy soldiers have not

[7] Statute of the International Criminal Court [as Corrected by the *procès-verbaux* of 10 November 1998 and 12 July 1999], Articles 7 and 8 (hereinafter, the Rome Statute).

[8] The Rome Statute, Article 8, sec. 2(e)(vi). Also see Kelly Dawn Askin, *War Crimes Against Women*, Dordrecht, The Netherlands: Martinus Nijhoff, 1997.

done anything wrong in attacking, because most of them act merely because they have been ordered to act. Therefore, even enemy soldiers are not owed a lethal response on our part. Indeed, for many centuries philosophers have accepted the moral equality of soldiers, that whether they serve on the aggressing or defending side, the soldiers themselves are no more or less guilty. Even in war, justice calls for restraints, and I would argue that more than justice is also required as soldiers seek honor during killing.

Humaneness, as we will see below, morally *requires* compassion and mercy, but only in certain circumstances. The most obvious case concerns confinement. The less obvious cases concern other statuses that a person has been thrust into, such as the vulnerable status of not having a weapon at all when others do, or of not having a certain *type* of weapon when others do. Even confinement is best seen as a special vulnerable status that changes what is morally required. On the other hand, soldiers who have no special vulnerabilities are not owed compassion or mercy as a matter of humaneness, although it is still often a very good thing for compassion and mercy to be displayed toward them. Humaneness becomes a duty, the violation of which counts as a war crime, only in special circumstances of vulnerability.

The general idea is that justice does not exhaust all of our duties, for justice typically concerns what is owed as a matter of what we have done. Justice often dictates what is owed as a matter of our equality, and thus justice can concern status, although normally only universal status, such as what is owed as a matter of our human rights. But there is no human right to be treated with compassion or mercy. Such considerations have to do with special status not universal status. Thus, I will talk of humaneness rather than humanity to make sure that we do not think of the duties of humaneness as extending to all human beings in all circumstances. Compassion and mercy are duties only in special circumstances, primarily when one person is vulnerable to another. It would indeed be good to display compassion and mercy to all humans, but this becomes a duty only when special circumstances of vulnerability obtain.

To say that the principle of humane treatment is the cornerstone of humanitarian law is to place it over the more traditionally recognized principles of discrimination, necessity, and proportionality.[9] These

---

[9] For a good preliminary philosophical discussion of these three principles, see Douglas P. Lackey, *The Ethics of War and Peace*, Upper Saddle River, NJ: Prentice-Hall, 1989, pp. 58–68.

principles are often understood as forming the entire basis for the laws of war. But unless we stretch these principles, it will be hard to make sense of the kind of prohibitions that are involved in many of the provisions in Common Article III of the Geneva Convention, what is sometimes called the "Convention in Miniature."[10] Necessity clearly calls for balancing or weighing restraining considerations against militarily necessary conduct. The principle of proportionality also involves a weighing or utilitarian calculation that seems very different from the prohibitions of the "Convention in Miniature." And discrimination, or distinction, which is clearly not about balancing, calls for a completely different treatment of civilians and combatants. So if I am right to think that the principle of humane treatment cuts across the divide between civilians and combatants, then the principle of humane treatment is not merely derived from, or a combination of, these other three principles.

If humanitarian law, or the law of war, is to have a grounding or cornerstone at all, the three traditional principles will not do the job. I suppose it is possible that the laws of war have no underlying principle of justification. Indeed, it sometimes seems as if what we have is merely a list of rules from different eras, cobbled together into increasingly lengthy instruments, where there is so little agreement about what their basis is that the list merely repeats previous lists verbatim, lest the original consensus about them be jeopardized by minor changes in wording.[11] Perhaps there is no cornerstone to humanitarian law. But then that branch of international law will be significantly more infirm than people generally think. The Geneva Conventions, for instance, at least until quite recently, have been considered the least controversial of all aspects of international law.[12] It would be odd if there were to be no underlying rationale for the various provisions of such a well-accepted document.

---

[10] Kenneth Watkins, "Controlling the Use of Force: A Role for Human Rights Norms in Contemporary Armed Conflict," *American Journal of International Law*, vol. 98, no. 1 (2004), p. 25, quoting the International Committee of the Red Cross's Commentary on the Geneva Convention.

[11] This seems especially apparent when examining the Rome Statute, which quotes verbatim from previous documents, such as the Geneva Conventions' Common Article III.

[12] Members of George W. Bush's administration have cast doubt on whether it is still true that the Geneva Conventions are uncontroversial. One member of this administration said that the Geneva Conventions were antiquated due to the rise of terrorism. I address this issue in the final chapter of this book.

In the next two sections, I will explore two components of the principle of humane behavior that are grounded in an understanding of what soldiers should do to maintain a sense of honor on the battlefield. These features will set the floor for the minimalist understanding of humane treatment. As I've argued, they are surely the most important conceptual and normative considerations for the grounding of humanitarian law. As we have seen in this section, there will also be broad overlap between this discussion and discussions of the conceptual and normative grounding of human rights law as well, although in the final section we will also see some differences between human rights law and humanitarian law.

III. COMPASSION AND MINIMAL SUFFERING

David Hume once famously asserted the connection between sympathy or compassion with the principle of humanity:

Would any man who is walking alone, tread as willingly on another's gouty toes, whom he has no quarrel with, as on the hard flint and pavement? There is here surely a difference in the case. We surely take into consideration the happiness and misery of others, in weighing the several motives of action, and incline to the former where no private regards draw us to seek our own promotion or advantage by the injury of our fellow creatures. And if the principles of humanity are capable in many instances of influencing our actions, they must at all times have some authority over our sentiments. . . . The degrees of these sentiments may be the subject of controversy; but the reality of their existence, one should think, must be admitted in every theory or system.[13]

There are two closely related reasons for this reaction. First, humans typically put themselves into the position of the other and imaginatively feel with the other – that is, feel what is imagined that the other is feeling at the time. And as a result of feeling with the other, literally what compassion means, we restrain our behavior based on our shared feelings with the other. Second, humans typically try not to inflict more suffering on one another than is necessary, because we subscribe to a principle of reciprocity whereby we do not do things to others that we would not want them to do to us. In particular, this means that we will go out of our way to minimize the suffering that is caused to another because that is how we would want others to treat us.

[13] David Hume, *An Enquiry Concerning the Principles of Morals*, 1751, sec. V. part II, para. 24, reprinted in *Hume's Ethical Writings*, edited by Alasdair MacIntyre, Notre Dame, IN: University of Notre Dame Press, 1965, p. 72.

Hume points out that sympathy, or compassion, will be limited in those cases where there is some private advantage to be gained at the infliction of injury on the other. But even in this case, the sentiments of sympathy and compassion continue to influence us, even in wartime. Indeed, from the earliest attempts to draw up a code of war, minimizing the suffering of others has been one of the key components. As I will argue later, even when our interest is affected – in those situations where the enemy soldier has been rendered vulnerable by us – our compassionate feelings should dominate our other sentiments.

The first modern codification of the laws of war were drawn up by Francis Lieber in the *Instructions for Government of Armies of the U.S. in the Field* and issued to the Union Army by President Lincoln in 1863. What is now called the Lieber Code says that "military necessity does not admit of cruelty – that is, the infliction of suffering for the sake of suffering or revenge."[14] One of the precursors of the Hague Conventions, the Project of an International Declaration Concerning the Laws and Customs of War expresses the hope that: "war being thus regulated would involve less suffering."[15] This sets the stage for the Hague Conventions of 1907, which placed the restraint on suffering at the core of the laws of war. It is interesting that the first modern attempt to codify humanitarian law specifically says that restrictions on extreme suffering in the form of cruelty are simply not compatible even with military necessity. This makes of the restraint on suffering something more than merely an injunction to engage in utilitarian calculations.

The Lieber Code seems to muddy the waters about how to understand the idea of minimal suffering in the laws of war when it also declares: "[T]he unarmed citizen is to be spared in person, property, and honor as much as the exigencies of war will admit."[16] This declaration creates a conceptual problem for understanding the earlier, seemingly absolute, prohibition on cruel treatment. Because cruel treatment is treatment of the person, it seems to be covered by and thus contingent on the provision that calls for a weighing in terms of what "the exigencies of war will admit." Luckily, there is also a definition of cruelty provided that seems to answer this objection. Cruelty is defined as "the infliction of suffering for the sake of suffering or

[14] Quoted in Leslie C. Green, "International Regulation of Armed Conflicts," in *International Criminal Law: vol. 1, Crimes*, edited by M. Cherif Bassiouni, 2nd ed., Ardsley, NY: Transactional Publishers, p. 363.
[15] Ibid., p. 364.   [16] Ibid., p. 363.

revenge." Thus, cruelty is given a fairly narrow meaning here, as a kind of superfluous suffering – at least in the case of suffering caused for revenge, it does not play a role in the military objectives of winning battles and wars. Once cruelty is given this narrow meaning, then it is understood as falling under an absolute prohibition, not merely being a matter of weighing that occurs when military necessity is added to the calculation. Indeed, the Lieber Code seems to define cruelty in such a way that it literally cannot overlap with military necessity.

It is possible, of course, that revenge could play a role in a militarily necessary strategy. Imagine a situation where the only way to over-come much greater troop strength is to motivate one's own troops into a fever pitch. Perhaps it is thought that the only way to do this is to instill a kind of blood-revenge, where the brutal killing of a cap-tured enemy soldier seems to be necessary to rally the troops for the ferocity that is needed. But even in this case, there would not be the creation of suffering merely for the sake of revenge. Rather, at least concerning this particular captured soldier, the main impetus for causing suffering is to motivate one's troops to do what is necessary to win a given battle. Cruelty is narrowly drawn here to include only superfluous suffering, at least superfluous to any military objective. And because most mistreatment of prisoners of war is claimed to have some objective connected to the war effort, there will unfortunately be very few cases of causing suffering that are banned as cruelty by the Lieber Code.

There is a debate in humanitarian legal theory about how best to understand minimal suffering. This debate begins in the context of a discussion about how to translate the French term *"maux superflus"* in the Hague Convention (IV) of 1907. Article 23 reads: "[I]t is especially prohibited . . . (c) to employ arms, projectiles, or material calculated to cause unnecessary suffering." *Maux superflus* here is translated as "unnecessary suffering." Originally, at the time of the adoption of Hague Convention (IV), *maux superflus* was given a more literal, and supposedly less subjective, translation as "superfluous injury." The term "excessive suffering" was thought to be a good compromise. "Unnecessary suffering" calls to mind the bright-line idea that only some tactics can be justified if they are militarily necessary, whereas both "superfluous" and "excessive" injury seem to be matters of degree. Indeed, both superfluous and excessive suffering are closely related to the idea of minimizing suffering, and this seems to be a utilitarian-inspired idea.

Minimal suffering does not have to be conceptualized in utilitarian terms. For minimal suffering could refer to a true minimum baseline beyond which our conduct should not fall. This is what I take it that *maux superflus* could have meant to the drafters of the Hague Convention (IV) – namely, a baseline beyond which the creation of suffering is prohibited because of the character of the suffering, not because of what it is, or is not, offset by. Minimal suffering can be seen as either a utilitarian notion that calls for us to weigh all factors before deciding whether we are permitted to act or as a more absolutist notion that sets a baseline above which acts are permitted and below which they are prohibited, or as something in between these two, as I will explain below.

I believe that the best way to view the requirement to avoid minimal suffering is closely related to what a person would feel to be required by compassion. It is not weighing per se that is at stake, but considering what it would feel like if I were the recipient rather than the perpetrator of the action. As a recipient, I would want as little suffering caused to me as possible given the circumstances. I would not necessarily be happy to learn that my suffering was offset by the greater happiness of someone else. But I might not mind it if I had to suffer a bit so that others would not have to suffer a lot. I would object if the level of my suffering went below what is acceptable, but I might not object if the level of my suffering was above this baseline and there was clearly greater suffering of others that was alleviated. So the idea of minimal suffering does not have to be conceived of as a utilitarian notion, and indeed it should not be if I am right to think that it is closely related to compassion.

Humane treatment calls for minimal suffering on the part of others who are affected by our actions. It would be inhumane to treat others in certain ways merely because I was made to feel some small happiness, or even a relatively large happiness. For then, we would fail to treat the other person as a fellow human whose status alone sets limits on how he or she can be treated. It is inhumane to make another person suffer when nothing of equal or greater importance is accomplished by that suffering. And beyond this, most people would not allow even for a trade of equal suffering and certainly not for the mere increase in happiness of the other. This is the baseline, and there will be other considerations as well, as we will see in subsequent sections of this chapter. At the moment, I want to investigate a bit more why international humanitarian law concerns itself at all with suffering, given that war always involves suffering and most of us would seemingly be better off without wars altogether rather than merely with restricting the practices of war.

In 1868, the first major international agreement prohibiting the use of a particular weapon in warfare was the St. Petersburg Declaration. It begins by declaring "that the progress of civilization should have the effect of alleviating as much as possible the calamities of war." And "the employment of arms which uselessly aggravate the suffering of disabled men" is said to be "contrary to the laws of humanity."[17] Here is a paradigm case of superfluous suffering, for if a soldier is already disabled, it is very hard to see how making him suffer now will advance the war effort. Perhaps it is believed that he has information about the next plan of attack, in which case there is a clear military advantage in making this soldier suffer. Otherwise, to continue to inflict suffering after the soldier has been incapacitated is surely cruel – not an action that would be in keeping with a soldier who cares about honor.

The idea is that some wars may be justified, especially when a State is being overrun by another State that seeks to subjugate its citizens. In such situations, once war has begun we would want to restrict the violence of war in such a way that suffering is minimized. Perhaps, some day far in the future, we will discover that wars could be fought like duels between two leaders of States who thought it was worthwhile to go to war. This would certainly minimize suffering because presumably these leaders would only authorize violence, especially given the likelihood of reciprocal violence by the other State, in the most extreme cases.

IV. MERCY, EQUITY, AND HONOR

Humane treatment calls for more than minimizing suffering, for when there are people who cannot defend themselves, or who are in some other way dependent on us, we owe more to them than just not making them suffer superfluously. In many cases, we might feel that we should not make them suffer at all, even if they have given us reason to hate them by their past behavior toward us or if the law permits it. In this way, the idea of mercy will restrain us further than will the idea of

---

[17] 1868 St. Petersburg Declaration Renouncing the Use in Time of War of Explosive Projectiles Under 400 Grams Weight, para. 2, quoted in Leslie C. Green, "International Regulation of Armed Conflicts," in *International Criminal Law, vol. I: Crimes*, edited by M. Cherif Bassiouni, Ardsley, NY: Transaction Publishers, 1999, p. 364.

minimal suffering. In addition, because mercy is linked to equity, there
is a sense in which merciful treatment is deserved in some other way
than what is deserved on the basis of justice, at least the kind of formal
justice that seeks to match praise or punishment with what one has
done. Mercy carves out a basis for treatment that is not necessarily
linked to what a person has done, but is more in keeping with that
person's status, the key generally to the idea of humane treatment.

My account of mercy coincides with some things that Claudia Card
has said on this subject, although we also differ a bit. In her 1972
article, Card said,

The basic point of mercy seems to lie in the recognition that, in the absence of
"cosmic justice," some of those whom a socially just community would have the
right to punish may be unusually more "sinned against than sinning," either by
other persons or, metaphorically speaking, by fate.[18]

For Card, employing mercy is "more just than it would be possible
to be in some cases were we to act in accord with institutional justice."
The reason for this is that acting mercifully forces us to consider "facts
about his character and suffering which may not be revealed simply by
looking at his offense."[19]

I support the general idea here that Card explains so well. We also
agree in thinking that the proper contrast is between "retributive"
justice and mercy, not between mercy and justice in general. We differ
only on the question of whether it makes sense to try to institutionalize
mercy, as seems to be done in the rules of war. Card thinks that the
reason why mercy makes sense is because "there seems to be no feasible institutional remedy for this state of affairs in the form of additional rules governing liability and punishment, which would not have
the effect of seriously undermining the common purposes for which
punishment is instituted."[20] Yet, it seems to me that mercy has indeed
been institutionalized, most obviously in the way that courts of common law regard the role of equity in decision making.

Equity has been opposed to formal justice since at least the time of
Aristotle. In this context, one can think of cases in which a captured
soldier truly deserves to be punished for having killed, perhaps in a
senseless way, many other soldiers. Justice, understood broadly, would
not warrant such punishment, for it would only be justified because of a
kind of gap that has opened due to the nature of war. But in fact,

---

[18] Claudia Card, "On Mercy," *Philosophical Review*, vol. 18, no. 2 (1972), p. 185.
[19] Ibid., p. 191.   [20] Ibid., p. 185.

because the whole idea of war is that soldiers are expected to try to kill each other, some response to the captured soldier other than retribution seems to be in order. Equity has traditionally been seen as that principle that fills the gaps left in formal justice. And mercy has often been the impetus behind filling those gaps in ways that are more restrained than they might otherwise be.

The idea behind this, on the account I have been developing, is that status rather than past behavior is supposed to be the basis of current treatment. Mercy has more to do with status than does justice. Mercy is what we owe to each other as fellow members of the human race with equal dignity and deserving of the same respect. But mercy is not only about status, it is also about the future. Displaying mercy shares with pardoning the idea of forgetting, or at least forgiving, what has been done in the past so that one can look to the future, to a time when peace is restored. Mercy is a gap filler in that it looks to status and the future in order to see what would be truly just in a larger sense than that captured by formal justice.

But when we move from considerations of formal justice to the largely informal considerations of mercy, the question arises about whether this is still properly within the domain of law, humanitarian or otherwise. Theodor Meron calls for a primary place for values such as "ethics, honor, mercy, and shame" in international humanitarian law, yet resigns himself to the idea that these values can only be properly instilled by "education, training, and persuasion" rather than by means of the law.[21] While I am in complete agreement with Meron about how human rights law and humanitarian law should be seen as having a common core, and that that core includes considerations of mercy and honor, I disagree with his claim, and seemingly that of Claudia Card, that much of this core has to be seen as extralegal. In the remainder of this section, I offer an argument against this restricted view of the purview of international law.

International law generally sits at the intersection between morality and law properly so-called, as the legal positivists were wont to say. Indeed, my view is that international law is a hothouse for experimenting with how to move from morality to legality. Many of the court opinions handed down by the ICTY and the ICTR liberally mix considerations of morality and legality, often creating law out of moral

---

[21] "The Humanization of Humanitarian Law," *American Journal of International Law*, vol. 94, April (2000), p. 278.

considerations, such as considerations of basic human rights. I think that Meron is too conservative in how he draws the line between international morality and international law in general. But I also wish to make a broader argument here, one that draws on my earlier discussion of minimal natural law theory. I wish to argue that the concept of equity has historically functioned, and can continue to function, as a basis for bringing such normally moral considerations as those of mercy and honor into a legal system.

In the late Middle Ages in England, considerations of equity were granted the status of law and set up as the basis for an alternative legal system to that of justice formally understood as involving the application of black-letter law. Courts of equity were set up as alternatives to the Common Law courts, and it was quite explicitly held that these alternative courts of equity were to issue judgments based on the conscience of the judges rather than on the strict application of black-letter law to the facts of a specific case. Bringing an action in equity allowed for a more individualized determination than in a common law court. In fact, the courts of equity were said to be outgrowths of the Lord Chancellor's conscience, where the point was to make sure that broad fairness was done.

Equity is still a major component of Anglo-American law, even though it has come under its share of criticism from those like Oliver Wendell Holmes, who was generally opposed to natural law theory. Whole areas of United States law, such as the body of law that arose after *Brown v. Board of Education* concerning school desegregation and busing, were premised on the idea of equitable remedies for violations of the equal protection clause's very broad moral injunctions. While the old courts of equity have been disbanded in most of the states, the ideas of equity were incorporated into the mandate of the restructured common law courts at the end of the 19th-century in the United States.

Conceptually, it makes sense to see equity as a part of law rather than existing outside of law's proper domain. Black-letter laws are necessarily very broad, and cases concern very narrow fact patterns. There will often be a mismatch here, and judges need to be able to use common sense and fairness in deciding what is the best result for the various plaintiffs and defendants. This is not to say that equitable considerations need not be carefully circumscribed, so that the large possibility for abuse of this concept is minimized. But it is also true that a fully fair legal system cannot operate without some conception of equity to allow judges to adjust the law to unusual or original facts, often not dreamt of by legislators.

Mercy enters into this picture in many ways already recognized as being inside rather than outside the domain of law proper. While pardons and amnesties are, strictly speaking, matters of executive and legislative function within the United States, mercy can be shown in judicial decisions in a host of ways, even when there are strict sentencing guidelines. For even when there are sentencing guidelines, there are also ranges of sentences that judges can choose among, and there is nothing extrajudicial about choosing one versus the other out of a concern for the character of the accused or even out of a concern that a particularly harsh sentence, while strictly called for, would not be humane in the circumstances.

Mercy can also be defended as part of the legal system, rather than being regarded as extrajudicial, from a natural law perspective. Natural law theory, even in the minimalist version that I defended in earlier chapters, already advocates a porous border between law and morality. The moral presumption in favor of security and well-being provides a grounding for basic rights to self-defense and subsistence, and these rights form the basis for legal claims. This is especially true of the way that international law traditionally has been conceptualized. As I argued in my book *Crimes Against Humanity*,[22] the core notion of international criminal law is the idea that certain norms are not derogable regardless of what occurs in the area of treaty and black-letter law.

Consider an example that has recently arisen about a supposed gap in the law of the Geneva Conventions that articulates the rights that protected persons have during wartime. The administration of President George W. Bush argued, as I will discuss in greater detail in the final chapter, that the prisoners at Guantanamo Bay's prisons had no status under international law, largely because they were illegal combatants who fell into a gap in the Geneva Conventions. They were not protected as prisoners of war, covered under Geneva Convention III, because they were not soldiers of a recognized state; and they were not protected as civilians under Geneva Convention IV because they were captured carrying arms and operating under a command structure.

---

[22] Larry May, *Crimes Against Humanity: A Normative Account*, New York: Cambridge University Press, 2005, Chapter 2.

Yet, this situation was explicitly addressed in the ICRC's Commentary on Geneva Convention IV's definition of protected persons:

[There] is a general principle which is embodied in all four Geneva Conventions of 1949. Every person in enemy hands must have some status under international law: he is either a prisoner of war and, as such, covered under the Third Convention, a civilian covered under the Fourth Convention, or again, a member of the medical personnel of the armed forces who is covered by the First Convention. *There is no* intermediate status; nobody in enemy hands can be outside the law. We feel that this is a satisfactory solution – not only satisfying to the mind, but also, above all, satisfactory from the humanitarian point of view.[23]

Here is where equity and mercy come together under the humanitarian point of view.

The Bush administration said that it does not recognize the legally binding status of the ICRC Commentary. Whether or not the commentary is binding international law is directly related to the question of what to think of equitable gap-filling strategies as sources of law in general. If one denies that they are part of international law, then one has the unenviable task of explaining what to do in those situations where there are such gaps. Are all States then free to act as they wish? And will the United States be happy with the prospect of fighting the war on terrorism against parties that have no incentive to treat U.S. troops humanely either?

What does honor add to the ideas of minimal suffering, compassion, mercy, and equity in our understanding of humane treatment. The main thing added by honor is the combination of conscientious reflection and motivation crucial for humanitarian law's requirement that soldiers act with restraint even when, as is usually the case in war, it is unlikely that penal sanctions will be brought against them. On this account, the primary motivation for humane treatment comes from a sense of self-worth of the person who acts humanely. Honor combines most closely with compassion, insofar as compassion has to do with feeling with the other, and with mercy, which has to do with seeing beyond what one has done to be able to see who one is. Honor generally calls for acting in ways that we would not only approve of, but that we would seek to emulate and use as a basis for educating our own children. In acting compassionately, we seek to do that which we would

[23] *ICRC Commentary on Geneva Convention IV*, published under the general editorship of Jean S. Pictet, Geneva: International Committee for the Red Cross, 1958, p. 51 (italics in the original).

heartily approve of if it were aimed not at the other but at ourselves. Yet, the behavior in question is not aimed at us but at the other, so there is still a need for some motivation. Similarly, mercy is a nice idea, but it generally lacks a firm motivation. Honor supplies the missing motivation for humane treatment.

Displaying a sense of honor is absolutely necessary in war because other emotions, especially anger, can run so high. If we instill a strict sense of justice – at least that form of justice that is based on what is owed to one another based on what we have done – the violence of war will spiral out of control as we move from one angry episode of revenge taking to another. Only if we see our own honor at stake in requiring restraint based on mercy and compassion for our enemies, now seen as merely fellow humans, can such a spiral be broken. We cannot count on the conditions of the battlefield, or even those of justice, to restrain such strong passions as anger and revenge.

Humane treatment is the cornerstone of humanitarian law in that minimal suffering, mercy, and honor are indeed the main ingredients in the normative conceptualization of the various traditionally recognized restraints on war. Not only does the principle of humane treatment operate to undergird the obvious restraints on how prisoners of war are to be treated, but it also makes sense of restraints on the use of weapons and even on the way that civilians are to be treated during war. Indeed, it is my contention, to be argued for in subsequent chapters, that the principle of humane treatment operates to ground and to limit the more traditionally recognized principles of necessity, discrimination or distinction, and even the principle of proportionality that many have thought to be the cornerstones of international humanitarian law.

The principle of proportionality is a principle of cool calculation that can somewhat restrain the passions of anger and revenge that are common during war. Soldiers are trained to act honorably on the battlefield, where the incentive to restrain oneself comes very deeply from a sense of one's self-worth, because there will be few other restraints that will succeed in overcoming the passions of the battle. Cool calculation will be important, but often only before or after the battles have been waged. And proportionality is notoriously slippery in any event, giving very different answers based often on only minor changes of circumstances. Proportionality calls for the kind of weighing that is hard to do when passions run deep, whereas the sense of honor is a passion that can provide a stop to forward momentum begun in anger or revenge. And honor, along with minimal suffering and mercy, are the considerations that encompass humane treatment, surely the true cornerstone of international humanitarian law.

V.   HUMAN RIGHTS AND HUMANE TREATMENT

In a 2004 article in the *American Journal of International Law*, Kenneth Watkin provides an interesting commentary on the relationship between humanitarian law and human rights law:

The normative framework of international humanitarian law differs in many respects from that of international human rights law. One fundamental difference is that humanitarian law requires the balancing of humanity with military necessity. . . . Because armed conflict largely consists of the application of deadly force, this balancing with humanity forms a major and highly visible part of international humanitarian law. . . . This aspect of international humanitarian law often leaves the impression that, in contrast, human rights law is absolute in nature. . . . [where] the use of deadly force is strictly limited by the requirement that a person not be "arbitrarily" deprived of life.[24]

Watkin goes on to say that this is not as large a difference as it might first appear, and in that assessment I would readily join. There is today an overlap concerning how to extend international law from conflicts that are truly international to those that are more properly said to be internal, as the various discussions of crimes against humanity have amply demonstrated. But the question I wish to pursue here will limit us to the hard case of international conflict.

Theodor Meron has argued that even in the case of international armed conflict there is a growing convergence between human rights and humanitarian norms. Meron cites the complete bans on the use of chemical, biological, and nuclear weapons as well as the ban on the use of reprisals as good evidence of this convergence. But his analysis turns on what I regard to be a faulty dichotomy. Both Meron and Watkin suggest that the major difference between human rights and humanitarian law is that the former has absolute prohibitions and the latter does not. They thus are easily able to show a convergence by pointing to examples of absolute prohibitions in humanitarian law and highly qualified norms in human rights law. This is too easy, especially because, as I will show in the next chapter, the prohibition on poisons

[24] Kenneth Watkin, "Controlling the Use of Force: A Role for Human Rights Norms in Contemporary Armed Conflict," *American Journal of International Law*, vol. 98, no. 1 (2004), pp. 9–10.

and chemical weapons goes back several thousand years, hardly demonstrating a recent convergence.

Another way to characterize the difference between humanitarian law and human rights law is in terms of who is the addressee of the law. Initially, humanitarian law was addressed to States specifying the way that States should act toward other States, where the soldiers who were not supposed to be treated inhumanely were understood as mere extensions of the State. In contrast, human rights law was addressed to everyone in the world, States as well as individuals, in proscribing mistreatment of individuals and groups. Meron also suggests this at one point in an essay.[25] Again, this is not quite right either because humanitarian law has clearly focused on the conditions not only of soldiers but also of civilians. And while it is true that those individuals who are not members of signatory States have had an ambiguous relationship to international humanitarian law, it is hard to see the various prohibitions in the two-thousand-year history of humanitarian law not as providing protection for individuals.

Both of these approaches are nonetheless on the right track in that humanitarian law has focused on what should be done during war, where States were once considered the main players in wars and Just War theory did not often condemn practices outright lest war itself be jeopardized. Because human rights law was not formed as a specific response to conditions of war, it did not need to be expressed with the nuances that humanitarian law did. And because we can trace humanitarian law back to long before human rights were conceived, to a time when States were indeed the only recognized actors on the international stage, it is also true that humanitarian law has focused more on States than has human rights law. What I want to argue, however, is that there is something deeper at stake that will need to be resolved if these two fields are going to converge.

The deeper difference between humanitarian law and human rights law has to do with different understandings of humanity in each field of law. Humanity has at least three different senses. First, it can refer to the *collectivity* of all humans – that is, to the animal species. Second, "humanity" can refer to the *quality* or property that is shared by each member of the collectivity, which makes them members of this species rather than another. In the case of humanity, it is often said that rationality is the key quality. Third, "humanity" can refer to

[25] Theodor Meron, p. 246.

characteristic behaviors and attitudes of the members of the species, such as compassion and mercy. While not unknown in other species and also not displayed by every member of the human species, these behaviors and attitudes are displayed in a greater extent in humans than in other species, at least in an understanding of the ideal member of the species.[26]

It is the third sense of humanity that is used in discussions – like my own earlier discussion of the principle of humane treatment – in accounts of international humanitarian law. But in human rights law, things are somewhat different, for the rights alleged are rights not by virtue of being ideal members of the species or even on the basis of having rationality, as opposed to the capacity to have, or once to have had, rationality. Rather, the rights are status rights in that they obtain whenever there is a member of the collectivity, a member of the human species. And typically, the behavior that is called for is not ideal but actual whenever there is a member of the human species who stands to be affected by certain actions.

Yet, even this seemingly clear difference is not quite as telling as it might at first seem, because humanitarian law also sets requirements for how members of the human species are to be treated that are not merely ideals. There are exceptions however: The Geneva Conventions, for instance, set a moral minimum that is certainly not merely an ideal way for soldiers to behave toward civilians and others who are not engaged in active fighting. Indeed, the requirements against torture in human rights law and the prohibitions against torture in humanitarian law are hard to distinguish from one another. This is not a statement about how humans ideally behave toward one another in either human rights or humanitarian law. The Geneva Conventions explicitly rule out military necessity as an excuse that can be used to justify such practices as torture.[27]

---

[26] There are very good preliminary treatments of this subject in recent literature. See Bernard Williams, "Making Sense of Humanity," in *Making Sense of Humanity and Other Philosophical Papers*, Cambridge: Cambridge University Press, 1995, pp. 79–89; Robin Coupland, "Humanity: What Is It and How Does It Influence International Law?" *International Review of the Red Cross*, vol. 83, no. 844 (2001); and David Luban, "A Theory of Crimes Against Humanity," *Yale Journal of International Law*, vol. 29, no. 1 (2004), 85–140.

[27] Jean S. Pictet summarizes the discussion at the Geneva Conventions concerning Common Article 3 as follows: Certain acts, including cruel treatment and torture "are prohibited absolutely and permanently, no exception or excuse being

Humanity understood in the third sense – namely, how humans characteristically do, or should, behave toward fellow humans – gives rise to the idea that certain forms of behaviour are humane and other forms are inhumane. The idea of inhumane behavior is the ground for at least some of the prohibited behaviors that are often listed as crimes against humanity and also many, if not most, of the behaviors listed as war crimes. It is not just the rational side of human nature that gives rise to these prohibited behaviors, but also the sentiment or feeling side, as we saw in the discussion of Hume. Humane treatment in both humanitarian and human rights law promotes the minimum amount of compassionate and merciful treatment that humans characteristically do, and should, display toward fellow humans.

What human rights theory provides for us, as a partial model for humanitarian legal theory, is the idea that there are indeed universal norms of minimally acceptable behavior that are grounded in the mere status of the recipient of the action as a fellow member of the human species. The minimalism is itself grounded in a certain understanding of human nature, of what Marx aptly called "species being." There can be aberrations, such as people who do not display compassion, but then we would be forced to say that those people are descriptively and normatively deficient in some sense. One of the characteristic features of humans is that they not only display compassion, but also hold other humans up to the standard and sometimes demand compassion as a necessary ingredient in what it means to act humanely.

But there is one significant difference between humanitarian law and human rights law having to do with status. As I have argued, humanitarian law primarily concerns the special not the universal status of humans. Humane treatment is a duty when humans have rendered other humans vulnerable. Compassion and mercy are good for all humans, but they are required only in special circumstances. Human rights involve duties that apply generally, not only in special circumstances, because they apply by virtue of a person being human. And while there is bound to be some overlap between human rights law and humanitarian law, as in the prohibition on torture, humanitarian law continues to focus on torture in cases of prisoners of war, whereas human rights law casts its net far broader and in an unrestricted way.

tolerated." *Commentary on Geneva Convention (I)*, Geneva: International Committee of the Red Cross, 1952, p. 55.

In Part A of this book, I have set up a normative grounding of the idea of humane treatment. I have provided two related grounds for the rules of humanitarian law. The collective responsibility of the society and the minimal moral idea of sociality combine to ground the special obligation to protect the vulnerable, especially when the vulnerability is the product of a State's action. To protect the vulnerable, compassion and mercy need to be displayed if soldiers are to act with honor. Rules of war that center on humane treatment, especially during wartime situations that are already so fraught with risks, are one of the best ways to protect the most vulnerable. The principle of humanity and the narrower principle of humane treatment are aimed at just this result. And from at least the time of Seneca, through the great thinkers of the 17th century and the Hague and Geneva Conventions today, humane treatment has been seen, as it should be, as the cornerstone of the rules of war, the violation of which will trigger prosecutions for war crimes.

In the second part of this book, I will indicate problems with how war crimes are identified in three types of cases: the killing of naked soldiers, the use of poisons, and the punishment of confined soldiers. In each of these cases, problems for the way we typically conceptualize necessity, discrimination, and proportionality will be identified. Then, in the third part of the book I will attempt to reconceptualize these three principles to overcome the problems discussed in the cases, in light of the principle of humane treatment I have just explicated. In the final part of the book, I will discuss in detail who should be prosecuted for war crimes and what defenses should be allowed.

PART B

PROBLEMS IN IDENTIFYING WAR CRIMES

5

Killing naked soldiers

Combatants and noncombatants

In 1625, Hugo Grotius argued that "war must be carried on with not less scrupulousness than judicial processes are wont to be."[1] Grotius' views form the normative ground for both modern Just War theory and contemporary international legal theory. In this Chapter, I will begin to discuss one principle that has often been seen as a cornerstone of both of these theories, the principle of discrimination, or distinction – namely that war tactics must not be employed that fail to distinguish the group of combatants from that of noncombatants, refraining from attacking noncombatants but justifiably attacking combatants. I will offer various reasons to reject the traditional principle of discrimination, on both conceptual and moral grounds. At the end of the chapter, I will offer an amended principle. It is my contention that if we follow Grotius' injunction that this principle be followed with minute scrupulousness, fewer military tactics will be justified than is normally thought.

Just War theorists contend that tactics are illegitimate unless they can be used in such a way as to distinguish combatants from noncombatants. Contemporary international legal theory also draws heavily on the principle of discrimination. The Geneva Convention IV, as interpreted in the Second Protocol of 1977, says, "The civilian population as such, as well as individual civilians, shall not be the object of attack. . . . Indiscriminate attacks are prohibited."[2] The principle of

---

[1] Hugo Grotius, *De Jure Belli ac Pacis* (*On the Law of War and Peace*) (1625), *Prolegomena*, section 25, translated by Francis W. Kelsey, Oxford: Clarendon Press, 1925, p. 18.
[2] Protocol Additional to the Geneva Conventions of 12 August 1949, and Relating to the Protection of Victims of Non-International Armed Conflict (Protocol II), 8 June 1977, Article 13.

discrimination also relies on the idea that it is possible to distinguish, in a morally significant way, those classes, or groups, of people who participate in wars from those who do not.[3] The categories of "soldier" or "civilian" and "combatant" or "noncombatant" are thought to be stable. Yet, there are serious conceptual and normative problems with identifying such social groups. In this chapter, I argue that, because of these problems, the traditional principle of discrimination offers no clear guidance because it offers no clear, morally relevant line between those who fight and those who do not. Nonetheless, I argue that a distinction of this sort should be maintained, although it should be one that will restrict tactics in war far more than is normally recognized.

When soldiers go to war, they are told quite explicitly not to attack civilians, though they can kill combatants. For instance, in the first Iraq War, in 1990–1, all U.S. soldiers leaving for Kuwait were given a Pocket Card on the Rules of Engagement. At the bottom of the card was the following summary of the rules governing U.S. soldiers in this war:

> Remember:
> 1. Fight only combatants
> 2. Attack only military targets
> 3. Spare civilian persons and objects
> 4. Restrict destruction to what our mission requires.[4]

These relatively simple rules reflect a long-standing principle of the moral and legal conduct of war: the principle of discrimination. And this principle is still interpreted traditionally. As one influential contemporary international law textbook puts it: "The principle of discrimination, about the selection and methods, weaponry, and targets . . . includes the idea that non-combatants and those *hors de combat* should not be deliberately targeted" for attack.[5]

The chapter proceeds as follows. I begin with some notes on the metaphysical issues that arise in discussions of collective identity and other attempts to delimit or define a social group. I then spell out first the conceptual and then the normative problems with the principle of

---

[3] On this point, see the excellent discussion in Michael Walzer, *Just and Unjust Wars*, New York: Basic Books, 1977, 2000, Chapter 9.

[4] "1991 Operation Desert Storm, U.S. Rules of Engagement: Pocket Card," reprinted in *Documents on the Laws of War*, 3rd edn., edited by Adam Roberts and Richard Guelff, Oxford: Oxford University Press, 2000, p. 563.

[5] *Documents on the Laws of War*, ibid., Introduction, p. 10. (*Hors de combat* literally means "out of the fight.")

discrimination, as it is traditionally understood. In the middle of this chapter, I consider the example of the naked soldier as a test case for thinking about how to draw the distinction between combatants and noncombatants. I then return to metaphysical issues, setting the stage for thinking that war should not be understood in a collectivist way. I explain why I think the principle of discrimination is nonetheless worth saving and offer a beginning attempt to provide a new restricted principle. In Chapter 8, I will address various objections to my revised principle and provide a revised understanding of using collective procedures in identifying who can be killed. Despite my misgivings about the traditional principle, throughout I argue that there is normally a major benefit to be derived from the principle of discrimination in that it makes soldiers stop and think and thus makes them less likely to use violence.

I.   SOME NOTES ON THE METAPHYSICS OF SOCIAL GROUPS

Social groups are, at best, medium-size objects. Social groups are somewhat like heaps of pebbles. Where a random assortment of individual persons ends and a group begins, and where one group ends and another begins, are difficult to determine and often largely a matter of convention. Perhaps there are a few naturally existing human groups, such as the group of women or men or the group of Blacks or Caucasians. And even for these groups, clearly there are so many fuzzy cases – hermaphrodites and biracial persons, for example – that the world does not naturally and neatly divide into just two groups, here along gender or racial lines. It is even controversial what would count as a clear demarcation of what constitutes a woman or a man: Is it genes, chromosomes, genitalia, reproductive capacity, etc.? And in the case of Blacks or Caucasians, is it blood, skin tone, intelligence quotient range, etc.? It is even more difficult to determine whether someone is a civilian or a soldier. Soldiers seem to be something social rather than natural.

But what is the difference between natural and social groups? Ontologically, groups are generally best understood as composed of individual persons in relations.[6] The relations or relationships cannot be reduced to individual persons, just as individual persons cannot be

---

[6] See Larry May, *The Morality of Groups*, Notre Dame, IN: University of Notre Dame Press, 1987, Chapter 1.

reduced to relations or relationships. Natural groups are composed of individual persons who are related by virtue of some essential characteristic, such as heredity, that links the members of a group across all possible worlds. Social groups are composed of individual persons who are related by contingent characteristics, such as being in a given place at a given time. And the specific contingent characteristic or property that constitutes their relatedness to each other is some feature of the external world, such as a given location in space or a feature that the individuals have assumed but can reject as well. Social groups are identified on the basis of such contingent matters, and these are often merely matters of convention.

There are two main difficulties with social groups that are relevant to an examination of the bifurcation of persons into groups, such as civilians and soldiers. The conceptual problem of social groups is that, like heaps of pebbles, it is often very hard to ascertain where one mere collection of individual persons ends and a group begins or where one group ends and another group begins. This problem is not insurmountable. There are many ways to define or delimit a social group, but unfortunately such strategies are problematic when it comes to groups like soldiers or civilians, combatants or noncombatants. The normative problem is that even if one can solve the conceptual problems involved in identifying social groups, one must then explain why the particular contours of a social group pick out persons who should all be treated the same way in respect to a particular end. The question of moral relevance arises when differential treatment is primarily based on membership in a social group, as in the case of how civilians or soldiers should be treated during war.

Social groups are not as difficult, or so it seems to me, as are comparative categories, such as tall or short, bald or hairy. For comparative categories to make sense at all, there must be some prearranged standard, such as a benchmark of a normal person in terms of height or amount of hair. Whether a social group exists is indeed often a matter of convention, but this is not by virtue of there being a benchmark cohesive group to which all other groups are to be compared. Rather than being a comparative category, social groups seem to be more stable, or differently stable, than comparative categories; but social groups do not necessarily have changing criteria for meeting the minimal existence condition(s) for being members. What does change from time to time, and this is a particular difficulty for social groups, is that group members tend to come and go with unpredictable ease: Civilians join the military and become soldiers, and sometime later the soldiers resign from the military and become civilians again.

In sociological circles, it is common to speak of either an in-group or an out-group – that is, a first-person or third-person approach to this question.[7] Social groups can be identified by either the felt cohesion of the members or by the way nongroup members identify the social group. In legal circles, where definitions are normally pragmatic, social groups are defined in terms of what are called "legal fictions."[8] We treat certain "assortments of people as a legal person", as a person who has rights and duties, just as if he or she were a natural human person, but this is only for legal convenience, not because there is anything metaphysically presumed by doing so. There is a kind of common sense metaphysics as well in that people often manage to identify members of groups quite easily, even though there is no clear articulation of criteria they can give for their identifications. As we will see in the next section, all of these approaches present various problems for identifying who is a combatant and who is a noncombatant.[9]

Discriminating or distinguishing members of one social group from members of another group typically involves both conceptual and normative considerations, for social groups are rarely distinguished merely in terms of what are conceptual considerations alone. There is often some particular moral point in drawing certain distinctions. More importantly, the use of various social group markers is often criticized in terms of moral relevance, where it is normatively

---

[7] Jurgen Habermas has done important work on the theory of groups from this perspective. See *A Theory of Communicative Action*, vols. 1 and 2, translated by Thomas McCarthy, Boston: Beacon Press, 1987.

[8] See Lon Fuller, *Legal Fictions*, Stanford, CA: Stanford Univerity Press, 1967.

[9] In my book *The Morality of Groups*, I spent several chapters wrestling with some of these questions about the ontological status of groups. Virginia Held wrote that I made the mistake of thinking that social groups were ontologically infirm because they were not as stable as individual human persons, although I was surely right to think that they did have some of the same features of human persons. Held pointed out that the ontological status of human persons was itself already quite infirm. Indeed, Held contended that who I am can, to a certain extent, change over the course of my life, just as group members can change over the "life" of the social group. I have over the intervening years come to agree with Held, in part because I have met so many people who are truly different persons depending on the time of the day or the year, that one interacts with them. Perhaps I was wrong to think that human persons were paradigmatically stable ontological entities and that social groups were more or less stable insofar as they approximated individual human personhood. In any event, I am still intrigued by how groups can be identified, especially when we are talking about social groups such as combatants and noncombatants.

appropriate to ask whether these markers should be used given the purposes to which they are put. Think of the famous early-20th-century U.S. Supreme Court case of *Plessy v. Ferguson*.[10] In this case, the state of Louisiana had decided to establish multiple racial categories at law, based on one's supposed percentage of "black blood." The plaintiff was an octoroon, that is, a racial group that was defined as having one-eighth "Black blood."[11] Such individuals were forbidden to ride in the train cars marked for whites only and could only ride in the train cars marked for Blacks, even though many octoroons could not be distinguished from whites by the naked eye. It seems clear that the social group identified by the one-eighth Black blood requirement could be criticized morally, for even though one could create such a social group, the question remains why the marker used to distinguish members of this group had any moral relevance for determining who could ride in various train cars. Moral relevance is used to try to sort out from the enormous number of possible social categories that we might construct, which ones should be used to determine appropriate behavior in a given society.

It is sometimes thought that metaphysics and morality can be kept separate from each other. The underlying stuff of the universe is thought to be just what it is, not at all a matter of what it ought to be. Whether this is true of so-called physical reality or not, it is hard to maintain this point when talking about social reality. For social reality is a function of the inventions of humans, and when, why, or even whether such inventions should be used for discrimination is itself not merely a matter of metaphysics or ontology. People come in many different colors. In fact, there are so many colors that it is odd to think that there are natural racial categories based on color. And even if one thought this, as a pure matter of ontology, one could still wonder why certain of these racial, or color, categories were given special status in the identification of persons eligible to ride in certain train cars. Indeed, one could assert that Plessy really was a member of a distinct racial group, an octoroon, and still wonder why he should be treated differently for being so.

---

[10] *Plessy v. Ferguson*, 163 U.S. 537 (1896).
[11] The category "octoroon" might appear to pick out a natural rather than a social kind, if the distinguishing characteristic of the group is that the members all have at least one of their eight great grandparents with "Black blood." But because there is no such thing as "Black blood" then this is not truly a hereditary group, but rather a mixture of a hereditary group and a socially defined group.

In the next two sections of this chapter, I will first describe some of the conceptual difficulties involved in group identification and then turn to normative considerations in determining what is a morally relevant basis for discrimination. In the end, I despair of establishing a clear, bright line, principle of demarcation between the groups of soldiers or civilians and combatants or noncombatants and urge that we adopt a more pragmatic view. Such a determination will almost surely have to be made on a case-by-case basis, rather than trying to make large-scale discriminations on the basis of fixed social group membership. Hence, I propose a new way to think of the principle of discrimination, where fine-grained rather than rough-grained determinations are made. In so arguing, something important is gained: Soldiers will be forced to think more carefully before they shoot, thereby shooting and killing less. I admit, though, that there is something lost along the way if we cannot discriminate in a rough-grained way between civilian and soldier, because fewer violent tactics will be justified. However, from the standpoint of a contingent pacifist perspective, what is lost is not necessarily a bad thing.

II.   IDENTIFYING SOLDIERS AND CIVILIANS

There are several obvious ways that the members of social groups can be identified. First, the members of such groups can be identified because they have a similar appearance. Consider the members of a baseball team. They all wear the same distinctive uniform, and the rest of the population does not wear this easily recognized indicator of group identity. Of course, anyone who has ever been to a baseball game knows that there is a problem here: The uniform, or parts of it, is worn by lots of people, called fans, who are not members of the relevant social group, the team. And when the members of the St. Louis Cardinals baseball team, for instance, take off their uniforms and put on their street clothes, they do not completely cease to be members of the Cardinals, just as the fans do not become members of the Cardinals team merely by putting on the "birds on the bat" uniforms. Of course, not much of importance turns on all of this.

But there is a significant and important problem of a very similar sort in war. How are soldiers to be identified and distinguished from civilians? It was once thought that the main basis was by reference to distinctive uniforms. But what if someone took off his uniform as a form of deception, as a way to fool enemy soldiers into dropping their guard toward him? Was this "kosher," and if it was revealed could the uniformless soldier nonetheless justifiably be shot as a soldier? Or as Michael Walzer famously asked: Was it legitimate to kill a "soldier" who was naked taking a bath? To put it more metaphysically, did the uniform establish group identity, or was it only one of several insufficient signs of such identity? The uniform once was the absolute determiner of whether one was a soldier. During the U.S. Revolutionary War, one of the first challenges to this doctrine occurred when the Red Coats, the name given to British soldiers because of the distinctive red coats they wore, faced men in regular clothes: the American revolutionaries. This irregular army nonetheless functioned as an army, even if its members intentionally did not don proper 18th-century garb worn by soldiers. In 20th-century terms, American revolutionaries were guerrillas, and the British might have claimed to be waging a war against terrorists.[12]

Another obvious way to identify members of a group concerns the tasks that each member engages in. Members of the St. Louis Cardinals perform various baseball tasks at such a high level of skill and sophistication as to distinguish themselves from even the most skilled of their uniformed fans. The ability – and, I suppose, the willingness – to perform certain tasks in a certain way can also identify members of a group. But what if the group member is injured? Is an injured Cardinals pitcher, no longer able to perform his appointed task at a high level of skill and sophistication, nonetheless still a member of the team? If I can now pitch better than the injured Cardinal, why is he still a member of the team while I still will never be considered one? Again, this question is of little importance, except perhaps to me, but in war it matters enormously.

Is a uniformed soldier still a soldier if she is so incapacitated that she cannot perform the tasks that define being a soldier, such as carrying and firing a rifle? Should she be treated now as a civilian or as a prisoner of war or some other nonfunctioning combatant? Can she be justifiably killed as a soldier even though she poses no threat to enemy soldiers? Of course, there are other rules of war prohibiting the killing of those who are sick or injured, but I am here focusing on whether the injury itself actually so disrupts the basis of group identification, in

---

[12] Today, U.S. Special Operation Forces – who do not wear uniforms, operate behind enemy lines, do not openly display their weapons, and generally fail to conform to the rules of war – also could be considered terrorists in that they are neither soldiers nor civilians.

terms of undermining one's ability to perform marking tasks, that the member ceases to be a soldier altogether. And what do we do with those who are so psychologically traumatized by war that they can't take up arms even though their legs and fingers still work sufficiently to allow them to march and shoot?

Third, members of a group can be identified by voluntary acts of joining. Of course, few join the group of civilians, but there is some kind of joining that normally precedes becoming a soldier. Even though the Cardinals may not always wear their uniforms or be able to perform the tasks normally associated with being a professional baseball player, they all sign contracts calling for them to become members of the Cardinals baseball team in exchange for a very lucrative salary, higher even than professors of legal and political philosophy. The contract normally makes everything quite clear: If a representative of the team has made an offer of compensation to a player for joining the team and the player has accepted the offer, then the player becomes a team member and remains so for the life of the contract. There are always cases of players who violate the terms of the contract, perhaps by refusing to pitch due to various muscle strains, who then may be shunned or even drummed off the team. Again, this makes for enjoyable breakfast table reading, but it hardly matters in the greater scheme of things.

Members of the military often do something like signing a contract, if not literally doing so. At the very least, they seem to assent to the terms of their conscription. Real problems arise when soldiers stop wanting to be soldiers. If they run away, they are normally regarded as deserters and either dragged back to the battlefield, shot in the back by their commanding officers, or court-martialed. This is true despite the fact that many soldiers do not voluntarily join the military. Walzer claims that every soldier "has allowed himself to be made into a dangerous man."[13] Just why such an acquiescence is morally important will be discussed later. At the moment, Walzer's claim is important for its attempt to get beyond the fact that many soldiers do not do anything like volunteering to be members of the military. Walzer calls attention to the fact that in one's acquiescence there may be an act of joining anyway.

We should be able to use this act of joining to discriminate soldiers from mere civilians. But what of those people who are too frequently

[13] Walzer, *Just and Unjust Wars*, p. 145.

forced into military service at a very young age, as young as 10 in some African countries, quite against their will and who remain in the military simply out of fear for their lives? The Statute of the Special Court for Sierra Leone says that children should not be recruited into the armed forces and identifies such recruitment as a war crime.[14] Are some of these children nonetheless members of the military, or are they mere slaves who happen to find themselves associated with armed factions? Should they be treated as having lost their civilian immunity? These are very hard questions, indeed, upon which a lot turns. There is a nearly irreconcilable problem if membership in the group "soldiers" is premised on having joined, given that so many soldiers do not do anything voluntarily to become members of the military.[15]

Fourth, members of groups can be identified by characteristics that they have no control over having, or cannot easily get rid of, such as racial, sexual, ethnic, or religious affiliations. Perhaps "soldiers" are a natural rather that a social group. Unfortunately, it is not possible to distinguish the members of the group "civilians" from soldiers on the basis of such considerations. Indeed, the main problem is that the group of soldiers is initially drawn from the group of civilians, and old soldiers ultimately return to being mere civilians. The principle of discrimination – or distinction, as the lawyers call it – as understood in the Just War tradition and in international law today, seems to require that there be a bright line separating civilians from soldiers, but that line is not drawn on the basis of what is indelible or even very hard to change. Members of volunteer armies can go in and out of membership over the course of just a few months or years. There is nothing that all and only soldiers essentially possess, unlike those who are women, Blacks, Asians, or Catholics. And there is no stigma to leaving the group of soldiers to return to the group of civilians. Such people are often welcomed home – and may even be nominated for president of the nation.

---

[14] Statute of the Special Court for Sierra Leone, Art. 4. See the commentary on this point in Jean-Marie Henckaerts and Louise Doswald-Beck, *Customary International Humanitarian Law, vol. 1: Rules*, ICRC, Cambridge University Press, 2005, pp. 482–488. The customary rule is that children under age 15 should be excluded from combat altogether. For them, incarceration for war crimes is precluded.

[15] There are also special problems of people who are conscripted but then refuse to serve on conscientious or other grounds. Some of these people are taken into the medical corps. Are they then civilians or soldiers? And what of those who are conscripted and fight for a while but then refuse to fight in a particular battle or even the war? Do they cease to be soldiers when they refuse to fight, even as they still wear military uniforms?

Another way to go seems far simpler: to make a definition by stipulation, marking the distinction between those who fight, or at least participate in fighting, and those who do not – between combatants and noncombatants, rather than between soldiers and civilians. Surely, this distinction can be maintained and defended as a relevant moral distinction, and thus provide us with a way to save the principle of discrimination. The 1907 Hague Convention's Regulations[16] provided the basis for the Geneva Conventions of 1949, both of which require four conditions for someone to be regarded as a combatant: "(1) that of being commanded by a person responsible for his subordinates; (2) that of having a fixed distinctive sign recognizable at a distance; (3) that of carrying arms openly; and (4) that of conducting their operations in accordance with the laws and customs of war."[17] Most recently, Ingrid Detter offers this definition of combatants: "[C]ombatant' is defined as someone who distinguishes himself from the civilian population, carries arms openly and is subject to an internal disciplinary system. . . . he must also act on behalf of a belligerent."[18] These definitions are useful, but it is unclear whether they provide the bright line that has seemed to be needed for a morally relevant distinction.

There are many conceptual and moral problems with this basis of the principle of discrimination. Not the least of the conceptual problems is that this basis fails to take into account "irregular" armed forces, such as guerrilla or terrorist groups that are surely just as morally worthy of attack, if anyone is, as regular soldiers are. There have been significant attempts to try to capture the nature of modern war, which is often waged by even such irregular forces as suicide bombers. What the definitions by stipulation lack is a morally relevant basis for drawing distinctions among classes or groups of people during war. For as I said above, we can form groups by stipulation in an infinite number of ways, but this will not yet tell us who should be morally distinguished from whom.

---

[16] Hague Convention (IV) Respecting the Laws and Customs of War on Land, Annex to the Convention: Regulations Respecting the Laws and Customs of War on Land, 1907, Sec. I, Ch. I, Art. 1. See Roberts and Guelff, *Documents on the Laws of War*, p. 73.

[17] Geneva Convention (I) for the Amelioration of the Condition of the Wounded and Sick in Armed Forces in the Field of August 12, 1949, Art. 13, reprinted in Roberts and Guelff, *Documents on the Laws of War*, p. 202.

[18] Ingrid Detter, *The Law of War*, 2nd ed., Cambridge: Cambridge University Press, 2000, p. 26.

III.   THE GUILTY AND THE INNOCENT

"Soldiers" is a group that is often hard to define conceptually and even harder to identify according to any morally relevant characteristics. Morally, the distinction between those who can be attacked and those who cannot is often thought to be better drawn in terms of the distinction between the innocent and the guilty, or at least between the innocent and the non-innocent, rather than between soldiers and civilians.[19] This distinction is suggested as a way to capture the obvious point that enthusiastic munitions workers participate more in war efforts than those reluctant conscripts who sit in desk jobs far from the front. What is needed, rather, is a morally significant demarcation. The one that many have seized on is the distinction between those who have done something wrong, insofar as it jeopardizes the security of others, and those who have not. It is the former but not the latter group that is a legitimate target of attack. Some have thought that a morally relevant distinction is between those who participate and those who do not participate in a type of harm. We could try to distinguish combatants from noncombatants on the basis of whether the individuals in question do or do not participate in an unjust war. If they do participate, then they were legitimate targets of assault by enemy combatants. If they do not participate, then they retain their immunity from such attack. And if they were nonetheless attacked, then this would signal a basis for a charge of war crimes. But this basis for distinguishing is also fraught with problems, especially if the distinction is to have any moral relevance, as we will next see.

Francisco Suarez, reacting against a long tradition to the contrary, tried to demarcate the truly innocent and separate them from those who are "guilty" in war. Earlier theorists, such as Averroes, had said that it is justifiable to kill any males who might take up arms.[20] Suarez instead held to the general principle that "no one may be deprived of his life save for reason of his own guilt." The innocent include "those who are able to bear arms, if it is evident that in other respects they have not shared in the crime nor in the unjust war."[21] Suarez says that

---

[19] See the important discussion of this issue in Robert Holmes, *On War and Morality*, Princeton, NJ: Princeton University Press, 1989, Chapter 6.

[20] Averroes, "Jihad" (from *Al-Bidaya*) (c. 1167), Para. 3, in *Jihad in Classical and Modern Islam*, translated and edited by Rudolph Peters, Princeton, NJ: Markus Weiner, 1996, p. 33.

[21] Francisco Suarez, "On War" (Disputation XIII, *De Triplici Virtute Theologica: Charitate*) (c. 1610), in *Selections from Three Works*, translated by Gladys L. Williams, Ammi Brown, and John Waldron, Oxford: Clarendon Press, 1944, pp. 845–846.

the innocent in war "neither consented to the war nor gave any assistance in it, but who on the contrary, urged the acceptance of peace."[22] This is an important point because if we allow, as Averroes did, that anyone who could take up arms is counted as guilty (or even non-innocent), then counterintuitively wars can be waged "indiscriminately," says Suarez.

In addition to considering the views of Suarez, we should also consider Grotius' views of who can count as innocent, views that could have led him to pacifism. In *On the Law of War and Peace*,[23] Grotius begins by articulating a very strong version of the principle of discrimination: "No action should be attempted whereby innocent persons may be threatened with destruction." He is led to support the view that the guilty can be released if it is "for the sake of the innocent."[24] Grotius defends this principle by reference to both mercy and justice, for from the standpoint of justice the innocent surely do not deserve to be killed and mercy dictates that in any event, "from humanitarian instincts," the innocent must be protected. All of this does not sound extremist today, but what Grotius says about who are innocent leads him almost to what Jeff McMahan and Robert McKim have called, in a different context, "a contingent form of pacifism."[25]

Grotius says that children, women, and old men are normally to be afforded the status of innocents, because they are generally "untrained and inexperienced in war."[26] For similar reasons, those whose occupation concerns religious matters or letters are not to be considered guilty,[27] as is also true of farmers and merchants.[28] Furthermore, those who have surrendered or who are prisoners of war are innocent rather than guilty.[29] For our purposes, it is especially interesting that Grotius says that "it is not sufficient that by a sort of fiction the enemy may be

---

[22] Ibid., p. 847.
[23] Hugo Grotius, *De Jure Belli ac Pacis* (*On the Law of War and Peace*) 1625, Book III, Chapter 11 ("The Right of Killing in a Lawful War"), Sections 8–19, translated by Francis W. Kelsey, Oxford: Clarendon Press, 1925, pp. 733–744.
[24] Ibid., p. 734.
[25] Jeff McMahan and Robert McKim, "The Just War and the Gulf War," *Canadian Journal of Philosophy*, vol. 23, 1993, pp. 501–541.
[26] Hugo Grotius, *De Jure Belli ac Pacis*, p. 735. On the general topic of whether women should be treated differently from men in combat situations, see Jean-Marie Henckaerts and Louise Doswald-Beck, *Customary International Humanitarian Law*, 2005, pp. 475–479; and on the special respect owed to children, see pp. 479–482.
[27] Ibid., p. 736.   [28] Ibid., p. 737.   [29] Ibid., p. 739.

conceived as forming a single body;" indeed, even "a quite obstinate devotion to one's own party, provided only that the cause is not alto-gether dishonorable, does not" mean that one should be grouped with the guilty.[30] This claim suggests that even when one is in a military unit, it cannot be assumed that one is guilty and can legitimately be killed. Rather, fine distinctions need to be made to see why one is serving in the military, for if one is merely serving out of patriotism, he is not to be grouped with the guilty. On Grotius' account, very few, if any, soldiers may be legitimately killed. And in any event, Grotius' arguments make it illegitimate to discriminate on the basis of large class categories at all. Grotius thus solves the problem of how morally to save the principle of discrimination, but he does so by calling for such fine-grained discriminations that as a practical matter it would be very difficult to satisfy the principle, lending credence to the view that Grotius ends up very close to a kind of contingent pacifism. My own view is similar to that of Grotius, as we will see.

Prior to Grotius, in war the guilty were those who were either members of a society or a subgroup that committed harms. This is why Averroes said that all able-bodied men could be slain, for he was speaking of members of an infidel society. As infidels, they were already guilty; and because the men were all able to fight, they could also be slain. It is interesting that Averroes does not think that all infidels – for example, children, women, and old men – could legiti-mately be slain in a jihad. It was assumed that even in a society of infidels, only those who could take up arms to defend their society could be legitimately attacked. Muslims could attack able-bodied infi-del men, regardless of whether they had taken up arms, because of the guiltiness of their beliefs, accompanied by the fact that they could take up arms and defend themselves. Generally, in the Middle Ages there was not such a fine line between soldiers and civilians, with people passing from one group into another quite rapidly without putting on uniforms. The point here is that Averroes is trying to establish a firm line, on the basis of guiltiness between those who can legitimately be killed and those who have immunity from attack. Today, many would readily dispute his criteria for guiltiness. What I want, however, is for us to rethink the whole strategy of using group identifications here.

There is a serious question of whether those who are currently taking up arms can morally be distinguished from those who would do

---

[30] Ibid., p. 741.

so if given the chance, as well as from those who perform other militarily necessary functions but do not take up arms. It is hard to see that merely carrying arms, especially if one has no intention of using them except in self-defense, is enough to make one morally guilty.[31] And it is harder still to see that those who do choose to take up arms can be seen as guilty, and yet those who choose to work in munitions factories cannot. There has been quite a lot of good argumentation by other theorists on this count, so I won't belabor this point here.[32] My point is only to indicate that guiltiness is a poor basis for providing a bright line between those who are subject to attack and those who are immune from attack.

I suppose someone could argue that we should distinguish being guilty in terms of having done some wrong from being guilty because one participated in an unjust war. Perhaps it could be argued that it is the latter group that is liable to be attacked.[33] I have indicated earlier, especially in Chapter 2, that I do not think that *jus ad bellum* considerations are relevant for *jus in bello* assessments. Rather than repeat those arguments here, let me only say that I do not regard soldiers who participate in a war, unjust or otherwise, to be guilty. While it may be true that soldiers who participate in an unjust war share in the collective guilt of their States, the share of guilt that soldiers must bear in such cases is normally quite small. Soldiers do not normally intend to do anything other than what they have been ordered to do. Lacking the requisite *mens rea*, soldiers are not personally guilty in a way that would make them liable to be attacked.

Not only is guiltiness a poor basis for giving us a bright-line basis for conceptually identifying social groups and making particular judgments about their members, but there are also serious questions about its general moral relevance in a discussion of war. Since at least the time of Augustine, it has been debated whether wars could justifiably be waged as a means of punishing the guilty, instead of being justified only on grounds of self-defense or protection of the innocent. It is

---

[31] Some might argue that it would matter if one were fighting an unjust war. I attempted to defeat such arguments in Chapter 2 above.

[32] The best recent essay on this topic is Christopher Kutz, "The Difference Uniforms Make: Collective Violence in Criminal Law and War," *Philosophy and Public Affairs*, vol. 33, no. 2 (2005), pp. 148–180.

[33] Jeff McMahan argued in a similar way to me in correspondence. This may not be his true opinion of the matter but rather something that he thinks is potentially defensible.

somewhat controversial that one State could seek to punish another
State; and it is highly controversial that one State could seek to punish
social groups within another State by means of war. The reason for the
second point is that one wonders why battlefields rather than court-
rooms are the appropriate place for punishments to be meted out.[34]
Even if we can distinguish those who are complicit in a war of
aggression and separate them out from those who are mere bystanders, a question remains: Why should this be the kind of morally relevant distinction that would justify the use of lethal violence against the
complicit without any attempt to ascertain whether all of the members
of a group are indeed guilty enough to make them liable to be punished by a State's armies?

The guiltiness of individual persons normally is judged in degrees,
as is the innocence of individual persons. When we make moral
judgments on the basis of rough-grained markers, such as large social
group membership, we necessarily must eliminate or diminish morally
relevant differences among members of a group. Individual combatants are not all guilty to the same extent, even if the basis of their guilt
is that they are representing an aggressing State. Indeed, I would also
challenge, although I cannot do so here, the idea that representing an
aggressing State makes an individual person liable to be punished in
any event. In the next sections, I will take up the question of whether,
given the conceptual and moral problems identified above, we should
merely dispense with the principle of discrimination altogether.

IV. THE CASE OF THE NAKED SOLDIER

The principle of discrimination is indeed worth preserving, on conceptual and moral grounds. In my view, one of its main benefits is to
force soldiers to think before they shoot, as is clear from the pocket
card handed out to all American soldiers in the Gulf War that I mentioned at the beginning of this chapter. And this will nearly always

---

[34] Indeed, the idea that punishment should be a justification for waging war was
seemingly laid to rest after the ratification of the United Nations Charter, where
Article 51 said that only matters of individual and collective self-defense could warrant
a State in going to war. The Bush administration has nonetheless recently claimed that
it was justified in waging the second Gulf War to punish Saddam Hussein for the
torture and murder of his own people. It also may be that the rationale for NATO's
bombings of the former Yugoslavia in light of ethnic cleansing in Kosovo, namely to
defend regional stability, signals a new interpretation of Article 51. I thank Mark
Drumbl for this point.

mean that soldiers will shoot less, normally a good thing in itself. In the current section, I will turn to the example of the naked soldier and offer a criticism of what Walzer says about such cases, while nonetheless arguing that the distinction that is at the heart of the principle of discrimination is indeed worth preserving. I will then say a bit about the distinction between justice and humanity, returning to Grotius' important work on this topic. I will end this chapter with a beginning discussion of what a revised principle of discrimination might look like.

Walzer defends the justifiability of shooting the naked soldier; indeed, he says that it is, strictly speaking, impermissible not to shoot him.[35] The example he uses, which is taken from Robert Graves, is the following:

> While sniping from a knoll in the support line, where we had a concealed loophole, I saw a German, about seven hundred yards away, through my telescopic sights. He was taking a bath in the German third line. I disliked the idea of shooting a naked man, so I handed the rifle to the sergeant with me. "Here, take this. You're a better shot than I am." He got him; but I had not stayed to watch.[36]

Walzer points out that Graves expresses dislike – a feeling, not a moral judgment. And in a related case, Walzer also points out that "[George] Orwell says, 'you don't feel like' shooting him rather than 'you should not' [shoot him], and the difference between these two is important." For Walzer, there is a "fundamental recognition" that it is permissible to kill the naked soldier.[37]

Walzer expresses much ambivalence about this position, but in the end he argues that war cannot be fought without discriminating between fighters and nonfighters, where the former "are subject to attack at any time."[38] The reason for this is that a soldier has allowed himself "to be made into a dangerous man."[39] A significant part of Walzer's argument justifying the permissibility of killing the naked soldier is directly relevant to our discussion of collective identity and discrimination in the previous sections of this chapter. For Walzer admits that soldiers "do not always fight; nor is war their personal enterprise. But it is the enterprise of their *class*, and this fact radically distinguishes the individual soldier from the civilians he leaves behind."[40]

---

[35] Michael Walzer, *Just and Unjust Wars*, p. 143.   [36] Ibid., p. 140.   [37] Ibid.
[38] Ibid., p. 138.   [39] Ibid., p. 145.
[40] Ibid., p. 144 (italics mine). By "class," Walzer does not mean socio-economic status but merely "group."

It is tempting to say that Walzer is relying on a notion of collective responsibility of the worst sort. And indeed, this is partly right. Walzer is arguing that the naked soldier is still a soldier, and as such he is subject to attack at any time, unlike civilians, who are only rarely subject to attack. Even though the soldier, as he sits naked in the bath, seems to be less dangerous than a normal, dressed, adult male civilian, the naked soldier will soon resume his role as a "dangerous man," and as part of a group of dangerous men he can be attacked at any time. It is because of his class that he can be shot; and because of her class, a civilian cannot be shot. But the classes are not clearly the only relevant moral basis for distinguishing one individual from another, especially if we are in effect talking about a liability to be killed for the one but not for the other.

Walzer admits that there are other morally relevant factors in the case of the naked soldier. Indeed, he says that a solider "alienates himself from me when he tries to kill me, and from our common humanity. But the alienation is temporary, the humanity imminent. It is restored, as it were, by the prosaic acts that break down stereotypes." In the case of the naked soldier, "my enemy is changed into a man."[41] As a man, I feel that he should not be killed; but I also recognize that because of his being still a member of a dangerous class, it is "less than is permitted" to spare his life.[42] Hence, Walzer comes to the conclusion that the group-based moral considerations override what he calls merely "passionate feelings." But it seems to me that Grotius is right to say that certain passions, especially humanitarian ones, should hold sway in such cases.

The group-based approach for determining who can legitimately be killed runs into problems when one asks why a particular member of the group deserves, or is justifiably liable, to be killed. Walzer says that all the members of the group have lost their immunity because they have allowed themselves to be made into dangerous men. If by this he means that each person in the group is dangerous by virtue of having taken up arms and joined a military unit, it is hard to see why a member of the group cannot take himself out of the group, even temporarily, and thereby regain his immunity not to be shot. We can see this most graphically when a soldier drops his gun and raises his hands. Surely, Walzer wouldn't maintain that that soldier still has no

---

[41] Ibid., p. 142.   [42] Ibid., p. 143.

immunity from being shot. So why is the naked soldier in the bath, who also has clearly dropped his gun and indicates by his behavior that at the moment he has no desire to shoot at us, not similar to the surrendering soldier?

Of course, it is true that the naked soldier, unlike the surrendering soldier, has indicated that he will still fight, and in the near future, too, whereas the surrendering soldier indicates that he will, for the foreseeable future, stop fighting. In this sense, the naked soldier is more dangerous than the surrendering soldier. But at the moment, the naked soldier is not a threat, either to other enemy soldiers or to the State against which he has been, and will later continue to be, fighting. It is thus difficult, although not impossible, to see the naked soldier as a threat who is liable to be killed. As I've indicated throughout this book, the best way to see such points is in terms of the principle of humanity rather than the principle of justice. I will make this argument in detail in Chapter 8.

Walzer may think that by not surrendering, the naked soldier indicates that he is still a member of the group and thus without immunity from being killed. But why are all of the members of the group to be treated the same? Why is the only way to regain one's immunity completely to remove oneself from the group? And what do we do with the fact that even those who surrender are legitimately seen as required to try to escape so they can rejoin their military units. If those who surrender are not permanently excluded from the class of dangerous men, it makes more sense to say that they have not regained their immunity, at least not fully. But then, it appears that the immunity from being killed is something that might vary over time and circumstance, disrupting the bright-line character of the principle of discrimination. If the principle has a variable status, then this would explain why it might be that the naked soldier is immune from attack but loses his immunity when he gets dressed and steps back into combat.

We might contrast the naked soldier with the soldier who does not otherwise appear to be threatening to us, but who may be scouting out our position so that he can later help target us for air bombardment. The latter may indeed be dangerous, too dangerous to our own safety to grant him the mercy that is otherwise due to those who appear to be merely human rather than members of a class of dangerous men. Walzer treats this case in the same way that he treats the case of the naked soldier taking a bath, who is seen in a telescopic lens at some distance and who presumably does not see his enemy. In both cases, Walzer says that the soldiers can – indeed, should – be killed. But unless Walzer is willing to take a thoroughgoing collectivist approach, and he seems unwilling to do so, he cannot argue that all soldiers can be targeted for attack. Thus, we must search for a way to reconceptualize the principle of discrimination.

The rough-grained approach that Walzer adopts is both conceptually flawed and morally unsettling. He admits that his view is morally unsettling when he indicates that there are people who are very hesitant to shoot the naked soldier. The conceptual flaw is not as readily apparent, but it emerges when we recognize that the members of the class of soldiers are not all dangerous all of the time, either to enemy soldiers or to the enemy State. Indeed, in the case of the surrendered soldier, who is expected to escape and return to battle, we recognize that soldiers can regain their immunity from being killed, even if only temporarily. This suggests, as we will see in the next section, that a fine-grained approach to the principle of discrimination might do a better job of capturing both the conceptually and morally intuitive idea of who has immunity than does the rough-grained approach taken by Walzer.

As one can see from the pocket card issued to U.S. soldiers during the first Gulf War, the principle of discrimination is understood as assigning to some an immunity and to others a lack of immunity. This is seen in the rules "spare civilian persons" and "fight only combatants." It is clear that individual soldiers are being told that they should not kill civilians, but that they are allowed to kill combatants. Individual soldiers are accused and tried for war crimes when they violate these directives. And while the principle of discrimination may speak differently to leaders than to soldiers, the principle of discrimination does speak loudly to individual soldiers, at least if one is on the ground, as it were. The question, then, is whether the principle of discrimination can be justified in such a way as to warrant the loudness with which it seems to speak.

V.   SAVING THE PRINCIPLE OF DISCRIMINATION

Despite all of the conceptual and moral difficulties, if there are going to be wars, then I believe the principle of discrimination is worth saving, although not in the form traditionally given. In this section, I provide a preliminary framework for a new way to understand the principle of discrimination. In recasting the principle of discrimination as a fine-grained rather than a rough-grained basis for drawing distinctions, I will urge that we greatly limit who can be legitimately attacked. I will first return to remarks by Walzer and Grotius, employing their arguments for somewhat different purposes than they might wish. I then turn to what it is about the principle of discrimination that is worthy of being saved.

First, consider the strategy adopted by Walzer that I mentioned earlier. If soldiers make themselves, or allow themselves to be made, into dangerous men and women, then perhaps they lose the right not to be killed. But as I have argued, not all, or even very many, soldiers actually are dangerous to other soldiers or to States.[43] If I am sitting in a foxhole and you come charging at me with your bayonet leveled at my heart and your finger on the trigger of your rifle, you are certainly a dangerous person for me. The principle of self-defense will surely allow that you have lost your immunity to be attacked by me. And if I am distracted at the moment and don't see you coming, then the principle of justice may allow a third party to kill you on my behalf. Notice, though, how few soldiers will be dangerous to each other in this way, especially in a high-tech war.

Second, following Grotius, we should recognize that it is a mistake to see the enemy as forming a single body, all the members of which are dangerous to the enemy State against which their own State is at war. Soldiers as a class do not make themselves dangerous, at least in the normal understanding of dangerousness. Many, if not most, soldiers never fire a shot and do not have any intention of doing so.[44] Indeed, as Grotius pointed out, many soldiers, especially those who are involuntarily conscripted, do not even support the war effort and have nothing to gain from shooting other soldiers. Of course, other soldiers, perhaps many others, support the war effort and more importantly are patriotically willing to do whatever the commander in chief asks of them. In this sense, they seem to be dangerous, but now as

---

[43] Another possible line of argument is that a person who fights in justified self-defense can never lose the right not to be killed. I myself do not argue in this way because I do not endorse the underlying premise here that *jus ad bellum* considerations affect *jus in bello* ones.

[44] Walzer notes this himself. See his, *Just and Unjust Wars*, p. 139: "In the course of a study of combat behavior in World War II, S. L. A. Marshall discovered that the great majority of men on the front line never fired their guns." Walzer provides the following citation: S. L. A. Marshall, *Men Against Fire*, New York, 1966, Chapters 5 and 6. Some scholars have called this claim into question.

representatives of those who are truly dangerous, not really in and of themselves.

Grotius offers us an important distinction in this respect. He proposes that the permissibility to kill is not the only or even the most important consideration in such cases. Rather, we should think about these matters from the perspective of the principle of humanity rather than that of justice and rights, as I argued in earlier chapters. In this respect, a Grotian position is one that stresses that the rules of war are supposed to display mercy, at least whenever doing so does not directly jeopardize our own safety. Indeed, if we embrace the principle of humanity, not merely the principle of justice, then it is even clearer that few people should be killed due to their putative dangerousness. While it may be that those who are members of a dangerous class do not deserve restraint on our part, the Just War tradition has also embraced a principle of humanity, from which the term "humanitarian law" is derived, where we are supposed to treat people with compassion and mercy, even when they are our enemies, as long as undue hardship is not created by this treatment. Treating people humanely will mean that their merely being in some general sense dangerous is not enough to justify killing them.

Yet, it is hard to see conscripts as having acted in such a way as to make themselves the representatives of the dangerous leaders of their States. It is more likely that such conscripts have been set up to be the targets of those who have grievances with the leadership. Representation is a voluntary act in which one person chooses another person to stand in for him or her, and the stand-in consents to be so regarded and to take on whatever duties are incumbent on someone in that role. Some soldiers – namely, those who volunteer to serve their States – might fit this account, but I would argue, along with Grotius, that this should not include those who join for patriotic reasons, but only those who choose to fight on behalf of their leaders because they truly believe in whatever the reasons are that the leaders have given for going to war. And even in this case, I would hesitate further if it turned out that the soldiers were fighting mainly for monetary support and only secondarily because they agreed with the supposedly just cause for fighting. For these reasons, we should not treat all soldiers as forming a single enemy unit of dangerous people.

If a person attacks me and she has not been provoked to do so, it seems quite plausible to say that she has lost the normal immunity from my assaults, an immunity that she had before taking this action against me. I may forgive her and not take advantage of her loss of immunity, or more likely I can fend off her attacks by, at least in part, the use of violent force that might otherwise be thought itself to constitute an unjustified attack. On this basis, it seems also quite plausible to say that we can construct a social category or group whose identifying characteristics are based on whether that person has demonstrated that he or she is a danger to others. But the members of such a social group, being hard to pick out of the crowded field of groups, will require fine-grained rather than rough-grained identification. If we stick to this basis, then the principle of discrimination would say that it is a war crime for a State to risk indiscriminately killing people who are not significant threats. And soldiers who demonstrate that they are a danger to others will also be subject to justifiable attack. But, as I have argued, because soldiers cannot be treated as merely members of undifferentiated units, it will be harder to ascertain whether they have in fact demonstrated their dangerousness. My proposal is for just this fine-grained, as opposed to rough-grained basis for determining who can legitimately be attacked. I will refine this proposal in Chapter 8.

There is a large philosophical objection to my criticisms of the rough-grained collective identification of social groups. Even though social groups are, at best, medium-size objects, people talk sensibly about them all of the time. Most people would not have thought that there is a general conceptual problem with talk about social groups or, in particular, with talk about civilians and combatants. And if ordinary people are not bothered by this talk, why should soldiers be any different? The principle of discrimination, as normally understood, is relatively easy to understand, and soldiers do not normally voice much of a problem in doing so. Despite what seem to be problems with the distinction, aren't we better off with this distinction in use than with no such distinction, or with one that is far harder to draw, such as what I am now pushing us toward in this chapter.

My response is not a frontal attack but a collateral attack on this objection. I agree that the use of groups in our practical decisions about how to treat fellow humans is a good thing. What is at stake here is whether social group categories should be used to ground absolute rules that are in themselves sufficient for action decisions, or whether the group categories are merely guides that inform but do not determine our actions. I do not think that we should abandon the category of combatants. What I object to is the rough-grained use of this category to determine who can be justifiably attacked in wars. I have argued instead that soldiers need to look further than the combatant category itself to see if certain combatants indeed pose a danger to them or to their States. Given my arguments against Walzer's naked-soldier example, one could then wonder why we should not dispense with the category of combatants altogether. My response is to say that – as in all human affairs – we cannot easily get by without some categories to frame our thinking.[45] This, in my view, is what the principle of discrimination should do for us. It should not be seen as itself a firm basis for making decisions, but rather as a framework within which decisions can be made about which actions to take.

Within the framework of what is permissible in terms of justice and rights, we then need to ascertain what actions would also be consistent with the principle of humaneness. The latter determination is a very particularized one, and perhaps in some cases, where danger is all around us, there will not be enough time to make this further determination, requiring us to rely only on the general framework. But in other cases, such as when viewing a naked soldier taking a bath – where one is far removed from the soldier, and he is unaware of our presence and not at all trying to harm us – it seems clear that the principle of humaneness would dictate that such a soldier should not be killed, even though he is truly a member of the group "combatants."[46] The framework that is based on rough-grained considerations, can only be the sole thing appealed to when the fine-grained determination of particular circumstances is somehow blocked – for instance, in emergencies. Collective identity strategies, such as the principle of discrimination, have their use, but it has a more limited use than has normally been recognized. I will return to this issue in Chapter 8.

In the next chapter, I will turn to a second example: shooting a poisoned arrow as a way to achieve a military objective. Examining such an example is a way to begin to understand the importance and the limitations of the traditional principle of necessity. As in this chapter, I will argue for a more fine-grained way to approach this topic than is normal. Indeed, I will argue that a complete ban on the use of

---

[45] One could dispute this move and argue that the Just War tradition is not so concerned about the consequences of its rules. I would simply point to Grotius and Suarez as the best examples of scholars in the Just War tradition who combine consequentialist and deontological considerations in defending the rules of war. See my discussion of this point in Chapter 3.

[46] For an opposing view, see Jeff McMahan's "Response to David Rodin's *War and Self-Defense,*" *Ethics and International Affairs,* 2004, pp. 75–80.

poisons in war cannot be justified without risking banning all bullets and bombs as well, adding further support to the doctrine waiting in the wings: contingent pacifism. For if a bright line must be drawn and justified concerning the people who can legitimately be targeted in war, then most wars, even those fought for purely defensive purposes, seem to be in jeopardy.

6

Shooting poisoned arrows

Banned and accepted weapons

Since the Nuremberg trials, it has become common to separate international criminal law into three divisions where war crimes were one of the three main categories of crime, along with crimes against humanity, and crimes against peace.[1] War crimes are violations of the rules of war, and the rules of war extend back in time for centuries. For example, almost since wars were first fought, there has been a complete ban on the use of poisons during war. The main reason seems to be that such tactics were thought to be inhumane or dishonorable in that they were unfair or caused unnecessary suffering, even when they otherwise appeared to be necessary for achieving a certain military objective. The area of international criminal law that we are investigating is often called "Humanitarian Law," because it concerns the violations of what is thought to be humane treatment during war. In this chapter I will explore the idea of inhumane treatment in war by reference to the use of poisoned weapons, such as chemicals and other weapons of mass destruction. I ask whether the idea of humane treatment can justify an absolute prohibition on poisons in war.

I will use the term "poisons" as a shorthand expression for "poisons and other chemical or biological weapons." Indeed, a U.S. military manual defines poison as "biological or chemical substances causing death or disability with permanent effects when, in small quantities, they are ingested, enter the lungs or bloodstream, or touch the skin."[2]

---

[1] See Belinda Cooper, editor, *War Crimes: the Legacy of Nuremberg*, New York: TV Books, 1999.

[2] U.S. Department of the Air Force, "*International Law – The Conduct of Armed Conflict and Air Operations*," AF Pamphlet 110–31, 1976, p. 6–5.

And the International Court of Justice Advisory Opinion on the legality of the use of nuclear weapons indicated that the term "poison" was now being used widely and could encompass nuclear weapons, thus linking poisons with most forms of weapons of mass destruction except for those involving conventional bombs.[3] I will follow this usage and employ quite a wide use of the term "poisons" in this chapter.

The structure of the chapter is straightforward. First, I discuss the status of international law in terms of poisons. Second, I examine one of the most thoughtful attempts to explain the prohibition on poisons during war, namely, that by Alberico Gentili at the end of the 16th Century. Third, I discuss how the Grotian idea of combat as a contest relates to the ban on poisons. Fourth, I take up the idea that compassion is central to humane treatment, and it requires that one not violate the principle of minimal suffering. I show that the use of poisons violates the principle of minimal suffering, but not if that principle is seen as an absolute principle. Finally, I try to explain how the idea of military necessity can be useful, but only in a more limited way than normally thought: in condemning the use of poisons in warfare. I ultimately conclude that the ban on poisons can only be justified if it is extended to include many uses of bombs and even bullets. This chapter takes up the challenge of trying to figure out what moral considerations the consensus against poisoning might be based on, if anything. In the end, I argue that the prohibition on poisoning is time- and place-bound and should not be seen as an absolute prohibition, lest we risk also condemning even defensive wars. I thereby set the stage for a reconceived principle of necessity.

I. AN ABSOLUTE BAN?

Most of the relevant documents in international humanitarian law mandate a complete ban on the use of poisons as weapons. The first codification of this prohibition occurred in the Hague Convention (IV) of 1907.[4] Article 22 reads: "The right of belligerents to adopt means of injuring the enemy is not unlimited." Article 23 then begins: "In addition to the prohibitions provided by special Conventions, it is

---

[3] International Court of Justice, Advisory Opinion on the Legality of the Threat or Use of Nuclear Weapons, July 8, 1996, paras. 55 ff.
[4] Hague Convention (IV) Respecting the Laws and Customs of War on Land, Done at the Hague, Oct. 18, 1907, 36 Stat. 2277, T.S. 539, 1 Bevans 631.

especially forbidden: (a) To employ poison or poisoned weapons."[5] In 1919, the Preliminary Peace Conference after the end of World War I listed "poisoning of wells" in its "List of War Crimes."[6] The 1993 Statute of the International Criminal Tribunal for the Former Yugoslavia (ICTY), Article 3, reads: "The International Tribunal shall have the power to prosecute persons violating the laws or customs of war. Such violations shall include, but not be limited to: (a) employment of poisonous weapons or other weapons calculated to cause unnecessary suffering."[7] And the 1998 Rome Statute of the International Criminal Court, Article 8, defines war crimes, in part, to mean: "(xvii) Employing poison or poisoned weapons; (xviii) Employing asphyxiating, poisonous or other gases, and all analogous liquids, materials or devices."[8] The assumption in these international documents seems to be that the ban can be justified because the use of poisons or analogous weapons is "calculated to cause unnecessary suffering."

Poisons in particular have been condemned for longer than there have been codes of war, but it is not always clear that the worry is with unnecessary suffering. To give an example, in India in 500 BC it was strongly condemned to tip one's arrows in poison, but not merely to use normal arrows, even if the arrows are aimed at the heart (or the eye) of the enemy.[9] If one used poisoned arrows then they would kill wherever they struck an enemy soldier, not merely when striking a vital organ. In this example it seems that the use of poisoned arrows is worse than the use of normal arrows, even though less suffering occurs with the poisoned ones because death comes more swiftly. To give another example, it would certainly be wrong to poison the wells of a city since many people would die horrible deaths and many civilians as well as soldiers would be killed. But it is seemingly also wrong to engage in "firebombing" of cities as was done by both sides in the Second World War. And while both uses of weapons (mass poisoning as well as firebombing) are condemned, the latter is not normally condemned in the

---

[5] Ibid., Articles 22 and 23.

[6] List of War Crimes Prepared for the Commission on the Responsibility of the Authors of the War and on Enforcement of Penalties, Presented to the Preliminary Peace Conference, Paris, March 29, 1919.

[7] Statute of the International Criminal Tribunal for the Former Yugoslavia, U.N. S.C. Res. 827, 1993.

[8] Rome Statute of the International Criminal Court, Adopted by the U.N. Diplomatic Conference, July 17, 1998.

[9] This condemnation was part of the Manu Laws of India. See Ingrid Detter, *The Law of War*, 2nd ed., Cambridge: Cambridge University Press, 2000, p. 151.

strong tones reserved for the former, and yet the latter cause greater suffering. It is tempting to say that there has been a mistake made here, but if there is a mistake it is one that has lasted for several thousand years.

Today, there is little debate about the wrongness of using weapons of mass destruction, which, as I indicated above, has been listed under the general category of the use of poisons.[10] Yet, despite the near unanimous condemnation of the use of weapons of mass destruction, many States, including the United States and many Western European States, have stockpiles of nuclear and biological weapons and even threaten their use from time to time. Every few years, the U.S. Congress debates the use of so-called tactical nuclear weapons. Indeed, the very same arguments in favor of the use of conventional weapons is often used to justify the use of weapons of mass destruction – namely, that there is some military objective that needs to be met, and can only be met, or at least without loss of significant life, by using the otherwise banned weapons.

Indeed, in a famous International Court of Justice Advisory Opinion on the Use or Threat of Nuclear Weapons, the Court was split concerning whether their threatened use in Iraq in the early 1990s could be justified as a counter to the threat to use chemical weapons by Iraq against the Kurds. Here the idea that almost any sort of weapon could be justified according to the principle of necessity comes to the fore. And those who argue for an absolute ban on the use of certain weapons will have to explain why some other type of weapon, one that caused less suffering, for instance, could not perform the same needed military task. As we will later see, it is incumbent upon those who defend an absolute ban that they show that the military objective is more significant than the damage done by the use of the weapon that advances that military objective.

In the current debates about so-called weapons of mass destruction, one of the most frequent arguments against their use is that they are inhumane because they do not discriminate between soldiers and civilians. Poisons are another example, especially when they are put in the water supply of a village containing enemy soldiers hiding among civilians.[11] Such weapons are aimed at, or at least have the clear effect

---

[10] Jean-Marie Henckaerts and Louise Doswald-Beck, *Customary International Humanitarian Law*, Cambridge: Cambridge University Press, 2005, p. 251. "The use of poison or poisoned weapons is prohibited. . . . The prohibition of poison or poisoned weapons is a long-standing rule of customary international law."

[11] Ingrid Detter, *The Law of War*, p. 253.

of, "destroying large groups rather than individual soldiers"[12] and therefore violate the principle of discrimination. As we saw in the previous chapter, the traditional principle of discrimination (or distinction) attempted to draw a clear line between soldiers and civilians. It is generally prohibited to attack civilians, so if weapons are used that do not distinguish between soldiers and civilians, then generally this is also prohibited conduct. Before applying this principle to the question of poisons, I wish first to revisit the rationale for having such a principle, a task I take up in much greater detail in Chapter 8.

As we saw in the previous chapter, whether it is the guilt or the dangerousness that causes a soldier to lose his immunity to be attacked, there remains a serious problem with the principle of discrimination. For just because a soldier carries a gun – indeed, is often forced to carry a gun – does not mean he will use it. And unless the soldier is likely to use his weapon, it is not clear why the soldier is guilty or even dangerous. Civilians, despite their lack of weapons, may sometimes play a larger role in the creation of danger than soldiers do. Especially in the case of political or civic leaders, who rarely carry a gun, there is no good reason to see them as innocent, even if they have been drafted into service, given how much harm they can cause by inspiring the nation to go to war. So, Walzer's attempt to save the distinction between soldier and civilian remains as problematic as the older basis for that distinction.

Nonetheless, there may still be great utility in maintaining the distinction between soldier and civilian and in continuing to support the principle of discrimination, for adherence to such a principle has prevented the kind of large-scale slaughter of civilian populations that war can make all too likely. It is in this light that we should examine the use of poisons to see whether there is a moral difference between their use and the use of bombs, for instance. It is undeniable that certain poisons, such as poison gases or poisons introduced into a town's water supply, kill indiscriminately. But it is also true, I believe, that most bombs dropped from high altitudes or delivered from cannons in ships hundreds of miles from the target, inevitably will kill indiscriminately. Such bombs are instruments of mass destruction, as most of the major wars since 1900 have amply demonstrated. Why, then, would the principle of discrimination prohibit the use of all poisons but allow the use of most bombs?

[12] Ibid., p. 251.

Such a strategy will not provide a ground for prohibiting all poisons, because many types of poison – for instance, those used in poison-tipped arrows or javelins – do not kill indiscriminately. These poisons are no more indiscriminate than any other weapon – for any weapon may go astray and kill a civilian no matter how carefully it is aimed how good the marksman is. Many forms of "conventional" weapons, such as aerial bombardment and perhaps all bombs delivered from a great distance, will have to be prohibited as well. Thus, such a solution gets us a much more rational policy concerning which weapons are to be prohibited even in war, but it does not get us an in-principle ground for distinguishing poisons from bombs.

The idea that we should not engage in indiscriminate killing could be useful in another respect. It might be maintained that poisons are not meant to cause injury or death to soldiers, but are more like terrorist tactics in that they aim to scare the general population into compliance. The term "poison" is connected to the term "drug," which is normally used to refer to medicines aimed at "treating disease, healing, or relieving pain."[13] Poisons are drugs that "cause illness or death when eaten, drunk, or absorbed in relatively small quantities."[14] Therefore, poisons could be viewed as medicines used for abnormal purposes, indeed for purposes so contrary to normal use as to be terrifying. Thus, the known use of poison assaults the population at large quite indiscriminately by causing fear, even panic. Yet, the principle of discrimination says that weapons should be restricted to attacking soldiers and those who provide necessary military support for soldiers. Perhaps in this sense, all poisons violate the principle of discrimination.

Unfortunately, this strategy also will not do the whole job, because while it might lead to the prohibition of all poisons, it won't help us distinguish poisons from most other forms of conventional warfare. For one of the main purposes of modern conventional warfare is that it appears to be so terrifying that civilian populations will either surrender or at least not continue to provide support for their own armed forces. So, while we might be able to use the prohibition on indiscriminate killing to show why all poisons are prohibited, we will not be able to show why all or most forms of bombing, indeed most forms of war, are not similarly prohibited.

[13] *Webster's New Twentieth Century Dictionary*, Unabridged, 2nd ed., New York: Prentice-Hall, 1983, p. 1118. "Drug" is defined on p. 559.
[14] Ibid., p. 1390.

I would maintain that the most serious problem with complete bans on poisons and weapons of mass destruction is that such bans will necessarily have to be grounded in principles that sweep so broadly that they would also ban most if not all other weapons. This leaves us, as we will see in subsequent sections of this chapter, with the problem that such an argument will support "contingent pacifism." This is the form of pacifism that is not grounded in absolute moral considerations on the value of human life or the abhorrence of war. Rather, contingent pacifism is grounded in the idea, first set out by Francisco Suarez, that one of the conditions of a war being just is that it can be conducted by just tactics. Not only must there be a legitimate authority, a just cause, and a rightful intent, but "the method of its conduct must be proper" as well.[15] Suarez thus linked *jus ad bellum* with *jus in bello* considerations in a very different way from that which we considered earlier in this book.[16]

If most or all weapons fall prey to the same absolute ban as that which attaches to poisons and weapons of mass destruction, then the justifiability of conducting war *at all* is called into question. I will have much more to say about this point as our discussion of the possible reasons for banning poisons continues to hit snag after snag. I am proposing the idea of a "contingent pacifism," both as a *reductio* for those who would flee from the very idea of associating with a putatively pacifist view, but also because I am intrigued by the idea of a contingent pacifism, perhaps understood on the model of a contingent objection to capital punishment, where capital punishment is considered immoral because there are no trial procedures that can be used that will not risk the execution of the innocent. There may be ideal conditions where capital punishment and war are justified, but in our non-ideal world it is unlikely that such conditions will ever obtain.

II.   GENTILI ON THE USE OF POISONS

Let us next consider Alberico Gentili's very helpful discussion of the question of why the use of poisons is inhumane in the chapter-length

---

[15] Francisco Suarez, "On War," in *Selections from Three Works*, (Disputation XIII, *De Triplici Virtute Theologica: Charitate*) (c. 1610), translated by Gwladys L. Williams, Ammi Brown, and John Waldron, Oxford: Clarendon Press, 1944, p. 805.

[16] In Chapter 2, I argued that *jus in bello* considerations did not vary based on whether one had *jus ad bellum* reasons, such as just cause for fighting the war. Now I take up the argument that wars may not legitimately be waged, even if there is just cause, if it is not possible to wage that war with justified tactics.

treatment "Of Poisoning" in his 1598 treatise *De Jure Belli*.[17] Gentili begins by proclaiming that there is a parallel between verbal deceptions and "guileful deeds" like poisoning.[18] In the previous section of his book, Gentili had argued that some falsehoods could be justified in battle. As Gentili argues, "[I]f they wish friends to be deceived by the falsehood of friends to their advantage, they also wish enemies to be deceived to their disadvantage. Thus indeed the enemy receives his due and evil is justly done to him; if good is justly done to friends."[19] It is odd, indeed, that Gentili begins his chapter on poisoning with the analogy to verbal deceptions, which can seemingly be justified in many circumstances, and then argues that poisoning can never be justified.

The chief reason seems to be that battles are supposed to be won by superior force of arms if war is to have "valour," as is true of a duel. War waged with poisons "is contrary to the manners of our ancestors," where the custom is to fight with "craft, ingenuity, and the like."[20] To fight with "drugs" rather than arms is "contrary to honour."[21] Unlike poisons, "arms and other things were invented or given for the safety of mankind, not for their ruin. They are useful to see if not to employ, ..." contrary to the use of poisons, which, in warfare, are indeed aimed at "the destruction of mankind."[22] The general idea seems to be that "war ought to be limited to things which it is within human power to resist." Indeed, poisons are so contrary to morality that they should never be used, even if their use is necessary for defending oneself from wrongful attack.

Gentili also offers other reasons against the use of poison even in wartime, some of which I will investigate in the next section. But his chief reason seems to be that it is not honorable to use poisons because they cannot be resisted with superior strength or ingenuity, thereby rendering the fight not a proper test of wills of the participants. As Gentili admits, this way of framing the issue relies on seeing warfare as a kind of duel writ large, where the participants fight for their honor and should not employ tactics that risk their honor. Gentili quotes Scaurus here: "It is better to be conquered than to conquer in an evil manner."[23] Yet, in the previous section Gentili admitted that lying to the enemy could be justified to prevent the enemy from unjustly conquering. The only way to reconcile these views seems to be that

[17] Alberico Gentili, *De Jure Belli* (*The Law of War*) (1598), Book I, Chapter 6, translated by John Rolfe, Oxford: Clarendon Press, 1933, pp. 155–161.
[18] Ibid., p. 155. [19] Ibid., p. 154. [20] Ibid., p. 156. [21] Ibid., p. 157.
[22] Ibid. [23] Ibid., p. 159.

Gentili sees the disvalue of poisoning to be something that always offsets the evil it might be aimed at resisting, whereas lying does not have this effect. As a result of this argument, Gentili thinks that there should be an absolute prohibition on the use of poisons, but not on lying, in war.

Perhaps we can focus on the claim about what it is in the power of humans to resist in order to understand the apparent inconsistency here – and a similar inconsistency in most of the writers who address these topics: The Hague Convention, for instance, also permits lying to the enemy, but disallows poisoning.[24] Indeed, Gentili ends his discussion of poisoning by similarly condemning the use of the "magic arts."[25] He argues that "the use of such arts are unlawful in war, because war, a contest between men, through these arts is made a struggle of demons."[26] The use of poisons, like the use of the magic arts, makes war into something different from what it should be. War is transformed from a contest of strength into mere killing. Somehow, the "contest" makes war justifiable, and such justification is lost when war is no longer a "fair" contest. It is not honorable, or consistent with humaneness, for a person to behave like a demon.

Here we see the analogy between a duel and a war in its most pristine form. Poisoning is thought to disrupt the honor of the participants to the contest. In Book I, Chapter 2, Gentili says that "the strife must be public; for war is not a broil, a fight, [or] the hostility of individuals. And the arms on both sides should be public, for *bellum*, 'war,' derives its name from the fact that there is a contest for victory between two equal parties, and for that reason it was first called *duellum*, 'a contest of two.' "[27] War is not merely "armed force" but must be just. For war to be just, "all of the acts of war must be just."[28] A "just war" is a "regular war" with regular soldiers, regular leaders, "and regular battle meaning a legitimate army as opposed to robbery and brigandage."[29] Such regularized battles are undone when poisons are used rather than conventional arms.

I have been exploring this first possible basis for the prohibition on poisoning in war because it well illustrates a very long tradition in the Just War theory of seeing the rules of war as meant to make the contest a fair one and because it seems to track with my earlier reliance on the

---

[24] Hague Convention (IV), Article 24: "Ruses of war . . . are considered permissible."
[25] Alberico Gentili, *De Jure Belli*, p. 160.   [26] Ibid., p. 161.   [27] Ibid., p. 12.
[28] Ibid., p. 13.   [29] Ibid., p. 14.

idea of honor. The Just War tradition has been seen as intuitively appealing because it reduces the enormously complex topic of war down to a manageable level by analogizing war with a conflict between two people. In this context, many thinkers in the 16th and 17th centuries proposed that war was essentially no different than a duel or was only a duel writ large, and honor was virtually the same in both contexts. There is a recent discussion in the literature about whether this way of understanding war is indeed fruitful or is deeply misleading.[30] At the moment, I only note that there is such a challenge being made today, one that will nonetheless partially follow the older tradition of thinking that dueling can be used as a model for understanding war. It is interesting to note that in this tradition lying is seen as justifiable in certain circumstances, but poisoning is not. Perhaps this is because the lie is to be expected and can be defended, but poisons cannot. Yet surely this is wrong. Poisons *can* be defended against, with antidotes or by simply not letting an enemy get close enough to use them. It is unclear why it is honorable to lie but not to use poisons in war.

Most troubling is that poisons are completely banned, whereas bombings are only partially restricted (such as the ban on carpet bombs or on bombing civilian centers). Yet, bombings also often make the contest not a fair one insofar as one side may have more resources for producing bombs or more control over their use. In this sense, the "contest" will rarely be fair when either bombs or poisons are used. In both cases, there is no sense in which it is "strength" that will determine the victor. But this should not be surprising because ever since the development of the most rudimentary of weapons – David's use of a rock against Goliath, for instance – physical strength did not determine the victor. If anything, it is craftiness, rather than craft, that has always determined the victor when there is a contest of arms other than bare arms and fists – and probably also in many of those cases as well. And it is often not skill either that is key, because it sometimes turns out that the dropping of a bomb requires less skill than the making of a poison.

If a contest pitting the strength of armories is a legitimate basis for a Just War, then why isn't a contest pitting the strength of stockpiles of poisons? If both sides use poisons, or could do so, why does this disrupt the Just War any more than when both sides use aerial bombs. Surely, bombs are no less likely to be resisted by humans than are poisons, for

[30] Of special note is David Rodin, *War and Self-Defense*, Oxford: Clarendon Press, 2002.

both can be delivered in ways that are meant to surprise. It is now an accepted tactic not to announce one's battle plans. If one's tactics call for the use of poisons instead of bombs, perhaps because the resources needed for one are more readily available than for the other, why should this taint the war? It cannot merely be that it is honorable to use the one but not the other tactic.

III. GROTIUS AND FAIRNESS IN CONTESTS

Gentili, and many other authors, focus on war as a "fair contest" and use this metaphor as a way to justify the restriction on the use of poisons. Hugo Grotius, writing just a few years after Gentili, claimed that poisons are prohibited by the law of nations but not by the law of nature. According to the law of nature, "it makes no difference whether you kill him by the sword or by poison." But the law of nations nearly universally condemns the use of poisons because he who is killed has no "chance to defend himself."[31] The law of nature does not have a clear basis for such a prohibition because combatants are not owed "fair" treatment, especially when one party is clearly in the wrong to begin with. In this section, I will follow Grotius in investigating whether the prohibition is one of the law of nations rather than the law of nature and why, even so, it is hard to justify the prohibition if we start with the fairness of the contest.

Grotius distinguishes the secretive use of poisons from the use of poison weapons, such as "the poisoning of javelins." Grotius admits that poisoning is "more closely allied with the use of force" that occurs in normal use of weapons and thus is harder to condemn. Indeed, placing poisons on javelins makes the javelin a more effective cause of death, because it is "a doubling of the causes of death."[32] But he says that European nations in particular have condemned such practices because they have looked to a "higher standard" for conduct during war.[33] Grotius does not explain what that higher standard is supposed to be, and he seems to be skeptical of it. Indeed, there seems to be little basis for condemning a form of weapon that is merely more efficient than another form, unless one believes that great disparities in the efficiency of weapons will make wars into unfair contests. Hence, we

---

[31] Hugo Grotius, *De Jure Belli ac Pacis* (*On the Law of War and Peace*) (1625), Book III, Chapter 4, Section 15, translated by Francis Kelsey, Oxford: Clarendon Press, 1925, p. 652.

[32] Ibid., p. 652.   [33] Ibid., p. 653.

return to the main idea behind the condemnation of poisons: their deceptiveness or inequality, which causes one party not to have a proper chance to defend against them.

The chance to defend oneself could be meant to apply to kings and princes or to the average soldier. The average soldier is disadvantaged by the use of poisons: For instance, if his food is poisoned he does not have the opportunity to preserve his life by fighting harder, for the poison is often not a force that can be seen and fended off. The 19th-century international legal scholar Henry Wheaton says that the problem is that poisons are such that they cannot be averted. But Wheaton acknowledges the conceptual problem we have been exploring when he says:

> As war will avail itself of science in all departments, for offense and defense, perhaps the only test, in case of open contests between acknowledged combatants is, that the material shall not owe its efficacy, or the fear it may inspire, to a distinct quality of producing pain, or of causing or increasing the chances of death to individuals, or spreading death or disability, if this quality is something other than the application of direct force, and of a kind that cannot be met by countervailing force, or remedied by the usual medical and surgical applications for forcible injuries, or averted by retreat or surrender.[34]

Wheaton gives a very good ground for condemning poisons, but, unfortunately, the same ground would condemn many forms of bombing. It is not possible to retreat or surrender after the bombs have been unleashed, nor is there often an obvious countervailing force, as was seen in the putatively unfair contest between the United States and Iraq in 2003.

The most hopeful part of Wheaton's test has to do with the business about the "application of the direct use of force." And here we also come to the main idea behind the "fair contest" issue. Poisons are problematic because they seem to be significantly different from arms in that poisons mostly do not act by means of increasing strength or force, but rather they operate in an indirect way by circumventing the struggle between two people, in a duel or on the battlefield. I suppose one could imagine a duel between two poisoners, each trying to outwit the other and inject the other first with a poison. But this would be completely separate from the use of force by these two combatants that

---

[34] Henry Wheaton, *Elements of International Law* (1836), Oxford: Clarendon Press, 1936, p. 360 n. Wheaton's treatise is considered one of the classic formulations of the principles of international law.

is supposed to characterize the fair contest of war. In a fair contest, each combatant uses his own force, or his force enhanced in various ways, to defeat the other. When poisons are introduced, it is as if one of the parties is cheating.

Unfortunately, the fair contest strategy will not help much in distinguishing poisoning from bombing. First, and most obviously, when combatants use sophisticated weapons, such as bombs, it is not the case that they are merely enhancing their own strength or natural force. Bombs are no more the extension of the strength of the person launching them than is the "launching" of poisons. Bombs have their own force, if you like, that is completely independent of the launcher's strength or force. It is not even like the use of rocks or javelins, where the physical strength of the launcher remains important because of the differences in how far the object will travel based on the strength of the launcher. When bombs are launched by the push of a button, the pulling of a trigger, or the lighting of a fuse, the strength of the launcher has no connection to the efficacy of the bombing, except in the most trivial ways.

Strength, or force, exerted by the use of muscles and tendons can be met by equal or greater strength, or counterforce. A boxing match, rather than a duel, is the best example of a contest of strength, although even here cunning can sometimes overcome greater strength. In duels, it is not strength that matters but accuracy and reflexes. A stronger dueler has no particular advantage over a weaker dueler, unless the weaker combatant cannot even hold the gun up and pull the trigger. Dueling does seem to be a contest, but not a contest of strength. Rather, it involves a contest of wills. This is not to say that it cannot be a fair contest nor that there is no room for cheating, but merely to say that what counts as cheating is not measured in terms of whether something other than strength is used.

Poisons may disrupt a fair contest if one side uses them and the other side is unaware that they are being used. Again, think of the duel, where everything appears to be out in the open. If one duelist uses poison-tipped bullets, unbeknownst to the other duelist, then wounding in any part of the anatomy will cause death for one, but only for one, of the duelists. This seems unfair for two reasons. First, there is the deception. Second, there is the advantage that one party has that the other does not. It doesn't seem to matter that much what the advantage is, because, as Wheaton says, for centuries combatants have used any tactic to gain an advantage in war and have done so without calling into question the fairness of the tactic. So, it appears that it is the deceptiveness that is key. But here there is a problem as well. All poisoning cannot easily be condemned by this method and distinguished from other more conventional methods of killing, because poisoning can also be announced in advance – limiting but not eliminating its effectiveness to be sure – and because it is obviously possible to use bombs that are not announced in advance.

And here we see just how badly the duel serves as a model for war, for new types of bombs and bullets have been secretly deployed for many centuries without anyone raising questions about justifiability. Earlier in the chapter, I supported the idea that war might be reasonably investigated by thinking of it as a duel writ large. Here, let me mention one of the most obvious disanalogies. War is really not a fair contest at all, at least not in the way that duels are supposed to be. In a duel, the weapons are preselected and agreed to by both parties. Wars are rarely, if ever, conducted in this way. There are certain weapons that are banned, but if one invents a new weapon that the other side does not have and cannot obtain, there is nothing wrong with using it, as we have seen in the use of tanks, submarines, airplanes, and helicopters in the last century or so.

Grotius gives a brief insight that could help us see what might be a cynical, yet true, ground for the ban on poisons. He suggests that the prohibition on poisons is about not putting kings or princes in an unfair position vis-à-vis insurgency groups, rather than about soldiers being put into an unfair advantage vis-à-vis other soldiers. "It is easy to believe that this agreement originated with kings, whose lives are better defended by arms than those of other men, but are less safe from poison."[35] Ordinary people will find it easier to buy or make poisons than fancy armaments, and poisons will bring ordinary insurgents onto a level playing field with kings and princes. Yet the kind of fair contest that is traditionally envisioned in war is a fair contest only among kings or princes. And in that contest, a premium is placed on weapons that are expensive or at least not easily obtainable by normal people. But this is to reduce the prohibition on poisoning to a cynical point – namely, to prohibit insurgency groups, like those in Iraq, from confronting large States, like the United States, by employing relatively cheap poisons and chemical and biological weapons so as to counteract the superior bombing power of the wealthy

[35] Hugo Grotius, *De Jure Belli ac Pacis*, p. 652.

State. But if we are reduced to such cynicism, not much is left of a moral basis for the prohibition on poisons, for it now appears that Carl von Clausewitz was right in saying that war is more like a game than a contest, where the rules are simply made up and changed from time to time based on who has the power to convince others to adopt the changes.[36] But if war is a game, then its rules are no more binding than any other positive law that can be easily changed over time.

IV. MINIMIZING SUFFERING

The most plausible ground for prohibiting certain poisons in warfare has to do with the effect that they have on those against whom poisons are used – namely, that certain poisons cause unnecessary suffering, as various international law documents allege. Such considerations will not easily justify a complete ban on all use of poisons, but they might provide a moral ground for prohibiting many poisons, especially those that are designed to asphyxiate.

I will focus on what the principle of minimal suffering entails. As a first approximation, the principle of minimal suffering restricts violence in war to those acts that are necessary to accomplish victory over an enemy. This characterization relies on it being clear what will produce victory, and this entails that in any given wartime situation it will be clear what is necessary and what is not for the ultimate victory over the enemy. It should be obvious that only the most egregious and unwarranted suffering will be ruled out by this principle, for even torture may be necessary to accomplish victory over an enemy. And it also seems that certain uses of poison may also be necessary, making it very hard to justify a complete ban on the use of poisons.

The principle of minimal suffering also seems odd in wartime because the whole point of most forms of military strategy is to inflict suffering on the enemy. If one supported a principle of minimal suffering in the sense that one supported a moral principle that urged that suffering be minimized to the limit, then one would hardly support wars at all. But, of course, some wars are fought to prevent the infliction of suffering on whole populations, and therefore some wars could be consistent with this principle. But then, given that causing

---

[36] Carl von Clausewitz, *On War* (*Vom Kriege*) (1832), translated by J. J. Graham, London: Penguin Books, 1968, pp. 116–117. Clausewitz allows a fairly minor role for morality in terms of the importance of certain virtues, like courage and self-reliance, but not as setting the limits on such things as the use of poisons.

some suffering must be engaged in to prevent larger suffering, it would be reasonable only to urge restriction on the use of certain tactics. The principle of minimal suffering would then require that tactics be chosen in war in such a way that suffering be minimized – that is, only that suffering that is militarily necessary would be permitted. But a complete ban on poisons could not be so justified.

The Hague Convention (IV) of 1907 prohibits any weapons that cause, either by nature or intent, unnecessary suffering. There is disagreement about the way the original French wording *"maux superflus"* of the convention should have been translated. Literally, the French term means "excessive suffering." Yet, the official English translation of the Hague Convention used the term "unnecessary suffering."[37] As we will see, there is quite a difference, especially when considering the use of poisons. There was also dispute about whether the convention was meant to prohibit weapons that "by their nature" caused such suffering, or whether the Convention required an intent to cause unnecessary suffering.[38] Again, this debate is very important for figuring out what was supposed to be condemned, especially concerning poisons. It should be pointed out, though, that the subsection that prohibits poisons contains a flat prohibition "to employ poisons or poisoned weapons," and that it is five sections later that the words concerning unnecessary suffering occur. But I will posit that there is a conceptual connection in our attempt to find a basis for the poison prohibition.

The difference between superfluous, or excessive, suffering on the one hand and unnecessary suffering on the other hand is important. The idea of unnecessary suffering recalls debates about the concept of military necessity. Soldiers can attack each other, but only with those weapons necessary for achieving victory. But what if victory is impossible to achieve by the use of normal tactics?[39] On the other hand, the idea of superfluous or excessive suffering does not seem to depend on a clear definition of military necessity. Rather it turns on what is disproportionate to a particular objective, regardless of what it is. If, for instance, one has been ordered to kill an enemy soldier, it would

[37] See my discussion of this dispute in Chapter 4, Section 3.
[38] Ingrid Detter, *The Law of War*, p. 165.
[39] On this topic, see Michael Walzer's interesting discussion of the difficulty of delimiting military necessity in his book *Just and Unjust Wars*, New York: Basic Books, 2000, pp. 144–151, 215–216, where he applies the discussion of military necessity to the rule prohibiting poison gases.

certainly be excessively cruel to torture the soldier before killing him. And indeed, it would be excessive to cut him and let him slowly bleed to death rather than to shoot him in the heart. Such comparisons make many people uncomfortable. But once we start down the path of discussing not the morality of military campaigns but the morality of the use of various tactics, such considerations are of paramount importance.

Superfluous (excessive) suffering can be understood on a piecemeal basis, whereas unnecessary suffering, at least when linked to military necessity, cannot. But there will still be many cases where it will be very hard to see whether a given tactic is indeed excessive. Consider again the case of the soldier who shoots an enemy soldier with a poisoned arrow, when the other side does not have such a tactic available. There is a certain immediate advantage in war if it becomes known that one side will not just kill swiftly but use poison against enemy soldiers. Such knowledge plays on the minds of soldiers and may make them considerably less likely to engage in combat against those soldiers who they believe will use poison against them. Of course, in some other cases this may backfire and provide a very strong incentive for soldiers to fight much harder so that they can attack first before poisons can be used against them.

The idea of military necessity is controversial and has been discussed in detail by various theorists. Unnecessary or excessive suffering seems to be an odd category during wartime, but only if one fails to distinguish between various forms of suffering. The point of war is to defeat the enemy. It may be possible to do this by merely threatening violence against the enemy. Or it may be possible to defeat the enemy by killing many of the enemy's soldiers. Or it may be possible to do this by threatening or producing intense suffering in these soldiers. Any of these measures are thought to be justifiable. What the prohibitions on war crimes seek to do is to limit, in advance, the type and amount of suffering that is caused during wars. For if there were no such agreements in advance, the idea of military necessity alone would not be able to restrict much at all. It is always worrisome whether one will indeed achieve victory and so always tempting to argue for more and more options in tactics.

A complete ban on all poisons, justified by reference to the prohibition on excessive, superfluous, or even unnecessary suffering, seems to imply that any suffering caused by poisons would be excessive or unnecessary. Yet, this is far from obvious, especially given the large range of poisons. Indeed, Ingrid Detter points out that "modern tear gas is so 'mild' that there is no reason why it should be prohibited."[40] We could compare the use of certain poisons that asphyxiate to other weapons that cause great pain. Think of certain fragmentation weapons, such as "flechettes, small arrows or needles [that] hit their target with such velocity and do not kill but cause multiple injuries and a very high degree of pain."[41] Because of the large number of very small parts involved, medical assistance is also made very difficult. Detter says that it "is questionable whether military necessity is ever great enough to outweigh the suffering caused by fragmentation weapons."[42] There are poisons of this sort, especially those biological agents that cause horrible, untreatable diseases. If indeed Detter is right that such a high degree of suffering can never be outweighed by military necessity, then certain poisons (or chemicals or biological weapons) could be banned on the same basis as fragmentation bombs.

The problem with Detter's argument is that it fails to account for the fact that the international instruments have banned all use of poisons, not merely those that act like fragmentation bombs in causing truly excessive suffering. Some poisons kill very quickly and nearly painlessly, just as some bombs do. If we are going to use the model of the ban on fragmentation bombs, for example, then we will indeed be able to ban some poisons. But we will not be able to sustain a complete ban on all poisons, just as the rationale for banning fragmentation bombs could not be used to ban all bombs. So, while Detter's strategy looks hopeful, it will not explain why poisons should be completely banned but only that certain bombs should be banned by the rules of war.

Walzer suggests that the complete ban on poisoned gases is necessary because it would be too easy to justify on a piecemeal basis the use of poisons in nearly every case.[43] So, we could argue that it is the rule against the use of poisons that is crucial rather than the prohibition of the use of poisons in particular circumstances. It may be thought that a complete ban is crucial because individual soldiers, or their leaders, will be inclined to make bad decisions if left to themselves, normally erring on the side of the use of more lethal tactics than less, on grounds of military necessity, so as to maximize their own defense. Rules that completely ban certain practices are established to take such decisions

---

[40] Ingrid Detter, *The Law of War*, p. 257. The United Kingdom has refused to follow the complete ban on poisons when it comes to teargas for just this reason.
[41] Ibid., p. 217.   [42] Ibid.
[43] Michael Walzer, *Just and Unjust Wars*, pp. 215, 275–276.

out of the hands of clearly interested parties and make it less likely that they will be tempted to do things that *ex ante* will normally produce the wrong results. Yet an absolute prohibition on poisons is hard to support even on the doctrine of minimal suffering because it is so hard to see, in advance, which poisons will be so clearly offset by suffering that they could not achieve justification when their use seems to be militarily necessary. And in any event, bombs or even bullets should probably also be banned if poisons are banned on this basis.

I have been investigating why, if at all, it could plausibly be maintained that during war killing by means of poisoning is always unjustified, while killing by means of bombing is justified. As indicated at the beginning of this chapter, nearly all of the codes and treaties to take up this subject hold that there must be an absolute prohibition against the deadly use of poisons even in war, where killing goes on regularly. The most obvious grounding for this claim would have to do with the type of death that is caused, where painful death is shunned. But this cannot be the basis, for some poison gases kill more quickly than, or at least *as* quickly and painlessly as, bombing does. Perhaps the ground for banning poisons is that they are surprises intended to catch the enemy off-guard. Of course, if everyone used them, they would not be surprises. In the final section of this chapter, I argue that it is a mistake to see the ban on poisons as absolute.

V. POISONING AND NECESSITY

The rules of war are based on many moral considerations, and perhaps the prohibition of the use of poisons is based on an accumulation of the moral considerations we discussed above. Perhaps the customs of war ultimately only hope to eliminate the element of surprise. But even here, it is not clear why allowing poisons would be so much different from allowing bombings from far distances. Surprise only seems to be eliminated when arms are limited to those weapons that are immediately present for inspection by those against whom they will be used, a situation not likely to happen very often for any weapons, conventional or unconventional.

Thinking about the ban on poisons as not grounded in absolute moral laws may help us ground the prohibition of some poisons in war. For instance, while it is not always true that poisons are a matter of unfair surprise, in certain conditions they are; and when these conditions obtain, it does seem to be dishonorable to use them. Similarly, while the use of poisons does not always cause unnecessary suffering, there are certainly situations where poisons cause such suffering, and it would be inhumane for poisons to be used in those situations. And while it is not always true that poisons kill indiscriminately, it is reasonable to say that when they will do so, it is inhumane and dishonorable to use them. Therefore, some of the reasons that we surveyed above could indeed be a basis for prohibiting poisons in certain circumstances. Furthermore, we could say that various moral principles prohibit the use of some poisons in war, just as is true for the use of certain forms of bombing and even the use of certain types of bullets.

Honor is key to situations where there are no absolute moral principles that ban all activities of a broad sort. When fine-grained determinations need to be made, it is often only the individual person who knows of the subtle change in circumstances that will trigger a duty to respond in a certain way. Duties of humaneness to others arise in such cases, but in ways where we would still want to have the added incentive of honor to make sure that the duties are met. For especially on the battlefield, soldiers will not much fear social sanction because things much more immediately important, their own lives, are on the line. If there were absolute prohibitions, then we would want to rely heavily on external sanctions of various sorts because we want all people to act the same. But in cases where rightful behavior will be quite disparate, rough-grained sanctions will not work that well and self-induced, fine-grained sanctions of honor may work best. Honor-based sanctions relating to humaneness might provide the best framework for enforcing a partial ban on the use of poisons in war. But it should by now be clear that humaneness and honor do not provide a basis for a complete ban on the use of poisons.

We could then ask whether there is any justification for using international criminal law to reinforce the assessments of conscience and honor. And the answer is that the sanctions of the criminal law can also be quite fine grained rather than rough grained. I will later provide a defense of international criminal sanctions in terms of the reinforcement of the core ideas of honor and humaneness that were discussed in detail in earlier chapters. What is best is that there is a code of honor that motivates all soldiers and their commanders to act humanely during war. Military necessity is such a strong pull that it must be countered by something equally strong. But because it is often true that tactics can be justified by reference to military necessity, what is needed is a moral grounding for the rules of war that is able to distinguish between cases where considerations of military necessity will or will not justify a certain type of tactic.

Ultimately, we must conceive the idea of military necessity in light of the principle of humane treatment, as I will attempt in greater detail in Chapter 9. By this, I mean that military necessity is not alone a ground for justifying the use of various tactics. Indeed, if it were so, few types of weapons could be ruled out, even such obvious cases as fragmentation bombs. The principle of necessity can be saved when it is understood as very much modified by and ultimately grounded in the principle of humane treatment. In this way, military necessity will be a kind of emergency exception to normal humanitarian considerations, but only when there are countervailing humanitarian considerations. Weapons and tactics may be employed when they are militarily necessary to thwart an even greater humanitarian crisis. In this way, we must understand necessity as intimately connected not only to humane treatment but also to proportionality, as we will see in Chapter 7, where we discuss torture of prisoners of war, and Chapter 10.

What follows from the above exploration is that there is no absolute moral, or natural law, basis for the prohibition against the use of poisons in war. Why the prohibition has remained for so long is still a question to be pondered, if only for a few more sentences. I mentioned earlier that one cynical interpretation is that poisons have been condemned because they were too easily manufactured and used, thereby making them easy tools of the masses, or insurgent groups, who might wish to revolt against States. If war and its implements are restricted to States, then State leaders will be secure from their own peoples, even if they are still at risk from foreign assault. Such an explanation would indeed allow us to distinguish between the use of poisons and bombs, especially high-tech bombs launched from great distances. But this cynical explanation will not allow us to provide a moral difference between them – and therefore our search for a moral difference between all forms of poisoning and all forms of bombing will ultimately be thwarted. The strategy of justifying the prohibition on poisons during war by reference to humaneness, honor, and nonabsolute moral principles is a promising approach, but it is not one that will provide a secure ground for the ban on the use of all poisons and weapons of mass destruction.

I have argued that, generally speaking, there is no basis for an absolute prohibition on poisons or weapons of mass destruction in war, with the possible exception that it would also rule out most if not all bombs and even bullets and thus, perhaps, rule out most if not all wars as well. The fact that the prohibition on poisons has been so strong for so long has led me to propose that mere positive law is also not likely to be its basis. Instead, I have argued that the ground of some of the prohibitions on poisons in war is best seen as related to honor and humaneness. Humanitarian law and prosecutions for war crimes would then be based on principles that only apply in certain circumstances. When there has been some human act or institution involving poisons that has created certain circumstances that increase vulnerability, then in all circumstances of that sort the use of poisons becomes a violation of what it means to act honorably and humanely. But the absolute ban on poisons and other weapons of mass destruction cannot be justified without risking the condemnation of all modern war.

In the next chapter, we will tackle another area of the rules of war: the treatment of confined soldiers. I will highlight conceptual difficulties with understanding the traditional way to view such rules and spend considerable time discussing the possible normative basis of this body of law as well. I will focus on another especially intriguing question: why torturing prisoners of war to obtain information that could stop even greater suffering seems to be unjustified. Like the discussion of shooting poisoned arrows and the killing of the naked soldier, the example of the tortured prisoner of war will set the stage for a more elaborate discussion that will bear fruit for an understanding of the general reasons behind the idea of proportionality, often thought to be the cornerstone of international humanitarian law. I will argue that proportionality needs to be reconceived, as have the other traditional *jus in bello* principles, in light of the principle of humane treatment, the *true* cornerstone of international humanitarian law.

7

Torturing prisoners of war

Normal and confined soldiers

Since the time of Hugo Grotius, torture and other forms of abuse of
prisoners of war, even if done to extract important information, has
been condemned. Despite the fact that torture of prisoners of war has
been condemned by every major document in international law, it has
seemed to some that terrorism creates a special exception to how
prisoners of war are to be treated.[1] The prisoner may belong to a "cell"
of those who have committed themselves to the use of tactics that risk
horrible consequences for many innocent people. The prisoner may
have information about future attacks on civilian populations that
could, if learned, be instrumental in the prevention of these attacks. In
addition, in a "war" against terrorists, it seems clear that the terrorist
side is not willing to play by the rules of war and thus that the terrorist
prisoners should not be afforded the privilege of humane treatment
that they deny to others. Nonetheless, in most cases even suspected
international terrorists should be treated humanely so that they are not
subject to torture when captured and imprisoned. Our humanity
demands as much. In this chapter, I will examine the very idea of
torturing those who have fought against us, but who are now confined

[1] See Neil A. Lewis and Eric Schmitt, "Lawyers Decide Bans on Torture Didn't Bind
Bush," *New York Times*, June 8, 2004, p. A1. Also see: "Memo for Alberto R. Gonzalez,
Counsel to the President," prepared by the Justice Department Office of Legal
Counsel, August 1, 2002; and "Working Group Report on Detainee Interrogations in
the Global War on Terrorism: Assessment of Legal, Historical, Policy, and Operational
Considerations," prepared for Secretary of State Donald Rumsfeld, March 6, 2003.
These and many other documents are collected in *The Torture Papers: The Road to Abu
Ghraib*, edited by Karen J. Greenberg and Joshua L. Dratel, New York: Cambridge
University Press, 2005.

under our care. In the end I argue that a properly focused principle of proportionality should rule out nearly all forms of abuse of prisoners of war.

Those who are captured on the battlefield where they had tried with all of their might to harm us are clearly our enemies. And on the assumption that they were the aggressors, what they deserve is retribution and even vengeance. Or if they have valuable information that could save lives, surely they should give it up, and it would not be unjust to extract that information by whatever means necessary. Indeed, justice-based considerations would make certain cases of torture unproblematic. Yet, traditionally the rules of war have been formulated to make cases of this sort paradigmatically subject to strict restraint on the part of the detaining army. The principle of humanity is said to be the ground of this restraint on the use of torture. Yet, proportionality complicates the picture in ways that will lead us to wonder whether any prohibition on torture can be justified. I will defend a nearly absolute ban on torture in certain limited circumstances by reference to the principle of humane treatment, but for other reasons than are normally given.

I shall begin with Grotius' discussion of the parallels between slavery and prisoners of war in order to see how the principles of justice and humanity might be employed in the case of confined soldiers. In the second section, I will examine why special restraint is called for in situations where soldiers have been confined, even when these prisoners might deserve to be severely punished. In the third section, I will argue that captors have a fiduciary or stewardship duty to prisoners of war. In the fourth section, I will discuss what reasons can be given in favor of punishment of those soldiers who are confined before a trial has determined their guiltiness. Finally, in the fifth section I draw some conclusions in light of the principle of proportionality when that principle is understood in conjunction with the principle of necessity.

I. GROTIUS ON SLAVES AND PRISONERS OF WAR

In the 17th century, Grotius began the task of considering what could be done to prisoners in wartime by setting out what he thought is true according to principles of natural justice and the then current law of nations. He began by pointing out that it was thought that prisoners of war were simply to be treated as slaves. Yet, "in the primitive condition of nature, no human beings are slaves."[2] No one can kill or limit the liberty of another person, as a matter of natural justice, "unless the latter has committed a capital crime."[3] Yet, many States have given to masters the absolute right over their slaves. According to the conventionally based law of nations, slaves may be justifiably killed or tortured; indeed, "there is nothing which a master is not permitted to do to his slave."[4] Grotius put the point starkly by saying; "[E]ven brutality on the part of masters towards persons of servile status is unpunishable," and then pointed out that "limits have been set to this power by the Roman law" nonetheless.[5]

Grotius also claimed that most States treat prisoners of war similar to their treatment of slaves. Indeed, "all without exception who have been captured in a formal public war become slaves from the time they are brought within the lines."[6] As a result, according to the law of nations there is no limit, even concerning brutality, to what may be inflicted on prisoners of war with impunity. Grotius signaled that he found this to be disturbing, but at this point in the text (Book III, Chapter 7) he did not disagree with the doctrine that prisoners of war have no customary rights at all, just as is true of slaves. Although, he did say that giving captors the right to punish prisoners of war would reduce the likelihood that they would feel the need to kill their prisoners outright, there was no attempt to limit this right of captors by considerations of what the captives deserve. From the perspective of the law of nations in the 17th century, there are apparently no restrictions on what can be done to prisoners of war.

Yet, Grotius argued that there should be severe restrictions placed on captors concerning prisoners of war. In Chapter 11 of Book III, Grotius begins by saying that there is "a limit to vengeance and to punishment." Grotius argues that "Even where justice does not demand the remission of punishment, this often conforms with goodness, with moderation, with highmindedness."[7] It is shortly after this remark that Grotius makes his famous allusion to "humanitarian instincts" that should govern how we treat our enemies.[8] Nowhere is this more important, in my view, than in the treatment of those who are confined by one party, especially when the party in question has every reason to want to exert vengeance or retribution on those who

---

[2] Hugo Grotius, *De Jure Belli ac Pacis* (*On the Law of War and Peace*) (1625), translated by Francis W. Kelsey, Oxford: Oxford University Press, 1925, p. 690.
[3] Ibid., p. 256.   [4] Ibid., p. 691.   [5] Ibid.   [6] Ibid., p. 690.
[7] Ibid., p. 731.   [8] Ibid., p. 733.

have been killing members of one's armed forces. Indeed, Grotius says: "To spare prisoners is commanded by the nature of goodness and justice." Even when burdened by too many prisoners of war, it is better to "release all rather than to kill them."[9]

According to Grotius, while prisoners should not be killed, they may in some cases be punished. But the punishment must be based on the specific crimes they have committed – that is, there should be no "retaliation except against those who have done wrong." On grounds of justice, those who have done wrong deserve to be punished only according to the extent of their wrongful behavior.[10] This is the basis of the contemporary view that prisoners should only be punished proportionately to what each has specifically done, for to do otherwise is for the captors to enforce an unjustified "sharing of punishments" upon the prisoners.[11] In particular, contrary to what was believed at his time, Grotius argued that hostages should never be put to death, no matter what their leaders do, unless the hostages "have themselves done wrong."[12] Considerations of justice plus the important idea of humanity combine to place severe restrictions on what can justifiably be done to prisoners of war, even if the prisoners are the enemy and have taken the lives of the captor's troops.

Grotius thus presents a strong case for thinking that prisoners of war, like slaves, should be treated humanely and should only be punished based on specific wrongs that they have done, not based on what others around them have done or what their leaders have done. What Grotius objected to, and what I described in earlier chapters as guilt by association, were reprisals taken against prisoners of war for what their leaders, or perhaps fellow soldiers, have done. It is unacceptable to treat prisoners merely based on their status as enemy soldiers. Grotius also objected even to treating confined prisoners as harshly as they may have deserved. For the principle of humanity required that to be honorable more restraint was needed based on seeing people as fellow humans rather than as enemies deserving of punishment. In the case of prisoners of war, who have been confined, a Grotian position is even stronger in insisting that extreme restraint be exercised.

When a soldier is captured or surrenders, one cannot continue to treat the soldier as a combatant who is subject to be injured or killed at any time. The moral universe changes from one of minimal rules governing those who are trying to kill each other to that of restrained

---

[9] Ibid., p. 739.   [10] Ibid., p. 741.   [11] Ibid., p. 537.   [12] Ibid., p. 742.

individuals, one of whom is strongly dependent on the other. In the next section, we will take up this changed situation and try to explain why the rules governing the treatment of confined people, such as prisoners of war, are vastly different from the treatment of soldiers who are not confined, despite the fact that prisoners of war are expected to try to escape so that they can again try to kill. It is their current situation of confinement that makes the moral difference.

Grotius insists that on the battlefield there is no other moral option but to exert punishment proportionate to wrongs that have been done. War is truly a state of nature, where no one has the authority to create judicial proceedings to determine whether a punishable offense has occurred and to what extent it should be punished. But after a soldier has been captured or has surrendered, that soldier is now under an authority that can provide a proper judicial basis for determining whether, and how, that soldier should be punished. On the battlefield, there is no authority to determine who is guilty and who is not, and quick decisions need to be made so that one's life is not jeopardized. In such situations, it is sometimes justifiable to punish someone who is not convicted of a crime. But once one is off the battlefield and there is a civil authority that can determine guilt and innocence, it is no longer justifiable to punish those who have not been convicted of a crime.[13]

The laws of nations seem to allow for abuse of prisoners of war as a kind of recognition that the conquering army could have simply killed these soldiers rather than spared their lives. The conquering army gets to treat prisoners of war as slaves for no other reason than as one of "so many advantages" from its victory over the captured soldiers.[14] Grotius is so focused on providing reasons for why prisoners of war should not be killed that he does not say much about other forms of treatment of these prisoners. But in a series of telling remarks in Chapter 14 of Book III, Grotius argues that severe punishment is not acceptable according to natural justice and "humane considerations."[15] Indeed, prisoners of war should be treated with moderation, rather than with severity, as the title of this chapter ("Moderation in Regard to Prisoners of War") indicates, because in the end they should be

---

[13] Ibid., p. 59. We might contrast this Grotian view with the claims made by the members of the administration of President George W. Bush that the enemies of the United States captured in Afghanistan could be treated harshly and held in captivity indefinitely without benefit of trial. I address this point later in the text, especially in the final chapter.

[14] Ibid., p. 692.   [15] Ibid., p. 764.

treated "as second selves, since they are human beings no less than we are."[16]

Humanitarian considerations are most at play when we are discussing confined soldiers who have unjustly refused to disclose information that is of military importance or soldiers who were fighting an unjust war. In both cases, justice-based considerations do not rule out abuse of these prisoners. If information is needed to save lives and it is unjustly withheld, extracting that information by the use of torture does not seem to be clearly unjust. And justice-based considerations having to do with what the prisoners deserve for fighting without just cause actually tell against restraint. Yet the laws of war should counteract the strong possibility of abuse, perpetrated by those who have weapons against those who do not. This is especially true of prisoners of war because there is also a strong tendency of armed captors to wish to act in unrestrained ways against those who have information that could save their comrades' lives or against those who were moments before being captured plotting the destruction or injury of the capturing soldiers.

So we have several important lessons from an examination of Grotius' 17th-century discussion of our topic. First, prisoners of war are not to be treated in an unrestrained way. Most importantly, these prisoners are not to be subjected to reprisals for what their leaders or comrades have done. Second, prisoners of war are not to be summarily dealt with, as might perhaps be justified on the battlefield, because these prisoners are now under the authority of the conquering army and subject to the same judicial adjudications of their cases as would be true of anyone else in society. Once off the battlefield, all parties are back in society and no longer in the state of nature. Third, captives are in a special moral situation because they are utterly dependent on their captors and are vulnerable in ways that soldiers on the battlefield are not. Fourth, considerations of humanity are especially apt in prisoner of war cases because the prisoners are utterly dependent and the capturing army is virtually unrestrained otherwise. We must be scrupulous about insisting that prisoners be treated humanely.

While justice-based considerations tell against some abuse of prisoners of war, such considerations will not tell against all such abuse. A Grotian argument can be advanced that humanitarian considerations, especially having to do with compassion and mercy, should rule out nearly all forms of abuse and torture of prisoners of war. In the next

[16] Ibid., p. 762.

section, I will advance that argument in more detail by considering the special status that prisoners of war occupy and the moral relevance of that status. From this "humanitarian" perspective, prisoners of war should be treated with moderation and not with the severity that might otherwise be deserved.

II. CONFINEMENT AND TORTURE

In Chapter 6, I followed 17th-century theorists like Gentili in considering the rules of war as attempts to make contests in battle fairer. On the model of a two-person battle, or a duel (a model that has problems to be sure), certain kinds of advantage bestowed on one party but not the other was thought to be unfair. If each played by exactly the same rules, then war as a contest of strength would be an acceptable way to settle disputes. According to Walzer and contemporary defenders of the Just War theory, if the contest is fair then soldiers have a kind of moral license to injure and kill each other.[17] Once the battle has ceased, different considerations of fairness apply. In this section, I want to spend some more time analyzing the significance of the changed circumstances of the soldier who is captured or who surrenders as far as fairness is concerned.

Assume that there is a convention in war as follows: If a soldier wishes to surrender, and to be spared from being killed in exchange for being removed from the battle, that soldier should throw down his or her weapons and raise a "white flag." Why would it be worse to kill him after he raised the white flag than before he did? In wartime situations, the surrendering or captured soldier is no longer able to defend himself in the ways he was before because he or she is now unarmed and has foresworn the use of weapons. The soldier now needs certain protections and restraints that were not needed before. And after placing himself or herself under the command of a previously belligerent force, other forms of restraint than merely not being killed are also called for.

Confinement, whether forced or voluntarily sought, makes a difference in how we are to treat a person. Imagine a boxing match in which one of the participants has had his hands shackled behind his back. The fight will not be considered to be a fair one, and any blows landed by the unshackled boxer will not be considered to be justified in

---

[17] Michael Walzer, *Just and Unjust Wars*, New York: Basic Books, 2000.

the way they would have been if his opponent was also unshackled. But what if one boxer voluntarily shackles himself and steps into the ring? That the act was voluntary would certainly make a difference, but it would still be considered inhumane for the unshackled boxer to land blows on the defenseless shackled boxer. Of course, when a soldier surrenders it is not as if he has shackled himself, because the soldier to whom he surrenders retains his or her arms and can take the surrendering person's life in a second. The soldier who surrenders is more like the boxer who resigns from a match but is still in the ring: He has taken himself out of the contest, and now we are back to a time when the rules are not that of a contest between adversaries who are roughly equal.

In life, as opposed to contests, people do not feel entitled to kill each other. Indeed, in life intentionally killing someone is considered one of the worst things that one person can do to another. So after a soldier is captured or surrenders, there is a very serious question about whether the soldier is still a soldier, and therefore still subject to the odd rules of contests, or not a soldier, perhaps some kind of civilian. One way to answer this question is to realize that soldiers are taught to try to escape and return to battle. So if a soldier has been captured, there are good reasons to think that he is still a soldier because he will try to return to battle. If the soldier voluntarily surrenders, things are much more complicated, for it is unclear why he would have surrendered if he still intended to return to battle. And yet, there certainly are situations where the soldier feels that surrender is the only hope, at the moment, of saving his life, but where the soldier also hopes to be able to return to the battle under more favorable terms than when he surrendered. In both situations, as long as the soldier is indeed confined he is not in a contest with anyone.

In American criminal law, it is thought to be an aggravating condition if an assailant first binds his victim or finds him incapacitated and then kills him. The idea is supposed to be that not giving the victim a chance to try to save her life makes the act of violence much worse than it would have been otherwise. When a person is confined and has little opportunity to defend herself, then injuries done to her seem especially unjustified. It seems clear that one person takes advantage of another person's vulnerability.[18] Indeed, even if a person

---

[18] See Robert Goodin, *Protecting the Vulnerable*, Cambridge: Cambridge University Press, 1984. Goodin seems not to pay attention to how the vulnerability occurred. I agree with him that it is the vulnerability that most matters, but I believe that circumstances that brought about the vulnerability are also sometimes morally important.

deserves to be injured, there is something especially nasty about preventing her from properly defending herself or even from striking back. It appears that one is taking advantage of another. At the very least, we would say that it is worse (an aggravation) to injure someone whom one is controlling than to injure someone who is not under one's control.

Think of one of the most disturbing pictures from the Abu Ghraib prison to have surfaced in the Iraq War in 2004. A prisoner huddles outside his cell. He is stripped naked and has no weapon with which to defend himself. His hands are tied. Two growling dogs on long leashes are snapping at him. Other prison guards, all fully clothed and holding weapons, surround the prisoner and seem to be encouraging the dogs to attack the prisoner. The prisoner cowers, almost in a fetal position, in expectation of the attack to come. This is so clearly an instance of inhumane treatment that when this picture appeared in newspapers and on television it caused outrage around the world.

Things look especially bad if the person in question has voluntarily placed himself or herself under the captor's care and the captor is now abusing the prisoner. One way to understand this is to see things as if there has been a kind of contract where the surrendering soldier offers to stop fighting in exchange for a guarantee not to be assaulted. By accepting the prisoner's surrender, the capturing army seems to accept the terms of the surrender. On this analysis, abusing the surrendering prisoner is a violation of an agreement. And the soldier who is forced to put down his arms and then cooperates with his captors also seems tacitly to accept a similar contract, where his or her cooperation is exchanged for a promise of good treatment while in captivity. But this does not fully capture the seriousness of the matter, for even if there was no contract it would still seem to be wrong for the confined soldier to be abused.

There is also a kind of fiduciary, or at least stewardship, duty that is quite independent of any explicit or implicit contract. Where one party has voluntarily assumed the role of protector and is in control of another person, an obligation of heightened care arises for the protector. If one surrenders, but also hopes to go back to the battle, or if one is forced into the dependent role by being captured, why should one be treated with restraint? At least in part, this is because one is forcibly placed under the care of another and that other then has a fiduciary, or stewardship, duty to provide care for the one who is dependent. Of course, the capturing army can refuse to accept the surrender or not attempt to capture enemy soldiers at all. But if it does accept them, it has placed them under its care, and then members of the army must treat prisoners with much more consideration than if the prisoners were still free to fight.

The fiduciary or stewardship obligation is clearest when the soldier has surrendered; but what of those who have been captured? While the captured soldier has not placed himself in the care of the capturing soldier, this is in effect what has happened nonetheless. By capturing, rather than merely killing, an enemy soldier, the capturing soldier could be understood to be merely securing a slave, as Grotius said was the custom in the early 17th century. But even slaves, or perhaps *especially* slaves, are owed humane treatment because their condition is so vulnerable. Indeed, it is the vulnerability rather than the voluntary act of the captured soldier that triggers the fiduciary or stewardship obligation. The fact of one's vulnerability combined with the voluntary acceptance of the vulnerable one as dependent upon the capturing soldier create the obligation to act humanely.

The confinement of soldiers as prisoners changes the rules of the game so that the captor goes from being a competitor of the enemy soldier to having a kind of fiduciary or stewardship responsibility for the soldier. And with this change, the idea of proportionality of treatment takes on a much greater prominence. Before capture or surrender, the enemy soldier should not be killed or injured unless this is somehow necessary for one's own survival. But the customs of nations (quite mistakenly, I argued in previous chapters) allowed for quite a wide latitude in terms of what was acceptable behavior in this domain, for it was assumed that soldiers were all on the same level, at all times ready to injure or kill one another. After capture, even on this (mistaken) view, it could no longer be assumed that soldiers are all ready to injure or kill one another, for among other reasons the captured soldier no longer has the ready means to effect this injury or killing.

While it seems to matter how it came to be that a soldier is currently in confinement, in all such circumstances the rules of war set severe limits on what can legitimately be done to a confined soldier. It is mainly the fact of confinement that changes the moral universe, as we will see in the next section. The question then is whether this change is enough to warrant the claim, often made throughout the centuries, that prisoners must only be punished in proportion to what they deserved, based on what they did while incarcerated. Why can't prisoners be tortured, either to obtain needed information, to set an example to others still fighting, or as representatives of those who unjustly tried to kill members of the capturing army?

III. FIDUCIARY AND STEWARDSHIP OBLIGATIONS

The confinement of soldiers as prisoners of war, as I said above, changes the rules of the game so that the captured soldier goes from being a competitor of the enemy soldier to being the enemy soldier's fiduciary or stewardship responsibility. The key consideration, I think, is that once a soldier is under the control of an enemy army, that soldier cannot be seen as a combatant and must be treated as a ward of the capturing army, with the rights that would be associated with someone who is now being forcibly subjugated by another. Once confined, the duty of the detaining soldiers is to treat detainees as their fiduciary or stewardship responsibilities, regardless of what they might have done or learned while on the battlefield. In light of our earlier discussion, it is interesting that one of the oldest English cases to discuss fiduciary obligations referred to the trust relationship as a "principle of humanity."[19] The status of the prisoner of war, as confined, dependent, and vulnerable, is crucial. Humanity requires restraint in such situations.

Fiduciary duties, as framed by the principle of humanity discussed earlier, normally attach in situations where a person has placed into another's hands his or her own life or a valuable piece of property that the fiduciary is trusted to take care of. It is the trust that one person expresses to another that generates the fiduciary duty. It is a violation of this trust to abuse the life or property that one has been entrusted to care for. Fiduciary duties can also arise when one person has been placed in a position of dependence vis-à-vis another person. Think of the guardian of a minor child. In general, it seems to me, the fiduciary duty originates in the dependence or vulnerability of one person toward another, either voluntarily or involuntarily caused. If this is right, or if there is a relationship somewhat like that of the fiduciary relationship that fits this bill, then I would argue that the prisoner/warden or detainee/confiner relationship is of this sort.

Stewardship relationships are slightly less stringent than fiduciary relationships, and I have said that I am not sure which of these models is best for understanding the relationship between prisoners of war

---

[19] *Hylton v. Hylton* (1754), 28 Eng. Rep. 349, 2 Ves. Sen. 547, at 549.

and their captors. Some see fiduciary relationships as incredibly stringent, where one party must place the interests of a second party over everything else, even the interests of the first party. As I will explain, I do not have this in mind when I talk of fiduciary relationships. For this reason, it might be better to think of these as stewardship relationships, which are not as well defined as fiduciary ones but seem to call for extra care on the part of the steward. While I think that a bit more than this is required of captors toward prisoners of war, I am willing to admit that this might be the best way to capture that relationship if the only alternative is a very severe understanding of fiduciary relationships.

A fiduciary relationship is a "functional relationship . . . not a contractual one since the expectations of the parties are not based on mutual promises, consideration or consent, for one party owns and has custody of the other party."[20] These are the words of the authors of *American Jurisprudence*, second edition, concerning the nature of the relationship between a parent and a subsidiary corporation. Interestingly, these authors then go on to say that this type of fiduciary relationship is "like the relationship between parent and child, warden and prisoner," which is also based on "the status of the parties."[21] While there are many forms of fiduciary relationships, they all have in common the idea that "a person in a fiduciary relationship is under a duty to act for the benefit of the other as to matters within the scope of the relationship."[22]

In a sense, it does seem appropriate to think of prisoners of war and their captors as existing in a fiduciary relationship because the captor certainly controls, and even could be said to own, the prisoner of war. If there are duties of the captor to the prisoner of war, they are certainly not based on a contract. And while it may seem to be too much of a stretch to think of the prisoner of war as a child or ward, this is not so important because there are many other forms of fiduciary relationships than those that are based on such total dependency. When one person is rendered vulnerable and the other person is assigned the care and protection of the vulnerable one, a fiduciary relationship can also arise. In the most dependent relationship, the duties are extremely strict, where the dominant party is to sacrifice his or her interests for the sake of the dependent party, as in the case of parents and

[20] 18A Am. Jur. 2d, CORPORATIONS, Sec. 773. [21] Ibid.
[22] Restatement of Trusts (3d), Sec. 2.

children. But when the dependency is not quite that great, then it makes sense to think that the duty is also less strict, perhaps where the dominant party must give slightly more weight to the dependent party's interests than to the dominant party's interests. And the idea here turns on status, as does the original Grotian idea of humane treatment that follows from the 17th-century idea of the principle of humanity.

To think that the person who captures another person becomes that person's fiduciary, or steward, is certainly not the normal way to think of the normative basis of the rules of war. And indeed, I have given a different and elaborate alternative construal in terms of mercy. But the mercy-based considerations do not get us a strong obligation of the sort that seems to be needed when discussing why captors should be prohibited from torturing prisoners of war. In my view, the case of prisoners of war is different from other battlefield cases.

Chemical weapons should not be used during battles, and naked soldiers should not be shot, but such considerations are weaker than the prohibition against torturing prisoners of war who have been taken off the battlefield. Those on the battlefield do not have a fiduciary/ stewardship obligation toward others on the battlefield, but they should display mercy toward them nonetheless. But the prohibition on torture of prisoners of war is not merely based on mercy. There is not a strong obligation on the part of the members of one side to treat the members of the other side as their fiduciaries or wards. But once one party has captured and rendered vulnerable and dependent members of the other side, a heightened form of protection is owed to these prisoners of war. Under such conditions of heightened protection, torture is certainly ruled out in virtually every case.

I think that prisoners of war are sufficiently different from normal soldiers on the battlefield, but also different from normal prisoners, so that my fiduciary analysis of prisoners of war does not necessarily have to be extended to normal prisoners. One difference is that prisoners of war have not been tried and convicted; indeed, most of them will not be tried because it is known that they did not do anything wrong. They will simply be released after the war is over. Of course, they might have killed or assaulted other people on the battlefield, but that is what all soldiers are supposed to be doing during war. Most prisoners of war are taken off the battlefield to get them out of combat, not because there is a prima facie criminal case against them. That is one fairly important difference between prisoners of war and normal prisoners: Not only are the former dependent on their captors, but there is normally no reason to think they deserve to be incarcerated for what they have done.

Also, the reasons for abusing prisoners of war are usually quite different from the reasons for abusing ordinary prisoners. Prisoners of war are often abused because they are still thought of as enemies and the abuse is a form of reprisal for what happened on the battlefield; and yet because most soldiers do pretty much the same things on the battlefield, on both sides, this is hardly a legitimate basis for abuse. There may be some information that these prisoners of war are thought to have picked up on the battlefield that they can convey and once known by their captors can help prevent future harms. Neither of these reasons is a common one for abusing ordinary prisoners, although this is not to say that abuse does not occur in normal prisoner cases, merely that the reasons for the abuse differ greatly. In any event, I think that there are differences that might lead us to treat prisoners of war as being in fiduciary or stewardship relationships with their captors that would not necessarily mean that the same relationship should be thought to exist for normal prisoners and their jailers. Therefore, I will restrict my comments about the fiduciary or stewardship relationship of guards and prisoners to the case of prisoners of war.

The moral argument for thinking that captors should not abuse prisoners of war hinges on the relationship of dominance and dependency between them. Once a person is in such a relationship, then it is status rather than behavior that counts morally. The captor is to treat the prisoner of war humanely, and to follow the specific restraints that that entails, because of the vulnerable, dependent position of the prisoner of war. The prisoner of war is to be treated mercifully, regardless of what he or she did or learned on the battlefield, because of the current status of the prisoner of war. Remember Grotius' comment that if there are too many prisoners of war to be treated humanely in a camp, then the captors have a duty to let them all go free. The fiduciary or stewardship relationship means that the captor must look to the interest of the prisoner with slightly more importance than is the captor's interests. The dependency status of the prisoner of war demands as much. I will say more about these status-based moral concerns at the beginning of the next chapter, especially as they relate to the idea of humanity. Suffice it here to say at least that something like a fiduciary relationship exists between the captor and the prisoner of war and that relationship generates duties on the part of the captor to treat the prisoner on the basis of this dependent status rather than on what the prisoner might otherwise deserve or on what justice might sanction.

IV.   THE MORAL EQUALITY OF PRISONERS OF WAR

Some have said that on the battlefield there is a moral equality of soldiers; I would contend that off the battlefield there is the moral equality of prisoners of war. It is common to say that on the battlefield all soldiers are morally equal, for they are each trying to kill the other and thus are equally deserving of being killed by the other in self-defense. Once on the battlefield, it does not matter whether one's State is in the right or in the wrong. I have given some reasons to question this principle. Most importantly, it seems to me that there are various situations where soldiers are not trying to kill one another and thus it does not make sense to say that they are justified in killing on grounds of self-defense. In Chapter 5, I argued for a more fine-grained basis for discriminating among combatants and noncombatants. What is supposed to make them all morally equal turns out to be rebuttable and not a good basis for determining when it is justified to kill, even on the battlefield. The moral equality of soldiers does make sense though, as I argued earlier, when thinking about how soldiers should be treated by one another, that is, humanely.

I now wish to defend a somewhat similar principle: the rough equality of all prisoners of war. While soldiers may do various horrendous things on the battlefield, once they have been captured (or have surrendered) it does not matter what they have done (at least before trial), for as confined prisoners they are all roughly equal in terms of how they should be treated. At the very least, those who hold prisoners of war must meet a minimum of morally acceptable conduct, regardless of what the prisoners of war have done on the battlefield. The main reason for this is that confinement transforms these previously dangerous soldiers into people who are not dangerous anymore and who are dependent on their captors for many of the essentials of life. Of course, it might be necessary to place some prisoners into special cells because of a greater risk of escape or of injuring the guards. But to punish prisoners of war based on what they have done on the battlefield, prior to any trial, is simply not acceptable, as I will argue below.

One of the main problems with punishing soldiers who are confined has to do with making sure that there are fair hearings to determine what those prisoners actually did and what would be appropriate punishment given the overall circumstances of the war. As I have just argued, the presumption (if ever there was one) that soldiers are ready to injure or kill one another is simply lacking in the case of confined soldiers. So the sort of rough justice of the battlefield, where one had to act quickly lest one be "acted upon," is missing. There is no longer even a hint of the "heat of battle" between two equal adversaries. We need to instill in the capturing soldiers the idea that they should exercise restraint toward enemy soldiers, especially restraint concerning the strong feelings of vengeance that many soldiers will feel toward their "enemies" who, just days earlier, were trying to kill them or their compatriots.

The principle of the rough equality of prisoners of war is the background assumption of the Third Geneva Convention. Article 3 leaves little doubt when it declares:

Persons taking no active part in the hostilities . . . shall in all circumstances be treated humanely, without any adverse distinction founded on race, color, religion, faith, sex, birth or wealth, or any other similar criteria.
To this end, the following acts are and shall remain prohibited at any time and in any place whatsoever . . .
a) violence to life and person . . .
c) outrages upon personal dignity, in particular, humiliating and degrading treatment. . . .

And Article 13 also is quite clear in saying that

prisoners of war must at all times be humanely treated. . . .
Measures of reprisal against prisoners of war are prohibited.

Thus, the Geneva Convention (III) subscribed to what I am calling the rough equality of prisoners of war by specifying that there is a minimum that all such prisoners can demand, regardless of who they are or what they did on the battlefield. They are not to be subject to reprisals. Although they can be disciplined for what they do while in custody, punishment for what they did on the battlefield must wait until after there has been a proper judicial proceeding.

So what normative considerations would justify the Geneva Convention, one of the least controversial of all of the international law documents, in condemning reprisals and other forms of extrajudicial punishment of prisoners of war? Once a soldier is under the control of an enemy army, that soldier cannot be seen as a combatant and must be treated as someone with the rights that would be associated with one who is being forcibly restrained while awaiting trial. A recent editorial about the Abu Ghraib prison scandal failed to understand the point of the Geneva Conventions' restrictions when it said: "No one expects U.S. troops to pat prisoners on the head."[23] What I am arguing is that this is indeed what is expected: that the troops who are running prisoner of war camps should treat their charges just as if they were any other soldiers who were being confined while awaiting trial. Once confined, the duty of the detainer is to treat the detainees with rough equality, regardless of what supposedly happened on the battlefield.

Of course, if by "pats on the head" one means some kind of praise for what the prisoners of war did on the battlefield, this is surely not required, just as it is not required in normal life. The moral equality of prisoners of war does not require that some prisoners be singled out for praise, just as it is not allowed that some prisoners be singled out for blame, on the basis of what was done on the battlefield. Prisoners of war, now no longer dangerous to their captors in the way they were while still on the battlefield, are owed what is owed to anyone else who is being confined and awaiting trial. Abusive treatment is not acceptable, regardless of how much it is believed that it is deserved for what that soldier or his or her military unit did.

Why think that prisoners of war should be treated as a class (an undifferentiated group), regardless of clear differences in deservedness for punishment? I argued in Chapter 5 that collective identification and treatment is generally not a good idea if there is some basis for finer-grained considerations. Yet, in the case of prisoners of war, at least when they are being held before trial, there is very good reason to resist differential treatment among them. During an ongoing war or in its immediate aftermath, it is highly likely that the detaining soldiers will have strongly negative feelings toward the detainees. There will be a significant possibility of physical abuse because the detaining soldiers will be so strongly predisposed to dislike, even hate, the detainees. Indeed, this is what both sides in wars always try to do: convince soldiers to hate the enemy. In such situations, the rough moral equality of prisoners of war is meant to force detaining soldiers to disregard these instilled feelings. I am arguing for a kind of strategic collective identity here, surely not an ontological one.

[23] *St. Louis Post-Dispatch*, Friday, May 7, 2004, p. B8.

There are, of course, sometimes very good prudential reasons to treat prisoners of war abusively so as to send a message to the other soldiers who are still fighting as one's enemies and trying to kill one's compatriots. It is also often true that there appear to be good reasons for torturing prisoners of war to get vital information to prevent the killing of these compatriots. But in addition to the principle of the *moral* equality of prisoners, there is also a closely related principle – namely, the *prudential* equality of prisoners of war. The prudential equality of prisoners of war makes it clear that for each side, and in most wars, there appear to be good prudential reasons to treat all prisoners of war abusively, including torturing them, whether they are my enemies or my compatriots. It is thus important to note that there are good prudential reasons *on both sides* to abuse prisoners of war. Therefore, there is a good prudential reason not to allow such treatment by recognizing the prudential equality of prisoners of war.[24]

The principle of the prudential equality of prisoners of war, like the principle of the moral equality of prisoners of war, is meant to indicate that there are good reasons for treating prisoners of war as an undifferentiated class, because there are overriding concerns that negate any differences among members of the class, at least until there have been trials. Collective-identity schemes are not in and of themselves conceptually or normatively problematical. We make collective identifications all the time, and indeed we must do so in order to survive the onslaught of information that comes our way in the course of any given day. What is problematical is when there are relevant differences among individual members of groups, and there are no overriding reasons to outweigh these differences, and yet collective identification occurs nonetheless.[25]

There is another moral reason not to abuse those who are under one's care, one that has to do with honor. Senator John McCain was a prisoner of war for five years during the Vietnam War, and he was

---

[24] The prudential equality of prisoners of war assumes that there is a kind of tit-for-tat situation that will occur in war time, where one side will retaliate for harm done to its prisoners of war by harming enemy prisoners of war. It is also assumed that when one sees one's own prisoners of war being well treated, one will be inclined to treat enemy prisoners of war similarly. It is always possible to mistreat prisoners of war and try to hide the mistreatment, but during war such secrets are often hard to maintain, and the risk to one's own prisoners of war if such information surfaces is such that the risk is hardly ever worth it.

[25] See the extensive discussion in Chapter 5, Section 1, about this point.

tortured. He strongly opposes the use of torture, even against terrorist detainees, not out of respect for who the prisoners of war are but out of respect for who *we* are. McCain's position aligns with the view discussed earlier concerning honor. Soldiers should act humanely out of a concern for themselves, for their own honor. Given that soldiers are already involved in morally questionable behavior – that is, killing – it is especially important for them to restrain themselves more than would be true for nonsoldiers.

In the present case, while there are differences among prisoners of war, especially in terms of what they are alleged to have done on the battlefield as soldiers, there are two reasons not to take these differences as definitive for overriding collective identity. First, the acts on the battlefield are only alleged acts until there has been a definitive court proceeding. And second, there are yet other, prudential, considerations that do not allow the simple overriding to go through. For these reasons, I believe that prisoners of war should continue to be treated as an undifferentiated class (until trials have been held), and they should all be subject to the Third Geneva Convention's prohibitions on the use of torture or other abuses against all prisoners of war, regardless of what they did on the battlefield. In the next section and in later chapters, we will take up another reason to differentiate among prisoners of war: that some of them have information that is vital for the war effort and yet they may only disclose this information if subjected to, or seriously threatened with, torture and other forms of abuse.

V.   REFOCUSING THE PROPORTIONALITY PRINCIPLE

Torture or other forms of physical coercion of prisoners appears to be unjustifiable in all circumstances, as the Geneva Conventions indicate, because such treatment violates the principle of humane treatment. Yet, the principle of proportionality actually opens the door to the possibility of justifying some physically coercive practices in those cases where there is no other clearly known way to stop terrorists and others who pose an extremely dangerous threat to the lives of many others. In such emergency situations, considerations of necessity and proportionality raise the question of whether causing a lesser evil, the torture of a few prisoners, can be justified by the prevention of a greater evil – for example, the killing of many people by a terrorist's bomb. These "lesser-evil" considerations seem to open the door to the justification of torture in some cases.[26]

Yet even in extreme emergency cases, there are worries about resorting to torture, for proportionality should not be our overriding guide in wartime. Michael Walzer states one of the main worries well when he says that while "[p]roportionality is a matter of adjusting means to ends . . . there is an overwhelming tendency in wartime to adjust ends to means instead, that is, to redefine initially narrow goals in order to fit the available military forces and technologies."[27] In this section, I will take up this worry, as well as Walzer's attempt to overcome it, and then offer a preliminary way to think about proportionality that will allow us to adjudicate disputes about how it is that prisoners of war should be treated even during times of extreme emergency.

The proportionality requirement at first appears to be a simple utilitarian principle, but on further reflection it appears also to involve a restrained form of utilitarian calculation. The simple way to understand the proportionality principle is that

the amount of destruction permitted in pursuit of a military objective must be proportionate to the importance of the objective.[28]

This principle is often combined with the principle of necessity:

that military forces should cause no more destruction than is strictly necessary to achieve their objectives.[29]

While necessity and proportionality may justify some military tactics, there are certain military policies that are ruled out if more bad is caused than the good achieved by the tactics, or if there are other tactics that could be used that produce less bad results and still attain the same good. Because of the addition of a restraint on simple utilitarian calculation that the principle of necessity calls for, Douglas Lackey calls the principle of proportionality an "attenuated" form of utilitarianism.[30] I will follow his lead in this respect for reasons that will become clearer later in this section and in Chapter 10.

---

[26] See Michael Ignatieff, *The Lesser Evil: Political Ethics in an Age of Terror*, 2004, for an excellent discussion of this general issue. Michael Walzer has also recently addressed these issues in his book *Arguing About War*, New Haven, CT: Yale University Press, 2004, Chapter 3.

[27] Michael Walzer, *Just and Unjust Wars*, New York: Basic Books, 1977, p. 120.

[28] Douglas P. Lackey, *The Ethics of War and Peace*, Upper Saddle River, NJ: Prentice-Hall, 1989, p. 59.

[29] Ibid.   [30] Ibid., p. 64.

Michael Walzer talks of a "war convention" that limits the tactics that soldiers are allowed to pursue, but that also allows the use of tactics otherwise prohibited. Walzer reconstructs the principles of pro-portionality and necessity – but then adds

The war convention invites soldiers to calculate costs and benefits only up to a point, and at that point it establishes a series of clear-cut rules – moral for-tifications, so to speak, that can be stormed only at great moral cost. Nor can a soldier justify his violation of the rules by referring to the necessities of his combat situation or by arguing that nothing else but what he did would have contributed significantly to victory.[31]

There is even a utilitarian reason to set absolute limits to the prin-ciples of proportionality and necessity – namely, that after wars are over, it is hoped that peace can be sustained, and yet this will be unlikely if the military tactics employed are thought to be "unneces-sary, brutal or unfair, or simply 'against the rules.' "[32] Such conduct during war will cause bitterness, Walzer claims, that will last after the fighting is over and that will potentially jeopardize lasting peace among previously belligerent States.

The Geneva Conventions and other documents of international humanitarian law provide clear-cut, anti-utilitarian rules. Over the centuries, however, many theorists have argued for exceptions to these rules, especially in situations of extreme emergency. The rules of war require soldiers to respect the rights of others. Walzer argues that when soldiers "come up against the basic rights of the people they are threatening to kill or injure, . . . then they are bound not to kill or injure them."[33] But in emergency situations, things change back to utilitarian concerns, although this does not mean that soldiers are left unrestrained:

Utilitarian calculation can force us to violate the rules of war only when we are face-to-face not merely with defeat but with a defeat likely to bring disaster to a political community. But these calculations have no similar effects when what is at stake is only the speed or the scope of victory.[34]

Even in situations of extreme emergency, Walzer claims, we should not expect to find good people who will do evil things. If it truly is an emergency, then perhaps "we must look for people who are not good, and use them, and dishonor them."[35]

---

[31] Michael Walzer, *Just and Unjust Wars*, p. 130.   [32] Ibid., p. 132.
[33] Ibid., p. 304.   [34] Ibid., p. 268.   [35] Ibid., p. 325.

I agree with Walzer that we should not subscribe to rule fetishism; it might possibly be justifiable to break the rules of war in some very extreme cases. But if we think we need to find already "bad" soldiers who are willing to break the rules of war and terrorize or torture in situations of extreme emergency, then it is unclear to me why we should ever be justified in punishing these individuals for what the emergency situations forced their States to do. I will return to this issue in Chapter 11. Suffice it to say here that the soldiers who must act in "evil" ways due to the orders that they receive are not the ones who should have to pay the most serious price for doing what appears to be required by the extreme emergency. It is far more appropriate to prosecute and punish the leaders, who admittedly are also forced by the circumstances to act, but who are at least the ones who have agreed to pay such prices in exchange for the increased status and monetary compensation that they receive compared to that of the ordinary soldier.

Leaving the general issue of who should be prosecuted until later, I wish to end this current chapter by addressing the question of whether it is justifiable to abuse prisoners in cases of extreme emergency. Here the classic case involves Bush administration officials who may have signed secret orders allowing for such prisoner abuse by the CIA in order to stop a future terrorist attack on the United States in 2004. If only these prisoners could be made to talk, they could tell who was planning such an attack as well as where and when it was to occur. Isn't this the classic case of extreme emergency, a basis for thinking that the rules of war could be suspended so as to achieve this clearly worthwhile military objective, despite the moral and prudential equality of the prisoners of war?

I wish to argue that if there are cases that are ever justified by the principles of proportionality and necessity, they are far fewer, and much harder to justify fully, than people like to think. The problem is the one we began to discuss above: that prisoners are completely at the mercy of the soldiers who guard them. Their being confined makes a huge moral difference. If these were soldiers in the field who could still defend themselves, then using banned tactics in cases of extreme emergency can more easily be justified, for the soldiers can at least fight back. It is again like the shackled boxer: It seems to be much harder to justify the use of brass knuckles here than in the case of a nonshackled boxer, despite the fact that in both cases brass knuckles are banned in boxing. Those who literally cannot defend themselves are owed much more in terms of what humane treatment morally requires than those who are not completely constrained.

There is an odd result when the conclusions of this chapter are juxtaposed on those of the previous two chapters. In this chapter, I have defended a more absolutist reading of the prohibition on torture and criticized interpretations of the proportionality principle that destroy virtually all absolutist prohibitions in the rules of war. Yet, in the previous two chapters I urged that we not adopt an absolutist understanding of either the prohibition on the use of poisons or the line between combatants and noncombatants. I suppose the simplest way to reconcile these various theses is to point out that I am not opposed to all absolutist principles in the rules of war. I accept absolutist or near absolutist principles when they are very narrowly tailored, as is true of the prohibition on the torture of prisoners of war. It is the very broadly construed absolutist principles, such as the prohibition on the use of all poisons, that I find especially problematic, unless one can find some way to separate such a broad category of prohibited acts from other acts that are quite similar, such as the use of bullets or bombs. This is why I was at pains to say why I was not in favor of extending the prohibition on the use of torture in war to everyone rather than merely to prisoners of war.

At the beginning of this chapter I pointed to Grotius, who said that prisoners of war were like slaves. We can do to them what we want, and do it nearly with impunity, because they are controlled by us. But because there has been no showing that they have done anything that warrants punishment, prisoners of war should be treated with restraint. Because of the dependency of prisoners of war on their captors, I have argued that there is a fiduciary or stewardship relationship between prisoners of war and those who detain then. In addition, the captors often see prisoners of war as deserving of vengeance for what they did to the detaining soldiers' comrades, making abuse even more in need of restraint. Then there is also the prudential argument that one should not abuse prisoners of war lest one's own soldiers who, if they become prisoners of war, may themselves be abused. And finally, there is the most important argument: that it dishonors soldiers to engage in cruelty toward those who cannot defend themselves. There are thus several reasons for treating prisoners of war with restraint. And while abuse might be justified in extreme emergencies, given that these cases are themselves extremely rare, it will also thus be rare indeed that captors are justified in torturing or otherwise abusing prisoners of war.

We can begin to see why abusing or torturing prisoners of war who are off the battlefield is worse even than the kind of killing that occurs on the battlefield.[36]

In the previous three chapters, I have discussed three of the main areas of conduct that are thought to violate the rules of war: killing those who are not engaged in combat, such as the naked soldier; using inhumane weapons, such as poisons and other chemical weapons; and torturing or otherwise abusing protected persons, such as prisoners of war. In each case, we used these examples as an occasion to consider the main principles of the *jus in bello* branch of Just War theory – namely, the principles of discrimination, necessity, and proportionality. In the next three chapters, I will embark on a more sustained examination of these principles, arguing that in each case there needs to be significant clarification and justification before these principles will be serviceable in helping us determine who has violated the rules of war and who is deserving of being prosecuted and punished for war crimes. In all cases, the principles of *jus in bello* should provide a very firm barrier to counter the tendency of soldiers everywhere to exert the full force of violence under their control. And when the barrier is crossed, it will normally make more sense to prosecute the commanding officers rather than the normal soldiers. The best way to conceptualize the change in these three traditional principles of the *jus in bello* branch of the Just War theory and the corresponding part of international humanitarian law is to see these three principles – the principle of discrimination or distinction, the principle of necessity, and the principle of proportionality – as grounded in and limited by the principle of humane treatment.

[36] See Henry Shue, "Torture," *Philosophy and Public Affairs*, vol. 7, no. 2 (1978), pp. 124–143.

PART C

NORMATIVE PRINCIPLES

8

The principle of discrimination or distinction

The principle of discrimination (or distinction, as it is sometimes called in legal circles) requires that soldiers treat civilians differently from fellow soldiers, generally not attacking the former except in extreme situations. The Geneva Conventions call for a clear separation of people into two camps: those who are protected from assault, including army medical personnel, injured soldiers, prisoners of war, and civilians on the one hand, and soldiers actively engaged in hostilities on the other hand. Since the Middle Ages, it has been common to differentiate these people into two large groups, although there has not been wide agreement about which of the following groups were the most salient: civilians versus soldiers; noncombatants versus combatants; or the innocent versus the non-innocent (the guilty). In this chapter, I will argue that the principle of discrimination or distinction is most plausibly defended as an extension of the principle of humane treatment, and only on that basis is it to be seen as providing a non-utilitarian basis for deciding how to act during war.

As I explained in Chapter 5, the principle of discrimination is often defended as itself a basis for rough-grained treatment, where there is an absolute ban on certain forms of violence against civilians, non-combatants, or the innocent, but where these forms of violence can appropriately be used against soldiers, combatants, or the non-innocent (guilty). I argued that the principle of discrimination could not sustain such a rough-grained, as opposed to a fine-grained, approach if the main consideration was whether a member of one group has indeed done something to threaten the lives of members of the other group. For in that case, the naked soldier could not be shot, and a whole host of people who do not clearly fit into the category of civilians, noncombatants, or the innocent would have to be protected, at least in certain circumstances. The principle of discrimination, therefore, could not sustain a bright-line approach to determining who was protected and who was not.

One of the most important difficulties with the principle of discrimination, as it is normally understood, is that it attempts to draw a bright line about who can legitimately be assaulted or killed on the basis of what the members of the group have done in the past or are currently doing. I will continue my attempt to show what is wrong with such a strategy, and I will begin to develop an alternative model that is closely linked to the model I established in Chapter 4 for understanding the principle of humane treatment – namely, to focus on status rather than on what one has done or is currently doing. The status-based model I will develop is often criticized for various reasons, some of which have to do with standard worries about collective responsibility that I will attempt to rebut.

In the first section of this chapter, I will return to my critique of the standard approach to the principle of discrimination offered by Michael Walzer and others. In the second section, I will then set out a different way to justify the principle of discrimination (distinction) in terms of humane treatment. In the third section, I will articulate a test for the principle of discrimination and discuss an application of the newly conceptualized principle of discrimination by returning once again to the problem of the naked soldier. In the fourth section, I turn to four criticisms of my account of the principle of discrimination. And then, in the final section, I address the most significant metaphysical problem with my account by addressing an important point made by Noam Zohar.

I.   FOCUSING ON STATUS RATHER THAN BEHAVIOR

The state of international law concerning how to treat combatants and noncombatants is controversial. I have been using the term "principle of discrimination," which is the term used in the Just War tradition. International lawyers tend to use the term "principle of distinction" to mark the requirement that combatants and noncombatants not be treated alike. The Institute of International Law adopted a resolution at its 1969 Edinburgh meeting concerning the principle of distinction.

The Resolution declared:

1. The obligation to respect the distinction between military objectives and non-military objectives as well as between persons participating in the hostilities and members of the civilian populations remains a fundamental principle of the international law in force . . . .
4. Existing international law prohibits all armed attacks on the civilian population as such. . . .
7. Existing international law prohibits the use of all weapons which, by their nature, affect indiscriminately both military objectives and nonmilitary objects, or both armed forces and civilian populations.

This extremely clear statement of the principle of distinction is not accepted by all States. In particular, the United States has said that it does not accept this statement of international law, despite the fact that a unanimous 1970 General Assembly Resolution embraced this formulation of the principle of distinction or discrimination.[1]

In international law, rationales for the principle of distinction or discrimination, when given at all, are primarily drawn in terms of humanity rather than immunity linked to behavior. Leslie Green, one of the foremost authorities on the law of war, puts the principle of distinction or discrimination into the general context of "considerations of humanity."[2] Dieter Fleck's *Handbook* states the point in a similar way: "[T]he principle of distinction belongs to the oldest fundamental maxims of established customary rules of humanitarian law. . . . The ICJ has recently reaffirmed, in the *Nicaragua* judgment, the particular dignity of these minimum rules, qualifying them as general principles of law which flow from 'elementary considerations of humanity.' "[3] And Ingrid Detter puts the point even more starkly: "The protection of civilians is, from the humanitarian point of view, the most important task of any legislative effort on warfare as such persons include the weakest members of the community most in need of protection, such as women, children and the aged."[4] Detter also mentions, but seemingly as a less important rationale, "that civilians must normally be assumed to have wished to abstain from involvement in the conflict."[5] In the next

---

[1] See Leslie C. Green, *The Contemporary Law of Armed Conflict*, 2nd ed., New York: Juris Publishing, and Manchester University Press, 2000, pp. 47–49.
[2] Ibid., p. 53.
[3] Dieter Fleck, *The Handbook of Humanitarian Law in Armed Conflict*, Oxford: Oxford University Press, 1995, p. 120.
[4] Ingrid Detter, *The Law of War*, 2nd ed., Cambridge: Cambridge University Press, 2000, p. 317.
[5] Ibid.

section, I will develop a rationale for the principle of discrimination or distinction in terms of the principle of humane treatment and in keeping with the dominant understanding of contemporary international law as a replacement for the behavioral rationale given by Walzer and others that is largely drawn in terms of justice rather than humanity. In the remainder of the current section, I will sketch some of the problems with the behavioral alternative.

In the first chapters of this book, I highlighted the difference between (retributive) justice and humanity as a basis for the rules of war. Justice calls for giving to a person what is owed as his or her due based on what that person has done or is currently doing. On the other hand, humanity calls for giving a person the benefit of the doubt and generally calls for acting toward the person as a fellow human being deserving of respect no matter what he or she has done or is now doing. As Grotius said, it is sometimes better to do more than what is required by justice, because we display our true humanity by doing so, especially when we are dealing with those who are our enemies. Wartime situations are obviously situations where it would be appropriate to appeal to the principle of humanity.

Focusing on what one has done is generally better than focusing on who one is, especially when we are talking about punishment. For punishment should normally reflect what one has under one's control, which is typically one's behavior, and not things out of one's control, such as one's status. There is a great likelihood of abuse when punishment is pegged to status. For this reason, U.S. Supreme Court cases have held that a person could not be punished merely for his or her status – for instance, merely for being drunk, for being homeless, or for just standing on a street corner.[6] In the liberal tradition that has developed since John Stuart Mill, punishment has been seen as apt only when a person does something harmful to another person that violates a law.[7] Wartime situations, though, are different from normal situations, especially because there are reasons to think that people are not going to act rationally toward one another.

In wartime, as I have suggested before, there is the problem of the heightened emotions of the participants to worry about. In wartime, commanders on both sides go to great lengths to make their troops

---

[6] See Wayne R. LaFave and Austin W. Scott, Jr., *Criminal Law*, 2nd ed., St. Paul, MN: West Publishing, 1986, pp. 195–200.

[7] John Stuart Mill, *On Liberty* (1863).

think of the troops on the other side as their enemies. Enemies tend to hate one another, even to seek vengeance against one another, making it very hard for individuals to be rational and to see what other individuals owe to one another. The emotional elements, especially anger and even rage, that are often standard fare in war make it imperative that narrow or natural justice not be the only basis for deciding how the "enemy" is to be treated. It is for good reason that Grotius argued, over three hundred years ago, for the priority of our "humanitarian instincts."

Also, in wartime it is not at all clear what individuals deserve, given that States rather than individuals typically wage wars. If individuals do not start wars, but are merely doing their patriotic duty by aiding their States in waging war, in what sense do they deserve ill treatment by enemy States? And even if they do, on some theory, deserve ill treatment, shouldn't it matter what their status was – namely, that they were merely followers of the leadership of a State or cogs in a war machine that was not of their own making? As I will explore in later chapters, especially Chapter 12, it might make sense to punish the leaders of a State based on what they deserve. But it might also make sense to relieve from punishment the soldiers who followed the orders of these leaders, even if the soldiers in some sense also deserve to be punished. Here we would let status override behavior.

In the Just War tradition, it is common to say that there is a rough moral equality of soldiers in wartime, in that each can kill and each can defend his or her life by trying to kill the enemy soldier. I have argued against this view in various respects in earlier chapters. Nonetheless, I think there is a grain of truth in this view: that soldiers all share the same status and for this reason generally should not be treated according to what is deserved based on their behavior. Soldiers rarely engage in behavior that has not been commanded, or at least sanctioned, by higher-ups. For this reason, it is usually a mistake to treat soldiers as if they were acting entirely on their own when they commit harms against others.

The principle of discrimination has been grounded in the behavioral rather than the status-based moral equality of soldiers. Walzer famously argues that all soldiers have "allowed themselves to be made into dangerous men," thereby losing their immunity from being attacked and killed.[8] This position seemingly links the loss of immunity

---

[8] Michael Walzer, *Just and Unjust Wars*, New York: Basic Books, 2000, p. 145.

to what the soldier has done, either by enlisting or allowing himself or herself to be drafted. I argued in Chapter 5 that it was insufficient to link loss of immunity to something as passive as allowing oneself to be drafted, especially because for many young men and women there were few reasonable alternatives at the time. But it seems to me that Walzer's argument is more at home with the status-based, rather than the behavioral, grounding of the moral equality of soldiers. For allowing oneself to be made into a dangerous person, except in unusual circumstances, is little different from having that status thrust upon one.

It is true that in some cases men and women could willingly resist allowing themselves to be made into dangerous men and women by not acceding to the draft. But it is hard to see why such a fairly minor form of behavior would carry with it such dire consequences. It is different, of course, if one decides to enlist, but even in that case one wonders what reasonable options the person had. Was enlistment due to overriding concerns about supporting a family or even overriding concerns of patriotism. If so, one can again raise the question of whether the "behavior" is sufficient to warrant the losing of such an important immunity, perhaps our most important immunity. For it takes little imagination to understand that the loss of immunity from being attacked and killed is perhaps the most important moral immunity a person has. It would seem to take a major behavioral argument to warrant the claim that one has by one's behavior lost that immunity. Let us next examine a status-based argument instead.

II.   HUMANE TREATMENT AND DISCRIMINATION

I will here construct a rationale for the principle of discrimination, or distinction, that is based on the status considerations of the principle of humanity and the discussion in Chapter 4 of the principle of humane treatment. Such a rationale will not result in a bright line between civilians and soldiers, because it will turn out that some soldiers, such as the naked soldier, are as much in need of protection (or more so) because of their status as many civilians are. Nonetheless, we will be able to get a strong rationale for the prohibition on indiscriminate killing in war, and thus we will be able to provide a rationale for the principle of distinction or discrimination that will mesh with the most important of the principles of humanitarian law: the principle of humane treatment.

Let us begin with Ingrid Detter's observation quoted at the beginning of the previous section. She says that the key consideration is that civilians during war are vulnerable and in need of protection. Of course, as Detter herself says, this is not necessarily true of everyone who is a civilian. The group of civilians "includes" those who are among the weakest, but it also includes others.[9] For some civilians may indeed have the means to protect themselves and may be as strong and effectively armed as members of the military. But typically, civilians are in a vulnerable position vis-à-vis armed soldiers. This is especially true of those who are very young, very weak, or very old. We need not endorse Detter's claim that all women fit into this category because many women function quite well as soldiers, and, even when not being soldiers, many women can defend themselves quite well. But Detter provides us with a good start by talking about the status of being vulnerable as the key to the principle of discrimination or distinction.

Being vulnerable is indeed a status not a behavioral characteristic, although there is a bit of a blending of these categories in some cases. Robert Goodin gives the following gloss on the dictionary definition of "vulnerable":

According to the Oxford English Dictionary, something is "vulnerable" if it "may be wounded," either literally or figuratively; it is "susceptible of injury, not proof against weapon, criticism, etc." . . . Conceptually, "vulnerability" is essentially a matter of being under a threat of harm; therefore, protecting the vulnerable is primarily a matter of forestalling threatened harms.[10]

While it may be that some people who are vulnerable have done something to place themselves in this position, there are many others who are merely born into this position or placed there by the commissions or omissions of others. Vulnerability may in some cases be connected to what one has done, but there is no necessary connection between one's behavior and one's vulnerability.

During war, civilians are generally vulnerable to attack and soldiers are generally not vulnerable because they have the means to fend off attacks. This is the starting insight that leads to the principle of discrimination or distinction. But it turns out that not all members of these groups are similarly situated, even if we focus on their status rather than what they have done. It is for this reason that I earlier

[9] Ingrid Detter, *The Law of War*, p. 317.
[10] Robert Goodin, *Protecting the Vulnerable*, Chicago: University of Chicago Press, 1985, p. 110.

proposed a fine-grained rather than a rough-grained way of understanding this principle. For if the key consideration is whether one is
vulnerable to attack or other forms of harm, it will rarely turn out that
all the members of a large group, all the time, are actually vulnerable.
But protecting those who are vulnerable may indeed be the underlying
rationale for having a principle of discrimination or distinction.

Humane treatment enters the picture because compassion and
minimizing suffering are ideas cognate to that of protecting the vulnerable. Compassion involves suffering with the other and makes one
especially prone to help the vulnerable because they are so clearly
prone to suffer. And, of course, minimal suffering is also very closely
related to protecting the vulnerable, for the main thing that the vulnerable need to be protected from is being made to suffer, whether
such suffering is deserved or not. Acting compassionately, like protecting the vulnerable, also seems to call for disregarding the behavior
of the individual so helped and focusing on the status of the individual,
especially the status that calls forth a response on our part as fellow
humans.

Our earlier discussion of the principle of humanity is therefore also
implicated for it is the status not the just deserts that count the most in
determining how people should be treated according to the principle
of discrimination or distinction. As Goodin indicates, a focus on vulnerability shifts the discussion from what the vulnerable person has
done to whether there is anyone who can help.[11] If there is a focus on
behavior at all, it is not one that looks back to what the vulnerable
person did, but one that looks ahead to what others can do to alleviate
the vulnerability, or at least to minimize its effects. The chief behavioral factor is what those who are not vulnerable, and who could exploit
this vulnerability, are capable of doing to protect those who are vulnerable.

It is, strictly speaking, not a matter of (retributive) justice that the
vulnerable be protected, but rather a matter of compassion and mercy,
the hallmark characteristics of the principle of humane treatment. For
it is largely irrelevant what the vulnerable have done in the past. What
matters is their current predicament and what it will take to protect
them from the ravages of that predicament. Here, "predicament" is a
kind of "status." Being vulnerable is not quite in the same category as
being human. Being human is never connected at all to what the

---

[11] Ibid., p. 126.

person who is human did in the past. But being vulnerable is not such a pure status category. There are often things that one could have done, or did, in the past that affect a person's status as vulnerable. Vulnerability is sometimes within the ambit of one's control, whereas humanity is utterly beyond our control by our behavior. But the important point is that for both cases of vulnerability and humanity protective treatment may be called for that would not be warranted by (retributive) justice, despite the differences between these two status categories.

The principle of distinction, or discrimination, can be defended initially by reference to status not behavior. Civilians clearly have not done anything to warrant attacks or to warrant immunity from attacks. Soldiers sometimes appear to warrant attack, but a closer look makes one wonder what the normal soldier has done that makes him or her lose one of the most important of immunities. Status is not to be seen as a basis for rough-grained distinctions because it also turns out that some soldiers are highly vulnerable and cannot at the moment defend themselves, such as when they are naked in the bath. And some civilians – even women, children, or the aged – are not vulnerable because they have the capability not only to defend themselves, but also to defend themselves better than some soldiers in certain situations. Because of these facts, the principle of discrimination will have to be a fine-grained basis for distinction. By that, I mean that it will be a good place to begin, but it will also not be sufficient for deciding how to treat people. A closer look at context and circumstance is necessary in order to decide whether the rough-grained categories are indeed a definitive guide to action in a particular case.

The principle of discrimination or distinction is nonetheless an important principle in wartime. On my construal of this principle, it sets a framework for deciding on what is likely to be humane treatment for two large topics: how soldiers should act toward civilians, where normally they should not attack them; and how soldiers should act toward "enemy" soldiers, where it is normally acceptable to attack them, as long as the force used is not disproportionate (another category we will discuss in detail in Chapter 10). But there will be many exceptions, and so there is no bright line that can be drawn here. Rather, the principle of distinction or discrimination is a "rule of thumb" that may be used in situations where there is no other information available, other than that the person one confronts is a civilian or a soldier or where there is insufficient time to get more information, due to an emergency, even though such information does exist. But if more information is available and there is no emergency, the principle of distinction or discrimination is only a rough-grained marker of appropriate action.

In the next section, I will present a test for the principle of discrimination or distinction and then apply the test to the hard case we discussed in Chapter 5: the question of whether it is justifiable to kill a naked soldier taking a bath. We will confront the practical question of how soldiers are to regard civilians as well as "enemy" soldiers in times of war. Unfortunately, the answer will not end up being the easy one that we mentioned at the beginning of Chapter 5, where we can state the rules in two or three bold-faced lines of type on the back of an index card, as was done for American soldiers entering the first Gulf War. With the exception of true emergency situations, it will not be possible to state an easy rule at all, but only a rule of thumb that helps in beginning to think about a very difficult topic.

III.   THE NAKED SOLDIER RETURNS

Except when there is no other information available, the test involved in the principle of distinction or discrimination is not an easy one. When there is an emergency and there is no other information available, it is appropriate for soldiers to use this simple rule: Attack "enemy" soldiers not civilians. But in all other cases, surely the vast majority of cases, there will be no simple test. One needs to begin by figuring out whether the person one is confronting is a civilian or a soldier. But then one needs to proceed to determine whether the civilian poses a threat at the moment or the soldier is not a threat. Such judgments will not be easy to make and will not necessarily follow any easy-to-learn rules. Indeed, even the naked soldier may have a gun ready-to-hand, and the child with a gun in his hand pointed at me may turn out to be holding a realistic-looking water gun.

The reason why the test is so hard to formulate, at least for the majority of cases, is that the status of civilian or soldier does not yet tell us whether the person in question is actually a danger to us or a vulnerable person who needs our compassion. Humanitarian instincts require more from us than a sense of justice, but there are certainly limits to what is required even as a matter of humaneness. It is generally not required that a person jeopardize his or her own security. So it will matter whether a given civilian is armed, or even whether the

civilian can defend herself or himself, obviating the need for the soldier to risk his or her own well-being to protect this civilian. And it will
also matter if it turns out that the "enemy" soldier I am confronting
has himself or herself been rendered vulnerable, due to being naked in
the bath or being wounded in a way that makes him or her no longer a
threat to my security and instead in need of my compassion and protection.[12]

Consider again the naked soldier taking a bath. I argued in Chapter
5 that such a soldier is surely no threat to the opposing soldier who
spies the naked soldier several hundred yards away through his
binoculars. Not only is the naked soldier no longer a threat to me, this
soldier is arguably in such a vulnerable position that if anything I owe
that soldier protection. For a naked soldier in the bath, just as is true
for nearly everyone who is naked in the bath, is supremely vulnerable
because he does not even have the normal protection of clothing and is
surely not in a position to keep his guard up looking for possible
attacks. And if I can see him but he cannot see me, then it seems truly
inhumane to suggest, as Walzer reluctantly does, that it is morally right
to kill this soldier. Indeed, Walzer argues counterintuitively that while
it would be kind not to kill this soldier, it involves "doing less than is
permitted."[13]

Despite what Walzer says, it is not mere kindness not to kill the
naked soldier who is taking a bath. Compassion is different from
simple kindness. Kindness involves what is literally optional for us to
do. Compassion falls below what is required as a matter of justice, but it
still can be in the domain of what is required as a matter of our
common humanity. Grotius makes a very interesting point in this
respect. He distinguishes, as we saw earlier, between two different
senses of what is permitted. There is what is strictly permitted as a
matter of justice, but there is also what is permitted when we consider
humanitarian concerns. Here the requirements may not look as steep,
but according to Grotius we are in the domain of truly "better"[14] moral
considerations than are typically involved when we only consider formal justice. By acting in this better way, we will be acting in a more
honorable way than if we merely act according to what is permitted as a

---

[12] In the final section of this chapter, I address the objection that it is not individual
security, but group security, that is the key. But I would reject the idea that this opens
the door for *jus ad bellum* considerations.

[13] Michael Walzer, *Just and Unjust Wars*, p. 143.

[14] Hugo Grotius, *De Jure Belli ac Pacis*, p. 716.

matter of strict justice.[15] Indeed, Walzer seems to confuse things by talking as if there are duties to kill opposing soldiers that override all other moral considerations. This only begins to make sense if the moral landscape contains strict justice-based duties or weak humanity-based considerations of kindness.

We should not lose sight of the connection between humaneness and honor. There is nothing honorable about killing a naked soldier who is taking a bath. Indeed, as Walzer recognized, most soldiers would find it repulsive and dishonorable to engage in this killing despite the fact that they would generally see killing on the battlefield as an honorable activity. As I have explained, retaining a sense of honor, especially while on the battlefield, is a crucial part of the moral landscape for soldiers. For without a heightened sense of honor, the soldier is merely a paid killer. And the sense of shame that is felt when a soldier acts dishonorably could act as a deterrent against the killing of the naked soldier, if the soldier has been properly socialized by the rules of war.[16]

Humane treatment is a requirement of all of us as fellow humans. As I argued in Chapter 3, the minimal natural law basis for *jus gentium* involves a kind of respect for the equality of persons. We owe each other respect, but not as a matter of what we have done or what the other person has done or is doing. We owe certain treatment to one another not because it is deserved in this behavioral way but because it is deserved in a status-based way. In this sense, there is a larger sense of justice that dovetails with the principle of humanity. For one could say that what is owed as a matter of status is so owed because of what a person has *not* done – namely, one has not done anything other than exist in a certain category of persons; and because of not having behaved in a way to have removed one's immunity, one is deserving of being treated only as a fellow human.

There is a kind of wide, as opposed to narrow, justice that can encompass many of the considerations of humane treatment I have been discussing in the last few chapters. For what someone deserves is not merely based on what one has done but on what one has refrained from doing. Against a baseline consideration that we should all be immune from being attacked or killed, it makes sense to say that justice and humanity are related. I am not fully happy with this character-ization, but if people want to hook all that is morally required to what is

---

[15] Ibid., p. 641.   [16] I am grateful to Mark Drumbl here.

demanded by justice, then I suppose I can live with this characteriza-tion, as long as we are in agreement that this is not the kind of strict justice, but rather the kind of equitable treatment, that the Greeks first discussed.

The thing that matters is whether there is a significant risk to the soldier if he or she would act to protect someone rather than to attack him or her. And part of making that determination is whether a given soldier, or civilian for that matter, is indeed a threat to the soldier. The test amounts to discovering whether the person one is confronting does, in fact, pose a threat. Part, but only part, of the test is to look at the status of the person one confronts. Then one must assess additional information to see if the person one confronts fits into an exception class, such as that of a child who seems to be concealing a weapon. This test is often very hard to use, because it turns on an appreciation of a nearly complete set of facts. We need a showing that our compassion will be met with significant loss of our own security before it is not the case that we are required to act compassionately, even toward our enemies.

Of course, there are two types of enemy that could be threatened by the naked soldier. We have been discussing the enemy soldier who spies the naked soldier at a great distance. To that enemy, the naked soldier hardly poses much of a threat at all. But it could be argued that the naked soldier nonetheless poses a threat to the enemy State. For the naked soldier will soon end his bath and resume his role as a danger to the enemy State. Perhaps this is why he can be killed. I will take up this larger issue in the next section, where I discuss a col-lectivist view of soldiers and the threats they pose. Suffice it to say that "at the moment" it is also not clear that the naked soldier is actually a threat to the enemy State. More information is needed here as well, and the information is of the same sort – namely, whether that solider will later play a major role in attacking the enemy State and how likely this is.

In addition, we need to examine closely whether a soldier is himself or herself in a vulnerable position that calls for our compassion. For in such situations, there may be competing motivations, as the case of the naked soldier makes clear: the motivation to attack due to a worry about the threat posed and a motivation to protect due to a worry about the vulnerability exposed. The case of the naked soldier taking a bath is a good example of the conflict just mentioned. This soldier is still a soldier – that is, someone whose job it is to try to attack or kill soldiers from the enemy camp. There is thus a motivation, as Walzer well argued, to attack or kill this soldier. But there is another motivation: to protect the naked soldier because of his clearly vulnerable position.

The question that arises is which motivation is stronger, and should be stronger, in the naked soldier case. As I said above, this is not immediately evident. Additional facts would be useful here, such as whether the naked soldier has his gun ready-to-hand or whether he could not conceivably mount an attack against us. If we have no additional facts, it is not at all clear that Walzer is right to say that the naked soldier can, indeed must, be killed. At the very least, Walzer should admit that there are competing motivations that have strong moral support. As I indicated above, it is surely at least permissible for the naked soldier's life to be spared. It will take quite a bit of information in order to justify killing the naked soldier. And there will not be many, if any, situations where there is the kind of emergency where we can straightforwardly justify killing the naked soldier without knowing whether he poses any threat at all to those who come across him. The competing motivations in the case of the naked soldier cannot be so easily resolved, and this is a telling example of why the principle of discrimination needs to be seen as much more nuanced than is often thought.

In the following sections, I will take up various objections to my proposal to weaken the strictures of the principle of discrimination or distinction so as to allow for many different contexts and circumstances. I then end by discussing a very serious conceptual and normative objection to the way that both Walzer and I have been proceeding, that is, working within the individualist perspective and not giving due consideration to the collectivist way that people have understood wars for centuries: as primarily battles between collectivities that are called States. Responding to the last objection allows me to return to metaphysical issues that I began to address in Chapter 5, but that I sidelined temporarily as I tried to work out an alternative normative basis for the principle of discrimination or distinction connected to the principle of humane treatment and generally to the principle of humanity with which I began this book.

IV. OBJECTIONS

One of the most significant objections raised to my proposal is that I have rendered effective fighting in war all but impermissible by reconfiguring the principle of discrimination. For, it would be claimed, I have put such a strict limitation on who counts as a true combatant that even fully justified defending soldiers must wait until they see not only the whites of the eyes of the enemy but also that the enemy is about to fire upon them before they can justifiably attack the enemy. In many cases, that will be too late to be able to stop an aggressing army from overrunning innocent armies or States. This is even clearer in the case of aerial bombardment. Defending soldiers often cannot see the source of these potential attacks and thus cannot figure out if these targets are themselves vulnerable, because the attacking soldiers are in airplanes too high to be spotted or in ships far out to sea. If such potentially vulnerable soldiers and their weaponry cannot be targeted, then it will be very difficult to wage effective war, even in defense of one's homeland. And even among those advancing armies, it will be very difficult to figure out which soldiers can be justifiably attacked, for the collectivity of the social group has been pierced and can no longer be treated as an undifferentiated unit.

This is quite a serious objection. One of the main points of the principle of discrimination or distinction was to separate two groups of individuals, the group that can be attacked, without worrying about what each individual member is doing at the moment, and the group that can never be attacked, again regardless of what is happening at the moment. Such a strategy of collective identity has not only simplicity in its favor; it also is a strategy that takes out of the hands of the soldiers the need to engage in fine-grained calculation that is quite likely to be mistaken. Advancing armies must be treated indiscriminately if successful defense is likely to occur. And civilian populations also must be treated indiscriminately if the inhumanity of war is to be kept within acceptable limits. For, as soon as such collective identification is disrupted and what is substituted for it is a highly individualized basis of treatment, we will find that soldiers are left in the very difficult position where they are more likely than not to make tragic mistakes. If combatants are to be treated all alike, and noncombatants are to be treated all alike as well, then all the soldier needs to do is to figure out which camp a given individual falls into. And while there will be difficult cases, the vast majority of cases will be clear-cut, and the soldier, who often has to make split-second life-or-death judgments, will be better served.

My response to this objection has two parts. The first is more clearly to indicate when rough-grained distinctions can still be made. In emergency situations, such as in the contemplated imminent attack, where one can literally see the whites of the eyes of the attackers, I certainly do not advocate that soldiers wait before firing. Also, I do not mean to restrict the idea of dangerousness so that soldiers can only attack when their own personal safety is threatened. For as I said, threats can also be made to the State that the soldier serves. There is no attempt on my part to render the waging of war impossible. But I am suggesting that concern for the normative underpinnings of the rules of war, specifically for the principle of discrimination, should indeed make wars harder to fight.

The second part of my response is that it is not clear to me that soldiers will be better off with the simplicity of the rough-grained distinction between civilians and soldiers. In Vietnam, many civilians posed as much danger for American soldiers as enemy "soldiers" did. The slightly better group category was that of combatants, a category into which apparently even some children fit. But then the ease of identification fades away as advantages of the group identity model. In addition, there is the problem of whether there is indeed a category of combatants at all that allows for meaningful discrimination in war. Think of what Averroes argued: that all able-bodied enemy men should be treated as legitimate targets of attack, because they could take up arms and threaten the lives of soldiers. This position is highly problematical, and my proposal does not countenance such rough-grained discriminations. Only those who are a real threat and not in a vulnerable position can legitimately be attacked, and identifying this group will require fine-grained discriminations, for it will not include all able-bodied men.

A second objection maintains that I have missed the point of the principle of discrimination, or distinction. This principle, at least as reasonably interpreted, only prohibits indiscriminate attacks – that is, attacks that pay no attention to who is being singled out for attack. According to this view, the idea is to make soldiers stop and think before they shoot, but because these are situations where the soldiers' own lives are often on the line, we cannot expect that they will stop for very long. For this to be a workable principle, discrimination or distinction can only be expected between large classes or groups, where the border between groups is rough-grained rather than fine-grained. My proposal, on the other hand, calls for such fine-grained discrimination that soldiers will either have to stop and think for so long that they render themselves vulnerable to attack or simply give up and ignore the distinctions altogether, surely a worse alternative, even if one is motivated by humanistic instincts.

My response is that I have tried to show that the traditional large groups in question are actually not that easily identifiable, at least not in a way that is morally significant. If we use the traditional category of soldier, what are we to do about the frequency of guerrillas and other irregular fighters who are just as dangerous, if not more dangerous, to soldiers of a modern army operating in a large, hostile city? If, instead, we shift to the slightly more helpful category of combatants, there are many problems in discerning who is part of the necessary support of the war effort and who is not. Not only do children and others who would normally fit into the noncombatant camp sometimes fit into the combatant camp, but so do munitions workers, for instance. Thus, if one sees a crowd of civilians, it will not be easy to pick out from that crowd those who are, and those who are not, noncombatants, as we have increasingly seen in the streets of the Middle East. Soldiers will still have to make fine-grained decisions according to the traditional view of the principle of discrimination or distinction, at least if those discriminations are to be morally justifiable ones. Even the traditional view will also have to make some fine-grained determinations, and so the pocket card technique for understanding distinctions will often be misleading.

A third objection is to ask why we should not merely be pragmatists (or even realists) about social groups. If there is some rough utility in using a particular distinction, then use it; otherwise, throw it out. And it does seem that there is such utility in the traditional way of understanding the principle of discrimination: that soldiers are caused to stop and think before they shoot their guns. A pragmatic way to approach collective identity is to give up any hope of discerning a natural kind that corresponds to any social group. Rather, look only for those categorizations that allow us to do various things we think are worth doing. Distinguishing between those who participate in a war and those who do not seems to be an eminently reasonable thing to do, especially if one is in a position where one might be attacked and is deciding how to defend oneself. As long as people can identify members of a group and the use of that group in making decisions has some utility, why not do so?

In general, I agree that talk of social groups is both omnipresent and quite useful. The problem I have tried to identify is that some talk of social groups is more misleading than useful. The distinction between civilians and soldiers is one such distinction. As I said in Chapter 5, one of the main problems is that the group of soldiers is drawn from the group of civilians, and after leaving military life soldiers return to civilian life. There are two problems. First, conceptually, can a clear set of criteria identify who is a soldier or combatant and who is a civilian or noncombatant given that these two groups are so intermingled with each other? Second, normatively, even if we can draw a clear distinction between these groups, should we use this distinction in our moral assessments? Based on the arguments advanced in several chapters, from both conceptual and normative perspectives, we should abandon the easy distinction between soldiers and civilians and be content with the distinction between those soldiers or combatants who are, and those who are not, a threat and are not themselves vulnerable.

I do not dispute that people talk as if they can make the conceptual distinction between soldier and civilian and that many also think that this is a morally relevant distinction. And I also do not dispute that something important might be lost if this version of the principle of discrimination or distinction were to be abandoned. My contention is that we can save some of what the principle of discrimination is best able to do: make soldiers stop and think before they act and, further, not to attack those who are not a threat to these soldiers. As it turns out, however, the people who are such a threat are not clearly so in very many cases. If this were acknowledged, then soldiers would not feel justified in shooting very often, just as is now true of police officers in the United States. Indeed, police in the United States and elsewhere are able to conduct most of their business by other than lethal means, so that when they do fire a gun they need to fill out special paperwork to justify it. Soldiers should also be inspired to try less lethal means than shooting. In general, the world would then be a safer place. Of course, this assumes – what I might not assume otherwise – that there are going to be some cases in which shooting is justified. The principle of discrimination was correctly envisioned to place limits on what tactics are justified in war. If we embrace my way to characterize the principle of discrimination, this objective will be met, with the added benefit that we will have less violence in the world.

V. INDIVIDUALISM AND COLLECTIVISM

In the debates about how to conceive the principle of discrimination or distinction, Noam Zohar has addressed one of the most difficult metaphysical problems in the way we see that principle:

The reality of international confrontations is not adequately described by reduction to individualistic terms. We are not only individuals confronting each other but also a nation confronting another nation.[17]

According to Zohar, we cannot justify killing in war "on a direct analogy to private self-defense. Where the basic analogy to self-defense does function is on the collective level, justifying self-defensive war itself despite its necessary cost in innocent lives."[18]

Zohar claims that war can only be understood if one appreciates the "dual reality" involved: what goes on at the individual level and what goes on at the national level.[19] Individual soldiers can rarely claim to be justified in killing in war on the individual level alone. Only by reference to collective self-defense can the individual be seen as justified in killing in most wartime situations. In this view, the principle of discrimination or distinction does not make sense unless one recognizes the reality of collectivities, such as States and armies. As Zohar says, "[I]f the individual and the collective are both taken seriously as facets of human existence, then the dual reality properly yields a dual morality."[20] And from this dual moral perspective, the best way to see the principle of discrimination or distinction is as prohibiting one State from "the pursuit of military advantage through killing non-combatants," not as somehow establishing an individual's absolute immunity from attack by another individual.[21]

I agree with Zohar that individual self-defense will not get us very far in justifying the attacks on combatants. Jeffrey Murphy has played out the individualistic position and come to the conclusion that combatants can be understood only as "all those of whom it is reasonable to believe that they are engaged in an attempt at your destruction."[22] I have tried

---

[17] Noam Zohar, "Collective War and Individualistic Ethics: Against the Conscription of Self-Defense," *Political Theory*, vol. 21, no. 4 (1993), p. 616.

[18] Ibid., p 615.

[19] Soran Reader argues that "although states are of course real, when it comes to violent action, there must be particular concrete, embodied individual moral agents, some of whom are responsible for the violent action." See his intriguing paper "Cosmopolitanism, War and Criminal Justice," scheduled at the Mini-conference on Global Justice at the A.P.A. Pacific Division Meetings in Pasadena, California, on March 27, 2004.

[20] Noam Zohar, "Collective War and Individualistic Ethics," p. 618.

[21] Ibid., p. 611.

[22] Jeffrey Murphy, "The Killing of the Innocent," in *War, Morality, and the Military Profession*, edited by Malham Wakin, Boulder, CO: Westview Press, 1979, p. 351.

to show that such a characterization will mean that even fewer enemy soldiers than one would normally think are justifiably subject to attack by opposing soldiers. Unless we talk of the self-defense of the State and somehow are able to translate that into individual terms, we are locked into what Zohar describes as a clash of perspectives.[23] The strategy preferred by Zohar is to see the combatants as "those marked by participating in the collective war effort."[24] But as I have argued, mere participation will not easily allow for the kind of rough-grained basis for distinguishing the groups of those who can be attacked and those who cannot. And in any event, appeals to the national self-defense do not clearly give us an individual basis for killing. In the end, despite Zohar's admonitions, I am willing to settle for what he calls the "moral vertigo" that arises when one views war as a matter of "aggregate individual confrontations" involving the violent use of force.[25]

There is here an important insight that might bear fruit none-theless. Perhaps soldiers can be seen as complicit in the evil or dan-gerousness of the State or of the State's leaders. States or State leaders would not be dangerous if they had no followers who were willing to try to implement their dangerous plans or if there were no others who provided what support they were forced to provide. But if we are going to base the principle of discrimination or distinction on complicity, then there is a problem about what to do about munitions workers and other ancillary support workers for the army. In many ways, these people – as well as the farmers who grow wheat and the bakers who bake bread for the army mess – are also to be treated as possible targets because they are surely as complicit in the sense that without them the leaders could not wage war. As a preliminary, and clearly incomplete, test, we might adopt a variation of the "but-for" test used in tort law. We could determine whether the work of a given person was causally necessary for the war effort by asking whether the war effort could be waged without her or his participation. But then, on grounds of complicity, we wouldn't have an easy way to hold all and only soldiers as a group accountable for the dangerousness of war. We will have to let many civilians be targets of attack, and, as we did in my version of the principle of discrimination or distinction, we will still have to restrict the targeting of many subcategories of soldiers.

[23] On this point, see David Rodin, *War and Self-Defense*, Oxford: Clarendon Press, 2002.
[24] Noam Zohar, "Collective War and Individualistic Ethics," p. 618.
[25] Ibid., p. 615.

Leaders formulate dangerous plans, and soldiers implement these plans. And because both are dangerous, then those who are defending themselves can legitimately attack both of these kinds of dangerous individuals. In this vein, one might begin with the most obviously guilty people the leaders of a State waging a war by the use of immoral tactics, and then see if one can eventually move to, perhaps only some of, the soldiers. The leaders of a State are often more at fault or guilty than are the soldiers of the State's armies, in that it is the leaders who have formulated the policies and the plans to initiate war and to implement those policies that create increased danger. It is for this reason, I believe, that State leaders are the ones who should primarily be tried for war crimes. I pursue this point in Chapter 12.

Whatever evil intent there might be to destroy the other's State is probably best laid at the doorstep of these world leaders. If anyone is ultimately an aggressor, or guilty rather than innocent, then it is much more likely that such a person is the State leader who has the guilty intent rather than a soldier whose normal intent is only to follow orders. State leaders who start wars and order the employment of immoral tactics toward their neighbors seem to have lost immunity from attack,[26] a position that can be extended to some, but not all, members of the group of soldiers who act in the service of the culpable leaders who have instituted these policies.

Despite all of these reservations, the principle of discrimination is indeed worth preserving, on conceptual and moral grounds. For one of its main functions is to force soldiers to think before they shoot. And this will nearly always mean that soldiers will shoot less, nearly always a good thing in itself. While it may be that no more than a few wars are truly justified, it is nonetheless true that during war minimizing death and suffering is still prized. But can a war be waged successfully if soldiers must wait to fire to see if they are about to be fired upon? In some cases, the answer is "Perhaps not." But in many cases, we can construct a distinction between those who are truly threatening to others and those who are not and treat those who are current threats as

---

[26] On this point, see Jeff McMahan, "Realism, Morality, and War," in *The Ethics of War and Peace*, edited by Terry Nardin, Princeton, NJ: Princeton University Press, 1996, pp. 88–91. McMahan says, "The case in which it is most obviously permissible to attack a non-innocent noncombatant in war is that in which the assassination of a political leader who bears moral responsibility for his country's unjust aggression would be sufficient to stop that aggression, thereby eliminating the need to kill a large number of the country's soldiers" (p. 90).

having lost their immunity from assault. Those who sit with their fingers ready to press the button launching cruise missiles are surely
threats as much as those who sit in a tank with its turret pointed at a
town.

It is true that the sum total of the acts of many people that do not
appear to be threatening, such as the acts of the munitions workers and
farmers, together constitute a collective threat when organized by the
leaders of a State into a war machine. We can even look at the naked
soldier taking a bath as playing a role in the State's collective war effort.
It is true that States are the ones who are most clearly threatening in
times of war. But I do not accept the view that soldiers are automatically to be treated as extensions of, or even clearly complicit in,
what States do.

In times of war, many soldiers are as vulnerable as civilians are. And
it is the State and its leaders that have created this vulnerability. It then
seems odd, indeed, to say that most soldiers can legitimately be
maimed or killed. Yes, it is true that wars can only be fought when
States enlist individuals to act in violent ways. But why should those
who are so enlisted be the ones who pay the price for what the State has
planned and is trying to execute? We do not punish a State effectively
by killing the soldiers of that State, because soldiers are so easily
replaceable. And similarly, we do not reward a State by sparing its
soldiers or its civilians from death. These individuals should be spared
or killed for reasons that have to do with them as individuals, for they
are not automatically to be seen as extensions of the State. Rather,
most civilians, and some soldiers, are rendered highly vulnerable by
war and by the actions of States during war. A properly understood
principle of discrimination or distinction will deal with this reality.

In this chapter, I have tried to set out a more nuanced understanding of the principle of discrimination or distinction than that
which is normally advocated in either the Just War tradition or the
contemporary international law literature. What I have advocated is
that the distinction between soldier and civilian, or between combatant
and noncombatant, be used as a beginning for determining whether
someone can legitimately be attacked or killed. According to this initial
group categorization, civilians cannot be subject to such attacks during
wartime, whereas soldiers can be. But such a determination provides
only an initial framework for decision. If there is time and there is
more information available, then there must be a more fine-grained
determination of whether the civilian or the soldier is currently a threat

or in a vulnerable position. Only in situations of emergency and inability to gather more information does the traditional principle of discrimination or distinction operate alone to justify violent action.

In the next two chapters, I will consider the other two most important traditional principles in the *jus in bello* tradition and in the contemporary international law of war: the principle of necessity and the principle of proportionality. In both cases, I will argue that these principles are justified because, and to the extent that, they connect with the principle of humane treatment. As in the case of the principle of discrimination or distinction, the principles of proportionality and necessity have been incorrectly thought to stand on their own merits as limitations on what can legitimately be done during wartime. I will also develop in more detail the discussion I began in Chapter 7 on how properly to understand the relation between the principles of pro-portionality and necessity and end with a general discussion of how these principles, along with the principle of discrimination, should connect together into a unified normative account of international humanitarian law.

9

The principle of necessity

In this chapter, I will discuss the principle of necessity, which in previous eras was thought to be a cornerstone of Just War theory. The principle of necessity seems to be simple indeed. In situations where the only way to achieve military victory in a Just War requires the employment of a certain tactic, say the bombing of cities, then that tactic is justified regardless of other normative considerations. I will explain what the basis and limit of this principle are, arguing that the principle of necessity is not simple or easy to apply. I will also argue that this principle should be seen as subsidiary to the principle of humane treatment. Military necessity should be seen as a kind of emergency exception, at best, and not as a guiding principle of humanitarian law.

When people say that humanitarian law is different from human rights law, as we saw in Chapter 4, they are primarily thinking of humanitarian law's utilitarian-sounding principle of necessity that seems to justify almost any tactic, including intentional killing and torture, as opposed to the human rights not to be killed or tortured, which seem to prohibit these tactics in all circumstances. If we are going to bring these two important areas of international law together, we will need to reconcile such differences. This is one of the main tasks of this chapter. I will argue that only in a very few cases does a properly limited understanding of the principle of necessity call for utilitarian calculation in an otherwise nonutilitarian sea of humanitarian law. And this is at least in part because the principle of necessity is itself limited by the principle of humanity and, as we will see in the last section, by the principle of proportionality as well.

Military necessity is often confusingly presented. It is often associated with a need that something be done lest a war be lost. In this sense, there is a military necessity that something be done. But sometimes there is more than one thing that *can* be done. So there may be a military necessity, and yet it may not be that a particular tactic is necessary for winning a war. Here, proportionality matters, because among those things that could avoid defeat, the one that involves less harm should be employed. Military necessity also sometimes means that one particular tactic must be employed lest the war be lost. In this sense, not employing that tactic means defeat. Proportionality seems not to intrude here, and yet it may because the winning of a war may itself not be morally significant, in which case it would matter how costly it is to win that war. Finally, even when it is believed that one particular tactic is necessary to win a war, this is often not certain; and because of this uncertainty, proportionality again enters into the picture, as we will see in detail in Chapter 10.

In the first section, I turn to the comparison of poisoning and aerial bombardment once again, arguing that there is not as much difference here as is often thought. In the second section, I show how a revised understanding of necessity fits into the kind of considerations that are involved in the principle of humanitarian treatment. Based on that analysis, I argue that the principle of necessity creates a very small class of cases that may be treated in an exceptional way. In the third section, I discuss how the principle of military necessity in international criminal law relates to the defense of necessity in domestic criminal law. In the fourth section, I attempt to formulate a test for the principle of necessity that is by and large consistent with what is today accepted in international humanitarian law and that is also normatively justifiable. In the final section, I return to the discussion at the end of Chapter 7 in an attempt to spell out how the principles of necessity and proportionality relate to each other. Here I argue that proportionality puts a restraint on the principle of necessity and that the two must be understood in tandem.

I. POISONS AND AERIAL BOMBARDMENT

Earlier in this book, I argued that if aerial bombardment seemed to be sometimes justified by reference to military necessity, so did using poisons and chemical weapons, and that if there were good reasons to ban the use of poisoned weapons, the same could be said of the use of aerial bombing. What is curious is that aerial bombardment has not been banned in international law, but there has been a complete ban on poisons and chemical weapons. I will take up various historical cases in an attempt to shed light on this issue in greater detail than I have so far, setting the stage for a consideration of how necessity and proportionality relate to each other, which will be the topic of the final section of this chapter.

One attempt to explain the ban on poisons and other chemical weapons was proposed by Richard Price.[1] He offers the prudential argument that a complete ban "added an extra burden of proof for the decisiveness of Chemical Weapons."[2] If a ban is in place, a State could not claim that it was stockpiling these weapons for some limited use that was not illegal. Instead, there is very little wiggle room for States caught stockpiling chemical weapons. The prudential argument is that "an absolute ban is less likely to be breached than a qualified restriction."[3] Of course, this presumes that we are better off with poisons and chemical weapons being taken off the table altogether. As I have been asking, wouldn't the same be true of aerial bombardment? Therefore, couldn't a ban on those weapons also potentially be grounded in such pragmatic considerations?

One way to distinguish the two cases might be in terms of the consequences of allowing one type of weapon versus another. It could be said that some bombing is necessary for some wars to be capable of being won by those who are fighting for a just cause. It would be odd, indeed, if poisons were ever necessary in this way, or so it might be claimed. And it could also be claimed that some poisons and other chemical weapons can cause truly horrible consequences, whereas most bombs do not have such horrific effects. This argument could be advanced to explain why the prudential argument in favor of banning poisons and chemical weapons makes sense in ways that it would not make sense similarly to ban aerial bombardment.

But just a bit of reflection will show what is wrong with such an argument. First, it is not at all clear that some very poor State that is fighting a truly defensive war might not need to use chemical weapons, or the threat of them, to repel a much stronger aggressive State. As I argued above, this was what Grotius pointed out when he said that

[1] Richard M. Price, *The Chemical Weapons Taboo*, Ithaca, NY: Cornell University Press, 1997.
[2] Ibid., p. 130.
[3] Barry Kellman, "Book Review and Note on *The Chemical Weapons Taboo*," *American Journal of International Law*, vol. 92, no. 1 (1998), p. 162.

poisons are much cheaper and can be obtained by those who cannot otherwise defend themselves against a State with a much more potent force in conventional weaponry. This is why insurgency movements have been one of the main groups tempted by the use of chemical weapons as they struggle against far superior, although not necessarily morally superior, forces aligned against them.

Second, it is also not clear that chemical weapons cause more horror and devastation than aerial bombardment does. Think of the kind of aerial bombardment often called "obliteration bombing" or "carpet bombing." Here is one account of this type of bombardment:

It is the strategic bombing, by means of incendiaries and explosives, of industrial centers of population, in which the target to be wiped out is not a definite factory, bridge or similar object, but a large section of the whole city, comprising one-third to two-thirds of its whole built-up area, and including by design the residential districts of workingmen and their families.[4]

It is hard to imagine that such aerial bombardment would be something that we would want to allow except in the worst emergency, and probably not even then.

The bombing of Coventry, England and Dresden, Germany during World War II involved obliteration bombing and is routinely condemned in almost the same strong terms reserved for the atomic bombing of Hiroshima and Nagasaki, Japan. That the Coventry and Dresden bombings used conventional bombs and the Hiroshima and Nagasaki bombings used nonconventional (nuclear) bombs does not seem to matter. Indeed, one could argue that there is a continuum here, with aerial bombardment placed nearly side by side with the use of certain nonconventional weapons. I would even raise the question of whether the bombings of Hiroshima and Nagasaki weren't instances of both aerial bombing and nonconventional weapons use at the same time. And I would also ask why it is that worries about nuclear bombing make us want to ban all chemical weapons rather than also making us want to ban all aerial bombardment, conventional and nonconventional.

It is very interesting to note that there is not a complete ban on the use of nuclear weapons in contemporary international law, even though there is a complete ban on the use of poisons and chemical weaponry more generally. The ICJ Advisory Opinion on the Use or Threat of Nuclear Weapons leaves open the possibility that

---

[4] John C. Ford, "The Morality of Obliteration Bombing," in *War and Morality*, edited by Richard Wasserstrom, Belmont, CA: Wadsworth Publishing, 1970, p. 24.

nuclear weapons could even be used as a form of tactical warfare. No international court has made a similar claim about the use of poisons. Yet, it does not make sense to maintain this distinction, allowing nuclear weapons but not other kinds of poisons, thus rendering the international position on poisons even more problematical.

Some theorists have indeed argued that worries about the use of aerial bombardment, which commonly risks large-scale destruction of civilian populations, calls into question the very justifiability of waging war with the use or threatened use of tactical nuclear weapons and that such considerations call into question the justifiability of waging war with bombs in contemporary times.[5] If we take the pragmatic approach recommended by those who urge a complete ban on poisons and other chemical weapons because of the horrible effects of some of these weapons, there seems to be no good reason not to extend such an argument to a complete ban on aerial bombardment because of the horrible effects of some of its usages.

Let us consider another distinction that is important in understanding the international law of war crimes. The rules of war are based on either justice or humaneness and seem to be intended to apply absolutely in all cases. Absolute prohibitions, whether grounded in justice or humaneness, would not vary based on who we are or even on the particular circumstances we face. But prohibitions in war seem often to be highly specific – for example, the prohibition on the use of nuclear bombs but not on the use of conventional bombs. If it is no violation of justice or humaneness to kill you with a *regular* bomb, it seems odd that it would be a violation of justice or humaneness to kill you with a *poisoned* bomb.

President Harry Truman rationalized even the use of certain banned weapons on the grounds of military necessity:

Having found the bomb we have to use it. We have used it against those who attacked us without warning at Pearl Harbor, against those who have starved and beaten and executed American prisoners of war, against those who have abandoned all pretense of obeying international laws of warfare. We have used it in order to shorten the agony of war, in order to save the lives of thousands and thousands of young Americans.[6]

If a weapon is available that can have such seemingly worthwhile and highly laudable effects and it is militarily necessary to use that weapon

---

[5] Ibid., p. 39, where Ford argues that the rights of the innocent have themselves been obliterated by obliteration bombs, and thus the morality of war is itself jeopardized.

[6] Address to the nation by President Harry S Truman, August 9, 1945, quoted in R. Tucker, *The Just War*, 1960, pp. 21–22.

to achieve these effects, why would we think that that weapon should not be used?

If what Truman says is justified, then there is no type of weapon that should be absolutely banned, because there could be circumstances, such as those concerning the bombing of Nagasaki and Hiroshima that Truman is addressing, that would defeat the otherwise good reason in favor of an absolute ban. And if Truman's point is correct, then at least in extreme emergencies, such as when the fate of the free world seems to hang in the balance, military necessity does, indeed, provide a reason to overcome the prohibition against certain tactics and weapons. As we will see, in the final section of this chapter and in the next chapter, considerations of proportionality still enter in and should have given even Truman pause as he considered the singular use of atomic bombs to stop Japan.

In the remainder of this chapter, I wish to raise the question of what we are to think of the principle of necessity. Does it so disrupt things that it eliminates absolute prohibitions on certain types of weapon during war? Or is the principle of necessity so restricted in its application that it rarely if ever comes into effect, a form of throat clearing where one says something like, "Well of course, there is always the theoretical possibility of exceptions to any rule"? My tentative conclusion is that the answer to these questions is unclear. And this is just one more reason to think that the principle of necessity is not best seen as a cornerstone of international humanitarian law, because it is so unclear what cases it affects.

It is considerably better to rest international humanitarian law on the principle of humane treatment, which at least has a much clearer scope of application and will restrain soldiers on the battlefield and make war less barbarous. So, the conclusion I wish to begin with is that there is no good basis for thinking that poisons should be treated differently than bombs. Military necessity makes one neither more nor less prone to be the subject of a complete ban. Indeed, military necessity seems to sweep quite even-handedly in making us aware that, at least in situations of emergency, hardly any tactic should be taken completely off the table.

II. NECESSITY AND HUMANE TREATMENT

The principle of humane treatment has two parts. The first has to do with how others are to be treated, and it captures what both compassion and mercy would require. As we've seen, compassion and mercy are at least as important, if not more so, in discussions of war crimes than (retributive) justice is. The other part of the principle of humaneness has to do with acting in ways that are true to, or respectful of, oneself, of one's honor as a decent person. Humaneness is about what is owed to others and what is owed to oneself. Even when it is unclear that anything is, strictly speaking, owed to another, it may display a lack of humaneness for us to act in a cruel way to that person in any event, for it would not be honorable to do so. It is in this way that the principle of humane treatment, as we have seen, often places quite severe restraints on the type of tactics that soldiers can use during war, even if they are pursuing a just cause.

On the face of it, the principle of necessity seems to be at odds with the principle of humane treatment. The principle of necessity is often characterized as holding that

Military forces should cause no more destruction than is strictly necessary to achieve their objectives.[7]

And while this looks like a limitation on what tactics can be employed, it is often understood as a kind of license to violate the normal prohibitions of the laws of war in those cases where the use of poisons or torture, for instance, is necessary to achieve a military objective. As with most principles, the principle of necessity both rules some things out as unacceptable and rules other things in as acceptable, or at least not unacceptable. The principle of necessity seems to rule some things in that the principle of humane treatment would definitely rule out, such as the use of torture.

But despite appearances, the principles of necessity and humane treatment can be reconciled. For the principle of humane treatment is not an absolute principle, and the principle of necessity is not a breaker of all absolute prohibitions in any event. Indeed, the principle of necessity carves out a remarkably narrow set of exceptional cases to the general prohibition on inhumane treatment, where it would be odd, indeed, if the principle of humane treatment were not amenable to such a class of cases, and on the very grounds of what humane treatment is all about. For if there is a tactic that must be employed in order to win a war and the winning of the war is morally very important, then it would be only the rule fetishist who thought that, on grounds of

---

[7] Douglas Lackey, *The Ethics of War and Peace*, Upper Saddle River, NJ: Prentice-Hall, 1989, p. 59.

humaneness itself, this exceptional case must be subject to absolute prohibitions.

Yet there is a legitimate difficulty that needs to be addressed. It seems to some that the principle of necessity simply destroys the possibility of there being any absolute, or near absolute, prohibitions during war, because a war may be merely a series of military necessities. Military campaigns proceed from one battle to another almost endlessly. And it can be argued that employing certain tactics is necessary for winning each battle and, in turn, that winning each battle is militarily necessary in the sense that if it is not won then the war will likely be lost. On this account, the principle of necessity does not have a narrow scope at all, and the gulf between acting humanely and doing what is necessary to wage war effectively seems very wide indeed. In this sense, humane treatment will often be trumped by military necessity.

But it turns out not to be true that in war situations of military necessity are rampant. Think of the use of torture to get militarily needed information. Of course, it is true that in wars more and better information is always needed. But the question is whether it is needed right here and now to win a particular battle or achieve a particular objective. Here there are two considerations that diminish the likelihood that such situations occur very often in war. First is the point that while information is always needed, it is not often obvious where the best place is to get the needed information. One needs to identify who might have reliable information, figure out how to capture the person who has this information, and then figure out how to extract the required information. Second, there is the problem that certain tactics – for instance torture – are not very reliable methods for obtaining information. In many situations, the torture victim eventually talks, but often what is revealed is what the victim believes that the torturer wants to hear, not necessarily what is actually reliable information. For these reasons, there will not be many situations where military necessity will justify the violation of the humanitarian prohibition on torturing.

To justify the use of torture, as I argued at the end of Chapter 7, one also needs to show that there was no other way to achieve the military objective that would involve less suffering for the victim. We will return to this issue in the next chapter, where we discuss proportionality. At the moment, I merely want to highlight the fact that it is not sufficient to show that there is a situation where it is necessary to get a certain military result. One also needs to show that using just torture is likely to accomplish the needed military objective and that it is the only means to accomplish the objective, in order truly to claim the emergency exemption to the torture prohibition. Along with the points made in the previous paragraph, this shows that at the very least there will not be a huge number of cases where military necessity will trump humane treatment considerations. And indeed, it is better to see the principle of necessity as working in tandem with the principle of humane treatment.

As I have argued throughout this book, the principle of humane treatment is the cornerstone of international humanitarian law as well as the bridge to human rights law. Humane treatment plays a significant role in our understanding of why military necessity has a strong normative pull and why military necessity needs to be tightly circumscribed. When wars are fought, it is crucial that soldiers on both sides retain their honor. If tactics are used that call for soldiers to destroy their honor, as happens in the use of torture, then often whatever military gains are achieved are offset by the loss of honor. Indeed, not all objectives that are militarily necessary have a strong normative pull. Winning a war by annihilating the enemy, even when this is the only way to win, does not in itself have strong normative weight. For if there is no prima facie basis for thinking that one side should win a war, the principle of necessity alone does not provide the strong normative pull for using certain tactics.

As Douglas Lackey has put it: "[T]he principle [of necessity] does not say that whatever is necessary is permissible, but that everything permissible must be necessary."[8] Two more things must be shown. First, the military objective itself must be normatively compelling in light of the overall objectives of the war, as well as in light of how humans should treat one another. It is here that humanitarian considerations can supply moral weight to the principle of necessity. Second, there must be no other, less objectionable tactics that are available that would achieve the same objective. This consideration moves us directly into discussions of the principle of proportionality, a principle that is designed to limit the principle of necessity and to do so by reference to humanitarian considerations. In the next chapter, we will see the full force of the principle of humane treatment when we

---

[8] Ibid., p. 59.

discuss the principle of proportionality's humanitarian constraints on the principle of necessity.

In the next section, I will look at the principle of necessity in criminal law generally, not merely as a military necessity, to get a sense of the reasonable restraints that have been proposed on using this principle as a means of justification of extraordinary tactics. Here we will discover that various considerations, most importantly that of imminence, greatly restrict the scope of the principle of necessity. In considering its scope, I will also need to reassess the principles of both necessity and proportionality. This will set the stage for an argument that proportionality needs to be linked to necessity for a reasonable basis for the rules of war. Such an argument will begin in the final section of this chapter and extend into the next chapter.

III. NECESSITY IN DOMESTIC AND INTERNATIONAL CRIMINAL LAW

In this section, I wish to draw two seemingly disparate sources of law together: the defense of necessity in domestic criminal law and the principle of necessity in international law. In domestic law, necessity functions as a defense – a way to block the normal attribution of criminal liability by denying that what was done really did constitute a legal wrong. In international law, necessity generally seems to be broader than this, justifying whole categories of behavior in advance, as it were. These different types of necessity are actually close to each other, and one of the best ways to see this is by examining the main elements of necessity in domestic law.

In domestic U.S. law, the Model Penal Code, Section 302, defines the criminal defense of necessity as follows:

Conduct the actor believes to be necessary to avoid harm or evil to himself or to another is justifiable, provided that:
(a) the harm or evil sought to be avoided by such conduct is greater than that sought to be prevented by the law defining the offense charged. . . .[9]

Stated so boldly, this defense seems to give a very broad defense to actions that would otherwise be punishable. It is common to understand this defense as a "choice of evils defense,"[10] that is, a defense

---

[9] Model Penal Code, sec. 302, and Comment (1985).
[10] See Wayne R. LaFave and Austin W. Scott, Jr., *Criminal Law*, 2nd ed., St. Paul, MN: West Publishing, 1986, p. 442.

based on the idea that while it would normally be prohibited to do a certain act, in certain situations it is justifiable to do the act given the negative consequences that will undoubtedly result from not doing the act. In Just War theory, necessity is also often discussed under the label of the "lesser of two evils."[11] Indeed, one can find such discussion extending back at least as far as the early 17th century.[12]

Notice, though, that even in its bold statement the Model Penal Code's authors build into the defense a restraint in terms of proportionality. For after it is said that there is subjective determination that a certain action is necessary to avoid a harm, there is then a second consideration: a weighing of harms. The harms, or evils, avoided by the act necessary to prevent them are weighed against the harms or evils caused by so acting. From the beginning, it is clear that necessity alone will not function to relieve from guilt or punishment without an assessment of proportionality, at least in this nearly canonical view of U.S. criminal law. Indeed, LaFave and Scott say that "necessity" is actually a misnomer. For it is not literally necessary "that a policeman speed after a fleeing criminal," but only that the law regards it as preferable for the policeman to do so, rather than to let the criminal escape.[13]

The idea that military necessity would itself both justify and limit behavior on the battlefield can be traced to the Lieber Code developed during the Civil War. Military necessity is there defined as "those measures which are indispensable for securing the ends of war."[14] The Lieber Code goes on to say that while military necessity "admits of all direct destruction of life or limb of armed enemies, and of other persons whose destruction is incidentally unavoidable in the armed contests of war, . . . [m]ilitary necessity does not admit of cruelty."[15] Thus, while military necessity may allow certain tactics otherwise prohibited, there were limits nonetheless. This was a major advance at the

---

[11] See Michael Ignatieff, *The Lesser Evil: Political Ethics in the Age of Terror*, Princeton: Princeton University Press, 2004.

[12] Francisco Suarez is well known for advancing such arguments. See his treatise "On War," in *Selections from Three Works* (Disputation XIII, *De Triplici Virtute Theologica: Charitate*) (c. 1610), translated by Gwladys L. Williams, Ammi Brown, and John Waldron, Oxford: Clarendon Press, 1944.

[13] Wayne R. LaFave and Austin W. Scott, Jr., *Criminal Law*, p. 441.

[14] Quoted in Burrus M. Carnahan, "Lincoln, Lieber, and the Laws of War: The Origins and Limits of the Principle of Military Necessity," *American Journal of International Law*, vol. 92, no. 2 (1998), p. 215.

[15] Quoted in ibid., p. 216.

time and led to a decrease in the amount of suffering that the Civil War produced. The idea was that certain kinds of tactics that seemed designed to cause suffering, even if otherwise militarily necessary, were ruled out, just as other tactics were ruled in.

Today, the portion of the Lieber Code that defines military necessity in terms of restricting tactics to what is "indispensable for securing the ends of war" is still recognized as the kernel of what the principle of necessity requires.[16] But over the last 150 years, things have been partially reversed. When Lieber first proposed the principle of military necessity, it was clearly thought to be a major advance in restricting the tactics that could be employed on the battlefield. But today, military necessity is often used to justify disregarding all restraint on tactics during war – for example, employing the chemical agent white phosphorous by the United States in the second Iraq war. As a result, today it is often thought that the principle of necessity is too wide in terms of what it allows, because so many things seem to be necessary for the successful conduct of war.

The Nuremberg trials expressed the idea that military necessity was severely limited. Indeed, following domestic law usage, the United States Military Tribunal sitting at Nuremberg, in the German High Command Trial, saw necessity as "an affirmative defense similar to the plea of self-defense in a murder trial." The tribunal went on to place severe limitations on the use of the idea of military necessity:

A bare declaration by the defendant that what was done was militarily necessary has no more probative substance than a statement contained in an answer or other pleading. In order to make out a valid defense of destruction or pillage on the ground of military necessity, the defendant must prove that the facts and circumstances were such at the time he ordered these measures that he would be justified in believing them to be necessary to save his troops from an imminent major disaster.[17]

Here, imminence is a key consideration.

In Chapter 1, I quoted Grotius as requiring that a harm be imminent for a State to be justified, in *jus ad bellum* considerations, in attacking on grounds of self-defense. The idea of imminence is not all

---

[16] Ibid., p. 215.
[17] *U.S. v. Wilhelm Von Leeb and Thirteen Others* (German High Command Trial), United States Military Tribunal, Nuremberg, December 30th, 1947–October 28th, 1948, quoted in The United Nations War Crimes Commission, *Law Reports of Trials of War Criminals*, vol. 12, London: His Majesty's Stationery Office, 1949; reprinted, Buffalo, NY: William S. Hein, 1997, p. 125.

that new, although perhaps it is true that it has not played a large role in past understanding of the narrower idea of the principle of necessity in *jus in bello* considerations.[18] The requirement of imminence makes it much harder to get to the stage of using the weighing considerations of the principle of proportionality than it might at first appear. This is very similar to the idea of imminence in discussions of preemptive attacks.

Nonetheless, it is true that imminence is often hard to define. Is sinking of a ship to be seen as imminent when a small hole is found that will eventually sink the ship? Such questions are often hard to answer, although some people have bitten the bullet and said that in the ship case this was already a clear case of imminence.[19] Here is how one author summarized the conditions necessary for the common law defense of necessity:

The defense involves a reasonable belief that an individual confronts an imminent and irreparable harm, a lack of legal avenues to avoid the evil, the commission of a criminal act which is reasonably calculated to eliminate the harm; and a proportionality between the crime and the threat.[20]

Here we have a clear statement of how necessity is limited only to cases where serious harm is imminent. While important, imminence is not the only limitation on the principle of necessity, for proportionality is also a major limit.

To understand how international law regards military necessity today, we will end this section with a very brief discussion of the International Court of Justice (ICJ) ruling concerning Israel's wall in the Occupied Territories. The wall was ostensibly built as a tactic in Israel's continued war with its neighbors, so as to keep terrorists and other insurgents from attacking Israeli population centers by crossing the border from the Occupied Territories into Israel.[21] But in building

---

[18] See Emanuel Gross, "Legal Aspects of Tackling Terrorism: The Balance Between the Right of a Democracy to Defend Itself and the Protection of Human Rights," *UCLA Journal of International Law and Foreign Affairs*, vol. 6, Spring/Summer (2001), p. 107.

[19] Ibid., p. 108.

[20] Matthew Lippman, "Conundrums of Armed Conflict: Criminal Defenses to Violations of the Humanitarian Law of War," *Dickinson Journal of International Law*, vol. 15, Fall (1996), p. 66.

[21] There is also a necessity issue that concerns *ad bellum* not merely *in bello*, that is, whether the security threat to Israel from its neighbors justified making war against these neighbors on grounds of self-defense. I will take up such questions in my book *Aggression and Crimes Against Peace*.

the wall, Israel also disrupted travel, agriculture, and commerce in the Occupied Territories. As the ICJ held:

To sum up, the Court, from the material available to it, is not convinced that the specific course Israel has chosen for the wall was necessary to attain its security objective. The wall, along the route chosen, and its associated regime, gravely infringe a number of rights of Palestinians residing in the territory occupied by Israel, and the infringements resulting from that route cannot be justified by military exigencies or by the requirements of national security and public order. The construction of such a wall accordingly constitutes breaches by Israel of various of its obligations under the applicable international humanitarian law and human rights instruments.[22]

The test used here will be examined below, but note that the question is whether the construction of the wall was "necessary to attain its security objective" as a tactic in Israel's ongoing war with its neighbors.

The ICJ then gave a gloss on how it understood the relevant part of the doctrine of military necessity:

In addition, it is not sufficient that such restriction be directed to the ends authorized; they must also be necessary for the attainment of those ends. As the Human Rights Committee put it, they "must conform to the principle of proportionality" and "must be the least intrusive instrument amongst those which might achieve the desired result."[23]

The key idea (one that I will explore in more detail later) is that the tactic not only must be likely to result in the achievement of a military objective, but also must be the "least intrusive instrument" of those tactics that could achieve the desired military objective. Although, as we will see, the ICJ has been criticized for not being explicit in specifying what test for military necessity it was employing.

The defense of necessity and the idea of military necessity share three important features. First, necessity is limited by imminence in that not any threat is one that will justify use of otherwise prohibited tactics, but only necessity that takes away other options because there is no time to try other things. Second, necessity is limited by proportionality in that even necessary action is only allowed if what is to be achieved is more significant than what is caused by the use of the otherwise prohibited tactic. And finally, following from the above

---

[22] International Court of Justice, Advisory Opinion, July 9, 2004, "Legal Consequences of the Construction of a Wall in the Occupied Palestinian Territory," General List 31, para. 137.

[23] Ibid., para 136, quoting CPR/2/21/Rev.1/ADD.9, General Comment No. 27, para. 14.

considerations, necessity does not trump all other factors and is not obviously the most important factor in deciding whether a tactic is justifiable.

IV. FORMULATING A TEST FOR MILITARY NECESSITY

There have been many attempts to formulate a test for the principle of necessity in international law. In the most recent formulation of the principle of necessity, many of the issues we identified so far have been addressed in a comprehensive account. I will use this account as a springboard for my own attempt to formulate a principle of necessity. In the final section of this chapter, I will attempt to explain why the principle of proportionality needs to be linked to the principle of necessity. Here is the test that is commonly employed in international humanitarian law to decide cases involving military necessity:

1. Do the "impugned measures violate an absolute prohibition"?
2. Is the State facing "an actual state of necessity"?
3. Is the impugned measure "the most adequate and effective response to meet the existing threat"?
4. Does the military advantage gained by the impugned measure "outweigh the damage done to the population"?
5. Was the "impugned measure adopted after due consideration of all of the interests involved and by the proper authority"?[24]

The second provision includes a consideration of imminence and the fourth provision is merely the insertion of the principle of proportionality into the core of the principle of necessity.

A debate has grown up about whether in 2004 the ICJ actually employed this standard test in deciding whether Israel's construction of a wall around the Occupied Territories was justified by military necessity. One reasonable criticism is that the ICJ did not explicitly employ these criteria – indeed, it did not explicitly employ any criteria at all in reaching its decision. In separate opinions filed by Judge Pieter Kooijmans and Judge Rosalyn Higgins, the correctness of the

---

[24] Here I draw liberally on the summary of the test proposed by Ardi Imseis, "Critical Reflections on the International Humanitarian Law Aspects of the ICJ Wall Advisory Opinion," *American Journal of International Law*, vol. 99, no. 1 (2005), pp. 111–113. Imseis says he is drawing liberally on an initiative of the Harvard University Program on Humanitarian Policy and Conflict Research.

ICJ's ruling was not disputed, but its inability to state the rationale for its decision in terms of the standard international law test for military necessity was heavily criticized. The ICJ had insisted that the principles of necessity and proportionality both had to be satisfied, but the court did not indicate how these principles were to be understood and related to each other.[25]

Another point is also worth noting in considering what is thought of as the standard test for military necessity in international humanitarian law. Notice that the first part of the test rules out immediately any possible use of military necessity to justify the use of banned tactics. But of course, from a normative rather than a strictly legal standpoint, there is no special negative weight placed on a tactic just because it is banned. Banning is merely a positive law or customary consideration, and we would need to investigate the reasons for why the ban was adopted and then assess these reasons in light of relevant normative principles before thinking that the banned tactic really should not be employed. What counts as a banned tactic can change and has changed over time. Of course, it is more than just a curiosity that over a very long span of time poisons and other chemical weapons have been banned. But even in this case, there is no necessity that special negative weight be attached to such a ban.

In contemporary international law, the use of poisons is banned, and so we would never get to a consideration of whether it could be used on grounds of military necessity. Yet, there are many occasions when poisons have been used for just these reasons of necessity. The above five-part test from international law can be distilled to four questions that can be listed in a kind of lexical order, where I have eliminated the idea of something being banned for the reasons just given. Thus, in the debates about the principle of military necessity, there are four questions that must be answered in this order:

Level One: Is there a serious harm (to self or others) that should be prevented?
Level Two: Is the harm imminent or extremely likely to occur?
Level Three: Is there no other, less problematical way to prevent the harm?
Level Four: Does the proposed means cause less harm than is prevented?

Only when positive answers can be given at each of these levels will military necessity be a possible justificatory basis for acting in ways that would otherwise be problematical.

---

[25] See ibid., p. 114, where Imseis summarizes these opinions and agrees that the court needed to state and apply the test for military necessity and proportionality.

At Level One, we need an operational definition of "significance." I would urge that we interpret this provision along the lines of those suggested by Michael Walzer when he said that not just any harm prevention would count, but only a disaster to a political community.[26] For in weighing harms, it is not enough to justify the use of a pro-blematical tactic that there is some very minor advantage and no overriding disadvantage in using the tactic. Military necessity concerns the justification of tactics that would normally not be considered jus-tified. And because the normative considerations that are usually cited for initially ruling out that tactic are serious, a similarly serious con-sideration is needed now to rule them in.

Military necessity is normally restricted to certain kinds of emer-gency situations. Indeed, the Nuremberg trials seemed to limit con-siderations of military necessity to cases of self-defense emergencies.[27] The Nuremberg courts said that there must be an "instant and over-whelming necessity for self defense" that is imperative, where this means that there is "no choice of means and no moment of delibera-tion."[28] Such emergency cases will be few and far between. However, military necessity can be claimed even when the war being fought is not just. The self-defense considerations are localized ones, not con-siderations of *jus ad bellum*. Either side in a war can claim military necessity, which is restricted to *jus in bello* considerations of tactical emergency, as one Nuremberg court says, and must be of the sort that would "be necessary to save . . . troops from an imminent major disaster."[29]

There is a time constraint as well, as we saw in the previous section. The Level Two requirement of imminence means that there must be a preponderance of evidence for thinking that serious harm will occur – and soon, normally in a few hours – unless the tactic is employed. The standard way to think about this requirement is in terms of the *Caroline* case's requirement of an "instant and overwhelming necessity for self defense leaving no choice of means and moment of deliberation."[30]

Level Three must be understood in light of Level Two: We are to consider whether there are other avenues open to us, within the time frame when we can still prevent the harm, and whether these avenues

---

[26] Michael Walzer, *Just and Unjust Wars*, New York: Basic Books, 2000, pp. 254, 268.
[27] See The German High Command Trial, quoted in *Law Reports of Trials of War Criminals*, vol. 12, p. 124.
[28] Ibid., quoting "The Caroline case."   [29] Ibid., p. 125.
[30] See *Moore's Digest of International Law*, vol. 2, p. 414, quoted in ibid.

are themselves legal, or at least less problematical, than the means under consideration. Notice that there is a difference between Level Three and Four. There are two sorts of weighing that must be done: first, weighing the chosen conduct against other options that could achieve the same result, and then weighing the consequences of the means to be employed against the harm to be prevented by those means. But in any event, the Level Two requirement of imminence makes it much harder to get to the stages of the weighing involved in the principle of proportionality than it might at first appear.[31]

We must not allow the invocation of military necessity to become merely "a callous way of violating basic human rights."[32] To make sure that necessity does not swamp other considerations that are at least as important, if not more so, necessity is restricted in both domestic and international law to some kind of an emergency, where the only acceptable way out of the emergency is to use tactics that would otherwise be considered inappropriate. And here the term "emergency" is meant to signal that it will only rarely be true that a certain tactic can be employed. There is no exceptional category that is hereby created, but only a rare exception to an otherwise rather firm rule. Necessity is not a blanket justification that can transform any rule into one that admits of an endless class of exception. The neo-realists were simply wrong to think that military necessity could be employed to explode the restraints of the Just War theory and its rules of war. International humanitarian law has also taken this stand.

The requirement of imminence is meant to restrict the cases that can fall under the justifying spotlight of the principle of necessity. Imminence is supposed to signal the idea that the emergency is truly upon us and there is very little time for us to contemplate other, more palatable options. But if there is more time, then it is quite likely that there are other tactics that could be pursued to achieve the same military objective. In addition, proportionality then enters into the picture to urge that only the strategy that causes the least suffering be chosen, as we will see in greater detail later, when we examine the relation between these principles. The idea is that imminence forces us to think about whether there was an emergency so serious that it could

---

[31] See Emanuel Gross, "Legal Aspects of Tackling Terrorism: The Balance Between the Right of a Democracy to Defend Itself and the Protection of Human Rights," *UCLA Journal of International Law and Foreign Affairs*, vol. 6, (2001), p. 107.

[32] Allen Gewirth, "War Crimes and Human Rights," in *War Crimes and Collective Wrongdoing*, edited by Aleksandar Jokic, Oxford: Blackwell Publishers, 2001, p. 53.

not be averted in any other, less costly way than the way that was chosen at the moment, and proportionality forces us to assess what the goal is to be achieved by the otherwise prohibited tactics.

V.   RELATING PROPORTIONALITY AND NECESSITY

The principle of necessity does not apply to every battlefield decision, for it kicks in, and possibly allows for the normal laws of war to be abridged, only when a very serious matter is at stake, such as where losing a battle will mean that a legitimate community is overrun or destroyed. Even wars that were not initiated for a just cause may indeed reach certain points where various otherwise inappropriate tactics seem to be needed and might be justified by the principle of necessity. But a normatively plausible principle of necessity will not automatically warrant such tactics. In this section, I begin a task that is continued in the next chapter: considering how necessity and proportionality should be related.

Let us next turn to further restrictions on the principle of necessity that its connection with the principle of proportionality might engender. For if necessity is to mean anything at all, it cannot mean merely that one has to establish that some action needs to be taken to achieve an important military objective, thereby justifying the taking of *any* action to accomplish this necessary objective. Rather, the objective must be tightly connected to the particular tactic employed. A political leader might be right that it is imperative that something be done to stop a terrorist threat. But this does not mean that the rules of war do not apply. For they will still apply as a means to restrict the tactics that can be legitimately selected by the political leader, in terms of pro-portionality, even in situations where something needs to be done.

Think about one of the classic cases involving terrorism. For several decades, there has been a debate about whether torture could be jus-tified to find the location of a ticking time bomb set to explode in a crowded area of a city. Here, torture seems potentially justifiable be-cause the good to be accomplished – the saving of thousands of lives – seems to be clearly greater than the harm to be done: the suffering inflicted by the torture of a few people thought to have information about the ticking time bomb. But to get the justification to work, there has to be no other, less harmful way to get the information that is needed in time to stop the tragedy. It is not merely that it is necessary to get information and that torture is quite likely to secure that information. Now there is a weighing of tactics, unless there is only one tactic that could achieve the significant and needed result. Even if there seems to be only one way to achieve it, we often don't know how certain it is that it can be achieved in this way. Thus, as I said earlier, it is rare that we know in advance that only one particular tactic will achieve a military objective.

Suppose there is a ticking time bomb and yet also the possibility of securing *needed* information to avert a tragedy by using torture. But if the threat is not imminent, we may miss the fact that other tactics can also achieve the needed result. In an attempt to get needed information, it may not be noticed that there are several ways to acquire what is needed. Of course, if there are other ways to acquire the needed information, then none of the ways are truly necessary to obtain the information. In addition, it might not be noticed that there was also the possibility – indeed, the likelihood – that the information could be secured by bribing the same people who are about to be tortured. If necessity is confused with what is needed, then there is no particular reason to use bribery rather than torture because either tactic will secure the information needed to find the time bomb. Yet this result is deeply counterintuitive. If the very same needed information can be secured by much less costly means, shouldn't it be required that one choose the less costly tactic? What could possibly justify the intentional choosing of a tactic that will cause such suffering when there are other, less costly tactics that could be used for achieving the desired result? We cannot appeal to the goal of ending the emergency if it is not imminent and there are other less costly ways to achieve this goal. Thus, the principle of proportionality must be seen as continuously relevant.

Think again of a political leader who claims that she was not getting needed information about where terrorists would next strike against innocent citizens. Could the necessity of getting this information justify breaking the provisions of the Geneva Convention and other rules of war that forbid the use of torture? The key consideration is whether there are any less costly tactics available that would achieve the same needed result – that is, we need to appeal to proportionality and imminence, not merely to bare necessity. Had the political leader seriously attempted to bribe, rather than torture, the people that were held in captivity? A difficulty arises if there were many possible tactics that could have been employed but were not. But what if they were running out of time and torture seemed likely to work, as did bribery, but torture was thought to be slightly more likely to succeed? Would necessity alone justify using it? Again, my response is that proportionality seems to matter. If the alternative was far less costly, then it is not at all clear that the political leader was justified in using torture, unless it truly was the last resort open to the political leader.

There are thus two ways to understand the relationship between the principles of necessity and proportionality. Either the principle of proportionality is itself one of the conditions of the principle of necessity, or the principle of proportionality is independent of but a serious limitation on the principle of necessity. The principle of proportionality is clearly at least a background constraint whenever there is a normatively plausible invocation of the principle of necessity in international criminal law, because the very thing that is said to require the otherwise prohibited tactic may not itself be worth the cost of the use of the tactic. In addition, it is rare that one knows for sure that other tactics will not also achieve the needed objective. To see this more clearly yet, I turn explicitly to a reconceptualization of the principle of proportionality in light of the principle of humane treatment. As we work out the problems of the principle of proportionality, we will again see how important it is that the principles of necessity and proportionality be linked in any reasonable account of the principles underlying the rules of war. And one of the best places to start is with a real-life ticking time bomb case from Israel, and with the attempt by the Israeli Supreme Court to address the question of proportionality and necessity in that case.

10

The principle of proportionality

The proportionality principle is on one level the easiest to understand, but on another level it is the most difficult. On the first level, the principle of proportionality simply says that the amount of force used as a tactic of war must be neither too strong nor too weak for the task to be accomplished. If a single enemy marksman is firing at two of one's own soldiers, it is not allowed to bomb an entire company of soldiers to stop the one shooter. On the second level, the problem is to identify the relevant ways in which tactics and tasks are to be related and how tasks themselves are to be individuated. The second level is enormously difficult. In this chapter, I will propose a relatively new way to think about the *jus in bello* principle of proportionality that sees it as intimately entwined with the principle of humane treatment.

Proportionality does not merely say that tactics must not cause more suffering than they prevent. Proportionality is only an attenuated utilitarian principle, for there is a core concern that sets a fairly rigid moral limit. There must be no morally less costly way to accomplish a military objective that is thought to be necessary. If there is such a less costly means availables, then the principle of proportionality forbids the use of the more costly tactic, regardless of how important the objective is – that is, no matter that we are in a situation of extreme emergency. The principle of proportionality, on this account, is thus a limit on the principle of necessity.

The scope of the principle of proportionality is properly seen only in conjunction with the principle of necessity. The other rules of war can be suspended only when suspending them is necessary. A certain tactic might be justified that would otherwise be unjustified then, but only when there is also no morally less costly alternative that would also achieve the necessary objective. Throughout this chapter, I will address tactics that are "thought to be" necessary. Of course, if a tactic is literally necessary to accomplish a result, then there is no less costly way to do so. But in war, as in most of the rest of life, we are never quite sure what is actually necessary. The principle of proportionality says that if there is time, one needs to pursue less costly alternative tactics in the hope that they will also accomplish the objective. Very few things are known to be literally necessary, and so I will address tactics "thought to be" necessary, with the odd-sounding result that even when it appears that something is militarily necessary, proportionality nonetheless sets limits that urge the consideration of less costly alternative tactics.

In this chapter, I complete the task of reconceptualizing the traditional principles of *jus in bello* in light of the principle of humane treatment. In the first section, I discuss an important case from Israel concerning torture of suspected terrorists in the Occupied Territories, one that implicates both proportionality and necessity. In the second section, I link the principle of humane treatment to the principle of proportionality, explaining how the latter needs to be reconceptualized. In the third section, I take up the special problem of how to understand the weighing of lives according to the principle of proportionality, now reconceived to fit better with humanitarian concerns. In the fourth section, I attempt a systematic sketch of how the three reconceptualized principles of proportionality, necessity, and discrimination all fit together. And in the final section, I explain how the rules of war connect moral and legal considerations into a system that regulates behavior in war.

I.   THE ISRAELI CASE

Torture and other forms of cruel and degrading treatment have been condemned by all the relevant documents in international law for over a century. Torture has been condemned so strongly that it is normally said that it is unacceptable even when seemingly required by military necessity.[1] I will mention here only the most significant of the

[1] Jean S. Pictet et al., *The Commentary on Geneva Convention (I)*, Geneva: International Committee of the Red Cross, 1952, pp. 134–135, points out that the prohibition on torture was to be an unconditional requirement as one of the main ways to give specificity to the idea of humanity and humane treatment in the common core of the

documents. The 1949 Geneva Conventions' Common Article 3 states that torture "shall remain prohibited at any time and in any place whatsoever."[2] The 1966 International Covenant on Civil and Political Rights, Article 7, declares, "[N]o one shall be subject to torture or to cruel, inhuman or degrading treatment or punishment."[3] The 1984 Convention Against Torture and Other Cruel, Inhuman and Degrading Treatment creates an absolute ban on torture.[4] And the 1998 Rome Statute of the International Criminal Court, in its own condemnation of torture as a crime against humanity as well as a war crime, refers to torture as one of the Grave Breaches of the Geneva Conventions.[5]

Adam Roberts, summarizing these and other documents, says, "[T]he laws of war . . . have helped to bring about a degree of acceptance and observance of certain valuable basic ideas: for example, . . . that there can be no justification for torture."[6] The standard cases of prisoners of war concern camps that have been established to hold soldiers recently captured on the battlefield. Torture in such settings is normally based on reprisals or merely sadistic tendencies of certain guards. In such situations, it is very easy to see why the torture of prisoners of war has been so roundly condemned.[7] It is widely viewed as the epitome of inhumane treatment for a confined soldier to be tortured or otherwise abused by vicious camp guards.

Yet in 1989 Israel's Landau Commission declared that "moderate physical coercion" could be justified as a tactic by Israeli security forces trying to prevent suicide bombings and other loss of Israeli lives in the Occupied Territories.[8] The commission report did not discuss

---

Geneva Conventions. This was understood to be an advance over earlier Geneva Conventions that did not clearly indicate that torture and other forms of inhumane treatment were to be prohibited even when seemingly required by military necessity.

[2] Geneva Convention (III), Article 3.

[3] The International Covenant on Civil and Political Rights, 999 U.N.T.S. 171, Dec. 9, 1966, Article 7.

[4] Convention Against Torture and Other Cruel, Inhuman and Degrading Treatment, 23 ILM 1027 (1984).

[5] Statute of the International Criminal Court, Article 8.

[6] Adam Roberts, "Introduction," *The Documents on the Laws of War*, 3rd ed., Oxford: Oxford University Press, 2001, p. 31.

[7] See Judgment, *Prosecutor v. Kvocka, et al.*, paras. 137–138, Case no. IT-98-30/1-T, T.C. I, 2, November 2, 2001.

[8] Report of the Commission of Inquiry in the Matter of Investigation Methods of the General Security Service Regarding Hostile Territory Activity (1987) (hereinafter, Landau Commission Report). Excerpts from the report were translated into English and published in the *Israel Law Review*, vol. 23 (1989), 146–188. Parts of this report,

particular cases, at least not in the part of the report that was made public. The Landau Commission's conclusion, interpreted to mean that some forms of torture could be employed by Israeli security forces, was exposed to widespread criticism, even outrage. Roughly ten years later, the Israeli Supreme Court sitting as the High Court of Justice rejected the Landau Commission's conclusions and held that torture and other forms of inhumane treatment, even in cases of military necessity, were contrary to Israeli and international law.

The case, *Public Committee Against Torture in Israel v. the State of Israel et al.*,[9] was brought by three human rights organizations and six individuals who had been interrogated by the General Security Service (GSS) of the Israeli government (hereinafter, the applicants). Various forms of physical coercion had been employed against the six individual applicants. The tactics employed by the GSS during interrogations of suspected terrorists bear enough similarity to those of Abu Ghraib and Guantanamo to make them especially relevant today. These tactics included forceful shaking; use of the "Shabach" position, whereby the suspect was seated on a low chair tilting forward, with his hands tied behind his back and his head covered by an opaque sack and subjected to powerfully loud music; use of the "frog crouch" position, whereby the suspect was compelled to crouch on the tips of his toes for repeated intervals; excessive tightening of hand or leg cuffs; and, excessive sleep deprivation.[10] The Court unanimously held that all of these tactics violated Basic Law 1992: Human Dignity and Liberty.[11]

What made the Israeli case so interesting was that the Court did not dispute the fact that Israeli security forces had thwarted suicide bombings with information obtained from torture of one of the applicants. In Section 5 of its September 6, 1999 decision, the Israeli Supreme Court noted that one of the applicants, Abd al Rahman

concerning what specific tactics could be employed, were never published in Hebrew or English and remain secret to this day.

[9] *Public Committee Against Torture in Israel and Others v. Israel and Others* (HC 5100/94, 4054/95, 6536/95, 5188/96, 7563/97, 7628/97, and 1043/99), Supreme Court of Israel, 7 BHRC 31, 6 September 1999.

[10] Ibid., Sections 9–13.

[11] Israel does not have a constitution. Instead, it has passed various Basic Laws that, because they articulate general principles defining rights in Israel, operate somewhat like a constitutional bill of rights, but that do not have authority higher than other statutes passed subsequently by the Knesset. See Mordechai Kremnitzer and Re'em Segev, "The Legality of Interrogational Torture: A Question of Proper Authorization or a Substantive Moral Issue," *Israel Law Review*, vol. 34, Fall (2000), 509–559.

Ismail Ganimat, "was involved in the bombing of the Café Appropo, in Tel Aviv, in which three women were murdered and 30 people were injured." According to the Court, "[A] powerful explosive device, identical to the one detonated at Café Appropo in Tel Aviv, was found in the applicant's village (Tzurif) subsequent to dismantling of the terrorist cell to which he belonged. Uncovering this explosive device thwarted an attack similar to the one at Café Appropo."[12] Thus, the Court acknowledged that the tactics employed by the General Security Service, "the main body responsible for fighting terrorism" in Israel, did stop a "ticking time bomb" but were nonetheless not justified.

On the basis of the idea of human dignity, the Court held that there were two relevant principles: "First, a reasonable investigation is necessarily one free of torture, free of cruel, inhuman treatment of the subject, and free of any degrading handling whatsoever. . . . These prohibitions are absolute. There are no exceptions to them, and there is no room for balancing. Indeed, violence directed at a subject's body or spirit does not constitute a reasonable investigation practice . . . [and] can potentially lead to the investigator being held criminally liable. . . . Second, a reasonable investigation is likely to cause discomfort, . . . [but] it is possible to conduct an effective investigation without resorting to violence." The "least restrictive means" necessary for an effective investigation must be employed.[13]

Depriving someone of sleep so that interrogations can be completed is allowed, but sleep deprivation as a means to some other end, such as "tiring him out or 'breaking' him," is not.[14] Uncomfortable physical restraint of an especially violent detainee may be allowed if it is necessary for the "investigator's safety," but restraint aimed to intimidate the detainee is not.[15] Covering the suspect's head with a hood, even if it is ventilated, is not allowed, even if the tactic is aimed at preventing contact with other inmates. There are other means of accomplishing this goal, if it is a legitimate investigative goal, that are less degrading. The question asked throughout – namely, is the investigation fairly conducted? – was key, and for all of these tactics the Court held that prohibited means were employed: "At times, the price of truth is so high that a democratic society is not prepared to pay

---

[12] *Public Committee Against Torture in Israel v. Israel,* 7 B.H.R.C. 31, Section 5. The government did not deny the use of these tactics.
[13] Ibid., Section 23. [14] Ibid., Section 31. [15] Ibid., Section 26.

it. . . . The rules pertaining to investigations are important to a democratic state. They reflect its character. An illegal investigation harms the
suspect's human dignity. It equally harms society's fabric."[16]

The Israeli Supreme Court decision is especially interesting for what
it says about military necessity. The Court distinguishes between *post
factum* and pre-emptory authorization based on necessity. The Court
rejected the idea that necessity can provide a pre-emptory authorization for torture or other forms of inhumane treatment.[17] At best,
necessity is

> an exceptional *post-factum* defense, exclusively confined to criminal proceed-
> ings against investigators. It cannot however, by any means, provide GSS
> investigators with the pre-emptory authorization to conduct investigations ab
> initio. GSS investigators are not authorized to employ any physical means,
> absent unequivocal authorization from the legislature pertaining to the use of
> such methods and conforming to the requirements of Basic Law 1992: Human
> Dignity and Liberty.[18]

Hence, these investigators can be subject to criminal prosecution.

The strategy of the Israeli Supreme Court is first to phrase the issue
as one of what investigative methods are allowed in interrogating
suspects and then to argue that any given methods are allowed only if
they are reasonable and fair. Normatively, this strategy is linked to the
importance of "preserving the human image" as one part of protecting
the dignity of the detainees.[19] No balancing is allowed when physical
violence is used, for these tactics are strictly prohibited. When lesser
forms of coercion are employed, the tactics employed must have a
close connection to a goal of the interrogation and must constitute the
least restrictive means available to achieve this goal. Proportionality
thus enters into the picture only in lesser forms of coercive interrogation. And necessity does not play a role in authorization, being
confined to its proper place as a *post factum* defense or mitigating
factor.

We can distinguish torture used as a form of terror, which is cate-
gorically condemned, from torture used as an interrogation technique.
Even in the second category, the Israeli Supreme Court held that
torture is illegal. The pain that is caused by normal means of securing

---

[16] Ibid., Section 22.   [17] Ibid., Section 14.

[18] Ibid. The court seems to imply that, in practice, authorization to use torture cannot be
    secured by reference to military necessity – that is, to the objectives that are being
    pursued by the investigative torture.

[19] Ibid., Section 22.

prisoners so that they will not attack their captors, or so that they do not cause grave harm to themselves, or the minor harm involved in keeping their attention during an investigation is acceptable. This is because torture is implicitly defined, as it was in the Torture Convention, "not to include pain or suffering arising only from, inherent in or incidental to lawful sanctions."[20]

If we think of torture as an investigative tactic for securing information, rather than as itself a form of terrorism aimed at deterring future terrorist acts, then the Israeli Supreme Court offers a reasonable approach. Here, the Court prohibits all forms of torture and other forms of physical violence because they simply are not consistent with a society that values human dignity and in any event do not often advance the goals of interrogation that cannot be attained by other means. In this sense, one can understand why the Court was not impressed by the fact that the use of torture against Abd al Rahman Ismail Ganimat had indeed thwarted a terrorist attack. For it was not clear that other tactics would not have achieved the same results. Having a ticking time bomb for which it is necessary to act quickly is not enough; there must be no other strategy open to finding the bomb but to use torture. And here it seems the Court believes that less physically coercive tactics could have been found. In any event, the Court found that certain kinds of information may have to be forgone in order to protect the values of a democratic society that respects individuals' rights to dignity.

The difficulty is that when we are faced with tactics that are less coercive than torture, we are thrown back into the problem of whether and when these tactics might be justified in so-called ticking time bomb cases. Proportionality seems to be a very problematical strategy to pursue because the ticking time bomb often threatens such massive destruction that it is unclear what tactics would ever be ruled out by a proportionality requirement. In subsequent sections, I will investigate

---

[20] Convention Against Torture and Other Cruel, Inhuman or Degrading Treatment or Punishment, Article 1. The convention's full definition of torture is as follows: "any act by which severe pain or suffering, whether physical or mental, is intentionally inflicted on a person for such purposes as obtaining from him or a third person information or a confession, punishing him for an act he or a third person has committed or is suspected of having committed, or intimidating or coercing him or a third person, or for any reason based on discrimination of any kind when such pain or suffering is inflicted by or at the instigation of or with the consent or acquiescence of a public official or other person acting in an official capacity. It does not include pain or suffering arising only from, inherent in, or incidental to lawful sanctions."

this point in more detail than did the Israeli Supreme Court. I do believe, though, that the analysis of the Court concerning torture seems plausible. Most, if not all, forms of physical coercion of prisoners of war must be prohibited on grounds of proportionality, and prosecutions of violations must be allowed. But beyond this important point, it is less clear whether there are at least some cases where even torture might be justified.

II. HUMANE TREATMENT AND PROPORTIONALITY

Michael Walzer points out that not all possible defeats at war trigger the principles of necessity and proportionality as bases for evading humanitarian considerations. In his view, only when the survival of a political community is at stake do military necessity and proportionality override those humanitarian prohibitions involved in the principles of humane treatment and discrimination or distinction. Considerations of the speed of victory or scope of victory are not relevant.[21] In this view, only certain forms of military necessity will count: those that are normatively weighty in some other respect. In addition, when necessity is combined with proportionality, even fewer cases of otherwise prohibited attacks based on military necessity will be justified.

Consider a commander who has determined that a civilian's house in a residential neighborhood is being used for military purposes by enemy forces and that the house needs to be bombed so as to achieve a military objective. Leslie Green says,

Even in such circumstances, however, the rule of proportionality must be observed. To minimize unnecessary or excessive suffering, those who plan or decide on an attack must do everything feasible, that is to say practicable or practically possible in light of all the circumstances, including those of a military nature, to verify that the objectives about to be attacked are neither civilians nor civilian objects, nor specially protected. . . .[22]

Here we see that the principle of proportionality is a restraint on the principle of military necessity. The principle of proportionality restrains military necessity even further than it would be restrained by considerations of otherwise proper targeting based on the principle of

---

[21] Michael Walzer, *Just and Unjust Wars*, New York: Basic Books, 2000, pp. 254, 268.
[22] Leslie C. Green, *The Contemporary Law of Armed Conflict*, 2nd ed., Manchester, England: Manchester University Press, 2000, p. 156.

discrimination or distinction. We also see how the pieces of the puzzle might fit together, how the various principles interrelate with each other, a task to which we will give full attention at the end of this chapter.

It is true, of course, that some States have used the principle of necessity as a complete defense against the use of otherwise inhumane tactics. For instance, in 2002, lawyers in the Bush administration argued that the doctrine of necessity could be used to breach treaties, especially concerning the use of torture.[23] This use of the principle of necessity, unrestrained by even the principle of proportionality, is odd indeed, for it makes it seem that military necessity is the most important principle of international humanitarian law. If this were true, then international humanitarian law would effectively cease to be anything other than prudential calculation, for, in wartime many decisions are made based on considerations of military necessity, which would trump all else in nearly every case.

By adding the principle of proportionality to the principle of necessity, we avoid the unhappy situation of losing any sense of restraint in times of war. Even though the principle of proportionality does not give anything like absolute prohibitions, it does operate as a significant restraint on even tactics believed to be militarily necessary. Proportionality is commonly defined by reference to what has already been determined to be a military target: "[T]he amount of destruction permitted in pursuit of a military objective must be proportionate to the importance of the objective."[24] Even when attacking a legitimate military target, disproportionate use of force is unacceptable. So what does it mean to use disproportionate force in relation to the importance of the military objective?

The principle of proportionality clearly calls for some kind of consequentialist or utilitarian assessment – namely, that it should be clear that more good than bad is done by the use of a certain military tactic. The rules of war are to be broken only when military necessity calls for it *and* when there is no less costly way to achieve the military objective than what is proposed. Strictly speaking, the proportion aspect calls for restrictions on tactics that are no more "important" than what is to be achieved by using those tactics. Importance is normally understood in

[23] Neil A. Lewis and Eric Schmitt, "Lawyers Decided Bans on Torture Didn't Bind Bush," *New York Times*, June 8, 2004, pp. A1, A10.
[24] Douglas P. Lackey, *The Ethics of War and Peace*, p. 59.

terms of minimal suffering, but it need not be. The Israeli case concerning where Israel's wall in the West Bank should be constructed makes this point well when it sets three secondary tests for proportionality:

1. the measures taken must rationally lead to realization of the objective;
2. the measure must injure the individual to the least extent possible;
3. the harm expected from the action should be proportional to the benefit gained from it.[25]

Importance can also refer to nonutilitarian factors such as those involving the values of liberty or autonomy. Hence, the principle of proportionality could be seen as involved in weighing, but not restricted to suffering.

The best way to understand the principle of proportionality is as a restraint drawn in humanitarian terms on the principle of necessity, whether this means minimizing suffering or producing goals or values at least as important as those of the other State that are undermined by military assaults. Humane treatment remains at the core of the principle of proportionality. This is best seen when proportionality is enlisted to require that even when in emergency situations tactics should be chosen that minimize injury or suffering. But humanitarian roots of proportionality can also be seen in the determination that proportionality calls for the weighing of the importance of the military objective versus the importance of what is lost on the other side due to the use of the tactics against them.

As in our earlier discussion of the principle of necessity, proportional treatment should be valued because it creates a more humane world. Certain tactics that are seemingly justified by military necessity are ruled out because they cause too much suffering, or more suffering than can be justified by the goal of the military campaign. However, one could argue that some kind of procedural fairness is at the heart of

---

[25] *Beit Sourik v. Israel*, Supreme Court of Israel, June 30, 2004, HCJ 2056/04 (ordering the State of Israel to modify the route of the wall/barrier that was being constructed in the Occupied West Bank). See Nidal Sliman, "Israeli High Court Decision on Location of West Bank Barrier," *ASIL-Insights*, July 6, 2004, p. 2. The Court affirmed the view that military purpose does not authorize the military commander to do anything thought to be militarily necessary, although it did not similarly state the conditions for military necessity.

the principle of proportionality, a fairness toward the other side in a military operation, for instance, and that this did not go so far as to involve the promotion of humane treatment. Perhaps proportionality is an aspect of the procedural fairness requirements of the rule of law rather than an aspect of humane treatment. However, the value of the rule of law seems to be precisely that it produces a more humane world. Indeed, I would argue that rule of law issues like those embodied in proportionality of treatment are related to the kind of fundamental fairness thought to be necessary for a humane society in any event.

Proportionality might be thought to be opposed to humane treatment if proportionality is wide-ranging in that it is thought to trump all other considerations on the battlefield. For one could imagine that the principle of proportionality would inspire soldiers constantly to be calculating whether their actions would actually advance important goals, and, if so, then nearly any tactic could be justified, except those few that caused even greater losses than what was achieved by a given military tactic. As a result, soldiers would not give much attention at all to whether the tactics employed were humane. There seems to be an opposition between thinking about war in terms of effects, characterized by respect for the principle of proportionality as it is currently understood, and thinking about war based on strong restraints of compassion, mercy, and honor and characterized by proportionality understood as respect for the principle of humane treatment. My proposal to see proportionality as involving respect for humane treatment will mean that proportionality is not thought of as wide-ranging.

My view is that proportionality does not range over all behavior on the battlefield. In the last chapter, I provided an argument showing that the principle of proportionality is not wide-ranging but merely a restraint on the principle of necessity, which is itself a very narrowly applied principle. Given this understanding, it is not the case that proportionality and humane treatment need to be seen as opposed principles. Rather, humane treatment is at the very core of why, even in situations of military necessity, tactics are to be chosen that minimize suffering or best promote other important human values. In this respect, like other restraints on tactical decision making, such as the principle of discrimination or distinction, the principle of proportionality makes soldiers stop and think before they act, and this is almost always a good thing indeed. Humane treatment is what should be at the heart of the stop-and-think of concern for proportionality. Except in the rarest of circumstances, the principles that underlie and limit the laws of war are aimed at restraining what soldiers can do and curtailing what these soldiers' superiors can legitimately order them to do.

Disproportionate treatment is almost always inhumane treatment of a certain sort – that is, inhumane treatment given the context. To engage in disproportionate treatment normally means that the tactics employed will make the soldier, or civilian, suffer unnecessarily. For example, disproportionate use of force against a confined enemy soldier often means that the suffering will be greater for that soldier than the possible lessening of suffering that the disproportionate use of force is aimed at alleviating. Those enemy soldiers who are deterred, as a result of learning about the confined soldier's suffering, rarely cause less suffering than what is caused to happen to the confined soldier by the tactic of inhumane treatment. It is like our earlier discussions of dishonorable treatment where one acted in a cruel way, going beyond what was reasonable to accomplish a certain objective – for instance, not merely tapping a person in the arm to get his attention, but breaking his arm when all one needed to do was to tap his shoulder to get his attention. Going beyond what was reasonable for the objective in question almost always involves excess suffering caused to other people, especially when one is in the pressure cooker environment of wartime. Hence, disproportionate treatment is often closely allied with inhumane treatment, and the condemnation of disproportionate treatment is often drawn in terms of the inhumanity of the treatment.

So, we have a new way to conceptualize the principle of proportionality. First, proportionality is a restriction on the principle of necessity, the former calling for tactics or treatment that are the least costly among those that are believed to be necessary to achieve a significant military objective. Second, proportionality, like necessity, only concerns situations of emergency, in which otherwise the normal rules of war still apply. Third, this makes the principle of proportionality quite similar to the idea that one should minimize suffering, itself a component of the principle of humane treatment. Fourth, proportionality involves the "weighing" of some lives against others, or some lives against property, only when such weighing is already seen as justified by humanitarian considerations. We will investigate the idea of weighing in the context of proportionality assessment in more detail in the next section.

III. PROPORTIONALITY AND WEIGHING LIVES

The moral equality of soldiers view expressed by Walzer and others that gives to soldiers the right to kill enemy soldiers seems to imply that there is no limit to how many enemy soldiers one can kill, for the right extends without limit as long as one is on the battlefield. Many theorists support the idea that a State "may kill any number of enemy soldiers to save just one of its own soldiers. Once a war has begun, enemy soldiers are essentially free targets that one may attack at any time."[26] This is the assessment of the Just War tradition given by Thomas Hurka. He does not himself support such an extreme view, although he does contend that a State "may give extra weight to its soldiers' lives because they are its own."[27] In this section, I will offer reasons, from within the Just War tradition, to reject the extreme view. I will also give reasons to reject, or at least modify, Hurka's more moderate principle. Proportionality has meant more than Walzer and his followers allow, and it sets the stage for at least modifying even Hurka's proposal.

As is common in discussions of the Just War tradition, considerations of justice are the only ones that are referred to. Walzer certainly exemplifies this strategy. But, as I have argued several times before, as early as 1625 Grotius broke from this tradition and urged that we also take into account considerations of humanity and honor. In Chapter 4 of Book III, Grotius writes about "The Right of Killing Enemies in a Public War" and at the end of the first page of this discussion makes it quite clear that more than even what is permissible is at stake: "For sometimes that is said to be permissible from every point of view and is free from reproach, even if there is something else which might more honorably be done."[28] Grotius then goes on to say that "it is permitted to harm an enemy" especially, but not merely, "for him who wages war for a just cause,"[29] and that "such persons may be slain with impunity."[30] What looks like a straightforward support of the Just War tradition turns into a kind of *reductio ad absurdum* when Grotius admits

---

[26] Thomas Hurka, "Proportionality in the Morality of War," *Philosophy and Public Affairs*, vol. 33, no. 1 (2005), p. 58. Hurka cites Walzer's *Just and Unjust Wars*, pp. 138–151.

[27] Ibid., Hurka, p. 163.

[28] Hugo Grotius, *De Jure Belli ac Pacis* (*On the Law of War and Peace*) (1625), Book 3, Chapter 4, Section 15, translated by Francis Kelsey, Oxford: Clarendon Press, 1925, p. 641.

[29] Ibid., p. 644.   [30] Ibid., p. 647.

that on this view "the slaughter even of infants and women is made with impunity."[31]

Grotius contends that those who act with a "sense of honor"[32] set limits and look to the intention of enemy soldiers in fighting.[33] For those who lack a wrongful intention do not deserve to be slain, even by those who fight a war for a just cause. And here is the test, which seems to be meant to be a reformulation of what was then, and still is now, considered the traditional proportionality principle:

Except for reasons that are *weighty and will affect the safety of many*, no action should be attempted whereby innocent persons may be threatened with destruction.[34]

Grotius then singles out prisoners of war, immediately after children and women as those innocents who "should be spared."

Grotius' view does not fit with what is sometimes thought to be the traditional Just War doctrine according to which civilians may be killed to save the life of one of one's own soldiers or even that many enemy soldiers can be killed to save the life of one of one's own soldiers. And if Grotius is indeed an exponent of the Just War doctrine, then the matter is more complicated than it might at first seem in understanding what the doctrine tells us about the principle of proportionality. Indeed, Grotius' version of the principle of proportionality, as was true of the view I endorsed above, sees proportionality and necessity operating in tandem, according to which the test of proportionality does not involve a simple weighing of lives on one side against lives on the other. At least on Grotius' view of Just War theory, neither Walzer's extreme view nor Hurka's moderate view is correct. On humanitarian grounds, we seem to be barred from giving any extra weight to our own soldiers' lives, even if we are fighting a war for a just cause.

The extreme position taken by Walzer might be supported by those who see only narrow issues of justice as germane in the assessment of the limits of proportionality. On this view, once war is begun, soldiers have an equal right to kill or be killed by other soldiers. They have made themselves into dangerous men, and as a result they can legitimately be targeted for attack or may attack those who are similarly dangerous. As Walzer puts it, soldiers have lost their immunity to be attacked.[35] All that matters are the rights of the parties, and once one

---

[31] Ibid., p. 648.   [32] Ibid., p. 716.   [33] Ibid., p. 723.   [34] Ibid., p. 737 (italics mine).
[35] Michael Walzer, *Just and Unjust Wars*, p. 145.

has lost the right or immunity not to be killed, one is then a legitimate target.[36] Walzer discusses all of this in terms of the principle of necessity,[37] but one wonders what has become of proportionality here – if all soldiers are legitimate targets, then it looks like proportionality does little normative work, as seems to be Hurka's interpretation of Walzer and this branch of the Just War tradition.

When Walzer comes to address proportionality directly, he says that it rules out "only purposeless or wanton violence."[38] But this, he tells us, "would eliminate a great deal of the cruelty of war."[39] Here Walzer is on the right track, for, as I have argued, the principle of proportionality is very closely aligned with the restraint on minimal suffering that is part of the principle of humane treatment. But as I conceive it, more is required than merely that purposeless or wanton cruelty be prohibited. Walzer's view is that to demand more is to fail to see that "the values against which destruction and suffering are to be measured are so readily inflated."[40] But Walzer is surely wrong to think that, for instance, we can justify killing many soldiers to save the life of one of our own. For proportionality, understood as grounded in humane treatment, does not allow us to weigh our own soldier's life as so inflated as to outweigh the lives of many others. Even if Hurka is right to suggest that we can place a bit more weight on the lives of our own soldiers than on others, this will normally not allow for the strong conclusions that Walzer wants.

In many ways, Hurka's proposal is quite a bit more plausible than Walzer's. Indeed, I would object only to the way that he reformulates the principle of proportionality concerning the weighing of lives. Recall that Hurka says that a State may give extra weight to the lives of soldiers that are its own. But the problem is still to figure out how much extra weight is justifiable. In order to avoid the clear problems of nationalist bias that Hurka himself acknowledged to be a major problem, the lives of one's own soldiers should be given only a very small amount of extra weight when applying the principle of proportionality.

In the end, the principle of proportionality does not tell us more than what was already contained in a somewhat expanded idea of minimizing suffering and thus already contained in the principle of humane treatment. And the idea that soldiers should feel honor bound to minimize suffering will surely not allow for many enemy soldiers or

---

[36] Ibid., p. 143.   [37] Ibid., p. 144.   [38] Ibid., p. 129.
[39] Ibid., p. 130.   [40] Ibid., p. 192.

civilians to be harmed or killed to prevent one of their own soldiers from being harmed or killed. Proportionality decisively sets a limit on how much harm and killing can occur even on the battlefield, indeed especially on the battlefield, where considerations of honor require restraint so as to make war not merely barbarous slaughter. As I have indicated, Hurka's arguments begin to move us in this direction and away from the extreme position often taken by Walzer. But Hurka needs to refine things so that the principle of proportionality is conceptually closer to the idea of minimizing suffering.

A beginning at such a refinement was made by the Prosecutor of the ICTY in the Report on the NATO Bombing Campaign in the former Yugoslavia in March and June of 1999.[41] The ICTY Prosecutor said that the "main problem with the principle of proportionality is not whether it exists but what it means and how it is to be applied.[42] The general idea is that "if there is a choice of weapons or methods of attack available, a commander should select those which are most likely to avoid, or at least minimize, incidental damage." The Prosecutor then cited the Kupreskic Judgment of the ICTY as providing a good rule of thumb. If there is one incident in which attacks against military targets cause collateral civilian casualties, this is not per se a violation of the rules of war. But if there are repeated attacks that have the same effect, they may indeed violate the principle of proportionality.[43] As a result of adopting this rule of thumb, the Prosecutor feels that the NATO bombings should not be seen as triggering an investigation for war crimes by her office because there was no pattern of military conduct that caused civilian casualties out of proportion to what was accomplished.

The Kupreskic Judgment of the ICTY justifies a similar assessment in light of the "demands of humanity."[44] Proportionality is one of those loose terms that needs to be further refined, and according to the Court the best way to do this is in terms of the "elementary considerations of humanity." Specifically, what that means is that rules "must be interpreted so as to construe as narrowly as possible the discretionary power to attack belligerents, and by the same token, so as

---

[41] Prosecutor's Report on the NATO Bombing Campaign, issued at The Hague, June 13, 2000.

[42] Ibid., para. 48.   [43] Ibid., para. 52.

[44] *Prosecutor v. Kupreskic et al.*, International Criminal Tribunal for the Former Yugoslavia, Trial Chamber, Case no. IT-95–16-T, January 14, 2000, para. 526.

to expand the protection afforded to civilians."[45] The idea here is that humane treatment must guide the interpretation of proportionality so that it is never interpreted to mean that it can give a wide-ranging discretionary right to kill enemy soldiers or to harm civilians.

IV. CONNECTING THE NORMATIVE PRINCIPLES OF *JUS IN BELLO*

In this section, I will try to put the pieces together and explain what one coherent set of principles of *jus in bello* rules of war would look like. As I said in Chapter 4, I regard the principle of humane treatment as the cornerstone of the rules of war. This principle is what underlies all of the other principles, and it makes of the other principles something less than absolute rules but more than mere utilitarian considerations. The principle of discrimination or distinction sets a rough normative framework for acting humanely by providing that civilians are generally not to be attacked, that soldiers can be attacked and killed during war, and that weapons should generally be designed in such a way that they discriminate or distinguish civilians from soldiers. The principle of necessity – along with its restraining condition, the principle of proportionality – provides a basis seemingly for limiting the principles of humane treatment and discrimination or distinction. But the principles of necessity and proportionality come into play only rarely, and even then they turn out to be largely based on considerations of humane treatment of a somewhat larger scope.

Humane treatment is closely related to the ideas of minimal suffering, mercy, and honor. In my proposal, these considerations are put into a framework where they have a different significance based on whether we are discussing the treatment of civilians or soldiers. We are to treat both categories of people humanely, but the treatments will differ at least prima facie. And we will rarely be allowed to disregard the components of the principle of humane treatment: minimal suffering, mercy, and honor concerning even enemy soldiers. In those cases where necessity seems to apply, we are still governed by proportionality, which itself calls for choosing that treatment which minimizes suffering. And the general idea behind necessity in any event is that it treats the whole of the political community humanely.

---

[45] Ibid., para. 525.

This way of setting the principles in line makes it seem as if there is a utilitarian orientation to the rules of war. Such a characterization, though, is only half right. As I explained in Chapter 7, the goal of minimal suffering, or better the prohibition on superfluous suffering, is only a baseline consideration. It is also true that the principle of discrimination could be thought of as anti-utilitarian in that it seems to set a prohibition, limited though it may be, on attacking and killing civilians. Yet, as I explained in Chapter 8, there are so many exceptions to the rule that it is better thought of as a beginning basis for further fine-grained reflections rather than itself a sole basis for deciding how people should be treated in wartime.

As with any system of principles, one particular principle needs to be given pride of place. Many have argued that that principle should be justice. In Chapter 4, and elsewhere in this book, I have argued that this is a mistake, at least if justice is understood narrowly to involve giving to each what he or she deserves. For during wars, we need humane restraint, which is more than merely focusing on what someone deserves, especially because it seems that in every war each side claims that the other side deserves nothing more than to be annihilated. It is for this reason that I proposed instead that the prime principle be related to humanity rather than to justice narrowly conceived and that we focus specifically on what I called the principle of humane treatment. Of course, as I admitted, one could construe the provisions of this principle as still falling within a broader conception of justice, one that centers on the respect that is due to each person, not as a matter of what is deserved from past behavior, but purely on the basis of one's status as a human being. Nonetheless, humaneness is still different from justice so construed because humaneness also concerns taking into account a person's special vulnerable status rather than general human status.

After setting out the prime principle, which itself incorporates elements that are consequentialist and absolutist, I turned to subsidiary principles. The principle of discrimination or distinction is the closest to an absolutist principle governing war, for it calls for a firm separation between how civilians and soldiers should be treated, where civilians generally should not be assaulted or killed. Yet it also turns out that there were exceptions to this principle and that we needed to see it as providing an initial rough-grained framework for thinking about wartime behavior, rather than itself a basis for fine-grained decision making. The fine-grained decisions had to take into account a lot of largely consequentialist considerations, such as what the circumstances of a particular battle were.

One way to understand the system of principles I have been articulating is to see the principles of necessity and proportionality as forming a basis for the class of exceptions to the nearly absolutist principle of discrimination or distinction. Necessity, seen as a principle rather than as a defense, carved out a class of exceptions to how civilians could be treated, as well as how soldiers could be treated, if it turned out that humane treatment caused battles to be lost, for instance. But within the domain of such consequentialist concerns, there were other consequentialist considerations that entered to restrict the range of the principle of necessity. Proportionality set consequentialist limits on the consequentialist principle of necessity in that it only made sense to break the rules of war if not only was it thought to be necessary to do so, but that no other less costly means were available. Indeed, if that mixture of necessity and proportionality did not occur, necessity itself seemed to be a particularly bad way to think about consequentialist allowances for some indiscriminate attacks.

I have tried to indicate why neither the principle of discrimination or distinction, nor some combination of the principles of necessity and proportionality should be seen as the prime principles governing the rules of war. Rather, humane treatment is the key principle because it both combines elements of consequentialism and absolutism and represents what has seemed to many over the ages to be true: that what is called for is a compound principle that meshes with our moral intuitions. The guiding idea that the minimization of suffering is to be encouraged and that, in doing so, mercy will often be extended to one's enemies is seen to rise above the other principles and to provide them with a guiding orientation.

Indiscriminate treatment is condemnable because it is clearly avoidable and will cause superfluous suffering in most cases. But when the suffering really is necessary, then the charge that it is superfluous at least partially falls away. Yet, if the only seemingly necessary action is not the least costly as well and thus violates the proportionality requirement, then it appears once again that it might involve superfluous suffering. The general condemnation of superfluous suffering is thus seen as the guiding orientation to all of the other principles traditionally listed in the *jus in bello* tradition. It is partially implicit in the principle of discrimination or distinction in that this principle tries to keep the ravages of war from encompassing civilians and noncombatant soldiers. And the principle of necessity, which seems to be a limitation on the ban on superfluous suffering, turns out not to be. For if torture is truly necessary and no less costly means are available, then the suffering involved in the torture is not superfluous. But it is my view that this will be true in relatively few cases, even in the most difficult of times.

There is nothing from a strict consideration of justice that calls for the minimization of suffering. And so we have to bring in considerations of compassion and mercy as well, and the idea of honor surfaces to add motivational impetus to what would otherwise be a pretty weak basis for restraint. All in all, there is a logic to these principles, although probably a fuzzy logic to those who look for tight systems. But war defies the kind of careful logic that people hope for – it is messy in multiple ways. For this reason, among others, the principles governing the rules of war will appear to be as much a matter of fuzzy-edged morality as of bright-line legality. Nonetheless, there are often relatively clear things we can say.

International law is a curious mixture of moral and legal norms. Nowhere is this more apparent than in the rules of war. International law is a matter of treaties, but it's also a matter of custom and of common law. Custom is not grounded in the way that treaties are, for it is grounded ultimately, if at all, in universal moral norms, such as so-called *jus cogens* norms. The rules of war have also been deeply rooted in codes of chivalry and honor, which are often regional moral norms, as well as universal norms, such as those concerning natural justice and humanity. The famous Martens Clause in the Hague Convention declares that international law should be connected to the conscience of the public and the duties of humanity. Such a declaration has had wide acceptance and has made of international law a fertile ground for mixing morality and legality.

The Abu Ghraib and Guantanamo prison abuse scandals in 2003–6 have highlighted how most people do not take a purely legalistic view of international law. It is not merely a matter of whether the Geneva Conventions technically applied to the inmates (which in my view clearly they did) but of whether humane treatment was provided for those inmates. Here humane treatment, which is largely a moral notion, has in some respects intersected with legality, but almost accidentally. The question is whether it is inhumane to strip people naked and then release dogs to attack them. Even those who might pause in answering this question in the negative are forced to draw on certain moral notions, such as utilitarian concerns about whether such treatment might not do more good for more people in the long run.

The principles governing the *jus in bello* constraints, or the rules of war, also have this curious mixture of morality and legality. It is no accident that there has been an informal international regime governing behavior during war and that this regime has been partially moral and partially legal. It is also not surprising that the ages-old debate in ethics between consequentialism and absolutism has dominated the debates about the principles governing the rules of war. Finally, it is also not surprising that there has been a serious effort over the centuries to construct a set of principles that would be firm and easy to employ, on the one hand, and yet flexible enough to take account of exceptional cases, such as emergency situations, on the other hand. I have attempted to reconstruct this system of principles with that understanding in mind.

In this third part of the book, I have attempted to add some order to the disparate and seemingly contradictory principles governing the rules of war. That I have not provided the kind of order that is encompassed in some systems of law, such as the tax code, is not sufficient to dismiss these rules. The rules of war constitute a system of norms for regulating the behavior of States and their agents in the absence of a World State. And the system of norms is meant to apply to probably the most stressful of times: when war has broken out and both sides not only call the other "enemy" but also can find no way to resolve the dispute other than to attempt to annihilate each other. In such times, any agreement about what the rules of the game are must be seen as a good thing. Every time one can get people who are sworn enemies to stop and think before they kill each other, surely much more good than harm has been achieved, even if the rules that produce the "stop and think" are themselves not as clear-cut as we might otherwise have hoped for.

In the final part of this book, I will tackle the question of who should be held legally liable for violations of the rules of war: for war crimes violations of international humanitarian law. Questions of criminal liability and punishment, rather than the question of moral guilt or innocence addressed throughout most of this book, raise somewhat different questions than we have yet seen. I take the view that our moral deliberations will serve us well for figuring out who should be held criminally liable and what sort of defenses we should recognize for them. But I recognize that others will find a much larger gulf between the morality of war and the legal rules of war. I have tried to address some of the worries that these theorists have expressed about the minimal natural law approach that I have championed in this book. But we can also leave that dispute aside and independently evaluate whether what I say in the following chapters about criminal liability of soldiers and commanders for violations of the rules of war is plausible.

PART D

PROSECUTING WAR CRIMES

11

Prosecuting soldiers for war crimes

We have spent most of our time so far trying to understand the normative foundations of the rules of war and of international humanitarian law. We have said very little about war crimes trials against individual defendants. The question that arises is whether individual criminal accountability can be assigned for violations of international humanitarian law. This is a serious question, indeed, for international humanitarian law, with the exception of the ICC Statute, is largely customary. And yet it is often said that mere custom is not sufficient to be the basis of a criminal proceedings, especially against someone who is not a head of state and is merely a normal soldier – or a civilian, for that matter. We will take up this issue, among others, in this chapter as we investigate what would need to be shown in order for a soldier to be criminally liable for violating the rules of war and international humanitarian law.

The controversy over the 2003–4 Abu Ghraib prison abuses brings to light the question of whether it is regular soldiers who should be primarily prosecuted for war crimes and, if so, what sort of proof of guilty intent is needed in such cases. I wish to argue that individual soldiers can indeed be held legally accountable for such things as the torture of prisoners of war, although the better case will be against the leaders who ordered or allowed such abuse to occur. Nonetheless, I will set out the case for holding minor players accountable for torture and other abuses of prisoners of war, paying special attention to the *mens rea* condition that needs to be established for successful prosecution of such cases. Of special interest is how individual *mens rea* should be related to collective criminality.

There are three main conceptual difficulties confronted in this chapter. First, how are we to think of the criminal liability of soldiers, given that they seem to lack any *mens rea*, for their main intention is to follow orders or to act in a patriotic way to do what is in the interest of their States? Second, how do we link the clearly harmful collective crimes, such as occur in prisoner of war camps, to the acts of the individual soldiers, given that the soldiers do not plan these larger crimes and often have only rudimentary knowledge of how their own isolated acts contribute to those larger harms? And third, even if the acts of soldiers can be considered criminal, why think that they should be the subject of international prosecutions? Throughout this chapter, I will discuss the case of a prison guard who tortures a detainee. Such cases illustrate what is right and what is wrong with prosecuting soldiers for violations of the principle of humane treatment.

First, I look at the recent case *Prosecutor v. Kvocka, et al.*, where Serbian camp guards were held criminally accountable for torture and other abuses of prisoners of war. Then, in Section II, I address the criminal intent element of such crimes. In Section III, I explain why individual criminal liability makes sense in such cases, especially in light of a soldier's fiduciary, or stewardship, duty not to abuse prisoners of war. In Section IV, I take up the problem of how to relate the criminal intent of the planners of a mass crime with the criminal intent of the minor players who are being prosecuted for such a crime, as well as the recent development of the idea of joint criminal liability in international law. In the final section, I discuss various objections to collective-responsibility schemes, such as joint criminal liability, and indicate the level of responsibility that I believe that minor players, as opposed to their leaders, have for torture in prisoner of war cases.

I. THE KVOCKA CASE

International criminal law is the field where prosecutions of individuals for violations of humanitarian law are most likely to occur. In this chapter, I will examine cases from the International Criminal Tribunal for the Former Yugoslavia (ICTY), of prosecution of camp guards who tortured prisoners of war. I will spend most of this section examining the case of *Prosecutor v. Kvocka, et al.*, decided on November 2, 2001.[1]

---

[1] Judgment of the Trial Chamber of the International Criminal Tribunal for the Former Yugoslavia, *Prosecutor v. Kvocka, et al.*, Case no. IT-98-30/1T, T.C. I, 2 November 2001

This is an especially interesting case because all of the defendants before the ICTY tribunal were minor players – policemen and reserve military officers – all "assigned to serve in various security or administrative positions within Omarska camp,"[2] one of the most notorious concentration camps in the Bosnian War in 1992. At least since the end of World War II, some of war's worst abuses have been found in such concentration camps, with camp guards often subsequently prosecuted for war crimes.

The Omarska camp operated for only three months during the summer of 1992.[3] Yet during this time, murder, torture, rape, and horrible abuse of prisoners was common. In the spring of 1992, Serb forces "conducted a bloodless takeover of the town of Prijedor" in the northeastern part of Bosnia Herzegovina.[4] The camp was originally organized to help suppress a rumored "armed uprising by local Muslims and Croats against the new Serb authorities" in the region.[5] By the end of the summer, camp inmates were so emaciated from poor food and the health conditions at the camp that authorities were forced to close it. But before its closure, detainees "were kept in inhuman conditions and an atmosphere of extreme mental and physical violence pervaded the camp."[6] Indeed, as the ICTY held, "an atmosphere of sweeping impunity and consuming terror prevailed. Few efforts were made to halt the beating of detainees."[7]

What made this case stand out was the sheer brutality of the conditions of the camp and how widespread the mistreatment of the camp inmates was. The Court cited the defense testimony of a physician, Dr. Slobodan Gajic, who visited the camp: Dr. Gajic said that

the "conditions were extremely bad." . . . The wounded had clearly been badly beaten. Dr. Gajic's diagnosis was that most of the injuries occurred from blows with blunt instruments "including, for example, an army boot, then the butt of a rifle, hands, fists." . . . Dr. Gajic estimated that he sent approximately 20 people to the hospital in Prijedor during the month he attended the camp. He further testified that the medical service would be called to the camp for emergencies at least once a day. The guards placed these calls to the emergency services. The vast majority of detainees, however, received no care for

---

[hereinafter, Kvocka Judgment]. In 2005, as I was finishing this draft, the ICTY Appellate Chamber handed down a decision in this case. The Appellate Court did not reverse anything from the Trial Chamber Judgment that affects my arguments.
[2] Ibid., para. 4.
[3] Ibid., para. 20. The camp operated from the end of May to the end of August, 1992.
[4] Ibid., para. 1. [5] Ibid., para. 2. [6] Ibid., para. 45. [7] Ibid., para. 43.

their wounds or ailments. . . . Dead bodies were left to fester outside for days at a time, and a terrible stench and fear pervaded the camp.[8]

Much of the abuse of prisoners was aimed at trying to get information from them.

The prisoners were regularly brought to "the administration building," where "mixed teams of investigators from the army and the state and public security services" attempted "to identify opponents of the Serb regime" in order to find "weapons and links to the Muslim opposition forces in the area."[9] Interrogations took place daily, and no one in the camp seems to have escaped interrogation. Whips and metal bars were found in the interrogation rooms. "A parade of witnesses described the terrible beatings they received during these interrogation sessions."[10] As the ICTY held, "[o]nly on rare occasions were interrogations conducted without any form of physical violence."[11]

So who were prosecuted for these crimes? Miroslav Kvocka and Mlado Radic "were professional policemen attached to the Omarska police station." Draglojub Prcac "was a retired policeman and crime technician." Two others, Milojica Kos and Zoran Zigic "were civilians, a waiter, and a taxi driver respectively, mobilized to serve as reserve officers." All five "were subsequently assigned to serve in various security or administrative positions within Omarska camp."[12] The Court ultimately convicted each of the five prison guards based on "the role he played in the functioning of the camp."[13] It is interesting that the ICTY Trial Chamber admitted that "[n]one of the accused was instrumental in establishing the camps or determining official policies practiced on detainees therein."[14]

Nonetheless, all five defendants were accused and later convicted of war crimes and held individually responsible for the atrocities at the camp.[15] They were sentenced to 5 to 25 years for their respective roles. Zigic seems to have been the lowest ranking of the group. He nonetheless received the stiffest of the sentences. Those who played more of a supervisory role received lesser sentences.[16] Because many of the

---

[8] Ibid., para. 64.
[9] Ibid., paras. 68–69.   [10] Ibid., para. 72.   [11] Ibid.   [12] Ibid., para. 4.
[13] Ibid., para. 7.   [14] Ibid., para. 4.   [15] Ibid., para. 5.
[16] Sentence of the Trial Chamber of the International Criminal Tribunal for the Former Yugoslavia, *Prosecutor v. Kvocka, et al.*, Case no. IT-98-30/1T, T.C. I, 2 November 2001. Of course, I do not know why the court chose to give the stiffest sentence to the lowest-ranking defendant. It is possible that it was because of the gravity of this defendant's offenses, although little in the record would support this conclusion.

detainees were "captured in combat or detained on the grounds of the Security Services,"[17] this case is a good recent example of individual guards prosecuted for torture and other abuses against prisoners of war. And because most of the abuse of detainees came as a result of interrogations, where "[e]veryone in the camp was interrogated at least once,"[18] this is an especially good case to consider in light of our previous discussion in Chapter 7 of the fiduciary or stewardship duties of prison guards for prisoners of war, especially during interrogation.

Early in its decision, the ICTY Trial Chamber set out a definition of torture that also provided the basis for the elements that must be proved to convict one of these guards of the international war crime of torture:

(i) Torture consists of the infliction, by act or omission of severe pain or suffering, whether physical or mental;

(ii) the act or omission must be intentional; and

(iii) the act or omission must be for a prohibited purpose, such as obtaining information or a confession, punishing, intimidating, humiliating, or coercing the victim or a third person, or discriminating, on any ground, against the victim or a third person.[19]

The Court held that State involvement was not necessary but that the victims must be protected persons, not combatants during war.[20] But the Court also seemed to say that the torture must be related to some purpose of war as part of the special intent that linked the acts of the guards to larger prohibited goals, as we will see in the next section.

II. THE *MENS REA* OF CAMP GUARDS

In this section, I will focus on the intent requirement (ii). For if, indeed, torture is to be prosecuted as an international crime, it would seem that what separates the normal crime of torture from the international crime of torture will be the intent, because the acts themselves – the beatings so as to obtain a confession, for instance – are virtually indistinguishable, whether as domestic or international crimes. For something to be a war crime, though, there must be some connection to armed conflict, and yet torture generally does not require this connection. The

[17] Kvocka Judgment, para. 17.
[18] Ibid., para. 19.   [19] Ibid., para. 141.   [20] Ibid., para. 139.

most obvious way, then, to distinguish garden variety cases of torture from international torture cases as war crimes would be to include a connection between the torture and the war effort as one of the elements of establishing *mens rea*.

It is seemingly for this reason that the Court interpreted the third torture element (iii above) as also involving a special intent requirement: namely, an intent to pursue a prohibited purpose during war. There must not only be an intent to inflict suffering, but also "a specific intent to punish detainees suspected of *participating in armed rebellion against Bosnian Serb forces* . . . [or] to obtain information or a confession . . . [or] to intimidate, humiliate, and *discriminate against non-Serb detainees*."[21] It is not at all clear from the Court's judgment that the words I have italicized are indeed meant to signal an additional intent requirement or whether they merely illustrate the specific acts of the defendants. I would suggest that the Court should list them as additional intent elements in order to mark torture as an international crime. These specific intents, seemingly, are what transform these acts of physical violence into the international crime of torture.

I do not mean to suggest that torture during war is somehow worse that garden variety torture in a domestic setting. Torture may very well be considered one of the most egregious of international crimes, but this does not mean that torture is any less wrong when committed outside of a war setting. Rather, all I am claiming here is that if torture is to be prosecuted as an international crime, rather than a domestic crime, then there must be additional elements proven to show why the international community should care about this torture.

The Court held that "in interpreting the prohibited purposes of torture, the Trial Chamber has regularly found torture existed when the perpetrator's intent was to punish or to obtain information or a confession."[22] Indeed, in the leading case to discuss torture, the Furundzija case, the Court held that the core issue was whether the individual "partakes of the purpose behind the torture (that is, acts with the intention of obtaining information or a confession)."[23] In the Furundzija case, a local commander of a group called "the Jokers" forced a female detainee to undress in his presence and threatened her

---

[21] Ibid., para. 157.   [22] Ibid., para. 154.
[23] ICTY Trial Chamber, *Prosecutor v. Furundzija*, Case No. IT-95-17/1-T, Judgment, December 10, 1998, para. 252. See the excellent commentary by William Schabas in *Annotated Leading Cases of International Criminal Tribunals*, vol. 3, edited by Andre Klip and Goran Sluiter, Antwerp: Intersentia, 2001, especially pp. 759–760.

with a knife. The accused then watched while subordinates raped her. They were trying to obtain information from her about "a list of Croatian names and the activities of her sons."[24] The Furundzija Court gives no hint that it is also looking for a connection to war in the intent of the defendant.

It is nonetheless interesting that the Furundzija Court endorsed the idea that the torture needed to be linked to the purposes of the prisoner of war camps, perhaps giving a way to link the torture to the war. The prosecution's argument, seemingly adopted by the court, was that liability of individuals in prison camp cases is based on participation in the prohibited activities. Such a "contribution does not necessarily require participation in the physical commission of the crime," but that liability "accrues where the accused is shown to have been intentionally present at a location where unlawful acts were being committed." This was sufficient to establish individual liability of the accused.[25] Furundzija did not rape the woman in question, nor did he do more than touch her with his knife, although to be sure in a very threatening manner. His individual criminal liability turns on his being present in the camp and at the site when the rapes occurred and when other physical abuse took place, at least on the prosecution's theory of the case.

The general problem is that since the 1995 Tadic Appellate Court's Decision on the Defense Motion for Interlocutory Appeal on Jurisdiction, the violation of international humanitarian law must be shown to be "serious," and the serious violation of international criminal law must be connected to "the individual criminal responsibility of the person breaching the rule."[26] Arguably, it is the prohibited purposes of the act that turn an otherwise nonserious violation into a serious one. And because the seriousness of the violation must also be linked to the *mens rea* requirement, there is a need to show that the accused perpetrator of the crime was aware that his or her act would advance the prohibited purposes and make those purposes his or her own. Proving such a connection has been very hard.

The difficulty in proving that minor players committed serious breaches of international humanitarian law and did so for prohibited purposes is that it often seems as if these minor players acted not

---

[24] Ibid., para. 40.   [25] Ibid., para. 42.
[26] ICTY Appeals Chamber, *Prosecutor v. Tadic*, Case no. IT-94-1-AR72, October 2, 1995, para. 94.

because they made the prohibited purposes their own but acted merely because they were so ordered to act. In the Furundzija case, the accused certainly understood that the actions of the others around him would have the desired, and prohibited, effect of coercing a confession or information out of the detainee and that such information would advance the war effort. But things are harder to see in the case of the camp guards in the Kvocka case. These very minor players, especially Zigic (who was punished most severely of all, even though he was the lowest in the chain of command) do not clearly intend to act in pro-hibited ways. They may know that their acts are part of a prohibited activity – the beating of the detainees to get needed information – but their intentions may only be to follow what those higher up on the chain of command have told them to do, not to advance the war effort.

In general, it is very hard to prove that an individual intentionally acted out of one set of purposes instead of another. In the case of a soldier or camp guard who tortures a detainee, it is not difficult to prove that the soldier intended to inflict serious physical or mental injury. But it is much more difficult to prove that the soldier intended to inflict injury so as to obtain needed military information as part of the war effort. For while the soldier may realize that someone else wants to get this information, it is often not the soldier's intention to get that information as a means to a military objective, as opposed to merely doing what someone else told him or her to do. Sorting out intentions and motivations, let alone proving which was primary, is a major difficulty in such prosecutions.

There are two strategies that could be pursued in light of the dif-ficulty of making the case against individual minor perpetrators. First, of course the prosecutor's office could choose to go after major rather than minor players. But this has been unsatisfying for a host of reasons. Primary among these reasons is that if we let the actual perpetrators off the hook, a message will be sent to potential perpetrators that they will be likely to be able to act with impunity. Yes, it is important to go after the major players, but it is also important to go after the minor players. The minor players will be the ones most likely to be deterred, because they have much less to gain otherwise from the prohibited action than do the major players.

The other strategy has two prongs, either showing that a minor player did have a purpose in torturing and thus advancing a military objective, or employing the theory of joint criminal liability, which we will discuss in subsequent sections of this chapter. The second prong is very controversial, but it does have the virtue of allowing for prosecution of many more minor players than would be true if one were restricted to the first prong. In either case, it is important to make it much clearer than it otherwise has been why certain actions are properly seen as international violations and hence potentially prosecuted by international criminal courts. This issue is an extremely important one, as I have argued in detail concerning crimes against humanity.[27]

We need to take quite seriously the general criticism of international law often made by U.S. politicians that international tribunals will overreach. To rebut this criticism, it is important to be able to indicate clearly what are the limits of international criminal law, and that means making it clear why certain acts are international crimes rather than being garden variety domestic crimes.[28] The first prong addresses this issue directly by requiring the showing that the minor player intended, by torturing, to advance a war aim. The second prong achieves this goal indirectly, but it also allows for bringing under the umbrella of the international crime of torture more of those minor players who are normally in the front line of such crimes.

III. CRIMINAL LIABILITY OF SOLDIERS

In previous chapters, I developed the idea that there are fiduciary or stewardship duties between guards and detainees during war, where the extreme vulnerability of the detainee calls for strict requirements on what could be done to a detainee by a guard. First among the requirements was that abuse, especially torture, by guards of detainees was simply unacceptable, even to gain needed information. This analysis tracks rather well with the holding of the Israeli Supreme Court addressed in the previous chapter. In the current section, I will explore in greater detail why individual soldiers should be held criminally liable for breaches of their fiduciary or stewardship duties and also begin to explain why the international community should care about such breaches.

---

[27] Larry May, *Crimes Against Humanity: A Normative Account*, Cambridge: Cambridge University Press, 2005.

[28] See the remarks by John Shattuck, former Assistant Secretary of State for Democracy, Human Rights and Labor, in an interview with the Center for American Progress about American Exceptionalism (July 24, 2004), http://www.americanprogress.org/site/pp.asp?c=biJRJ8OVF&b=130841.

When soldiers take on the role of prison guard or interrogator, they assume a fiduciary or stewardship duty for the detainee who is under their care. Even if they have been ordered to perform this role and there is a legitimate chain of command that has been followed in the issuing of those orders, soldiers still have duties toward the detainees. Any violations of these duties certainly open up the possibility of prosecution of this soldier, especially when the violation of the fiduciary or stewardship duty results in harm to the detainee. Of course, for criminal liability to be assigned, there must have been a statute that enshrined the duty or proscribed torture and other forms of harm committed by soldiers toward detainees. We will have to consider quite seriously various defenses, such as superior orders and duress, which will be taken up in Chapter 13. The idea that soldiers could be held criminally liable for abusing detainees, such as by torturing them, is certainly not a far-fetched idea. What causes difficulties is the idea that such soldiers could be held criminally liable for violating *international* law, as we will see in this section.

When individual soldiers, especially as minor actors, engage in torture of prisoners of war, there is a significant skeptical question that must be addressed squarely: Why is the international community the entity that should prosecute such individuals? To answer this question, there must be a good reason offered for not focusing merely on the leaders who have transformed these individual acts into a mass crime. There must be a way to characterize the crime that has consequences far-reaching enough to make the international community the appropriate forum and also the forum interested in prosecuting that crime. One clear way to meet this challenge is to show that there was a kind of criminal conspiracy in which many people participated at different levels, but where each of the individual participants did things that were enough wrong so as to make the international criminality of his or her acts transparent. The camp guards may well have violated their duties as prison guards, but we still need to know why such violations are also violations of international criminal law.

If we are talking of crimes like persecution or genocide, there are normally so many people affected and such a far-reaching plan is needed to accomplish this crime that one can begin to see why the international community would be interested in prosecuting these cases. The crime often affects humanity by its sheer scale and by the systematic involvement of a State, or State-like, actor. Torture appears to be different because it is committed by one individual person upon another individual person, often without State involvement. While there may be far-reaching consequences of some acts of torture, there is nothing about torture per se that would make it likely to be widespread in its reach. In my book *Crimes Against Humanity*, I raised the question of whether torture should be seen as an international crime since it seems to be so isolated.[29]

One way to answer such a challenge is to point out that the definition of torture as an international humanitarian crime requires that the infliction of severe pain or suffering be done for only certain prohibited purposes. Let us look again at each of the prohibited purposes listed in the ICTY Trial Chamber's definition of torture in the Kvocka Case:

1. obtaining information or a confession;
2. punishing;
3. intimidating, humiliating, or coercing the victim or a third person; or
4. discriminating, on any ground, against the victim or a third person.[30]

As noted earlier, the ICTY Trial Chamber decided not to add the additional dimension from human rights law that there must be a State actor involved. For this reason, it is crucial that something about the prohibited purposes distinguish torture as an international crime from the garden-variety domestic crime of torture. And yet, the purposes listed above do not seem to accomplish this task. Each of the purposes could have been pursued by solitary individuals acting against other solitary individuals without any special interest on the part of the international community.

The first three categories could easily encompass quite isolated behavior. While obtaining information could be for some larger goal, as is also true of punishing or coercing, there is no reason why these purposes could not be isolated from anyone other than the perpetrator of the torture, as we can see in cases of sadistic individuals throughout history who have tortured their victims. In the final category of purposes, there is a hint of larger group involvement, because the purpose addresses discrimination, which would normally involve group-based treatment. But even in this category, the phrase "on any ground" opens things up to such a broad range of discriminations that it is

---

[29] Larry May, *Crimes Against Humanity*. [30] Kvocka Judgment, para. 141.

unclear what would be the international interest in all those forms of torture.

The violation of fiduciary or stewardship duties that results when soldiers torture prisoners of war does not display what would make such torture into a crime that should be prosecuted internationally. Violating such a duty is normally thought to be a nearly paradigmatic domestic crime. For fiduciary or stewardship relationships are normally quite "personal" in that they are defined by the status of the parties. These relationships are primarily ones of trust and vulnerability, definitive of how individual humans respond to one another – one by one, as it were. International crimes are normally characterized as crimes that in some sense affect humanity, or at least some significant part of the international community. It is thus hard to see torture as the kind of crime that should be prosecuted internationally.

But humanity comes in various shapes and sizes, as do crimes that affect it. One of the salient difference between crimes against humanity and war crimes is that war crimes have not been thought to be literally or figuratively crimes that *assault* humanity. Crimes against humanity are supposed to assault a population and thereby, arguably, to assault humanity. As I have argued, war crimes are crimes against humaneness. They must be linked to an armed conflict, whether international or internal, and during such armed conflicts the principle of humane treatment applies. So, for instance, it is thought to be inhumane to use weapons that cause superfluous suffering. Causing superfluous suffering is inhumane, it assaults the principle of humane treatment, which is the cornerstone of international humanitarian law. But it is unclear that this means that the international community has more of an interest when torture occurs in armed conflict than when not.

And here is the idea that may allow us to make progress on why torture could be seen conceptually as an international crime. During war, there is already international instability. This is often true even when we are only in the midst of internal armed conflict, for revolutions and struggles for secession are just as destabilizing as traditional wars between sovereign States are.[31] And when fiduciary violations

---

[31] As Leslie C. Green has said, "[S]ince 1945 it has become obvious that many or most of the conflicts that had occurred or were likely in the foreseeable future were not international conflicts in the normal inter-state sense, but rebellions, revolutions or struggles for national independence." See his essay "International Regulation of Armed Conflicts," in *International Criminal Law, vol. I: Crimes*, edited by M. Cherif Bassiouni, Ardsley, NY: Transnational Publishers, 1999, p. 371.

occur during war, there is already prima facie inhumanity, for the laws of war are meant to try to make wars not as much an assault on humanity as they would normally be, in addition to the prima facie wrongness of the violation of trust. Inhumanity is about lack of mercy and compassion toward those who are vulnerable. During wars, the international community has a special interest in humane treatment that may not exist when we are not in the midst of war or other armed conflicts.

In my view, the idea that there are fiduciary or stewardship duties when one person is superior to someone else who is utterly dependent on him or her is grounded in the principle of humane treatment. And for the principle of humane treatment to be the cornerstone of international humanitarian law, there must be a way to hold individuals liable for violations of this principle. The most obvious way for this to occur is for prosecutions to be authorized when violations of the principle of humane treatment occur. But there must nonetheless be some way to link the isolated act of torture, for instance, to the larger war effort. In the next section, we examine the strategy recently developed at the ICTY of establishing the international nature of the crime by establishing that there is a link between what the individual soldier did and what others who were pursuing war objectives did.

IV. JOINT CRIMINAL LIABILITY

In the Kvocka case, much of the Trial Chamber's Judgment is taken up with the analysis of what the prosecution called "the joint criminal enterprise theory."[32] While this is not as clear as one would like, it seems to me that the reason that the prosecution and the Court took up this theory has to do with the fact that the defendants in this case were fairly minor players – some of whom did terrible things, and others of whom could have stopped them – none of whom established the camps or in the larger scheme of things instigated the abusive treatment that occurred therein. While minor players clearly did conduct some of the abuse, it is difficult to show that they had the requisite *mens rea* requirements for international humanitarian law violations. Regardless of what the court was doing, I argue that this is what it conceptually and normatively should have been doing: trying to link the acts of the individual defendants to a larger plan that could

---

[32] Kvocka case, paras. 265ff.

cross the threshold into being the kind of crime that the international community should concern itself with and for which the ICTY should prosecute individuals in the name of that international community.[33]

The Court cites the ICTY Appeals Chamber in the Tadic case as establishing the following elements of joint criminal enterprise liability:

1. a plurality of persons;
2. the existence of a common plan, which amounts to or involves the commission of a crime provided for in the Statute; . . .
3. participation of the accused in the execution of the common plan.[34]

In concentration camp cases, the Court held that the joint criminal enterprise liability theory was especially apt in establishing criminal participation on the part of camp guards "in a detention facility which operates as a joint criminal enterprise."[35] For those who were, in the words of the Court, "co-perpetrators" as well as aiders or abettors, the theory of joint criminal enterprise can play a significant role in individual prosecutions in establishing the *mens rea* of individuals in camp cases.

While it is far from clear in the opinion, it does seem that the court agrees with the prosecution that for individuals who did not establish or plan the concentration camps, establishing "violations of international law" was made easier if it could be shown that the defendants were "participating in the common plan."[36] Indeed, the Court cited a case from the Nuremberg Tribunals where individuals were successfully prosecuted under this theory even though their "participation" in a common plan was conducted "under duress."[37] For it is much easier to show that minor players intended to participate in a common plan than that they intended to pursue the specific purposes of that plan. Even if one is merely following orders under duress, if an order is to follow a plan, then it is not unreasonable to say that one intends to follow the plan. But once we ask about one's intention to follow the

---

[33] For criticisms of the joint criminal enterprise theory, see Mark Drumbl, "Sands: From Nuremberg to The Hague: The Future of International Criminal Justice," *Michigan Law Review*, vol. 103, no. 6, (2005), pp. 1305–1311; and Mark Osiel, "Shared Responsibility for Mass Atrocity: Aligning the Incentives," unpublished manuscript.

[34] Kvocka case, para. 266.   [35] Ibid., para 268.   [36] Ibid., para. 304.

[37] Ibid., citing Trial of Alons Klein and Six Others, U.S. Military Commission Appointed by the Commanding General, Western Military District, USFFT, Wiesbaden, Germany, 8–15 October, 1945, UNWCC, vol. 1, p. 49.

details of a plan, it is very unclear that there is an intention to accomplish those particular purposes.

In a significant admission, the Court recognized that "during periods of war or mass violence, the threshold required to impute criminal responsibility to a mid- or low-level participant in a joint criminal enterprise as an aider and abettor or co-perpetrator of such a joint criminal enterprise requires a more substantial level of participation than simply following orders to perform some low-level function in the criminal endeavor on a single occasion."[38] In addition to following orders, one must also be aware that the orders are linked to a plan and that the plan involves a prohibited purpose in the case of torture prosecutions. I would add that more than merely following orders of others is needed in order to establish *mens rea* of an international crime in such cases and that the joint enterprise liability can be a key consideration in linking the acts of minor players to the commission of an international crime at all.

The problem is that for the individual to intend that his or her act advanced a prohibited purpose, he or she would normally have to know quite a bit about and intend to advance these prohibited purposes. This is a very difficult standard to meet, not merely because low-ranking individuals do not normally commit lots of abusive acts, but mainly because they do not know about or intend that those acts be for certain prohibited purposes. Normally, it is the leaders not the low-ranking individuals who have knowledge about or intention to advance, those prohibited purposes. Both the prosecution and the Court in the Kvocka case seem to accept the idea that in camp cases conviction of minor players for the international crime of torture will be easier if it can be shown that the camp "functioned as a joint criminal enterprise." For then, individual prosecutions will only have to show that the defendant, as in a conspiracy case, was merely aware that he or she was indeed participating in such a joint enterprise. Increasingly, the ICTY prosecutor's office has relied on the theory of joint criminal liability, especially when we are looking at fairly minor players.

William Schabas has raised a set of objections to the increasing use of the theory of joint criminal liability, especially in cases like the Kvocka case. He points out that "in the case of secondary offenders or accomplices, the acts of assistance are often quite ambiguous, and it is

---

[38] Kvocka case, para. 311.

not as easy simply to presume the guilty mind from the physical act."[39] Schabas rightly says that the joint criminal liability theory is being increasingly relied on so that the accused can be convicted "not only for the crimes that he or she actually committed, with intent, but for those committed by others that he or she did not specifically intend but that were a natural or foreseeable consequence of executing the crime that formed part of the collective or common purpose of the enterprise."[40] This weakens the generally recognized requirement that criminal liability should only fall on those who had a guilty mind. Making the case rhetorically, Schabas says: "It is just a bit like the famous prosecution of gangster Al Capone, who was sent to Alcatraz for tax evasion, with a wink and a nod, because federal prosecutors couldn't make proof of murder."[41]

For Schabas, " 'joint criminal liability' . . . has become the magic bullet of the Office of the Prosecutor."[42] Schabas's main worry is that individual liability is being undermined and in its place is being substituted "collective responsibility."[43] Because I hold a much more complex view of collective responsibility than Schabas does, I would not make the same kind of charge, although I would agree with him that there is a significant worry that the Office of the Prosecutor could be leading us toward "guilt by association" and away from bedrock principles of individual guilt in criminal prosecutions.[44] As long as we keep the general subject of collective responsibility – which can have various positive formulations, as in conspiracy law – conceptually distinct from the normally unjustified "guilt by association," I would follow Schabas in expressing worries about the diminution of individual guilt in a international prosecutor's use of the joint criminal liability theory.

Nonetheless, I think there are various positive reasons to explore joint criminal liability theory in international humanitarian law. For camp guards to recognize that they have fiduciary or stewardship obligations to the detainees in a camp, there must be some recognition that the camp functions as more than merely a random collection and distribution center. In addition, the camp guards must also come to see

---

[39] William A. Schabas, "Mens Rea and the International Criminal Tribunal for the Former Yugoslavia," *New England Law Review*, vol. 37, Summer (2003), p. 1019.
[40] Ibid., p. 1031. [41] Ibid., p. 1034. [42] Ibid., p. 1032. [43] Ibid., p. 1035.
[44] My views on collective responsibility have been set out in several previous books, most significantly for the current discussion in *The Morality of Groups*, Notre Dame, IN: University of Notre Dame Press, 1987.

that there are common, and criminal, purposes being advanced by the camp in which they work, in order for these guards to incur international criminal liability. This is the view that I will try to support in the next section. If international humanitarian law can justifiably prosecute individuals who are not "State actors" for war crimes – unlike human rights law, which requires that torturers be State actors – humanitarian law must face the significant conceptual and moral questions of why individual acts of abuse or torture rise to the level of *international* crimes.[45] This is especially important so that we do not engage in mere guilt by association and so that we show respect for the situation of the soldier or other minor player who often is placed into a situation where it is hard not to participate in events that are totally outside the orbit of control of that soldier.

V.   COLLECTIVE LIABILITY AND INTERNATIONAL CRIME

Many people confuse collective responsibility with guilt by association. I suppose it could plausibly be argued that guilt by association is indeed one form of collective responsibility, namely, a form of responsibility in which anyone who is a member of group, by virtue of merely having an association with the group, is held personally and indiscriminately liable for what is done in the group's name. For example, if a State's leader says that he will hold all of the members of a town responsible for the killing of one of his soldiers in that town, we are repulsed by the very idea. For it is normally the case that many people who are members of a town have nothing to do with what goes on in the town and couldn't have prevented what goes on. Therefore, to hold each member personally responsible for what he or she did not do and could not have prevented seems to be a caricature of responsibility ascriptions. Such forms of collective responsibility give responsibility itself a bad name.[46]

It is useful to set out what is abhorrent in guilt by association schemes of responsibility ascription in order to see how it might be that some other forms of collective responsibility might be justified. First, there is the problem of holding individuals personally responsible for what is done by a collectivity. This looks like a simple category mistake.

---

[45] See Kvocka case, para.138, for a brief discussion of this difference.
[46] See Hannah Arendt's 1968 essay "Collective Responsibility," reprinted in Hannah Arendt, *Responsibility and Judgment*, edited by Jerome Kohn, New York: Schocken Books, 2003, pp. 147–158.

If a collectivity acts, then it is the collectivity (not yet any of its members) that should be held responsible. If the collectivity is so loosely structured that it is really nothing more than the sum of its members, then there is a strong practical reason to treat the collectivity as if it were nothing more than a bunch of individuals personally acting. But this would also be a serious mistake. For if there is any sense to assigning the *action* to the collectivity, then there should also be a basis for assigning the *responsibility* to the collectivity as well. In any event, even if one finds it necessary to assign responsibility to individuals, there is no reason to think that this should be personal individual responsibility instead of role-based individual responsibility. Of course, individuals can be prosecuted as soldiers, but we need then to think hard about what we expect of those in that role. Taking care with such fine distinctions would obviate most counterintuitive aspects of some forms of collective responsibility.

A second problem is that collective responsibility of the guilt by association form tends to ignore important individual differences among members of collectivities. Most collectivities have leaders and followers; indeed, most collectivities have members who are completely silent or inactive concerning many of the group's activities. At the very least, such differences need to be taken into account when we move from collective action to individual responsibility. Guilt by association makes membership the only relevant moral concern, which unjustifiably diminishes the very important moral considerations of what role particular members played, if any, in terms of commission or omission in the collective action. When we come, if we do, to distribute individual shares of responsibility for what a collectivity has done, it seems counterintuitive to ignore what each of the members actually did or did not do. Again, taking care to match individual shares of responsibility to what each member of a collectivity did obviates this glaring problem. Perhaps the best way to take this into account is to give to those who played minor roles more possible defenses or ways to mitigate punishment than those who performed major roles.

Third, there is the charge of unfairness in that guilt by association schemes tend to "punish" all members of a group in the same indiscriminate way. Even if all members did in fact play a role in the collectivity's action, it is rare for each member to play the same role or to bear the same guilt for what the group has done. But of course one does not have to distribute responsibility in such an indiscriminate manner. One could assign individual shares of responsibility, or guilt, based on what role the individual member played rather than merely on the fact of one's membership. Such a basis of responsibility ascription is not "personal" but is still group-based because the role is best understood in terms of the relation between the individual and the group rather than a characteristic of the individual standing alone. This is what can be done when trials focus on both the joint enterprise and on what each individual did and intended to do.

The above considerations point toward a model of how collective responsibility could be understood that does not fall prey to the obvious problems of guilt by association. Membership is important as one factor in determining whether a person played a role in a collective action, but one also needs to consider what specifically a person did or did not do. To avoid the most pernicious aspects of guilt by association schemes, we need to make membership only one of several factors that are considered morally relevant in assigning individual responsibility. As long as collective-responsibility schemes do not try to set out how to distribute responsibility to individuals, or do not do so based on membership alone, then it will be possible to have a putatively acceptable form of collective responsibility. This is the optimal way for us to think of joint criminal liability, for we should resist the idea that individual members bear any individual responsibility for what the group did based merely on group membership. Rather, there has to be something that the individuals intended to do that counts as participating in what the group was intending to do so that we can talk about the individual's intentions and acts linked to those of the group.

It is at this stage that one might want to revisit the idea of a joint criminal enterprise that often characterizes the pattern of abuse that occurs in prisoner of war camps. Surely, it is easy to see that the infliction of suffering one on one, as it were, is quite different from the infliction of the same kind of suffering that is part of a larger enterprise and organized for a particular political objective. When there is a joint enterprise such as a concentration camp or a series of camps, and when the aim of having the camp, or camps, is to intimidate a group of people or achieve some other war aim, then we are now much more clearly into a parallel situation to that experienced in the arena of crimes against humanity, when we look to see whether the individual assaults are all part of a plan that is widespread or systematic.

Once prisoner camps have been established and individuals are given roles that involve or allow for serious abuse of the detainees, a kind of conspiracy has been established. We must be very careful to pay

attention to what specific individuals do, not holding them responsible
for what others do unless there is a true melding of individual acts into
a common enterprise. In subsequent chapters, this issue will continue
to be quite prominent. Leaders will be easier to prosecute according to
the theory of joint enterprise liability because it is normally so much
clearer that they join in such an enterprise by what they do. For
individual soldiers, what counts as being a member of the joint
enterprise will be harder to prove, because in many cases the soldiers
are merely following orders rather than intentionally choosing to join
any kind of criminal venture. We must avoid what Schabas calls the
"wink and a nod" theory, where we do not really have evidence of
international criminal activity on the part of soldiers but we try to use
joint enterprise theory to prosecute them anyway. Such an abuse will
open up the charge of guilt by association, rather than allowing joint
enterprise liability to be an acceptable form of collective responsibility.

In general, wars or other armed conflicts intensify the interest that
the international community has in what would otherwise be private
wrongs, or at least wrongs that are best solved by domestic adjudica-
tion. Soldiers and other minor players who torture people or otherwise
violate the laws of war can legitimately be prosecuted in international
courts, but normally only when they have been part of a larger
enterprise aimed at advancing the objectives of a war. It isn't merely
that it is easier to prove *mens rea* when individual solders participate in
such enterprises. It is also because the joint enterprises that are most
evident in prisoner of war camps make it much more likely that the
abuses that occur are ones that affect the international community. For
the creation of prisoner of war camps is normally aimed at a particular
purpose, and that purpose is the kind of thing that is often seen to be a
destabilizing part of the war or other armed conflict.

Creating prisoner of war camps is normally creating a very risky
environment for potential abuse. When a soldier abuses a prisoner, a
fiduciary or stewardship duty has indeed been violated. But when a
prisoner of war camp is established, then the likelihood and extent of
abuse is much greater. Whenever there is the potential for systematic,
serious inhumaneness in a situation, then that situation is open to
legitimate intervention by the international community. This is
because inhumane treatment systematically accomplished on a large
scale undermines whatever hope there was of containing violence so
that the rest of the world is not ultimately dragged into it. Inhumane
treatment is always wrong, but it is especially apt for international

prosecution in such times as when it is specifically linked to a war or other armed conflict and the abuse is widespread or systematic. In the next section, we will see that it is even more appropriate to prosecute the leaders than the individual soldiers or other minor players when abuses like torture take place during times of armed conflict. But I hope to have shown that it is sometimes not unreasonable to prosecute minor players for torture and other inhumane acts during wartime.

Prosecuting military leaders for war crimes

In the previous chapter, I argued that soldiers can be held individually responsible for violating international humanitarian law, but I believe that leaders should be the primary targets of international prosecution for war crimes. While soldiers can be held individually responsible for violating international humanitarian law, normally it should be difficult to do so unless there was a joint criminal enterprise. Even in such cases, the *mens rea* component of criminal liability will be difficult to prove. It is the leaders rather than the normal soldiers who more often display the kind of *mens rea* that is looked for in criminal cases. When we come to consider the criminal responsibility of the leaders, there are two conceptual problems nonetheless. In this chapter, I argue that military (and political) leaders should normally be those who are prosecuted for war crimes. In so arguing, I will offer solutions to two main conceptual problems with such prosecutions.

The first conceptual problem concerns how difficult it often is to establish the *actus reus* component of criminal liability, for it is normal soldiers rather than the commanders who actually do the killing of civilians or torturing of prisoners, for instance. The two strategies normally employed for solving the *actus reus* problem correspond to the two main provisions on criminal liability of the ICTY Statute. First, issuing orders to do the killing, torturing, etc., is itself a criminal act that directly links the commander to the normal soldier. Second, failing to prevent soldiers from doing what it was known that they were doing or would do is a failure to act that also could link the commander to the acts of the normal soldier. The second conceptual problem concerns the *mens rea* component especially when we are discussing leaders who did not themselves intentionally plan the larger criminal enterprise. The questions concern whether having knowledge is sufficient and whether negligence can be seen as sufficiently grave to warrant individual criminal liability for violations of international humanitarian law. I will focus mainly on the *mens rea* issues.

I believe that it is *mens rea* that should be key in war crimes prosecutions, and thus it is the leaders not the minor players who should be the primary subjects of prosecution for international crimes. I will also discuss some serious difficulties in determining the level of *mens rea* that needs to be proved in order to convict political and military leaders for international crimes. In this respect, I will focus on cases where the claim is that leaders commanded that these crimes occur. I will not consider the somewhat easier cases concerning the criminal liability of leaders for the lesser crimes of aiding or abetting a crime. The particular case that I will focus on is that of the prosecution of General Tihomir Blaskic, the commander of the Croatian Defense Council. Blaskic was prosecuted for his part in the mass crimes committed against Muslims in Bosnia, especially for inhumane treatment in the taking of hostages and the use of human shields, from 1993–4.

In Section I, I will set out the key facts of the case and the basis of the ICTY Trial Chamber's conviction of General Blaskic. In Section II, I will set out the basis of the ICTY Appeals Court's overruling of the Trial Chamber's decision. In Section III, I will focus on the issue of *mens rea* concerning those who commanded others to do such crimes as the taking of hostages and the use of human shields. In Section IV, I will set out a limited argument in favor of negligence as a type of *mens rea* in international criminal law. And finally, in Section V, I discuss the relevance of the idea of the theory of joint criminal liability (discussed in the previous chapter), in such cases. Throughout, while arguing in favor of holding leaders responsible for international crimes, I worry quite a bit about what would be a fair standard of *mens rea* for these leaders.

I. THE CASE AGAINST GENERAL BLASKIC

General Tihomir Blaskic was one of the few non-Serbs to be prosecuted for war crimes by the International Criminal Tribunal for the Former Yugoslavia. Blaskic

was appointed commander of the HVO [the Croatian Defense Council] armed forces headquarters in central Bosnia on June 27, 1992 and occupied that position throughout the period covered by the indictment. In this position and pursuant to Article 7(1) of the Statute, he was accused of having, in concert with members of the HVO, planned, instigated, ordered or otherwise aided and abetted in the planning, preparation or execution of each of the crimes alleged . . . . and that he had not taken the necessary and reasonable measures to prevent the said crimes.[1]

Among the crimes that Blaskic was accused of participating in were persecution, unlawful attacks upon civilians and civilian objects, willful killing and serious bodily injury, destruction and plunder of property, destruction of institutions dedicated to religion or education, inhumane treatment, taking of hostages, and use of human shields.[2]

The Trial Chamber of the ICTY notes that the Blaskic prosecution concerned "the criminal responsibility of a military commander."[3] Involved in this prosecution were two related forms of individual responsibility. The first was the planning, instigating, ordering, or aiding and abetting of a crime. This is covered under Article 7(1) of the Statute of the ICTY and is not necessarily restricted to "persons who directly commit the crimes in question."[4] Blaskic was not accused of having committed the *actus reus* of any of the crimes just mentioned. Rather he was prosecuted for having ordered, planned, or instigated the acts of others who directly committed the crimes in question. It is interesting that the Trial Chamber commented that to be convicted of ordering, the "order does not need to be given in writing or in any particular form," or that the "order be given by the superior directly" to the person who performs the *actus reus*.[5]

Second, Blaskic was accused, in the alternative, of having known that crimes were about to be committed, or had been committed, by a subordinate, and he had failed to take the necessary steps to prevent, or punish, the commission of the crime.[6] This is covered under Article 7(3) of the ICTY Statute. The Trial Chamber then went on to list the proof that was necessary:

1. there existed a superior-subordinate relationship between the commander (the accused) and the perpetrator of the crime;
2. the accused knew or had reason to know that the crime was about to be committed or had been committed; and

---

[1] *Prosecutor v. Tihomir Blaskic*, Judgment of the Trial Chamber of the ICTY, March 3, 2000, para. 9.

[2] Ibid., paras. 10–16.   [3] Ibid., para. 261.   [4] Ibid., para. 263.

[5] Ibid., paras. 281–282.   [6] Ibid., para. 289.

3. the accused failed to take the necessary and reasonable measures to prevent the crime or punish the perpetrator thereof.[7]

The Trial Chamber also held that "the commander need not have any legal authority to prevent or punish acts of his subordinates. What counts is his material ability, which, instead of issuing orders or taking disciplinary action, may entail, for instance, submitting reports to the competent authorities in order for measures to be taken."[8]

One of the key factual findings of the Trial Chamber was that Blaskic ordered an offensive against Loncari and Ocehnici, directly implicating him in the "cleansing" of these areas.[9] The Trial Chamber also found that when Blaskic gave these orders "he knew full well that there were criminals in its ranks, [and] the accused [Blaskic] intentionally took the risk that very violent crimes would result from their participation in the offensive."[10] In addition, to choose just one of the crimes, the Trial Chamber also found that General Blaskic "ran the risk that many detainees might be taken hostage"[11] and that "[he] ordered civilians from Gaćice village to be used as human shields in order to protect his headquarters."[12] Thus, Blaskic was found either to have ordered many of the atrocities or in the alternative to have run the risk that they might occur and then failed to prevent them.

The Final Conclusions section of the opinion was unusually harsh. The Trial Chamber accused Blaskic of having given "genuine attack orders" to kill civilians and to slaughter livestock and destroy mosques.[13] The court concluded:

At no time did he even take the most basic measure which any commander must at least take when he knows that crimes are about to be or have actually been committed. The end result of such an attitude was not only the scale of the crimes, but also the realization of the Croatian nationalists' goals – the forced departure of the majority of the Muslim population in the Lasva Valley after the death and wounding of its members, the destruction of its dwellings, the plunder of its property, and the cruel and inhuman treatment meted out to many.[14]

For these reasons, the Court, by majority vote, convicted Blaskic and sentenced him to 45 years in prison, certainly one of the stiffest penalties ever meted out by the ICTY.[15]

---

[7] Ibid., para. 294.   [8] Ibid., para. 302.   [9] Ibid., para. 590.   [10] Ibid., para. 592.
[11] Ibid., para. 741.   [12] Ibid., para. 743.   [13] Ibid., paras. 749–750.
[14] Ibid., para. 754.
[15] Ibid., disposition following para. 802. A life sentence is actually the stiffest punishment, but given that Blaskic was in his late thirties when the alleged crimes were committed, he would face the equivalent of a life sentence.

One of the most interesting aspects of this case is the way that the Court tried to prove that orders were given as a way of substantiating Blaskic's individual responsibility under Article 7(1) of the ICTY Statute and the way that it established the riskiness of his behavior in not intervening when he could have as a way of substantiating his individual responsibility under Article 7(3) of the Statute. In both cases, the Court drew inferences from a somewhat spotty evidentiary record. As in many cases that go before international and domestic criminal tribunals, courts look for what is beyond a reasonable doubt, but not what is certain. It is thus very interesting that, as we will see in the next section, the Appellate Court's reversal was also unusually harsh.

General Blaskic, as a commander of Croat national forces, clearly had a duty to exercise care in the way that he issued orders. But the question becomes whether he should be held criminally liable for not exercising *extraordinary* care. I am inclined to agree with the Trial Chamber that we should hold commanders to a very high standard. Especially when they know that there are miscreants under their command, commanders must be extraordinarily vigilant not to let these potential criminals engage in abuses or atrocities, which have been so common over the centuries when ethnic wars were being fought. With only a bit of hindsight, it also seems reasonable to hold people responsible for what are the obvious problems that result from attempts at ethnic cleansing.

In terms of war crimes, the command structure should not be something that military leaders can hide behind, for it is hard to prove that a general order is interpreted in just one way by others down the line. Then the very difficult problem becomes that of deciding what standard of *mens rea* to use in such commander cases. Everyone agrees that strict liability is not sufficient for criminal liability in such cases, that it is not enough merely to show that a general was indeed the commander at the time. At the very least, it must also be shown that the general had knowledge of the likelihood of a massacre occurring. But at various points, the Trial Chamber seems to signal that actual knowledge or intent is not required, only a certain kind of negligence on the part of the general. However, as we will see in the next section, it is highly controversial to use a negligence standard of *mens rea* in criminal law and even more controversial about how to understand that standard. It seems to be not enough to seek a conviction on the ground that reasonable people would have seen the possibility that harms could result from the issuing of various orders, but too much to require that it be certain that such harms would result. We will see that the Appeals Chamber took issue with the Trial Chamber on just such grounds, ultimately reversing the conviction of General Blaskic.

II. BLASKIC'S APPEAL

In 2004, the ICTY Appeals Chamber surprisingly ruled that the Trial Chamber in the Blaskic case had made very serious mistakes in law. Based on newly discovered evidence, it voted to exonerate Blaskic from most charges and released him based on the eight years he had already served in prison. The main alleged mistake of law that caused this reversal concerned the *mens rea* component of individual liability for leaders who participate in war crimes. Before addressing the important ruling of the Appeals Chamber on negligence as *mens rea*, I first want to say something about the *actus reus* issue, that is, whether there was sufficient reason to think that Blaskic's behavior constituted unjustified ordering of the acts that the soldiers under Blaskic's command subsequently committed.

The Trial Chamber drew the inference that because the towns in question, especially Ahmići, had no significant military significance, attacking the towns was not based on a military objective. While the Appeals Chamber seemed to agree with this assessment, it nonetheless declared that

The Trial Chamber gave no significant weight to the argument that the road linking Busovača and Travnik had strategic significance, and with respect to the fact that AbiH [Muslim] soldiers were reported to be traveling toward Vitez . . . additional evidence submitted on appeal shows that there was a Muslim military presence in Ahmići and the neighboring villages, and that Appellant had reason to believe that the AbiH intended to launch an attack along the Ahmići-Santici-Dubravica axis.[16]

Thus, the Appeals Chamber concluded that the Trial Chamber misinterpreted the order to attack that General Blaskic gave. Evidence of the imminent Muslim attack and that individuals other than Blaskic gave the order to attack makes Blaskic harder to link to an *actus reus*

---

[16] *Prosecutor v. Tihomir Blaskic*, Appeals Chamber Judgment, Case no. IT-95-14-A, July 29, 2004, paras. 331, 333. For a very insightful commentary, see Mark A. Drumbl, "ICTY Appeals Chamber Delivers Two Major Judgments: *Blakic* and *Krstic*," *ASIL Insights*, August 18, 2004.

and casts reasonable doubt, that a judge could have determined, that Blaskic was criminally culpable in this case.

More important conceptually is the Appeals Chamber's ruling concerning Blaskic's *mens rea*, especially whether he was aware that civilians would be killed during the attack on Ahmići. Even if Blaskic did give various orders, the question is: What was his state of mind in so acting? Here is how the Court characterized the relevant *mens rea* standard:

In the absence of direct intent . . . a person who orders an act or omission with the awareness of the substantial likelihood that a crime will be committed in the execution of that order, has the requisite *mens rea* for establishing responsibility under Article 7(1) pursuant to ordering. Ordering with such awareness has to be regarded as accepting that crime.[17]

The Appeals Court reversed the judgment of the Trial Chamber and held that the orders "at most, [are] sufficient to demonstrate the Appellant's knowledge of the mere possibility that crimes could be committed by some elements" but not "a substantial likelihood that crimes would be committed in the execution of" the order.[18]

As noted earlier, there are two ways to establish the *mens rea* component of criminal liability of leaders under the ICTY Statute. The first way, which was addressed in the previous paragraph under the rubric of Article 7(1) of the ICTY Statute, concerns whether a commander gave orders that were known to create a substantial likelihood that a crime would be committed. The second way, under Article 7(3) of the Statute, concerns whether reasonable steps were taken to prevent crimes that the commander had reason to know were being committed, or would be committed, by those who were under his or her control. In this second respect, the Appeals Chamber initially agreed that Blaskic had effective control over the military personnel who committed crimes against civilians. But the Appeals Chamber disagreed with the Trial Chamber in the analysis of what it means to say that Blaskic "had reason to know" that crimes were being or would be committed.

In the Appeals Chamber Judgment, substantial time was spent explaining what it means for a commander to have "reason to know" that a crime would be committed that could be prevented. The Trial Chamber addressed this issue in terms of negligence, which the Appeals Chamber agreed is "likely to lead to confusion of thought."[19]

---

[17] Ibid., para. 345.　　[18] Ibid., para. 347.　　[19] Ibid., para. 63.

Indeed, the Appeals Chamber remarked that the International Criminal Tribunal for Rwanda (hereinafter, ICTR) "Appeals Chamber has on a previous occasion rejected criminal negligence as a basis of liability in the context of command responsibility."[20] So in rejecting a negligence standard of *mens rea*, the ICTY Appeals Chamber turned to the jurisprudence concerning the idea of "had reason to know" as a standard of *mens rea* for commanders.

The Appeals Chamber adopted the view of the ICTY's Celebici Appeals Chamber that commanders have a duty to be informed of the behavior of their subordinates, but that it cannot merely be assumed that they had been so informed simply because they occupied a superior position of authority.

The Celebici Appeal Judgment has settled the issue of the interpretation of the standard "had reason to know." In that judgment, the Appeals Chamber stated that "a superior will be criminally responsible through the principles of superior responsibility only if information was available to him which would have put him on notice of offenses committed by subordinates." Further, the Appeals Chamber stated that "(n)eglect of a duty to acquire such knowledge, however, does not feature in the provision of Article 7(3) (as a separate offense) and a superior is not therefore liable under the provision for such failures but only for failing to take necessary and reasonable measures to prevent or to punish."[21]

Thus, the Appeals Chamber endorsed the Appellant's claim that actual knowledge must be proved, not merely a showing of possible knowledge that a reasonable person should have obtained. The criminal liability of a commander requires proof that the commander had actual knowledge of what the subordinates were doing, not mere negligence that the superior should have had such information. As the Court said, the "had reason to know" *mens rea* standard does not reduce to a "should have known" standard.[22]

The Appeals Chamber thus reached the judgment that General Blaskic was not liable for the criminal acts of those under his control. The Appeals Chamber held that Blaskic did not have knowledge of what his soldiers were doing. In addition, the Appeals Chamber concluded that "the Appellant took the measures that were reasonable within his material ability to denounce the crimes committed" and that in any event Blaskic lacked effective control to prevent or punish these crimes.[23] For these reasons, the Appeals Chamber exonerated Blaskic

[20] Ibid. [21] Ibid., para. 62. [22] Ibid., para. 59 [23] Ibid., paras. 420–421.

of most of the serious charges alleged against him. Thus, the highest ranking Croat leader to stand trial for mass crimes committed against Muslims in Bosnia was released, with the Trial Chamber receiving a rather stiff admonishment for having incorrectly stated the *mens rea* standard for commanders in such cases involving Article 7(3) of the ICTY Statute.

The Appeals Chamber Judgment in the Blaskic case is likely to have far-reaching effects in the development of international criminal law. For it is hard to see how the ICTY Appeals Chamber action will not make it harder to convict military (and political) leaders of war crimes. As is true for corporations, the negligence standard rejected by the Appeals Chamber has often been seen as the only practicable standard for achieving convictions of their leaders in such cases. I will return to the general issue of negligence in subsequent sections of this chapter. In the next section, I will survey the most important *mens rea* considerations in holding commanders responsible for war crimes and begin to explain why negligence has often been appealed to.

III.   THE *MENS REA* OF LEADERS

Normally, it is thought that the hard part of obtaining convictions of leaders concerns the fact that they do not actually do the proscribed deed: They are not the ones who torture or kill. But it is also thought that leaders, not soldiers, are the ones who intentionally issue the orders and therefore have the *mens rea* requisite for criminal liability. While this is how it appears, the reality is that it is often very hard to find evidence of orders to torture or kill. Instead, the norm seems to be that there are generalized orders, such as the order to "secure an area" or "clear civilians from an area," and these orders do not appear to be based on a guilty mind, at least not on their face. Therefore, establishing the *mens rea* of leaders is, in many cases, harder than it might seem at first. As the ICTY Appeals Chamber has said, it does not appear to be fair to hold leaders criminally guilty just because they gave generalized orders and a crime occurred on their watch. To take this route would be tantamount to adopting a strict liability standard of criminal liability for leaders, an idea that is abhorrent to most.

It is important to try to explain why strict liability, in its various forms, is considered so abhorrent. There are three ways that liability can be strictly assigned. The most severe form concerns a disregard for both *mens rea* and *actus reus*. Think of a parent who is held strictly liable for what his child does. Under such a scheme, criminal liability is assigned regardless of what the parent did to try to stop the child from acting, and what were the parent's intentions or knowledge concerning the child's actions. While there may be good reasons to hold parents liable, as a way of motivating them to minimize the risky actions of their children, it does not seem fair to a particular parent to disregard what he or she has intentionally done, or intentionally tried to do, to minimize these risks.

Perhaps it could be argued that parents have indeed done something to warrant liability: They have procreated and created a child. But for the act of procreation, there would be no child whose risky or harmful behavior is now at issue. Even this form of strict liability is not completely strict because it is still based on something the parent did, perhaps even something that the parent did intentionally or with knowledge of the risks being created. But this is not the normal kind of action that connects a perpetrator to a harm and triggers possible criminal liability. For we normally look for proximate rather than remote causal influence. Remote causal influence, extended to its limit, would involve so many people's actions in harms that liability would be diffused beyond recognition, perhaps extending back several generations and holding all living relatives responsible for what the current child has done. Thus, the liability that is most strict makes little sense, at least as a form of criminal liability.

A second form of strict liability is one that disregards only the intentions of the person held liable but still requires action that is not remote. A classic example of this form of strict liability concerns the manufacture of explosives. We might hold the manufacturer criminally liable for anyone who is injured in the manufacturing process, no matter how careful the manufacturer is and regardless of the fact that it was no part of the manufacturer's intention that people would be harmed during the manufacturing process. Again, it seems that this is unfair because the manufacturer not only hasn't tried to harm anyone but may have tried exceptionally hard to minimize the likelihood of harm. On the assumption that the manufacturing process was considered a trigger for criminal liability, it is true that the manufacturer did something wrong, thus establishing *actus reus*. But the lack of any *mens rea* seems to mean that there isn't the kind of willfulness that is often thought to be the hallmark of responsibility, the larger category under which criminal liability falls.

Criminal liability, unlike civil liability, involves the risk of loss of liberty. To warrant loss of liberty, it is normally thought that willful misconduct is required, not merely accidental misconduct, as it were. For if an agent causes harm, but did so intending to do good or perhaps without even understanding that one's conduct could cause harm, it then seems unfair to take liberty away from the agent. To be fair, punishment requires responsibility, and yet responsibility is blocked when an agent did not act willfully. Again, it might be appropriate to levy a fine for accidentally harmful behavior, but punishment, and its attendant loss of liberty, seems to require more from the agent than mere action without any guilty mental state.

The third kind of strict liability disregards only the actions of a person, focusing instead on the person's knowledge and intentions. This is indeed the form of strict liability that normally is assigned to leaders. For as I said above, the leader normally doesn't do the torturing or the killing, but may nonetheless have come up with the plan that called for just such actions by others. And yet, despite the fact that the leader did not commit the guilty action, we might hold him or her criminally liable based on intentions and planning alone. For it seems that having a guilty mind is the most important dimension to being guilty. Even if this is true, however, there seems something odd in not requiring proof of some sort of action on the part of the accused, because without requiring action we would start down the slippery slope that might end in the punishment of mere thoughts.

The way to stop from sliding down this slippery slope is to require some action, even if it is relatively remote from the actual perpetration of the torturing or killing. In many contexts, the issuing of a verbal command or the drafting and dissemination of a written plan, no matter how long ago, is thought to be enough of an *actus reus* then to let *mens rea* dominate in the assigning of criminal liability. But in that case, because there is both action and intention, we are not really in the domain of strict liability at all. In the General Blaskic case, the prosecution tried to prove that Blaskic issued an order to assault the civilian population or, in the alternative, that he failed to act (an act of omission) to prevent what he knew, or should have known, would result. These acts of commission or omission stop the possible slippery-slope slide, but the Appeals Chamber still thought there was a problem.

The Appeals Chamber focused on another issue that arises in cases concerning the *mens rea* of leaders – namely, whether potential knowledge is ever sufficient to constitute a guilty mind. By virtue of being a military commander, Blaskic was in a position to know certain facts and had a duty to know what his troops were doing or were about to do. The Trial Chamber had held that it was sufficient to establish that the knowledge was available and that Blaskic had the duty to obtain the knowledge. But the Appeals Chamber reversed and held that actual knowledge had to be proved. The main reason for this was the fact that the *actus reus* was already so diminished and the intent part of *mens rea* was seen as being of diminished importance. To get a better grip on this matter, we next turn to the question of whether negligence should be sufficient to generate criminal liability in international tribunals.

IV. NEGLIGENCE IN INTERNATIONAL CRIMINAL LAW

Negligence has played only a limited role in criminal law, although it has played probably a disproportionate role in those few cases of chief executives prosecuted for white-collar crimes. The main reason for this general neglect of negligence in criminal law is that it is not thought that punishment can be administered in all fairness if the accused has not done something willful. Negligence does not involve willfulness, and it is unclear whether negligence is even a state of mind at all, rather than merely the absence of a certain state. The terms "carelessness" and "inadvertence," sometimes thought to be synonyms with "negligence," clearly indicate a lack – that is, "care-less-ness" and "inadvertence," the mere negation of states of mind rather than states of guilty mind themselves. In this section, I will explore the idea of negligence in international law, especially in international criminal law.

One recent textbook in international criminal law, written by the renowned jurist Antonio Cassese before the Blaskic Appeals Chamber Judgment, argues that there has been a

broadening of the range of acts amenable to international prosecution . . . in keeping with the general object and purpose of international humanitarian law. This modality of *mens rea* [gross or culpable negligence] may for instance apply to cases of command responsibility where the commander should have known that war crimes were being committed by his subordinates.[24]

[24] Antonio Cassese, *International Criminal Law*, Oxford: Oxford University Press, 2003, p. 58.

Cassese admits that mere "negligence is the least degree of culpability. Normally, it is not sufficient for individual criminal liability to arise."[25] Given what is at stake in international criminal prosecutions, only gross or culpable negligence will generally meet the standard of *mens rea*. Gross or culpable ignorance arises, according to Cassese, when the person

(i) *is expected or required to abide by certain standards of conduct or take certain specific precautions*, and in addition
(ii) is aware of the risk of harm and nevertheless takes it, for *he believes that the risk will not materialize owing to the steps he has taken or will take.*

In addition, for international prosecutions, there must be "some specific conditions relating to the objective elements of the crime, that is, the *values* attacked are fundamental and the *harm* caused is serious."[26]

While Cassese argues that there has been a broadening of how *mens rea* is understood, he nonetheless recognizes that negligence is used in a fairly limited set of criminal cases. Cassese does argue, though, that in some cases a superior can be held criminally liable for the acts of his subordinates "if he did not know, but 'should have known' that they were about to commit, or were committing, or had committed crimes."[27] This analysis is at odds with that provided by the Blaskic Appeals Chamber of the ICTY, which clearly required more than proof that Blaskic "should have known" what his subordinates did or were about to do. Rather, the ICTY Appeals Chamber required proof of actual knowledge of what the subordinates did or were about to do. In effect, the ICTY Appeals Chamber said that negligence of any form would not be sufficient for international criminal liability. By requiring actual knowledge, the ICTY effectively required at least recklessness for *mens rea*, not merely culpable negligence.

Admittedly, the border between gross or culpable negligence, on the one hand, and recklessness, on the other hand, is often difficult to see and even harder to prove. In corporate cases, proof of what a CEO knew is often very hard to fathom, especially because CEOs often either intentionally blind themselves to what their subordinates are doing or make sure that there is no paper trail concerning what they have been informed. For this reason, the standard often employed is what a reasonable CEO would have or should have known. This moves us more toward negligence, but it is often a standard used because of

[25] Ibid., p. 172.   [26] Ibid.   [27] Ibid., p. 173.

the suspicion that the CEO was actually reckless but the proof of the CEO actually having relevant knowledge is just too difficult to get, especially when CEOs are so well insulated from observation by their subordinates.

I move now to the question of whether there are good normative grounds for not allowing gross or culpable negligence to satisfy the *mens rea* requirement of criminal liability for commanders concerning war crimes. Gross or culpable negligence is often morally serious enough for us to think that those who have this "mental state" are guilty in some sense. Think here of the case of those who are given the task of caring for children who have been separated from their parents. If those put into the position of standing in for the parents disregard the needs of the children, why would we need to show that these people actually knew that disregarding their needs would produce suffering in the children? Isn't it enough to show that they certainly should have known?[28]

Even in the case just sketched above, it is unclear whether what was described was gross negligence or recklessness. For those in charge of the children not only should have known that the children would suffer, but in some sense did know as well. "Must have known" is of course somewhere between "did know" and "should have known." While it would be reckless to know this information and yet not to act on it, it is only gross negligence not to know what one should have known and not act on it. But "must have known" does not fit into this divide. One of the reasons why gross negligence seems to be sufficient to many people is because they believe that the defendant actually *did* know, because anyone in that situation must have known, but merely that it couldn't be proven.

The normative question is why we would demand that it be proven that a superior actually did have the knowledge that we assume he had and that any normal person would have had in these circumstances. At least part of the answer to this question has to do with what criminal trials are generally supposed to be about: the unique facts of a case rather than the general tendencies of human nature. Indeed, in criminal trials in the Anglo-American system of law, talk of tendencies for how people behave is generally excluded by the rules of evidence.

---

[28] Cassese cites the case of Heinrich Gerike and Others (the Velpke Baby Home trial), where a British court found the defendants guilty on grounds of gross negligence – a case similar to the one I just sketched. See ibid., p. 203.

What must be proven is what the defendant did or knew at the time of the incident in question. It is generally considered irrelevant to discuss what others knew or what people generally would have known. This seems to be the basis of the Judgment by the Blaskic Appeals Chamber.

Normatively, the principle is that criminal liability only attaches to willful acts. It could be contended that if a superior is required to know certain things and does not come to know them then this looks like "not knowing" is a willful act. But the difficulty is that it would only be willful if it could be shown that the superior chose not to know what he should have known. If, instead, the superior simply forgot or was not alert, then his failure to learn the required information is not necessarily willful. And while we may want to make an exception to the general principle requiring willfulness, we must recognize that such an exception will render the criminality and subsequent punishability of the defendant suspect as well.

Let me say just a few more words about why the principle requiring willfulness is so important to criminal liability. At least in part, such an investigation might discover in which areas exceptions might be more justifiable than in other areas. From the time of the ancient Greeks, it has been thought that responsibility and punishment attach to the willful acts of agents. If the agent had no choice in the matter or acted accidentally, the agent is typically not held morally responsible for his or her behavior and its consequences. Similarly, only when a choice has been made to cause or risk harm does it make sense to hold someone criminally liable. If the behavior and its consequences were not the result of a willed action, there was no clear decision to do something wrong and thus no clear reason for responsibility or punishment to be assigned. What we should hold people morally and criminally responsible for is freely choosing to do something wrong. Without the act of will, it is hard to see why punishment would be justified.

The key component in any defensible use of negligence as a *mens rea* condition in international criminal law is that the commander not only should have acted as any normal person would have acted but had the capacity so to act and chose not to do so. We can bring willfulness back into the equation of *mens rea* in negligence cases by proving that the commander knew that he or she was under a duty to act a certain way – for instance, to supervise carefully his or her subordinates – had the capacity to meet his or her duty, and yet chose not to do so. The difficulty is to show that the omission to do "that which any ordinary reasonable man could and would have done," namely, "a standard requiring him to take precautions against harm," was chosen.[29]

One of the most difficult normative problems is whether it is sufficient to prove that there was information that could have been available and that should have been known, but was not actually known by the accused. Is it sufficient to prove that there was a duty to get this information and it wasn't gotten, or must it be proven that there was specific information available that was disregarded? In the Blaskic case, the ICTY Appeals Chamber required a showing that General Blaskic had knowledge of the likely bad conduct of some of his subordinates. Why wasn't it enough to show that a reasonable person would have and should have known this information? This is really a question about whether something very close to recklessness is required rather than simple negligence.

I am of two minds about this issue, and as a result I am inclined to proceed cautiously. On the one hand, I think there can be clear willfulness in choosing not to be informed, even though one should have become informed, or in choosing to omit to supervise when one should have been supervising one's subordinates. For this reason, I do not see any reason in principle to rule out negligence as a *mens rea* standard. On the other hand, I do not think that it is sufficient merely to infer such willfulness from one's failure to do that which one had a duty to do. In law, if not also in morality, I think we do need to distinguish inadvertence from negligence, where the difference is not merely whether one had a duty in the latter but not in the former case. From the mere lack of doing x, it does not follow that one has omitted to do, in the sense of willfully chosen not to do, x. We should not be too quick to draw the inference that one has chosen to omit to do x, rather than that one has merely inadvertently not done x.

H. L. A. Hart argues that "negligence is gross if the precautions to be taken against harm are very simple, such as persons who are but poorly endowed with physical and mental capacities can easily take."[30] Hart gives the example of a workman who does not look to see who might be below before throwing slate tiles off a construction site to the ground below. Hart thinks that this is a case of gross negligence that could form the basis for the *mens rea* element in a criminal prosecution

---

[29] See the most important essay on this topic: H. L. A. Hart, "Negligence, *Mens Rea*, and Criminal Responsibility," reprinted in H. L. A. Hart, *Punishment and Responsibility*, Oxford: Oxford University Press, 1968, esp. pp. 147–148.

[30] Ibid., p. 149.

of the workman. As long as there was no incapacity, then a person "can
be punished in effect for a failure to exercise control."[31] Hart then
posits a two-pronged test for when negligence is criminally punishable:

1. Did the accused fail to take those precautions which any reasonable man with normal capacities would in the circumstances
   have taken?
2. Could the accused, given his mental and physical capacities,
   have taken those precautions?[32]

The question I am raising is whether in addition we need:

3. Did the accused choose not to take those precautions?

One way to address this question, made popular by Hart, is to ask
whether we are demanding more than we would demand when the
mens rea standard is intentional wrongdoing rather than negligence.
Hart says that just as the workman could say, "My mind was a blank,"
so the murderer could say "I just decided to kill."[33] But while this
argument works well against those who think that negligence is not
sufficiently a mental state at all, it also works against the claim that
negligence might not manifest sufficient willfulness to be culpable. The
question that I am raising is not whether negligence could be a *mens rea*
standard by being a state of mind, but whether it is sufficiently willful to
be regarded as a culpable state of mind upon which a criminal prosecution could be based. My general answer is that it could be, but that
what is needed is to prove that the neglect was chosen, and yet this is
incredibly difficult to show in most cases (although not in all cases, as
we will see in the next section).

Hart thinks that it is often hard to prove that a person chose to
commit murder as well. It is possible that the person was forced to do
so or couldn't help but kill. But this would be very odd, barring special
circumstances. We would want to know what could possibly have
motivated him to kill and how it could possibly be that he killed
without foresight. Similar kinds of things can be said, Hart thinks,
about the person who omitted to do what any reasonable person would
have and should have done. Again, barring special circumstances, we
want to know what could have been the motivation not to do what was
plainly one's duty to do.

[31] Ibid., p. 153.   [32] Ibid., p. 154.   [33] Ibid., p. 151.

But the lack of a motivation does not, in and of itself, allow us to infer that a person had willfully chosen to omit what he should have done. A compromise has sometimes been proposed in which only gross negligence will count as satisfying the *mens rea* requirement of criminal liability. This is roughly what the drafters of the U.S. Model Penal Code attempted when they gave the following qualification:

The risk must be of such a nature and degree that the actor's failure to perceive it, considering the nature and purposes of his conduct and the circumstances known to him, involves a gross deviation from the standard of care that a reasonable person would observe in the actor's situation.[34]

But questions still arise about whether and when we should be entitled to infer willfulness even in gross deviations from what reasonable people would do? Can't even such gross deviations be due simply to lack of thought – that is, to thoughtlessness of the kind that is non-culpable?

The debate about whether negligence should count as a sufficient *mens rea* for criminal liability is at least in part a debate about whether neglect can be presumed to be willful. Neglect can certainly be willful, but it is often not clear whether it is or is not in a particular case. Neglect can be merely due to an absence of thought, or it can be due to a decision not to act. If one has a duty to act, then it is more likely that one's failure to act is willful, but it is not always the case. So here is the problem in a nutshell: Mere neglect or negligence is not clearly willful and therefore not clearly something for which the agent should be held responsible. And because criminality carries with it such serious consequences, I am cautious about holding leaders responsible for what subordinates do unless there is some indication that the leaders *chose* to neglect their supervisory roles. In the next section, I will discuss a possible way to get around this problem concerning negligence, although it is not a foolproof way.

V.   BENIGHTING ACTS, WILLFULNESS, AND PRECOMMITMENT

When it is unclear what role each person plays in a concerted effort, it is sometimes easier to parse guilt and blame if it is clear that all parties entered into an enterprise together realizing what was likely to happen

---

[34] Model Penal Code, Section 2.02(2)(d). See the very perceptive commentary on this sentence in George P. Fletcher, *Basic Concepts of Criminal Law*, Oxford: Oxford University Press, 1998, pp. 114–117.

and how each person's part would contribute to the joint effort. In military matters, as is true in corporate matters, often all of the members voluntarily and willfully join into a common undertaking. Because of these willful acts, then certain questions about particular responsibility or liability are not quite as difficult because of the willful act of joining into the enterprise. Then when a negligent or benighting[35] act occurs later, it may be easier to infer willfulness. As we will see in this section, the use of the joint enterprise liability theory can help us resolve some of the problems we identified above concerning the liability of military leaders for what their subordinates have done or are doing. There will still remain problems, but most of the problems get somewhat easier to solve.

The main difficulty with a negligence standard of *mens rea*, within a general theory of command responsibility, is that normally we can only infer, not prove, that omitting was indeed willful; and yet if omissions are not willful then it is not clear why they are sufficiently guilty to be the subject of criminal liability and punishment. But if people have joined an enterprise and clearly committed to do certain things identified as their duties, then it seems to be more justifiable than not to infer that when they fail to do their duty it is because they have chosen this path. It is still possible that in a given case the reason the person didn't do *x*, even though he had committed to doing *x*, was not that he chose not to do *x*, but that he was at a given moment thoughtless in how he was behaving.

But the most important question, as Holly Smith has shown, is whether there was a culpable act that preceded the benighting or negligent act and that itself colored the benighting act and the unwitting act that followed and caused harm. Let us take up an example to illustrate the general problem. Consider a commander who fails to discover that his troops are planning to cause harm to civilians, and as a result the commander does not move to prevent them from doing this harm to civilians but only goes about his job as he otherwise

---

[35] Holly Smith, in her paper "Culpable Ignorance," *The Philosophical Review*, vol. 92, October (1983), first uses "benighting" in this way when she discusses the first act of doing what would make one ignorant of certain facts that later prove important in one's harmful behavior. The dictionary gives as its third definition of "benight" this definition: "to involve in moral darkness or ignorance, to exclude from intellectual light; as absorbtion in routine benights of the mind." Smith often uses the term also to mean the first act that then colors all others, calling to mind a kind of "knighting" act that colors the rest of one's actions.

should, and then the soldiers do cause harm. The initial failure to discover information is the benighting or negligent act. The failure to prevent harm is an unwitting act that gives rise to, or at least significantly contributes, to the perpetration of harm. The main question, as Smith formulates it, is whether the benighting act is both objectively wrongful and also culpable. It is objectively wrongful insofar as it is a violation of a duty that the commander had. But it is unclear whether it is culpable because we do not know whether the commander had bad motives in not doing his duty.

Two things could make a difference. One is the motive behind the benighting act. The other is whether there was a prior act that so greatly colored the benighting act as to make the act culpable. Smith focuses on the former, pointing out that it is not merely a question of whether at the time of the benighting act the agent had reprehensible motives, but also whether the agent had "reprehensible motives at the time of some earlier act that indirectly gave rise to the unwitting act and which render it blameworthy."[36] I will focus on the latter factor that could make a difference. If I promise to do *x* realizing that failure to keep my promise will cause harm and then forget that I made the promise and act in an otherwise blameless way, my previous promising act, which is not itself blameworthy, colors the situation to such an extent that the subsequent act is clearly blameworthy because it is an instance of promise breaking that one realized previously to be something that would cause harm.

My view, which takes off from Holly Smith's but then diverges from it, is that the key to using negligence as a form of *mens rea* for criminal liability turns on whether the act of negligence is preceded by an act or set of acts that make(s) the negligence blameworthy independent of whether we can prove anything about the state of mind of the agent at the time the act of negligence occurs. Think of one of Smith's own cases: A doctor ought to have read his medical journals, yet he did not, and as a result he did not know that the use of high concentrations of oxygen causes severe eye damage. On her analysis, the prior act that colors the rest, the failure to read the medical journals, is wrongful, if it is, because it displays a wrongful motive. The key question for Smith is whether the doctor had reason to foresee that his earlier act would spill over to color his later acts and yet took that risk.[37] My own take on this case is somewhat different from Smith's, and in setting out those

---

[36] Ibid., p. 566.   [37] Ibid., p. 554.

differences here I will also begin to sketch my own view. I will then connect that view to the theory of joint criminal enterprise liability discussed in Chapter 11.

I would argue that the key is whether there is a willful act that is causally connected to the negligence that then caused the harm in question. For regardless of whether the willful act is itself blameworthy, it is the willfulness that transfers, at least in some cases, to the negligent act, making of the negligent act not merely something done thoughtlessly but something done willfully. The doctor has the duty to read medical journals because of his role as a physician, and perhaps also because of a specific duty based on his maintaining board certification in his specialty. In any event, what is key is that he has committed himself to read these journals. The wrongness of his failure to read them can be construed independently of whether he recognized the risk to his patients of not doing so. So when he fails to do so, the wrongness of doing so turns on the violation of a duty he has expressly committed himself to perform rather than on the foreseeabilty of the risk.

In the cases we examined in this chapter so far, the key question is whether the negligent act displayed wrongfulness, which I understand to mean a willful choosing. The problem that needed to be resolved was whether the negligent act was neglect caused by thoughtlessness or by something willful. But it isn't necessary that the willful act itself be wrongful or even that the benighting act would encompass the risk in the sense that the perpetrator of the benighting act recognized the risk at the time. On my analysis, what is wrong is that by not reading the journals the physician violated a duty he committed himself to serve. In the typical commander case, commanders commit themselves to be part of a larger campaign of a certain sort and to follow certain rules of war. As with the physician, it does not matter whether they can or cannot foresee that by not following the rules harms will result. Rather it is the violation of duty that is key.

Of course, one could still wonder whether the violation of duty is itself willful or merely thoughtless. The physician might say that he just didn't think. But like the person who makes a promise and then fails to keep it, the defense or the excuse of just not thinking, is generally not applicable if one has committed oneself in advance, where pre-commitment means, among other things, that such defenses or excuses will not be recognized. This is a kind of strict liability, to return to one of the ideas expressed earlier, but perhaps not one that is especially obnoxious because it is one that the agent could have avoided completely on his or her own merely by not engaging in the precommitment.

Let us return to the idea of joint criminal enterprise liability. One way to understand joint criminal enterprises is as large-scale instances of precommitment. People in joint enterprises commit themselves to the goals of the enterprise by making the collective goals of the enterprise their own personal goals. This means that they precommit to do what it takes to achieve the goals of the group enterprise. Later, when individuals unwittingly act to advance those goals by simply doing what they are told, or if they fail to do things that turn out to advance that goal, they are linked to those goals almost as surely as if they had intended that their acts would advance those goals. Once it is proven that there was a joint criminal enterprise, then it is significantly easier to show that the failure to supervise is not merely a thoughtless act, especially in those cases where that failure facilitates the achievement of the goals of the enterprise.

Let us return to the Blaskic case. If he was part of a joint enterprise whereby some people put miscreants into positions where they could terrorize camp prisoners or civilians and where not properly supervising these miscreants was part of the plan, then when they are in fact not supervised this certainly no longer looks like simple negligence based on thoughtlessness. And even if it is truly thoughtlessness, it still looks like the precommitment counts to allow us to disregard the thoughtlessness and hold General Blaskic strictly liable nonetheless. But again, this is not an especially obnoxious kind of strict liability, for in effect Blaskic has by his own earlier acts endorsed just such a scheme of liability, as had the promise maker.

Another route leading to the same result is that the commander by accepting the assignment as commander also precommits to follow the rules of war. Such precommitment also acts as a kind of license to others to hold the general strictly liable for following this self-assumed duty. It may still be true that some commanders act out of thoughtlessness rather than willful wrongness when they do not properly supervise their subordinates. But the precommitment to follow the rules of war, including the proper supervision of troops to make sure that they do not commit crimes, looks like a transferred willfulness for the later negligence. The category of willful negligence sounds like an oxymoron until it is recognized that the willfulness comes earlier and the benighting or negligent act comes later. We still do not have willfulness at the same point in time as the benighting or negligent act, or else it wouldn't really be negligence. But the earlier willfulness involved in precommitment does, in fact, color the negligence and makes of it something culpable.

I agree with the ICTY Appeals Chamber that there are significant hurdles to overcome in cases like that of General Blaskic, hurdles that require different moves than those employed by the Trial Chamber. But I have tried to indicate how a commander like Blaskic could still be properly prosecuted for war crimes even if it turns out that Blaskic simply didn't think when he left miscreants unsupervised to torture and kill civilians in Bosnia. Blaskic's negligence could still be based on willfulness, although admittedly much earlier in time than the act of negligence of not supervising would be. This is a form of transferred willfulness – or even of strict liability, if you like – for in a sense Blaskic has little defense open to him concerning the acts of negligence. But it is important also to recognize that the reason Blaskic would not have these defenses or excuses open to him has to do with his own acts in joining the criminal enterprise or in simply agreeing to be a commander in the first place. Thus, while this strategy does not solve all of our problems, it possibly does allow us to hold Blaskic criminally liable even though his most important acts may not have arisen out of willful malice at the time.

13

Commanded and commanding defenses

In the previous two chapters, I argued that both soldiers and commanders can be held liable and prosecuted for war crimes, but that *mens rea* creates various problems that are often hard to get around. I now wish to investigate superior orders, duress, and necessity, the leading bases for mitigation, and even for a complete defense, of criminal liability in war crimes cases. In the case of soldiers, it is initially very easy to see why superior orders, duress, and necessity are so important, because soldiers clearly do not plan or even intend to commit harm but only to do their duty; rather, it is their superiors who do the planning and who order the soldiers simply to comply with their orders, often under significant threat. But it is also true of commanders that they are often responding to what seems to be necessary to win a battle, or even the war, or to do what is necessary to protect their troops. Thus, they are simply attempting to do their duty rather than intending to do wrong. In both cases, the crimes that are committed are so clearly group crimes that it is difficult to see who individually is to blame, especially if we are thinking about *mens rea* considerations. Indeed, in wartime this is especially true because wars are not planned or executed by individuals but by very large groups of people, operating collectively, as it were. For this reason, it seems that soldiers and even their commanders would be able to mitigate their guilt or even defend against it altogether by reference to the fact that these individuals were forced to do what they did or that they were merely doing their duty rather than intending to do wrong.

While it is often thought that soldiers are those most likely to be able to use coercion-based defenses, I will also explain that a very similar defense, or at least a source of mitigation of punishment, is also open to some commanders. In the previous chapter, I explained how commanders could be held criminally liable based on the roles that they voluntarily assumed. It is for this reason that I am especially aware of the potential for mitigation of punishment if it can be shown that commanders, like soldiers, were also coerced or merely doing their duty in following what those whom they serve had ordered or assigned them to do. I do not wish to overemphasize this point, but I do think that some commanders may have defenses open to them very similar to those open to soldiers and camp guards. Just as soldiers can sometimes claim to be operating under duress, commanders can sometimes claim to be operating under necessity, and in both cases they have a defense, or at least a strong basis for mitigation of punishment.

In the first section, I examine a World War II case where a commander claimed the defense of necessity. In the second section, I examine a recent case from the Yugoslav Tribunal, *Prosecutor v. Erdemovic*, where a soldier/guard attempted to employ a superior-orders and a duress defense. In the third section, I look at how these ideas of duress and necessity might play a role as mitigating factors in war crimes cases, as opposed to cases of crimes against humanity. In the fourth section, I look at how *mens rea* is affected by these claims. While the old superior-orders defense is generally rejected today in international criminal law, duress and necessity do have an effect on the *mens rea* of both commanders and those commanded. In the final section, I return to the discussion in the earlier chapters of this book to see how the principle of humanity, as opposed to the principle of justice, affects the use of these defenses, arguing that these coercion-based defenses should be expanded in war crimes, as opposed to genocide or crimes against humanity cases, by reference to the principle of humane treatment.

I. MILITARY LEADERS AND NECESSITY

In Chapter 9, we examined the general doctrine of military necessity as a reason to justify certain sorts of tactics in war. Now we ask whether military leaders can use the idea of military necessity either to avoid or mitigate liability in international criminal trials. The Lieber code of 1863 speaks of prohibitions on "cruelty and bad faith," but also on acts of "private revenge."[1] The code singles out one class of combatants as

---

[1] Instructions for the Government of Armies of the United States in the Field, General Orders no. 100 (1863), Article 11.

especially deserving of punishment for violations of the rules of war: "Offenses to the contrary shall be severely punished, especially so if committed by officers. . . ."[2] But the Lieber Code also talks quite a bit about military necessity, here defined as that which is "indispensable for securing the ends of war."[3] As the code articulates this: "Military necessity admits of all destruction of life and limb of armed enemies and other persons whose destruction is incidentally unavoidable in the armed contest of the war."[4] Therefore, while military necessity can never justify cruelty,[5] it can justify a range of tactics that might otherwise be condemnable.

The question then arises of whether officers and other military leaders can use military necessity as a defense against various charges of war crimes. The Lieber Code seems to block such a move, when the definition of military necessity involves those acts "which are lawful according to the modern law and usages of war."[6] The addendum seems to rule out the use of military necessity by officers as a defense to war crimes charges. This is made abundantly clear when, at the end of Article 15, the Lieber Code proclaims: "Men who take up arms against one another in public war do not cease on this account to be moral beings, responsible to one another and to God."[7]

There is another potential basis of defense open to officers and other military leaders having to do with necessity. There is a defense similar to duress that might justifiably be used even by military leaders, namely, "threat to life and limb emanating from objective circumstances." Necessity, unlike duress, "covers situations other than those where one is faced with threats or compulsion of a third party."[8] In cases of necessity, the person "intends to cause an unlawful harmful effect" but offers as a defense that it was the only practicable way to overcome some greater tragedy, and thus the person should not be punished. The classic case of necessity is of a person who is shipwrecked and floating in a one-person boat. If another person tries to climb on board, the first person may justifiably push the other person overboard, even though his or her intent is to cause "the death of the other" person.[9] Another classic case is of a ship's captain who needs to beach his ship in a storm, and the only available dock is privately

---

[2] Ibid.   [3] Ibid., Article 14.   [4] Ibid., Article 15.   [5] Ibid., Article 16.
[6] Ibid., Article 14.   [7] Ibid., Article 15.
[8] Antonio Cassese, *International Criminal Law*, Oxford: Oxford University Press, 2003, p. 242 [hereinafter, Cassese].
[9] Ibid.

owned. Again, necessity relieves the captain of what would otherwise be an unjustified trespass upon the dock owner's property.

Like preemptive war, necessity only operates as a defense in those situations where there is an imminent threat and the chosen action is the only means available to avert the threat. Cassese helpfully summarizes the elements as follows:

1. the act charged is done under an immediate threat of severe and irreparable harm to life and limb;
2. there is no adequate means of averting such evil;
3. the crime committed is not disproportionate to the evil threatened . . . ;
4. the situation . . . must not have been voluntarily brought about by the person coerced.[10]

In such situations, even military leaders may be relieved of culpability for intentionally causing the kind of suffering that would normally constitute a war crime, although it is highly controversial in contemporary international criminal law that such defenses are available for acts of killing.

I wish to argue that we should indeed recognize such defenses, even though I also think that military leaders are those who should normally be the ones prosecuted for war crimes. It may be the case that there are situations thrust upon commanders where committing war crimes is the lesser evil, although I also suspect, as with our earlier discussion of torture, that these cases will be few and far between. Nonetheless, the ICC Statute opens the door for such defenses in Article 31. The statute declares that criminal responsibility will not be assigned if the "person acts necessarily and reasonably to avoid" a threat of "imminent serious bodily harm against that person or another person." Such a threat may be either made by third parties or "constituted by other circumstances beyond that person's control."[11] This wording tracks rather well with the traditional way to understand the defense of necessity.

Consider briefly a case from World War II. In the case of Flick and Others, managers of various German companies were accused

of having employed conscripted foreign workers, concentration camp inmates, or prisoners of war allocated to them through the slave labor program of the

---

[10] Ibid.
[11] Statute of the International Criminal Court, Adopted by the U.N. Diplomatic Conference, July 17, 1998, Article 31(d).

German Government. The defendants claimed that they had done so "under the circumstances of compulsion under which such employment came about." The US Military Tribunal upheld the plea. It noted that the defendants lived "in a reign of terror." "The Reich, through its hordes of enforcement officials and secret police, was always present, ready to go into instant action and to mete out savage and immediate punishment against anyone doing anything that could be construed as obstructing or hindering the carrying out of governmental regulations or decrees." The tribunal therefore found that the defendants had acted "under clear and present danger" and acquitted them.[12]

In this case, we have civilian and military leaders acquitted because they were living under circumstances that necessitated that they commit war crimes against civilians and prisoners of war so as to save their own lives. If it is true that there was a clear and present danger to the defendants if they had not committed these war crimes, that the risks to them of not committing these war crimes was indeed greater than to the people whom they harmed by committing these crimes, then this is a possible case where leaders could employ the defense of necessity.

The main normative justification for a defense of necessity against war crimes charges for military leaders is that even leaders face situations not of their own making, where they or others will be harmed more by not committing certain war crimes than by committing them. This is especially easy to see if we think of war crimes that concern violation of property rights. Surely, a commander can be excused for having trespassed so as to save the lives of his troops. But the much more difficult question is whether a commander could use the defense of necessity to avert criminal responsibility for killing civilians as a way to save his own troops. This was, in fact, the strategy in the Lt. William Calley case during the Vietnam war. No particular person was applying duress against members of Company C in the My Lai incident. Rather, the claim was that the general circumstances in the Vietnamese hamlets was one that made it very difficult to tell who was an enemy and who was not. Thus, giving orders to kill civilians was claimed to be necessary to preserve the lives of U.S. soldiers in these situations.

I am inclined not to accept such a defense for military leaders.[13] Rather, in cases where war crimes concern loss of life, rather than merely loss of property, I would be much happier saying that necessity

---

[12] See Cassese's discussion of this case on p. 244, quoting Flick and others at 1199–1202.
[13] See my more extensive treatment of the Calley case in my book *Crimes Against Humanity*, Chapter 10.

could be used as a mitigating factor for punishment rather than as an exculpatory factor. With few exceptions, military leaders are not themselves subject to loss of life; rather, it is others whom they are protecting. But in that case, I would rather grant exculpation to the soldiers whose lives are jeopardized and who actually commit the war crimes than to the leaders. It is important for leaders to think that violating the most serious rules of war will nearly always get them convicted. But to be fair, the full force of punishment should not necessarily be meted out against them if they were trying to save their own soldiers. Deterrence will function better at the commander level, where there is time to reflect on one's choices and where commanders, unlike soldiers, are rarely found in the heat of battle.

II. SOLDIERS AND DURESS

Michael Walzer and others maintain that all soldiers have the right to protect their lives on grounds of self-defense, whether they fight for the defending or aggressing side in a war.[14] In addition, it does not seem to matter what reason a soldier has to act for fear of loss of life. Whether the fear is generated from the opposing soldiers or from his own commanders, that soldier seems to have reasons to be relieved of responsibility, on grounds of duress, for doing what he or she is required to do. The defense of duress, as we have just seen, is similar to the defense of necessity, except that the coercion to act contrary to the rules of war comes from a third party, not merely from the general circumstances surrounding a person. The difficulty with the defense of duress in times of war is that it seems to provide a defense for so many soldiers' acts that would otherwise be punishable war crimes. In fact, the very idea of war crimes is called into question, for most of what soldiers do is driven by fear either of what the enemy will do or of what their commanders will do if the soldiers do not act in a certain way.

The life of a soldier is generally not his or her own, but is taken up with reacting to justified fears of various sorts, especially of what will happen to the soldier if he or she does not follow orders. It is for this reason that many feel that soldiers are not the ones to be held primarily responsible for war crimes, for it is their leaders who are the ones giving orders. The recent history of war crimes prosecutions is a history of attempting to motivate soldiers to see themselves as being in

---

[14] Michael Walzer, *Just and Unjust Wars*, New York: Basic Books, 2000.

charge of their own lives and as the front guard to resisting war crimes orders. But such a history, as otherwise admirable as it may be, often unfairly seeks to punish soldiers as the ones who have brought about war crimes when it is their leaders who should more appropriately be punished.[15]

Let us consider one court that has tried to come to grips with the problem of whether soldiers can legitimately employ the defense of duress for prosecutions brought against them for war crimes. The ICTY case of *Prosecutor v. Erdemovic* is certainly one of the most interesting. Drazen Erdemovic was accused of personally killing 10–100 unarmed civilian Bosnian Muslim men on or about July 16, 1995 at a collective farm in Pilica, near Srebrenica.[16] Erdemovic was 23 years old at the time of the incident.[17] He was "a professed pacifist and claims to have been against the war and nationalism. He said that he had to join the Bosnian Serb Army (BSA) in order to feed his family."[18] In addition, Erdemovic said at the trial: "Your Honor, I had to do this. If I had refused, I would have been killed together with the victims. When I refused, they told me: 'If you are sorry for them, stand up, line up with them and we will kill you too.' "[19] Thus, Erdemovic admitted participating in the killing of unarmed civilians, but he said, in defense: "I had no choice. . . ."[20] He testified that from the time he realized he would have to kill civilians until the shooting stopped he had no "possibility to avoid taking part in this shooting without jeopardizing" his life.[21]

The Erdemovic case is truly a classic case of duress as a defense against war crimes.[22] Yet the Yugoslav Trial Chamber did not accept the defendant's plea of duress, or what it called "extreme necessity."[23] This judgment was upheld on appeal, as we will next see, although several prominent appellate judges strongly disagreed with the ruling

---

[15] See Hannah Arendt's 1966 essay "Auschwitz on Trial," reprinted in Hannah Arendt, *Responsibility and Judgment*, edited by Jerome Kohn, New York: Schocken Books, 2003, pp. 227–256, for an argument that is opposed to mine.

[16] *Prosecutor v. Drazen Erdemovic*, International Criminal Tribunal for the former Yugoslavia, Sentencing Judgment of the Trial Chamber, March 5, 1998, para. 13.

[17] Ibid., para. 16.   [18] Ibid.   [19] Ibid., para. 14.   [20] Ibid.   [21] Ibid.

[22] Erdemovic pleaded guilty to having committed a crime against humanity. Because this was a more serious crime, and the war crimes charge was in the alternative, technically the court only ruled on the crime against humanity, although the ruling is relevant to war crimes as well as to crimes against humanity.

[23] *Prosecutor v. Erdemovic*, International Criminal Tribunal for the former Yugoslavia, Sentencing Judgment of November 29, 1996, para. 91.

by the majority. The ICTY Trial Chamber allowed duress to be used as a mitigating factor in deciding punishment, but not as a defense against the charge of war crimes. In the remainder of this section, I will explore the reasoning of the court and of the dissenting judges. Then I will examine the idea of duress, or necessity, as a basis for mitigation.

The original trial court judgment stressed evidentiary concerns as it denied Erdemovic's plea of duress or necessity as a basis of *mitigation*. On appeal, the defendant alleged that the Trial Chamber committed an error in law by not considering the duress plea as a complete *defense*.[24] In a split decision (3–2), presented in a "Joint Separate Opinion of Judge McDonald and Judge Vohrah and in the Separate and Dissenting Opinion of Judge Li, the majority of the Appeals Chamber [found] that duress does not afford a complete defense to a soldier charged with a crime against humanity and/or a war crime."[25] In rehearsing the arguments in this fascinating and controversial case, we will get a good idea of what counts as duress and why it was thought not to apply to war crimes cases.

In the separate appellate opinion by Judges McDonald and Vohrah, after a very lengthy survey of a wide range of authorities on the status of duress as a complete defense to the charge of murder, the idea was rejected based on the court's "mandated obligation under the Statute to ensure that international humanitarian law, which is concerned with the protection of humankind, is not in any way undermined."[26] The judges explicitly rejected utilitarian calculation of the sort that would excuse conduct if it did not really make a difference – that is, if the murders would have been committed without the defendant's participation. Indeed, the court quite explicitly argued, as stated in a head note, for the "[r]ejection of utilitarianism and proportionality where human life must be weighed."[27] As these judges put their conclusion: "[w]e give notice in no uncertain terms that those who kill innocent persons will not be able to take advantage of duress as a defense and hence get away with impunity for their criminal acts in the taking of innocent lives."[28]

---

[24] *Prosecutor v. Erdemovic*, International Criminal Tribunal for the former Yugoslavia, Judgment of the Trial Chamber, October 7, 1997, para. 12(c).

[25] Ibid., para. 19.

[26] *Prosecutor v. Erdemovic*, International Criminal Tribunal for the former Yugoslavia, Appeals Chamber Joint Separate Opinion of Judge McDonald and Judge Vohrah, October 7, 1997, para. 88.

[27] Ibid., head note to para. 80.   [28] Ibid., para. 80.

It is hard to see Drazen Erdemovic as getting away with impunity, especially if we accept, as the court did, that the facts were as Erdemovic claimed. Indeed, the judges did accept his duress as a mitigating factor. So the issue is the narrow one of whether Erdemovic should be completely exonerated on the basis of this plea, not whether his punishment should be lessened. And on that issue, it is true that Erdemovic would not be punished at all if the defense of duress were accepted. But the normative question is whether someone like Erdemovic should be punished at all for what each side admits he was forced to do. At the end of this section, I will mount an argument against what Judges McDonald and Vohrah have claimed, but before doing so I wish to give a sense of what was argued by Judge Cassese in dissent.

Among many arguments mounted by Judge Cassese, one of the most normatively compelling concerns the question of whether a court should presume that a defendant should sacrifice his or her "own life at the expense of others."[29] Cassese cites the Einsatzgruppen case from the Nuremberg trials:

Let it be said at once that there is no law which requires that an innocent man must forfeit his life or suffer serious harm in order to avoid committing a crime which he condemns. . . . The test to be applied is whether the subordinate acted under coercion or whether he himself approved of the principle involved in the order.[30]

There is a strong normative argument embedded in this position, one that I will attempt to flesh out and defend.

Judge Cassese discusses the defense of duress in the Erdemovic and Einsatzgruppen cases as involving the question: Is there a duty to prevent harm to others even when preventing another's harm puts one's own life in jeopardy? This is not the same as the duty to rescue, where one is asked to act positively rather than merely to refrain from harming. Stated in this way, it appears that there is a huge difference between these two cases. But if one adds that direct harming is not done out of one's own free will but from coercion, then our intuitions about the two cases might come closer together. For the question of whether one has a duty to drop other things and go to the aid of others

---

[29] *Prosecutor v. Drazen Erdemovic*, International Criminal Tribunal for the former Yugoslavia, Appeals Chamber Separate and Dissenting Opinion of Judge Cassese, October 7, 1997, para. 24.

[30] Ibid., para. 27.

is similar to the question of whether one has a duty not directly to cause harm to others when one is being forced to do so. Indeed, the latter is a case that admits of ready excuse, whereas the former is much harder to see as involving a legitimate excuse or defense, because dropping other considerations involves much less serious consequences normally than not doing what one is being coerced to do under threat.

The general question in both cases, although more forcefully put in the case of duress, is what costs an individual can be expected to bear in order to avoid harm to others. Morally speaking, we may wish to demand quite a lot of fellow members of a community. But legally, with criminal punishment on the line, it is hard to fathom that we would demand adherence to a strict duty to risk our own lives to avoid harming others. In general, this position also follows from application of the principle of *favor rei* ("favoring the accused").[31] As the ICTY Trial Chamber put it in the case of *Prosecutor v. Krstic*: "[w]here there is a plausible difference of interpretation or application, the position which most favors the accused should be adopted."[32] On the basis of *favor rei*, we should not interpret our duties not to cause harm to apply in those cases where doing so risks significant harm to us.

The defense of duress is important in international humanitarian law, for it calls on us to be not only fair but also humane, in the sense of being merciful, in considering the plight of soldiers who might be accused of war crimes. I will have much more to say about this in the final section of this chapter. Here I wish only to note that duress, which can be seen as either a complete defense, a partial defense, or merely a mitigating factor, is important because it forces us to consider things from the standpoint of the accused. According to that standpoint, it often seems as if there are simply no other morally legitimate choices but to obey a particular order. And while a superior order itself is not enough to excuse or even to mitigate behavior, when orders are joined by serious threats to the life of the subordinate, it seems inhumane to demand that the subordinate risk his or her own life so as to protect others. It may very well be good to do so, but it is highly questionable that criminal law should require such behavior on pain of punishment.

---

[31] See Antonio Cassese's discussion of this principle in his book *International Criminal Law*, Oxford: Oxford University Press, 2003, pp. 156–157.

[32] *Prosecutor v. Krstic*, International Criminal Tribunal for the former Yugoslavia, Trial Chamber Judgment, Case No. IT-98-33-T, August 2, 2001, para. 502.

III.   MITIGATION OF PUNISHMENT FOR WAR CRIMES

The ICC Statute says that superior orders will not be allowed as a defense to crimes against humanity or to genocide. But, as several commentators have pointed out, political considerations militated against ruling out superior-orders defenses for war crimes. This was because of legitimate concern for fairness to soldiers. International courts continue to treat war crimes charges quite differently from other international crimes, especially crimes against humanity. But issues of whether punishment should be mitigated are harder to dismiss, because they do not involve the worries about extending impunity to killers that we faced in the previous section. I will try to explain why the superior-orders defense as well as questions of mitigation of punishment should be handled differently in war crimes prosecutions as opposed to other international criminal prosecutions. Let us return for a moment to a subject we discussed in Chapter 1 – namely, what are the salient differences between war crimes and crimes against humanity?

The ICTY Appeals Chamber in the Erdemovic judgment cited the Einsatzgruppen case to help draw this distinction:

> War crimes are acts and omissions in violation of the laws and customs of war. By their very nature they can affect only nationals of belligerents and cannot be committed in time of peace. The crime against humanity is not so delimited. It is fundamentally different from the mere war crime in that it embraces systematic violations of fundamental human rights committed at any time against the nationals of any nation. They may occur during peace or in war. The animus of criminal intent is directed against the rights of all men, not merely the right of persons within a war zone.[33]

Therefore, crimes against humanity are said to be "graver" than war crimes, although curiously the court goes on to approve of the way that Dusko Tadic's crimes were handled in the ICTY case, where Tadic was given only an additional year of punishment when the prosecution proved that he had committed a crime against humanity rather than merely a war crime concerning the same act.[34]

Another important consideration is that when crimes are committed during wartime or other armed conflict, as opposed to peacetime, there are almost always special considerations that should make us more sympathetic to people accused of crimes than we would normally

---

[33] *Prosecutor v. Erdemovic*, Joint Separate Opinion of Judge McDonald and Judge Vohrah, October 7, 1997, para. 24.

[34] Ibid., para. 25.

be. During wartime, soldiers and even their commanders are often faced daily with serious assaults on their lives. The accumulation of such threats is sometimes enough to change the attitudes and dispositions of the soldiers and their commanders. When our lives are on the line, we tend to become, of necessity, more self-centered and less able to respond empathetically to the needs of others because our own needs are so overwhelming. This can be seen most clearly when we realize that soldiers on the battlefield are able to claim to be acting out of self-defense most of the time, whereas in peacetime such claims of self-defense are extremely rare.

War crimes concern acts committed in a chain of command, and the fact of that chain of command would seem to be relevant to the assessment of guilt. If one acts merely as a link in that chain, it would seem that one's guilt, as opposed to that of the person who constructed the chain, would be minimal. This is what the superior-orders defense has been constructed to do. And when considering mitigation, as opposed to guilt, the surrounding circumstances of a crime are also seemingly relevant. If a person is in dire poverty and engages in theft, while we may not wish to relieve him or her of guilt, most would admit that the severity of punishment should be diminished because of these surrounding circumstances. It seems that just as poverty can transform how severely we react to theft, so wartime conditions can transform how severely we react to killing and other assaults.

Duress and necessity have been widely recognized as important mitigation factors in criminal law. The ICTY Appeals Chamber opinion of Judges McDonald and Vohrah in the Erdemovic case is illustrative here. These judges state:

[I]t is, in our view, a general principle of law recognized by civilized nations that an accused person is less blameworthy and less deserving of the full punishment when he performs a certain prohibited act under duress.[35]

So while it may be controversial that duress, or necessity, would completely exonerate in cases of killing and other serious offenses against persons, it is relatively uncontroversial that duress would act as a strong mitigating factor in decisions about severity of punishment for those offenses.

The only possibly controversial question is whether wartime situations actually provide the requisite duress or necessity to mitigate

[35] Ibid., para. 66.

punishment even in cases of killing. Here it is interesting to note what the ICC Statute says about duress resulting from a threat of imminent death or serious bodily harm:
Such a threat may either be:

(i) Made by other persons; or
(ii) Constituted by other circumstances beyond that person's control.[36]

Within the same article, the ICC Statute makes it clear that war crimes cases are to be treated differently from other international crimes, allowing defense of self to take the form of seizing property essential for survival or for achieving a military objective.[37] Wartime situations are more inherently threatening than peacetime situations, and generally more leeway is given to criminal actions in such situations.

There is a countervailing consideration that needs to be addressed when comparing wartime with peacetime mitigating circumstances. In wartime, there is a much greater possibility of abuse, with much greater possibility for serious bodily harm or loss of life, than in peacetime. This is largely due to the fact that in wartime many more people have the capacity, because of their proximity to armaments, to cause devastating loss of life to civilians. For this reason, we would want to treat soldiers fighting during war with a stricter set of standards and subject them to more severe punishment than would be true of civilians during peacetime.

This countervailing consideration speaks more to the question we addressed in the previous section, namely, whether duress should completely exonerate soldiers who kill civilians. For this may send the wrong message to very dangerous individuals concerning deterrence. But I am not persuaded that such considerations should not have the same weight when discussing mitigation of punishment. It is true that mitigation can affect deterrence, but as long as one expects at least some punishment (and where the actual severity of punishment is not fully clear), there remains a significant deterrence, as much as there ever is, to the perpetration of crimes.

The fact remains that wartime situations create the paradigmatic "circumstances beyond [the] person's control" that cause a severe risk

---

[36] Statute of the International Criminal Court, Adopted by the U.N. Diplomatic Conference, July 17, 1998, Article 31(d).
[37] Ibid., Article 31(c).

to that person. The day-to-day exposure to those circumstances can cause syndromes rarely seen outside those circumstances. Duress enters into this picture as the most severe of the circumstances. And as we have seen, it is the worry that you will be killed by enemy soldiers, enemy civilians, or even by your fellow soldiers that creates the basis of mitigation. And because "superior orders" is recognized as a defense for certain war crimes, when conjoined with duress it should certainly be a mitigating factor in sentencing.[38]

In peacetime situations, even when conflicts arise that eventually lead to crimes against humanity, the basis of mitigation is not nearly as great as it is during wartime. This is perhaps best seen by reference to necessity rather than to duress. In Chapter 10, I discussed reasonable criteria for deciding when necessity applies:

Level One: Is there a significant harm that should be prevented?
Level Two: Is the harm imminent or extremely likely to occur?
Level Three: Is there no other, less problematical way to prevent the harm?
Level Four: Does the proposed means cause less harm than is prevented?

I argued that only when positive answers can be given at each of these levels will military necessity be a possible justificatory basis for acting in ways that would otherwise be prohibited.

Once necessity has been proved, then there are overwhelming reasons to treat it as at least a significant mitigating factor in punishment. The strictness of the test for necessity is meant to indicate that only in exceptional cases will it be applied, even though it might appear that necessity is the standard operating condition for all wartime situations. Once necessity is so constrained, nearly all legal authorities allow it to be at least a mitigating factor. Even in cases of the killing of innocent civilians, necessity will apply as long as the conditions, especially the fourth condition, are met. In the cases we have been discussing, where the soldier's life is jeopardized if he or she does not follow orders and kill a civilian, the fourth condition seems to be met. But in the Erdemovic case, where in order to save his life the defendant said he had to kill at least 10 people, it is not at all clear that the conditions for necessity are indeed met. In the Erdemovic case, duress rather than necessity will be the main basis for mitigation. And even though duress is somewhat more controversial than necessity, it is nonetheless a well-recognized basis in international criminal law for

---

[38] *Prosecutor v. Erdemovic*, Joint Separate Opinion of Judge McDonald and Judge Vohrah, October 7, 1997, paras. 62–65.

mitigating an otherwise severe sentence, largely because of the way that duress tends to negate moral choice.

It is only somewhat controversial that soldiers could use coercion-based defenses as a way to defeat or mitigate charges of criminal liability. But it is highly controversial that commanders might do so. In this section, I will first explain how war creates much more coercion than people generally face in their day-to-day lives and how this should affect how we approach punishment for war crimes. If war does create serious coercion of soldiers and commanders, this will have an obvious effect on punishment because we tend to punish much more severely those acts that are committed freely and intentionally than those acts that are not truly free. When the connection between war and coercion is properly understood, then one can see more clearly why duress and necessity are important considerations in determining guilt and punishment for war crimes.

In his powerfully evocative book, *The Warriors*, J. Glenn Gray speaks of the fear felt in wartime as one of the most powerful of forces:

Here death is an intimate and repugnant enemy before whose threat and presence one can only flee in terror. There are soldiers in nearly every unit who can endure every hardship and humiliation of military life without flinching, yet cannot face personal death with any composure at all.[39]

Notice that there are two parts to the environment of combat that are relevant to our discussion of coercion. First, there is the obvious daily fear of death, either from a bullet or bomb aimed at you or from a stray bullet or bomb that finds you as its target. Second, there is also the "hardship and humiliation" of being regulated and disciplined for the most minute forms of behavior.

The battlefield experience of many soldiers and commanders is one of constant tension, if not downright fear. These experiences create a cumulative effect that makes otherwise normal people into killers. As Gray puts it: "[T]he warrior who slays an impersonal enemy has traditionally not been regarded as a criminal, a murderer."[40] Then Gray quotes a soldier: "We all figured we might be dead in the next minute,

[39] J. Glenn Gray, *The Warriors: Reflections on Men in Battle*, New York: Harper and Row, 1970, p. 111.
[40] Ibid., p. xvi.

so what difference did it make what we did?"[41] Here again, there are
two rather good bases for why war crimes are committed: They will not
be regarded as wrong, and in any event deterrence won't mean much
because either a soldier will be dead or will gain more than he or she
could lose because he or she avoided death by so acting. The concern
that death will result unless one takes forbidden action is a strong basis
of coercion, which helps explain why massacres of civilians and other
atrocities occur.[42]

As we know from sociological accounts of military training, another
dimension of the military environment is the tremendous respect for
rank and authority that is instilled in each soldier through basic
training.[43] One's own judgment is diminished in importance and
overshadowed by the judgment of one's superiors. The superior is not
only an object of respect but of fear, which is intensified on the battlefield, where one worries that one might be shot in the back by one's
commanding officer if one disobeys the superior's orders. The respect
and fear of superiors that is instilled in soldiers in basic training and
later in field training makes the tense environment on the battlefield
much worse for the individual soldier, who now cannot trust his or her
individual judgment but must trust another person to know what is best
to do.

Soldiers are coerced by the above-mentioned factors in that their
options are restricted against their wills. Quite a bit of good work has
been done to make sense of the conceptual elements of coercion. On
the most plausible account, one has to first find a prethreat (or pre-
offer) baseline. Then the question is asked: Are the options available
on one side of the baseline worse than they were before? If so, then one
has been coerced. Coercion becomes a major factor in moral assessment of an agent's action when there are no longer acceptable options
for the agent after the threat has been made. Of course, in military
situations it is not just one threat but a series of threats plus a very
threatening overall environment that is the key to seeing why soldiers
are coerced in ways that affect the moral and legal assessment of their
actions.

---

[41] Ibid., p. xvii, quoting from David Lang, *Casualties of War*, 1966.
[42] In my book *Crimes Against Humanity: A Normative Account*, New York: Cambridge
University Press, 2005, Part D, I also argue that punishment for crimes against
humanity, for similar reasons, should be diminished as well.
[43] See my discussion of this phenomenon in my book *Masculinity and Morality*, Ithaca, NY:
Cornell University Press, 1998.

While it is well documented that *soldiers* feel constrained and even coerced on the battlefield, it is not often recognized that many of the same factors that go into that coercion are also true for *commanders*. After all, commanders were socialized in the same way as soldiers, because all of them were either soldiers first or went through a very elaborate indoctrination and training in officers' school. Commanders are also themselves commanded by those who are even higher up the chain of command. And while it may appear that commanders are able to make of their lives something better than what they had prior to joining the military, there are still situations where their options are reduced to the point where there are no morally acceptable alternatives open to them. In this sense, we can speak of commanders being coerced, especially on the battlefield, in ways similar to that of soldiers, even though it might first appear that commanders are in a very different moral position than soldiers are, and even though commanders often participate in the coercion of other soldiers.

War is a coercive force for myriad reasons that coalesce to make people more likely to commit acts they would normally not countenance. Of course, it is rare when a coercive environment removes choice altogether. What is more likely is that acceptable choices will be limited or even eliminated. In disobeying orders, one is faced with the unenviable possibility of being court-martialed or shot for one's disobedience. Surely, we want people to stand up and refuse orders that are patently illegal or immoral, but what cost is it reasonable to expect them to pay for this? It seems to be too much, as was argued earlier, to punish people who do not risk their lives or bodily integrity to stand up against illegal or immoral superior orders.

If we care enough about deterring war crimes to want to punish these crimes even when the perpetrators were merely following orders, and if we similarly want to deny exculpation when pleas of duress and necessity can be substantiated, then we still face the question of mitigation. It seems to me that war and all its surrounding circumstances coerce and intimidate, but perhaps not enough in many cases to support exculpation. Yet it is very hard to see why war's coercive environment would not mitigate the guilt of soldiers and even their commanders. Mitigation of punishment does not necessarily diminish the international law's deterrent effects, whatever those might be.[44]

---

[44] It is beyond the scope of this book to address the very important question raised here, namely, whether international law in general and international humanitarian law in

Indeed, if no mitigation is allowed for any reason, the law will not necessarily deter at all because people may simply give up trying to conform when they realize that no matter what they do they will still be held fully responsible and subject to the most severe punishment.

Commanders are to be treated somewhat differently than regular soldiers in that commanders often have more options when faced with an illegal or immoral order than do regular soldiers. Commanders often have channels of communication open, due to socializing with higher-ups than do regular soldiers. And there are certainly avenues open to commanders to enlist media support to publicize bad policies and orders, whereas such avenues are largely closed for regular soldiers. It is also much less likely that a commander's superior would shoot him or her in the back for disobeying orders, at least in part because the orders are likely to be much less specific and much more subject to interpretation.

The coercive nature of military units, explicitly perpetrated by heavy emphasis on obedience within a chain of command as well as realistic fears of serious injury or death at the hands of the enemy, create an environment that seems extremely well suited to support claims of mitigation during sentencing for war crimes. It is less clear whether to let these factors count as full-scale defenses, although there were some good arguments to this effect explored earlier in this chapter. Soldiers are the ones who can most clearly make a claim for mitigation of a sentence based on such coercion. But as we have seen, commanders can sometimes make out this case as well. War normally creates an extremely stressful environment, especially for regular soldiers who end up with not much control over their options. When options are diminished to the point where they are worse off than before, then coercion has occurred. And when coercion intensifies to the point where there are no morally acceptable options remaining, then this coercion should become a basis for mitigating sentences that would normally be handed out to soldiers and commanders. And as we

---

particular are likely to be effective deterrents of crime. Mark Drumbl has proposed that codes of honor and more localized dispute resolution mechanisms might be better at deterring war crimes than fear of international prosecution. I do not necessarily disagree. This is why throughout this book I have moved back and forth between these two models. See Drumbl's recent work, which bears on this topic: "Sands: From Nuremberg to The Hague: The Future of International Criminal Justice," *Michigan Law Review*, vol. 103, no. 6 (2005), pp. 1305–1311; and "Collective Violence and Individual Punishment: The Criminality of Mass Atrocity," *Northwestern University Law Review*, vol. 99, no. 2 (2005), pp. 101–179.

will next see, there is another powerful moral reason that reinforces this conclusion.

V. TREATING SOLDIERS AND COMMANDERS HUMANELY

Another reason to think that soldiers and their commanders should at least have their punishment mitigated because of coercive forces during wartime is that it would be inhumane not to do so. In this final section, I wish to return to our various discussions of the principle of humane treatment. It will turn out that while the principle of humane treatment supports strong rules of war, that principle also supports lenient treatment of those who are accused of violating the rules. And the leniency extends from soldiers to commanders, although precisely how far up the chain of command it extends is initially unclear. If it is true that the principle of humane treatment is the centerpiece of international humanitarian law, it will have a profound impact on punishment of war criminals as well.

Hugo Grotius defined punishment as "an evil of suffering which is inflicted because of an evil of action."[45] He followed Seneca in thinking that "'everyone must be punished who has a base and malicious nature.'"[46] But as Grotius pointed out, "Scarcely any one is bad for no purpose, while if any one delights in wickedness for its own sake he is beyond the pale of humanity. . . . Most people are led to sin by their desires."[47] If "great and pressing grounds for punishment are lacking, we should be the more ready to mitigate the punishment." Such a strategy will allow us to "weigh on the side of humanity."[48] If there is no evil intent, then it makes much more sense to punish with moderation than with severity.[49] According to Grotius, moderation and mitigation of punishment are what the principle of humanity calls for unless we are dealing with someone who acts maliciously, and that is rarely true in wartime situations.

Grotius is especially concerned about behavior that lacks "freedom of action."[50] Such behavior is not properly guilty and should not be punished, at least not with the severity reserved for malicious conduct. As I have been arguing in this chapter, many of the actions taken that cause harm during wars are not based on malice but simply on duty. As

---

[45] Hugo Grotius, *De Jure Belli ac Pacis* (*On the Law of War and Peace*) (1625), translated by Francis W. Kelsey, Oxford: Clarendon Press, 1925, p. 462.
[46] Ibid., p. 488. [47] Ibid., p. 494. [48] Ibid., p. 501. [49] Ibid., p. 523.
[50] Ibid., p. 488.

we saw earlier, Grotius believed that pardons and clemencies are justifiable, especially in the case of someone who acts without malice.[51] In certain cases, it may be permitted to punish those who are without malice, but the punishment is not deserved. And in those cases, Grotius was concerned that the punishment inflicted be mitigated by reference to the state of mind of the person committing the harmful act.

Following Grotius' lead, as I have done throughout this book, I would also argue that especially in wartime it is important to look at why harmful actions were taken. If the person acts out of a desire to do his or her duty or is constrained by fear to act, that person does not deserve to be punished or, if punished at all, not as severely as the person who causes harm out of malice. And the main reason for this is the principle of humane treatment, which calls for compassion as well as mercy in the way that people are treated, especially those who are dependent on us. The principle of humane treatment calls on us to treat fellow humans with respect. Unless they act in ways that are "beyond the pale of humanity" – that is, in a truly monstrous way – they should be treated as fellow humans to whom we would give the benefit of the doubt (see Chapter 4).

Wartime situations are not those where we normally find harm being done out of malice. Of course, when there are malicious acts, severe punishment of those responsible makes sense and may even be sanctioned by the principles of humanity and justice. But when harms are caused to civilians, for instance, because there is some military objective that is thereby served, those who are commanded to act, and even those who do the commanding, are normally not malicious. In such cases, humanitarian concerns should dominate. This does not necessarily mean that the perpetrators should not be punished at all, but on the Grotian account of the principle of humanity that I have defended in this book, mitigation of punishment will make sense when there is no malice involved.

We should at least acknowledge a hard case of someone who acts during wartime from mixed motives, that is, the person is commanded to act a certain way and is also motivated to do so out of a hatred for the ethnic group that he or she has been ordered to harm. This can be an especially hard case if the soldier's hatred has itself been caused by indoctrination from superiors in the chain of command. Malice instilled by others also makes of the act of the soldier something that is

---

[51] Ibid., pp. 489–491.

not fully free. It is for this reason that even some forms of malice, as in this case, may not be subject to severe punishment. Unfortunately, it is very hard to tell what a person's motives are and even harder to tell what has caused those motives to exist. Nonetheless, when it can be ascertained, the case of mixed motives, of malice plus duty, can sometimes be treated as we treat simpler cases of actions from duty. Many of us act from mixed motives, but rarely do we act solely from malice.

Humane treatment, as the cornerstone of international humanitarian law, concerns those who are accused of war crimes as well as those who merely fight in times of war. In fact, our discussion of prisoners of war in Chapter 7 can help us understand how those who are confined and accused of war crimes should be treated. Remember that those who confine persons are to act as fiduciaries or stewards, and the confined should be treated as innocents until trial. Even after trial, while there may be strong incentives to retaliate against these prisoners for what they have done on the battlefield, we should still exercise restraint and treat them humanely. Here we can turn to Grotius, again quoting Seneca, who said, " 'Vengeance is an inhuman term, although accepted as just, and only differs from insult in degree. He who avenges his grief, sins, although with more excuse.' "[52]

The pleas of duress and necessity should be given due consideration as defenses and even more as the basis for mitigation of severe sentences otherwise deserved in war crimes trials. If humane treatment signals that people are to be respected as fellow humans and treated with mercy and compassion, then surely this means that sentences are to be mitigated whenever such action is warranted. Even when not strictly deserved, as a matter of justice, sentences should be mitigated if compassion or mercy calls for it. For example, if a soldier has participated in an atrocity against a group of civilians, compassion for his claim to be only acting upon orders and so that his family will not starve, as in the Erdemovic case, should be heard. It would be heartless not to hear the plea of an Erdemovic, even given that he killed at least 10 people. Again, this is not to say that an Erdemovic should necessarily be granted impunity, but only that mitigation should be seriously considered in light of the circumstances.

Throughout Part D of this book, I have argued that it makes sense to prosecute individuals for war crimes, but I have also argued that it

[52] Ibid., p. 468.

normally makes more sense to prosecute military leaders than regular soldiers for such crimes because of considerations of *mens rea*. I indicated that it was significantly easier to prove the elements of a crime, for both leaders and regular soldiers, if it is possible to use the joint criminal enterprise theory. For if the leaders and soldiers are all part of a larger scheme that they are aware of and have come to endorse, then it is much easier to show criminal intent than it would be otherwise. Although I also warned against the possible abuses to which the joint enterprise model could be put.

While I have argued that punishments can be legitimately meted out for war crimes, I have been sympathetic to the pleas of duress and necessity, as well as the plea of superior orders – pleas that can often be made in wartime as possible bases for defense or mitigation of punishment. This final part of the book has brought us to the point of seeing how the principle of humane treatment can be used to substantiate charges of war crimes while placing limits on what punishments are reasonable for those convicted of war crimes.

The idea of a war crime is not, as some have thought, a contradiction in terms. There are legitimate rules of war that apply, even though war itself looks like a major violation of moral rules. War crimes may not be viewed as being as serious as crimes against humanity or genocide; but when civilians are targeted for attack, for instance, the crimes are very serious indeed. It is quite appropriate for individuals to be held accountable for such crimes, because, after all, it is individuals who commit them. But unlike many other kinds of crime, war crimes are almost always planned by, or at least permitted by, States. Thus, while international criminal tribunals are appropriate arenas for prosecuting war crimes, other political arenas may also be appropriate places to deal with the States that normally orchestrate war crimes.

14

Epilogue and conclusions

Should terrorists be treated humanely?

Since the terrorist attacks in New York City and Washington, DC on September 11, 2001, many people have said that the way they thought of Just War theory changed.[1] While these attacks seemed to be directed at the government of the United States, they were not conducted under the auspices of another State. And more importantly, those who took part in the attacks were not normal soldiers, at least as this category had previously been understood. Indeed, most saliently, the "terrorists" did not recognize the rules of war, failing almost grotesquely to conform to the principle of discrimination or distinction, even as I have reconceptualized that principle. In this final chapter, I will try to explain why even terrorists should be treated humanely, contrary to what most politicians said at the time of the World Trade Center and Pentagon bombings. In so doing, I will summarize some of the main conclusions reached in this book.

In many ways, the principle of humane treatment in international law is like the principle of due process in domestic law, in that both principles aim at treating everyone with a minimum of humanity. As I have said several times, war crimes are best seen as crimes against humaneness. In the case of terrorists, it appears that they have clearly engaged in war crimes by denying to their victims any sense of humanity. So, as the argument goes, these terrorists do not deserve any

---

[1] Cf. Joseph Boyle, "Just War Doctrine and the Military Response to Terrorism," *Journal of Political Philosophy*, vol. 11, no. 2 (2003), pp. 153–170. For worries about how terrorism has affected international law, see Antonio Cassese, "Terrorism Is Also Disrupting Some Crucial Legal Categories of International Law," *European Journal of International Law*, vol. 12 (2001), p. 993.

better treatment than the treatment they have displayed toward their victims. And if one of the main rationales for subscribing to the principle of humane treatment is that it will be most likely to produce similar behavior toward one's own troops, this rationale seems highly questionable in the case of terrorists because they have shown no sense of restraint toward civilians, let alone toward fellow fighters. Perhaps the only way to secure our own civilians and soldiers from the inhumane treatment of terrorists is to act even more harshly toward them than they act toward us, thereby deterring the terrorists from future horrific acts.

At the beginning of this book, I said that changes in the way that warfare is conducted might cause us to change the way we think of the rules of war. The case of terrorism is a very good test case. Terrorism is not well contemplated by the traditional Just War doctrine. That tradition was set during a time when wars were fought exclusively by the soldiers of States, and these soldiers were in uniform and recognized the chain of command. Terrorists do not wear uniforms and rarely fight under the direction of commanders with ultimate authority from the head of a State. Nonetheless, terrorists are fighters who are even more in need of the traditional protections of the rules of war, for they inspire emotional reactions that are themselves often inhumane.[2]

In this final chapter, I will mount an argument, drawing on the ideas I have advanced in previous chapters, supporting the view that terrorists should be treated humanely. In the first section, I will articulate several problems for the Just War theory that are raised by the phenomenon of terrorism. In the second section, I make a stab at explaining who are the terrorists and how the term "terrorism" should be defined. In the third section, I explain the difficulties of answering the question "What are terrorists owed?" In the fourth section of this chapter, I argue that the rules of war, especially the principle of humane treatment, need to be instilled in all soldiers concerning all those who are fighters "on the other side," even when the sides are not as clear-cut as they were once thought to be. In the fifth section, I address the argument that politicians today seem too ready to give: that any wrong done in our fight against terrorists can be justified because terrorists also do wrong. And in the sixth section, I provide

[2] For a discussion of how terrorists associated with the September 11, 2001 attacks should be conceptualized, see Mark A. Drumbl, "Victimhood in Our Neighborhood," *North Carolina Law Review*, vol. 81 (2002), pp. 1–113.

some brief final thoughts about Grotius and the Grotian project I have been engaged in.

I. THE PROBLEM OF TERRORISTS

Karl Rove, President George W. Bush's right-hand man, put the case quite clearly when he said that the difference between liberal Democrats and conservative Republicans is that Democrats' reaction to September 11 terrorism was to "prepare indictments and offer therapy and understanding for our attackers," whereas Republicans' reaction to September 11 terrorism was "to prepare for war."[3] One could make the same response to my proposals advanced in previous chapters. Many people react to scenes of terrorist violence with feelings of retribution rather than mercy. Unfortunately, it has been the reaction on both sides of most controversies, for hardly anyone's first reaction is mercy or compassion toward those who act as one's enemies. Rove is correct to imply that most people would seek retribution, if not revenge, in such situations. But, it seems to me, this is only the first reaction, and like most first reactions it is not necessarily the reaction that will be seen as justifiable after cool reflection.

The rules of war are meant to make both soldiers and leaders stop and think before they react as their emotions may initially direct them. This creates a reciprocal respect for the rules of war that translates into a minimal respect for the participants in a war. But if terrorists do not recognize the rules of war, why should their victims restrain themselves by the rules that the terrorists ignore? This is one of the main problems posed by terrorists for the Just War tradition. It was assumed in that tradition that if one side kept to the rules of war, it would likely mean that the other side would also keep to these rules. If there is unlikely to be reciprocity, why should soldiers voluntarily restrain themselves in the face of terrorist violence?

It might be useful at this stage to look back to the time in history when the rules of war were quite vigilantly subscribed to and yet there was little or no reciprocity. It is often said that the Allied soldiers in World War II, especially the American soldiers, were scrupulous in keeping to the rules of war, even as they came to realize that the Axis soldiers, especially those from the Third Reich, utterly disregarded

---

[3] Jim Abrams, "Democrats Say Rove Should Apologize or Resign," *Washington Post*, June 23, 2005, p. A1.

those rules.[4] Was this a foolish strategy on the part of the Allies? Why didn't the Allies declare that the Nazi soldiers were terrorists who did not deserve to be treated humanely? Perhaps the Nazi soldiers should have been seen as illegal combatants and tortured or otherwise abused if it was thought that this abuse could perform some kind of deterrent purpose in winning a clearly just war.

There is a reason for keeping to the rules of war, even though it is clear that one's opponent will not do so: a concern for instilling the general idea of the importance of obedience to the rules of war. According to this belief, it is not an immediate tit-for-tat response that is the reason for keeping to the rules of war, but something more long-run. The world is generally a better place the more people believe that they should restrain themselves even, and especially, during war. As has been recognized for several thousand years, the rules of war prevent the ravages of war from destroying the humanity of those who fight in them.

It could be objected, though, that if in World War II the Axis powers had won the war because they did not feel that they had to restrain themselves in the use of tactics, the Allied powers' restraint would definitely not have made the world a safer place: The Allied soldiers would have felt better about themselves morally, but they would most likely have been subjugated under an oppressive rule. When a war is worth fighting for and one's enemy does not conform to the rules of war, it seems counterintuitive to engage in unilateral self-restraint. Morally important wars need to be fought with all of the material that is available, and that includes the use of all available tactics.

My response to this important point is to concede that it is indeed difficult to maintain support for the restraints of the rules of war in the face of an enemy who shows disregard for those rules. But doing what is right is often difficult and seemingly counterintuitive. Think of the easy case of stealing. Why don't more people simply take the opportunity to increase their own wealth any way that they can? Is it only because they are afraid of getting caught? It's true that this is sometimes the motivation, but it cannot be the whole story, given that there are many opportunities for stealing where the chances of getting caught range from minuscule to nonexistent. It is also true that people believe that not stealing is the right thing to do, and they take pride in

---

[4] I do not share this view, but I introduce it as the example most often cited. In my view, there were significant violations of the rules of war on both sides during World War II.

the knowledge that their own property was obtained in ways that they find conscientiously acceptable. The rules of war provide a basis for pride and honor for soldiers who would otherwise not be able to distinguish themselves from simple murderers.

It could also be objected that in any event the Allies did not respect the rules of war throughout World War II. The fire bombing of Dresden and the atomic bombing of Hiroshima and Nagasaki were all conducted toward the end of the war. These tactics were used as a way to make sure that the Nazis and Japanese did not gain an advantage with their own breaking of the rules of war by the firebombing of Coventry, England and the attempt to develop the atomic bomb. Even World War II, often cited as an example where one side, the Allies, kept to the rules of war despite good evidence that the other side would not, is not a good model for those who think that the rules of war should be kept against terrorists. The rules of war, while acknowledged for several thousand years, have also been systematically violated during that same time period.

At this stage, I must admit that there have probably not been any cases where one side observed the rules of war throughout a war while the other side was clearly violating those rules. But that does not mean that there are not good normative grounds for doing so nonetheless. The case of terrorists is indeed problematical for both the Just War tradition and international humanitarian law. If I am right to argue that we are better off for keeping the rules of war than not, then we should not be overly swayed by the historical fact that the rules of war have been broken by both sides in nearly every war.

The problem of terrorists is that they don't violate the rules of war only occasionally. George W. Bush said that terrorists posed a special problem because they totally ignore the rules of conventional warfare.[5] As I have argued throughout this book, it is not the rules of conventional warfare, but the rules of war of the Just War tradition, that are key, and it is those rules that terrorists seem to ignore. In the next section, I will examine whether it is true that terrorists are by definition incapable of keeping the rules of war and thus pose an especially difficult problem for those, like myself, who argue in favor of those rules as applicable to all people, even terrorists.

---

[5] Ron Hutcheson, ""Bush Uses Sept. 11 to Rally U.S. for War," *St. Louis Post-Dispatch*, June 29, 2005, p. A1.

II.   WHO ARE THE TERRORISTS?

There has been a serious debate about how to define "terrorism" and "terrorists" that has not approached anything like consensus in the last 25 years. One of the central questions in this debate is whether "terrorism" can be defined in a neutral way. Michael Walzer has defined it as a strategy that recognizes no moral restraints.[6] Specifically, Walzer claims that the "victims of a terrorist attack are third parties, innocent bystanders; there is no special reason for attacking them. . . . The attack is directed indiscriminately against the entire class."[7] Others have defined "terrorism" as a form of unjustified attack, again because of the indiscriminate targeting of civilians.[8] If "terrorism" is so defined, then it appears that terrorists will necessarily violate the rules of war and they will indeed pose a serious problem for Just War theory and international humanitarian law.

Robert Fullinwider rightly points out that some terrorists do not act indiscriminately.[9] Take the case of the kidnapping and murder of Aldo Moro by the Italian group the Red Brigades. According to Fullinwider, "the abduction had been planned over several months and followed a period of kidnappings and kneecappings of industrialists and lesser political figures. There was nothing indiscriminate about the taking of Aldo Moro."[10] Fullinwider also argues that terrorists can be engaged in a moral quest for justice. Of course, one can argue about whether the Red Brigades were indeed terrorists, but this would be difficult because at the time, in the late 1970s, they were considered a paradigmatic case of terrorists. In any event, it seems right to think that terrorists often target quite specific individuals or groups for their assaults and do not merely attack civilians indiscriminately.

I will attempt to provide a morally neutral definition of "terrorism." This does not necessarily mean that terrorists won't still violate the rules of war, but only that this will not be true by definition. Andrew

---

[6] Michael Walzer, "Terrorism: A Critique of Excuses," in *Problems of International Justice*, edited by Stephen Luper-Foy, Boulder, CO: Westview Press, 1988, pp. 237–247; reprinted in *The Morality of War*, edited by Larry May, Eric Rovie, and Steve Viner, Upper Saddle River, NJ: Prentice-Hall, 2006, pp. 297–305.

[7] Ibid., p. 297.

[8] See Burton M. Leiser, *Liberty, Justice, and Morals*, 2nd ed., New York: Prentice-Hall, 1979, pp. 375–397.

[9] Robert Fullinwider, "Understanding Terrorism," in *Problems of International Justice*, edited by Stephen Luper-Foy, Boulder, CO: Westview Press, 1988, pp. 248–259; reprinted in *The Morality of War*, edited by Larry May, Eric Rovie, and Steve Viner, Upper Saddle River, NJ: Prentice-Hall, 2006, pp. 306–315.

[10] Ibid., p. 308.

Valls proposes a definition of "terrorism" that I find the least objectionable of those proposed lately: "[V]iolence committed by nonstate (or state) actors against persons or property for political purposes."[11] The only problem with this definition is that it loses the sense of why the term is used in the first place by leaving out the idea that the point of terrorism is to instill fear in the population. Valls says that there are other kinds of tactics that would still count as terrorist ones, and I suppose he is right. But by defining "terrorism" in this way, we lose that etymological base, although what is gained is much greater than any of the competing definitions.

Valls and Fullinwider are surely right that terrorism does not necessarily involve indiscriminate violence or killing. Indeed, when high-ranking politicians are targeted by terrorists, two things are accomplished that are significant for the moral assessment of their actions. First, the targeting is not indiscriminate. Second, the targeting may not even violate the discrimination or distinction principle because the politician may be responsible for injustice or the conduct of an unjust war and thus is not, strictly speaking, innocent. This type of terrorism nonetheless often does accomplish the objectives of terrorists in that it instills fear in the population at large. After all, if their leaders can be targeted, anyone can be.

The issue of whether terrorists necessarily violate the rules of war does not exhaust the issue of whether terrorism can be justified. But a justification is indeed what is needed by those who say that terrorists in general, not just some specific terrorists, have violated the rules of war and do not deserve to be protected by those rules. Once we move to discussions of particular terrorists, the issue is reopened. For nothing that I have said so far is aimed at defeating the claim that specific terrorists can ignore the rules of war. I would agree with the emerging international consensus that terrorists who engage in indiscriminate killing should be condemned. But then we come to the second question related to who the terrorists are: Are terrorists enough alike that it is important to confront them all in the same way or at least to worry that the way they are confronted in one case will not affect how they act in other cases.

---

[11] Andrew Valls, "Can Terrorism Be Justified?" in *Ethics and International Affairs*, edited by Andrew Valls, Lanham, MD: Rowman and Littlefield, 2000, pp. 65–79; reprinted in *The Morality of War*, edited by Larry May, Eric Rovie, and Steve Viner, Upper Saddle River, NJ: Prentice-Hall, 2006, p. 318.

We have no good reason to think that terrorists are all alike or that they think of themselves as enough like other terrorists that treating them humanely in one case will mean that other terrorists will be more likely to commit mayhem. Indeed, we have already seen that some terrorists engage in indiscriminate violence and others do not. It is not at all clear that both groups should be treated the same and that the way to treat them both is by suspending the rules of war. Indeed, it is much more plausible to think that differentiating among terrorists would be justified both morally and prudentially. This seems to be true, unless there is something about terrorists that makes them not prone to act rationally.

As I have argued throughout this book, what is needed is a fine-grained rather than a rough-grained determination. Some terrorists, such as members of al-Qaeda, deliberately and intentionally disregard the rules of war. Other terrorists, such as the Red Brigades or the ETA (Euskadi Ta Askatasuna), try to stay within the bounds of those rules by, for instance, phoning first before bombs are detonated so as to give civilians the chance to be evacuated.[12] Given the wide disparity in types of terrorists, we should not merely lump them all together in a rough-grained way. Rather, we should also pay attention to salient differences among them.

If we think of suicide bombers, it is tempting to say that they are simply not rational beings at all, or at least not enough so that it would matter to them how we treat them. After all, they are willing to die for their cause, so why should they care whether we might act humanely toward them if, but only if, they acted in a more discriminating way, perhaps by not targeting civilian centers but instead choosing military barracks, for their assaults. Notice that this position does not argue for indiscriminate treatment of terrorists, but only for worrying about how some will react to how others are treated. And here we have no reason to think that treating some terrorists humanely will make it more likely that other terrorists will act more brazenly.

There is a reason for thinking that all terrorists should be treated the same that is based on who they are and that will tell against disregarding the rules of war in how they should be treated. Terrorists are like other types of accused criminals in that until there has been a trial it is unfair to treat them as if their status as terrorists had been conclusively determined. If some terrorists have been convicted of assault

---

[12] I am grateful to Mark Drumbl for this example.

or murder, then it is perfectly plausible to punish them or otherwise discriminate against them for what they have done. But if suspected terrorists have been captured and not yet convicted, they should not be treated according to their status as terrorists. Or perhaps the point could be put this way: We should treat suspected terrorists according to their status as "suspected" terrorists, much as we would treat anyone else who is suspected of a lesser crime. Here the "war on terrorism" is utterly at odds with my arguments advanced in earlier chapters. There is no reason to try to kill suspected terrorists rather than to capture them and bring them to trial. Therefore, there is no reason to think that Karl Rove was right to say that the correct response to the terrorism of September 11, 2001 in New York and Washington was to prepare for war rather than to seek indictments. But even if war is the answer, there is still no reason to think that the rules of war do not apply to the treatment of terrorists.

III. WHAT ARE TERRORISTS OWED?

Given how I have framed the issues so far in this book, the question of what is owed to terrorists must be addressed from both the standpoint of justice and the standpoint of humanity. If we restrict ourselves to considerations of retributive justice, it turns out that terrorists could be owed severe punishment, although I will argue that even this is not fully clear. From the standpoint of wider justice considerations, especially from considerations of humaneness, terrorists would be owed something else, perhaps protection. The question I will address in this section is what terrorists are owed, all things considered. I will argue that terrorists are not owed punishment unless they are convicted of a crime and that terrorists are owed humane treatment, especially before they have been convicted.

Even from the standpoint of retributive justice, terrorists – and all others, for that matter – are owed the procedural due process considerations that are involved in establishing what they have done. As commonsensical as this may sound, this has indeed been challenged since the September 11, 2001 terrorist assaults in New York and Washington. The alternative, as Karl Rove famously put it, is to plan for war immediately rather than to put accused terrorists on trial. Is there something about terrorism that makes its perpetrators different from those who engage in other crimes? I suppose Karl Rove and others would try to assimilate terrorism to war rather than to crime. On this model, we do not have to wait to identify the perpetrators but are entitled to strike out at those who we believe are attacking us, as a simple matter of self-defense.

One major difference between the law/crime model and the war model is that in the war model the assumption is that which individuals are assaulted does not matter.[13] The war model assumes that there will be other individual combatants who will rise to replace any fallen or captured combatants. The law/crime model assumes that the individual perpetrators will not necessarily be replaced by others, so that the key is to capture and prosecute the right individuals, for only if the wrong ones are captured will there still be others out there that might attack again. In most war situations, no matter who is captured, there will be others ready to attack, so the only thing that matters is deterring the others by what is done to the one who has been captured. Of course, this sets the stage for thinking that even torturing the non-guilty could be justified as deterrence. In the law model, there does not appear to be any incentive to capture and punish those who are non-guilty.

Should terrorism be best viewed on the law/crime or the war model? I'm inclined to think that the war model makes more sense. Terrorists are more like regular combatants in that they are replaceable. This is especially true because there is rarely any direct personal payoff for the terrorist, as there would often be for the normal criminal. But this also means that, as in war, it will be hard to deter terrorists from future attacks because they are not motivated by personal considerations of gain and probably won't be motivated by personal considerations of loss. Nonetheless, I am inclined to think that the war model makes more sense than the law/crime model in how we initially think about terrorists.

But then what are terrorists owed from the perspective of the war model? Those who would argue that individual terrorists are owed retribution now have a more difficult task than they may have thought. For unlike standard criminals, terrorists do not do what they do out of a hope for personal gain, and someone else probably would have replaced them if they had not been able or willing to do what they did.

---

[13] For more on the differences between the war model and the law/crime model for dealing with terrorism, see David Luban, "The War on Terrorism and the End of Human Rights," in *War After September 11*, edited by Verna V. Gehring, Lanham, MD: Rowman and Littlefield, 2003; reprinted in *The Morality of War*, edited by Larry May, Eric Rovie, and Steve Viner, Upper Saddle River, NJ: Prentice-Hall, 2006, pp. 413–421.

Because terrorists do not generally engage in violence unless others have told them to do so, they are like combatants in that they are not really proper subjects of retribution. Rather, it is their leaders, if anyone, who are subject to retribution.

Even if on the war model individual terrorists are not due retribution, what, if anything, is their due? This is the crux of the matter, for unless it is claimed that terrorists are neither criminals nor combatants, they will be owed what is normally owed to people in one or the other category. If terrorists are combatants, then they are owed the type of mutual respect that is paid to all combatants according to the Just War tradition. If we are to use the law/crime model, then terrorists are owed the full due process considerations that apply to any criminal suspect. This is why the administration of George W. Bush has tried to create an intermediate category for terrorists, because on either of the reigning categories terrorists are owed quite a lot. For terrorists to be subject to abuse or torture, they could not fall into either standard category.

The idea that terrorists are not criminals or combatants is an imaginative way to get out of the bind articulated above. The term "illegal combatant" is meant to signify this intermediate status. But even if we agree that this is the proper way to characterize terrorists, it is not at all clear that this category involves fewer rights than either of the categories that it lies between. For this intermediate category could be one that incorporated protections from both categories rather than having the protections of neither. The chief reason to disagree has to do with the idea that terrorists have waived whatever protection they might otherwise have by refusing to conform to the rules of war.

Even if terrorists are illegal combatants, this does not mean that they should be treated without restraint from either the perspective of the rule of law or the rules of war. I suppose that someone could claim that terrorists are simply outlaws and thus outside any system of rules. Such a view is like treating terrorists as pirates were treated in the 16th and 17th centuries, where their voluntary acts were thought to have waived any rights that they would otherwise be entitled to. But as with similar views about other types of criminal acts, it is not at all clear that we should endorse the view that a waiver has occurred especially because the people in question surely don't recognize what they have done as constituting such a waiver.

If a State's soldiers violate the rules of war but are not categorized as illegal combatants, why should we believe that terrorists who do not accept the rules of war are best categorized as illegal combatants? What

is typically thought is that soldiers who violate the rules of war should
be tried as war criminals and that such trials should themselves be
conducted according to the rules of war. This is similar to what is
thought about domestic criminals: We do not hang suspected criminals
from trees, as was tragically done in the Ox Bow Incident, but instead
we treat them according to the rules that apply to anyone who is
standing trial. It is normally thought that those who have broken the
law, even if cavalierly done, still deserve the law's protection. Indeed,
this is the hallmark of a liberal society that recognizes the rule of law, as
opposed to a vigilante-based society.

In the end, I see no reason to think that terrorists are not owed what
is considered the minimum for all humans, and I believe that this
should be drawn in terms of both considerations of justice and
humanity. Once one is convinced of this claim, then it is just a short
step to believing that terrorists, like everyone else, are owed a minimum amount of compassion, mercy, and justice, at least procedural
justice as epitomized in rule of law considerations. This conclusion is
largely a negative one – namely, there are no good reasons to reject
this claim on behalf of terrorists. In the next section, I take up some
positive reasons for thinking that it is a good thing for terrorists to be
treated humanely. In advancing this argument, I will return again to
the idea of honor, an idea as old as Homer and central to the thought
of the theorists whom I have been most strongly influenced by in this
book: Seneca and Grotius. For on my account, both the Just War tradition and contemporary international humanitarian law are deeply
entwined with considerations of honor and conscience.

IV.   HONOR AND INSTILLING HUMANENESS

At the U.S. military academies, students are quickly socialized into an
honor code that governs their lives first as students and then as soldiers. According to one former West Point cadet:

> The honor code was not just a way to fight a better war. In the Army, soldiers
> are given few rights, grave responsibilities, and lots and lots of power. The
> honor code serves as the Bill of Rights of the Army, protecting soldiers from
> betraying one another and the rest of us from their terrifying power to destroy.
> It is all that stands between an Army and tyranny.[14]

---

[14] Lucian K. Truscott IV, "The Not-So-Long Gray Line," *New York Times*, June 28, 2005,
      p. A23.

This cadet called the honor code the Army's DNA and worried about whether it will survive if the moral code of the Army is not respected and is not continually instilled into each new generation of cadets.

As I have argued, the principle of humaneness is crucial to this code of honor, which has come down to us in the rules of war. Instilling the provisions of this code is a difficult matter, but it is especially difficult if soldiers are told to treat terrorist combatants differently from other combatants on the battlefield – or in the streets, as is increasingly the case today. The rough equality of soldiers is so ingrained in military cadets and boot camp soldiers that we would risk significant trouble by urging that some soldiers, the "terrorist" ones, be treated completely differently than the rest. Soldiers would be allowed to mistreat the "terrorist" soldiers, even though the decision about which category a given group of soldiers fit into would be difficult to make. Indeed, this would be an especially difficult task while engaged in active fighting.

It could be argued that I have already called for a rewriting of the rules of war, especially how soldiers understand who is a civilian and who is a combatant liable to be attacked, that involve finer-grained determinations than were called for in the traditional characterization of the rules of war. So, given this, why would I resist rewriting the rules of war concerning who counts as a "legal" combatant. If a soldier's sense of honor can withstand finer-grained decision making in terms of who is a civilian versus who is a combatant, then why couldn't a soldier's sense of honor withstand finer-grained decision making concerning who is a legal combatant versus who is an illegal combatant?

One of the problems is that the distinction between a legal and an illegal combatant is not merely a definitional matter but is supposed to justify quite radically different treatment. If one is a legal combatant, then all of the rules of war apply; but if one is an illegal combatant, then seemingly few of the rules of war apply. Hence, the distinction between these categories is monumental in terms of how a combatant is to be treated. And most importantly, soldiers would be encouraged to disregard the equality of soldiers, which they have been trained to think protects them and other soldiers and makes their assaults something more than acts of violent aggression. Such a difference between categories is problematical, and of course it calls into question whether acts perpetrated against terrorists would themselves now count as acts of retaliatory barbarism rather than the kind of acts of courage and bravery that soldiers aspire to. Indeed, the recent abuse of so-called illegal combatants by American soldiers seems very close to a return to barbarism.[15]

A soldier's honor is deeply entwined with a conscientious sense that the soldier is doing the right thing by engaging in violence. For centuries, this idea has been instilled by reference to a set of restraints that soldiers are bound by, most significantly that they would not allow their own sense of hatred or revenge to dictate how to act toward fellow combatants.[16] One could wonder why it is that soldiers could not get their hands dirty just as is true for many other role-based professions.[17] Politicians, for instance, seem to have little difficulty seeing that in certain cases it is important, indeed necessary, that they act in ways that would otherwise be considered immoral. Why not think that soldiers could also conceive of themselves this way when confronting terrorists?

The problem is that soldiers are already engaged in a profession that has dirty hands on a massive scale. Soldiers assault and kill as a matter of professional training, even of professional duty, where such behavior would otherwise be considered immoral. So to argue that they should have dirty hands also in the way that they carry out their terrible duty toward terrorists is truly troubling. For this would mean that soldiers would lose any sense that their own actions are conscience- or honor-based, and conscience and honor only "work" if there is some line that should not be crossed.[18] If soldiers are permitted to treat terrorist combatants, or anyone for that matter, inhumanely, then there is no line that cannot be crossed.[19] The soldiers then will find it difficult to see themselves as anything other than paid killers. And it will be increasingly hard for them to see that what they did as soldiers was something that they could accept after the war is over, as they tell their war stories to their children or even to themselves.

Grotius was well aware of such problems when he wrote during the first half of the 17th century that the law of nature is linked with the

[15] See the various reports of the International Committee for the Red Cross about conditions in Abu Ghraib and Guantanamo prisons, collected in *The Torture Papers*, edited by Karen Greenberg and Joshua L. Dratel, New York: Cambridge University Press, 2005.

[16] See Shannon French, *The Code of the Warrior*, Lanham, MD: Rowman and Littlefield, 2003.

[17] See the excellent collection of papers on the problem of dirty hands, *Cruelty and Deception*, edited by Paul Raynard and David Shugarman, Peterborough, Canada: Broadview Press, 2000.

[18] French has an especially good discussion of this issue in Chapter 9 of her book.

[19] See Larry May, "On Conscience," *American Philosophical Quarterly*, vol. 20, no. 1 (1983).

sense of honor. Honor provides the motivation for the laws of nature, a sense of inner restraint that is crucial for the maintenance of the various duties that are stipulated by natural law.[20] Good people, who are deserving of praise, will restrain themselves beyond what is required by justice, says Grotius.[21] Even in war, good people will not merely look to what is permissible, but also to what will give credit to them. Grotius also suggests that a sense of honor can replace a sense of fear on the battlefield, thus contributing to the success of armies. But the overriding consideration is that a sense of honor leads people to exercise greater restraint than would be required by law or even by considerations of justice.

We can think of the question "How should terrorists be treated?" as a question of how we should act from a sense of honor rather than from a merely legalistic approach. In fact, it seems plausible to think that the current designation of terrorists as illegal combatants is just the kind of legalistic approach that is opposed to the approach focused on honor and conscience. Because the combatants are somehow "illegal," they can be assaulted and otherwise abused with impunity. This is just the kind of view that Grotius rejects when he says "that many things are said to be 'lawful' or 'permissible' for the reason that they can be done with impunity" but which should not be done "on higher grounds."[22] We could recharacterize the dispute about how to treat terrorists as one about whether terrorists should be treated in terms of what is merely permissible or what should be done from honor "on higher grounds."

Seen in this light, terrorists should be treated humanely if we are not merely looking to what is permissible. As I have argued throughout this book, humane treatment is the key consideration in the rules of war, where those rules go beyond what is dictated by (retributive) justice. Of course, one can look at wartime behavior merely through the lens of mere permissibility, but surprisingly this is not how soldiers have looked at their own behavior in war over the centuries. Indeed, some of the first strongly negative reactions to the disclosure of prison abuse in Iraq were from members of the military, who insisted that this was not how good soldiers were supposed to behave.

---

[20] Hugo Grotius, *De Jure Belli Ac Pacis* (*On the Law of War and Peace*) (1625), translated by Francis W. Kelsey, Oxford: Clarendon Press, 1925, pp. 716–717.
[21] Ibid., p. 716.   [22] Ibid.

V.   *TU QUOQUE*

I wish to return to an argument with which we began this book: whether it matters what enemy soldiers are doing in terms of how we should characterize the appropriate normative response on the part of opposing soldiers. There is both a general and a more specific way to understand this point. The general point, discussed in the first three chapters, concerns whether the rules of war, *jus in bello*, change based on the justness of why one engages in war, *jus ad bellum*, in the first place. I argued, in keeping with the dominant treatment of our topics for the last several thousand years, that *jus in bello* considerations were not dependent on *jus ad bellum* considerations.

The specific point is that "the fact that an adversary has also committed similar crimes offers a valid defense to the individuals accused."[23] This defense is often referred to as the *Tu Quoque* Principle. While *tu quoque* is often regarded as a straightforward informal fallacy, because it seems to respond irrelevantly or to shift the argument to the character of the person, it is not clear that it is always a logical mistake when it is used as the basis of a defense. It could be perfectly legitimate to give as your defense for why you hit me on the arm that I had just a moment before hit you on your arm. Given that arm hitting is not itself always wrong, but only when one hits first, it is indeed a legitimate defense to say that one was hit prior to hitting back. But things change if the conduct one is trying to defend is always wrong.

This is the position taken by the ICTY Trial Chamber in the Kupreskic case. The issue arose when the defense counsel "gave a list of Croatian villages from which Croats were allegedly expelled and their houses burnt, supporting the inference that the Croats justified the massacres in Ahmíci in terms of revenge (Trial Transcript 3344–3346)."[24] The Court offered two responses. First, it pointed out that it has never been considered to be a defense to a criminal charge to say that the victim also committed a criminal act. "Indeed, there is in fact no support either in State practice or in the opinions of the publicists for the validity of such a defense."[25] At least since the time of the Nuremberg Trials, in the *High Command* trial, an accused cannot

---

[23] *Prosecutor v. Kupreskic et al.*, International Criminal Tribunal for the Former Yugoslavia, Judgment of the Trial Chamber, Case no. IT-95-16-T, January 14, 2000, para. 515.

[24] Ibid., note 767.   [25] Ibid., para. 516.

exculpate himself from a crime by showing that another has committed a similar crime.[26] The ICTY Trial Chamber said that the reason for this is that international humanitarian law imposes absolute prohibitions.

This brings us to the second response that the ICTY gave to the defense counsel's use of the *tu quoque* argument, which is also the most relevant to our discussion of how terrorists should be treated. I quote from the Court's opinion:

After the First World War, the application of the laws of war moved away from a reliance on reciprocity between belligerents, with the consequence that, in general, rules came to be increasingly applied by each belligerent despite their possible disregard by the enemy. The underpinning of this shift was that it became clear to States that norms of international humanitarian law were not intended to protect State interests; they were primarily designed to benefit individuals *qua* human beings.[27]

The example thought to best exemplify this shift in normative principle is the nearly unanimous agreement that reprisals are legally prohibited.[28]

Reprisals raise serious problems for both the Just War tradition and international humanitarian law. There is some sense to the idea that individuals or States that break the rules with impunity will only stop such practices if they are confronted in kind. The *tu quoque* principle may be defended as a kind of variation of the "turnabout is fair play" principle.[29] If one side to a war ignores the rules of war, it may be that "turnabout" is indeed fair on the part of the other side. The problem is that this argument only works in those cases where there are no independent reasons for thinking that the behavior in question is already prohibited. "Turn about" is not an especially strong moral principle in light of substantive moral considerations, if it is a moral principle at all, for it is procedural not substantive. The *tu quoque* principle merely gives a small moral nod in favor of a practice directed against one party who has already accepted this principle by dint of having engaged in the very same practice. Reprisals, even in-kind reprisals, thus have only very limited moral appeal when confronted by substantive moral principles.

[26] *U.S. v. von Leeb et al.* (the *High Command* trial) (1948), *Law Reports of the Trials of War Criminals*, vol. 12, Boston: William S. Hein Publishers, 1997, p. 64.
[27] Kupreskic case, para. 518.   [28] Ibid., para. 520.
[29] See the discussion of this interesting connection between these two ideas at the following website: http://www.cuyamaca.net/bruce.thompson/Fallacies/tuquoque.asp.

It is in light of this argument that we can now summarize our response to the topic of this chapter – namely, how should terrorists be treated in international humanitarian law? There is a perhaps uncharitable way to see the Bush doctrine regarding terrorists: as a simple form of the *tu quoque* argument.[30] We are justified in the use of otherwise prohibited tactics against terrorists because they have engaged in prohibited behavior toward us. The response to such an argument, sketched out above, takes two parts. First, *tu quoque* arguments are generally not persuasive when used to justify otherwise prohibited behavior. It is no defense to say that the other person also engaged in prohibited behavior. Second, the rules of war are not themselves mainly grounded in reciprocity, although as we saw in the second chapter there is certainly a strong hope of reciprocity nonetheless. There is a different normative grounding as well, as we saw in the third chapter, that is substantive and universal in character, and that provides the grounding for the principle of humanity, as we saw in the fourth chapter. *Tu quoque* arguments fail because they disregard the importance of treating people not as they deserve but on the basis of their status as human beings and as vulnerable in various ways. Terrorists who are imprisoned are no less human and vulnerable than non-terrorists.

Terrorists should be treated humanely for their own sake but also, at least as importantly, for the sake of the soldiers who have to treat them. There is a sense in which the torturer, for instance, is also a victim of the torture. And in a larger sense, those who violate the rules of war lose their sense of honor and are thus victimized as well. My book has tried to make the case for this conclusion. In so doing, I have tried to give expression to a long-standing view, but one that is not always appreciated today, that the principle of humane treatment, not justice, is the cornerstone of how soldiers should behave in war.

VI.   CONCLUSIONS AND THE GROTIAN PROJECT

In this final chapter we have seen that the argument of the book has the implication, perhaps to some a counterintuitive implication, that even terrorists need to be treated humanely. The conscience of humanity demands as much, as does the honor code of soldiers, in so

---

[30] The Bush doctrine fails to note that many of those it incarcerated in Afghanistan and Iraq were not terrorists but lawful combatants in an armed conflict.

far as these have been enshrined in the traditional rules of war of the Just War tradition and by various provisions of international humanitarian law. There is even some evidence that Grotius would have made a similar assessment. In any event, there is ample evidence that this conclusion is consistent with the Grotian project I have sketched. I will end with some discussion of Grotius on pirates, the 17th-century equivalent of terrorists, and then say a few final words about the Grotian project of this book.

Grotius did not discuss terrorism per se, but he did say a bit about piracy, perhaps the closest thing to terrorism in the 17th century. Grotius separated those who are merely wicked from pirates when he remarked: "So great is the distinction between a people, however wicked it may be, and those who not forming a people, associate together for the sake of a crime."[31] Pirates and others who "associate together for the sake of a crime" are on a different plane from those who are merely wicked. Grotius here implied that pirates could be treated worse than those who are merely wicked because they pose a greater threat. Of course, this is in the context of the claims made in his great work that humanitarian considerations are always relevant, especially when we are talking of those who are likely to be retaliated against.

In his earlier writing, Grotius was quite explicit about how one is permitted to treat pirates:

While Caesar (he who afterwards became Dictator) was still a private citizen, he pursued with a hastily raised fleet the pirates by whom he had been captured on an earlier occasion. Some of their boats he put to flight, some he sank; and when the Proconsul neglected to punish the guilty captives, Caesar himself put out to sea again and crucified the culprits, influenced undoubtedly by the knowledge that the judge to whom he had appealed was not fulfilling the functions of the judicial office, as well as by the consideration that it was apparently possible to take such action guiltlessly upon the seas, where one is governed not by written precepts but by the law of nations.[32]

But Grotius went on to say that even though it is no sin for one private person to punish another private person, this is always on the condition that such situations are rare – for instance, in cases of necessity – and in any event, the one punishing the pirates "should observe the scrupulousness of a judge in the act of chastisement."[33]

---

[31] Hugo Grotius, *De Jure Belli ac Pacis*, p. 632.
[32] Hugo Grotius, *De Jure Praedae* (*On the Law of Prize and Booty*) (1605), translated by Gwladys L. Williams, Oxford: Clarendon Press, 1950, p. 95.
[33] Ibid.

Grotius was judicious in his approach to the subject of how to treat pirates, and I have proposed a similar approach to how we should treat terrorists. In both cases, there is a tradition of thinking that these people can be treated without restraint. The idea was that there were no limits to what could be deployed *contra barbarum* ("against the barbarians"). M. Cherif Bassiouni traces this idea back to Roman times and connects it to the idea of humanity, the guiding idea of this book. He says that pirates

were referred to as *hostes humani generis*, the enemies of humanity, a concept which derived from Cicero's writings, reflecting a philosophical perspective of Roman law. Publicists from the 17th to the 19th centuries used the term to refer to perpetrators of international crime. The concept of *hostes humani generis* was a consequence of the Roman law's *jus naturale* and *jus gentium*. . . . The *jus naturale* and the *jus gentium*, as well as the concept of *hostes humani generis*, presupposed the existence of a universal human community and universal values. Obviously, it is different from the contemporary notion of an international community as we have now come to know it, but it evidences the existence of a communal notion that applied to nations and peoples, and it stands for the proposition that those who transgressed certain fundamental universal values would be both enemies of that community and transgressors of the law of nations and peoples, namely, *jus gentium*.[34]

Bassiouni helpfully links the discussion of piracy to our earlier discussions of *jus gentium* and natural law theory, as well as to the principle of humanity. Yet, it seems to me that pirates and terrorists should not be treated as international criminals unless there has been a trial. Before trial, there is every reason to treat them with restraint. Indeed, if they are captured and rendered utterly dependent on us, then they should be treated with the utmost decency.

I wish to make three points about this discussion of the "enemies of humanity" to conclude the book. First, we should note that Bassiouni distinguishes a universal human community from an international community, as we understand it today. The international community today need not be seen as the same as a cosmopolitan world society. Instead, as I indicated at the beginning of this book, we could see it merely as a loose solidarity of people with common interests, as those followers of Grotius in the so-called English School of International Relations have understood it. Indeed, the push for war crimes tribunals

---

[34] M. Cherif Bassiouni, *Introduction to International Criminal Law*, Ardsley, NY: Transnational Publishers, 2003, pp. 109–110.

and for a general strengthening of the rules of war can be defended without supporting a universal human community in a strong sense.

Second, there is a distinction between *jus gentium* and *jus naturale* on the one hand and the principle of humanity on the other hand. I have followed Grotius in thinking that the principles of humanity and humane treatment require more of us than merely conforming to the laws of nature (understood in terms of justice) or of nations. The principle of humane treatment calls for mercy and compassion, regardless of whether the person is a fellow citizen or an enemy soldier. And this principle holds even if, in some way, it could be argued that natural law and the law of nations does not require such restraint. From a Grotian standpoint, we all need to be scrupulous in how we behave toward those whom we are strongly motivated to hate, even when they seem to be the worst type of human being. Even if we sometimes act without restraint, it should only be done in the rarest emergency case if we are to act with honor.

Third, there is no category of people who "fall through the cracks" and to whom we should not act with honor. As I write this at the beginning of 2006, certain political leaders in the United States continue to portray terrorists as not deserving of humane treatment. Those who are our enemies, even those who seem to have no regard for the normative principles I have discussed in this book, are still deserving of certain consideration on our part. There is no category of "barbarians" or "enemies of humanity" that falls outside the restraints imposed by the rules of war. In this limited sense, there is a solidarity among peoples, but this does not necessarily mean that there is a cosmopolitan world order.

The system of principles I have described is best seen as a combination of morality and legality, rather than strictly and exclusively legal. It is for this reason that I, and others, have sought the roots of these principles in what has been called natural law theory. Natural law theorists have traditionally not been as bothered by a porous border between law and morality as have other theorists. Indeed, natural law theorists have championed the view that this is the correct way to understand that border. The codes of honor and chivalry have also been based on a combination of morality and legality, especially as the codes have been connected with natural human feelings of compassion and mercy. Such codes were premised on the idea that legal codes of conduct should reflect the moral virtues. In wartime, the chief virtue that legal codes are to be modeled on is that of humaneness.

Throughout this book, I have argued for a conception of humanitarian law that truly places humaneness at the center of a legal regi-
men. When I discussed crimes against humanity in my previous book, I
also stressed the idea that to understand these crimes we have to take
seriously what it means to harm humanity. Now for war crimes and
humanitarian law, I stress the idea that during wars people must display humaneness if they are not to be subject to prosecution. Humaneness involves a respect for people as fellow humans and a discounting
of what they have done as discrete individual persons. Harming
humanity also has this characteristic of undifferentiated treatment of
the human race as a whole. If there is to be a truly global international
law, it would seem that certain crimes must be of the sort that affects all
of humanity and that certain forms of treatment are seen as especially
well suited for humans interacting with each other as fellow humans
and not as discrete individuals.

Of course, one of the signs of respect for a person is that that person
be treated according to that person's unique characteristics. But
another equally respectful form of treatment is, in some circumstances,
to disregard those differences. The situation of war, as I have been
arguing, is the kind of circumstance that calls for a disregard of what
the individual has done. This is mainly because the circumstances of
war make all of us into different people than we would be otherwise.
Especially in the case of soldiers, these men and women become
trained killers, when in their previous lives such behavior would have
been anathema. In addition, there is the instilled anger and hatred
that cloud our judgment about the actions of others and what is their
due for so acting. In addition, there is the seeming need to respond
right away lest our own safety be jeopardized. All of these factors make
the case for rules of restraint, especially in war, as the best sign of our
humaneness.

When the world is a blur of emotions and violence, the best thing is
to get people to stop and think, to shake them out of their normal ways
of reacting. And one of the best methods is to get people to stop
reacting to each other as unique individuals and instead see each other
as just fellow humans. That is what is involved in getting a child to stop
reacting meanly toward another child with whom he has been feuding
over the loss of a toy. And in a time where grown children similarly
react to one another based on real or perceived insults and harms, we
similarly hope for a stop to the feuding and revenge taking by focusing
on what we all share rather than on what divides us. Humanitarian law

is about just this attempt to reconfigure the way people think, so that it is possible that peace might be restored, and that in the meantime suffering is reduced.

The Grotian project on the subject of war crimes importantly argues for restraints on multiple levels and from multiple normative perspectives. In this book, I have followed the Grotian project in this and many other respects. In a deeply pluralistic world, we need Grotian common sense even more than ever. We need to understand the rules of war as the collective responsibility of States that send their citizens into harm's way, as the embodiment of humanity, and as the chief way for soldiers to retain a sense of honor on the battlefield. We need to deal with the real facts of war and the ideal that humans can aspire to even in the midst of this reality. The conscience of humanity demands as much, but so, too, does common sense in an increasingly dangerous world.

Bibliography

Abrams, Jim. "Democrats Say Rove Should Apologize or Resign," *Washington Post*, June 23, 2005, p. A1.

Advisory Opinion on the Legal Consequences of the Construction of a Wall in the Occupied Palestinian Territory, 43 I.L.M. 1009, International Court of Justice, July 9, 2004.

Advisory Opinion on the Legality of the Threat or Use of Nuclear Weapons, 197 I.L.M. 814, International Court of Justice, July 8, 1996.

Arendt, Hannah. "Auschwitz on Trial" (1966), reprinted in Hannah Arendt, *Responsibility and Judgment*, edited by Jerome Kohn, New York: Schocken Books, 2003, pp. 227–256.

Arendt, Hannah. "Collective Responsibility" (1968), reprinted in Hannah Arendt, *Responsibility and Judgment*, edited by Jerome Kohn, New York: Schocken Books, 2003, pp. 147–158.

Askin, Kelly Dawn. *War Crimes Against Women*, Dordrecht, The Netherlands: Martinus Nijhoff, 1997.

Augustine, *The City of God* (c. 420), Book 19, translated by Henry Bettenson, New York: Penguin Books, 1984.

Averroes (ibn-Rushd), "Jihad" (from Al-Bidaya) (c. 1167), para. 3, in *Jihad in Classical and Modern Islam*, translated and edited by Rudolph Peters, Princeton, NJ: Markus Weiner, 1996, pp. 29–33.

Bassiouni, M. Cherif. *Introduction to International Criminal Law*, Ardsley, NY: Transnational Publishers, 2003.

Beit Sourik v. Israel, Supreme Court of Israel, June 30, 2004, HCJ 2056/04.

Bentham, Jeremy. *Introduction to the Principles of Morals and Legislation* (1789), edited by J. H. Burns and H. L. A. Hart, Oxford: Oxford University Press, 1970.

Bernard, Suzanne M. "An Eye for an Eye: The Current Status of International Law on the Humane Treatment of Prisoners," *Rutgers Law Journal*, vol. 25, Spring (1994), pp. 759–798.

Boyle, Joseph. "Just War Doctrine and the Military Response to Terrorism," *Journal of Political Philosophy*, vol. 11, no. 2 (2003), pp. 153–170.

Brandt, Richard. "Utilitarianism and the Rules of War," *Philosophy and Public Affairs*, vol. 1, no. 2 (1972), pp. 145–164.

Bull, Hedley. *The Anarchical Society: A Study of Order in World Politics*, London: Macmillan, 1977.

Bull, Hedley. "The Importance of Grotius in the Study of International Relations," in *Hugo Grotius and International Relations*, edited by Hedley Bull, Benedict Kingsbury, and Adam Roberts, Oxford: Oxford University Press, 1990.

Card, Claudia. "On Mercy," *Philosophical Review*, vol. 18, no. 2 (1972), pp. 182–207.

Carnahan, Burrus M. "Lincoln, Lieber, and the Laws of War: The Origins and Limits of the Principle of Military Necessity," *American Journal of International Law*, vol. 92, no. 2 (1998), pp. 213–231.

Cassese, Antonio. *International Criminal Law*, Oxford: Oxford University Press, 2003.

Cassese, Antonio. "Terrorism Is Also Disrupting Some Crucial Legal Categories of International Law," *European Journal of International Law*, vol. 12 (2001), pp. 993–1001.

Clausewitz, Carl von. *On War* (*Vom Kriege*) (1832), translated by J. J. Graham, London: Penguin Books, 1968.

Commission on the Responsibility of the Authors of the War and on Enforcement of Penalties, List of War Crimes Presented to the Preliminary Peace Conference, Paris, 29 March 1919.

Convention Against Torture and Other Cruel, Inhuman and Degrading Treatment, 23 ILM 1027 (1984).

Cooper, Belinda, editor, *War Crimes: the Legacy of Nuremberg*, New York: TV Books, 1999.

Corn, Geoffrey S., and Michael L. Smidt, "'To Be or Not to Be, That Is the Question': Contemporary Military Operations and the Status of Captured Personnel," *Army Lawyer*, vol. 1, June (1999), pp. 1–13.

Coupland, Robin. "Humanity: What Is It and How Does It Influence International Law?" *International Review of the Red Cross*, vol. 83, no. 844 (2001), pp. 969–990.

Detter, Ingrid. *The Law of War*, 2nd ed., Cambridge: Cambridge University Press, 2000.

Draper, G. I. A. D. "Grotius' Place in the Development of Legal Ideas About War," in *Hugo Grotius and International Relations*, edited by Hedley Bull, Benedict Kingsbury, and Adam Roberts, Oxford: Oxford University Press, 1990.

Drumbl, Mark A. "Collective Violence and Individual Punishment: The Criminality of Mass Atrocity," *Northwestern University Law Journal*, Winter 2005, pp. 101–179.

Drumbl, Mark A. "ICTY Appeals Chamber Delivers Two Major Judgments: *Blakic* and *Krstic*," *ASIL Insights*, August 18, 2004, pp. 1–3.

Drumbl, Mark A. "Sands: From Nuremberg to The Hague: The Future of International Criminal Justice," *Michigan Law Review*, vol. 103, no. 6 (2005), pp. 1305–1311.

Drumbl, Mark A. "Victimhood in Our Neighborhood," *North Carolina Law Review*, vol. 81 (2002), pp. 1–113.

Finnis, John. *Natural Law and Natural Rights*, Oxford: Clarendon Press, 1980.

Fleck, Dieter. *The Handbook of Humanitarian Law in Armed Conflict*, Oxford: Oxford University Press, 1995.

Fletcher, George P. *Basic Concepts of Criminal Law*, Oxford: Oxford University Press, 1998.

Ford, John C. S. J. "The Morality of Obliteration Bombing," in *War and Morality*, edited by Richard Wasserstrom, Belmont, CA: Wadsworth, 1970, pp. 15–41.

French, Shannon E. *The Code of the Warrior: Exploring Values Past and Present*, Lanham, MD: Rowman and Littlefield, 2003.

Fuller, Lon. *Legal Fictions*, Stanford, CA: Stanford University Press, 1967.

Fullinwider, Robert. "Understanding Terrorism," in *Problems of International Justice*, edited by Stephen Luper-Foy, Boulder, CO: Westview Press, 1988, pp. 248–259; reprinted in *The Morality of War*, edited by Larry May, Eric Rovie, and Steve Viner, Upper Saddle River, NJ: Prentice-Hall, 2006, pp. 306–315.

Geneva Convention III, Relative to the Treatment of Prisoners of War, August 12, 1949, 75 U.N.T.S. 135, 6 U.S.T. 3316, T.I.A.S. No. 3364.

Geneva Convention IV, Relative to the Protection of Civilian Persons in Time of War, August 12, 1949, 75 U.N.T.S. 287, 6 U.T.S. 3516, T.I.A.S. No. 3365.

Gentili, Alberico. *De Jure Belli (On the Law of War)* (1598), translated by John C. Rolfe, Oxford: Clarendon Press, 1933.

Gewirth, Allen. "War Crimes and Human Rights," in *War Crimes and Collective Wrongdoing*, edited by Aleksandar Jokic, Oxford: Blackwell, 2001, pp. 48–56.

Goodin, Robert. *Protecting the Vulnerable*, Cambridge: Cambridge University Press, 1984.

Gray, J. Glenn. *The Warriors: Reflections on Men in Battle*, NY: Harper and Row, 1959, 1970.

Green, Leslie C. *The Contemporary Law of Armed Conflict*, 2nd ed., New York: Juris Publishing, and Manchester University Press, 2000.

Green, Leslie C. "International Regulation of Armed Conflicts," in *International Criminal Law: vol. 1, Crimes*, 2nd ed., edited by M. Cherif Bassiouni, Ardsley, NY: Transnational Publishers, 1999, pp. 355–380.

Greenberg, Karen J., and Joshua L. Dratel, editors, *The Torture Papers: The Road to Abu Ghraib*, New York: Cambridge University Press, 2005.

Gross, Emanuel. "Legal Aspects of Tackling Terrorism: The Balance Between the Right of a Democracy to Defend Itself and the Protection of Human Rights," *UCLA Journal of International Law and Foreign Affairs*, Vol. 6, Spring/Summer 2001, pp. 101–113.

Grotius, Hugo. *De Jure Belli ac Pacis (On the Law of War and Peace)* (1625), translated by Francis W. Kelsey, Oxford: Clarendon Press, 1925, p. 722.

Grotius, Hugo. *De Jure Praedae (On the Law of Prize and Booty)* (1605), translated by Gwladys L. Williams, Oxford: Clarendon Press, 1950, pp. 12, 26.

Haberle, Anne Christine, et al. "Nature of Duty or Relationship," *American Jurisprudence*, 2d, vol. 18A, 2d CORPORATIONS sec. 773.

Habermas, Jurgen. *A Theory of Communicative Action*, vols. 1 and 2, translated by Thomas McCarthy, Boston: Beacon Press, 1987.

Hague Convention (No. IV) Respecting the Laws and Customs of War on Land, Done at the Hague, Oct. 18, 1907, 36 Stat. 2277, T.S. No. 539, 1 Bevans 631.

Hart, H. L. A. "Negligence, *Mens Rea*, and Criminal Responsibility," reprinted in H. L. A. Hart, *Punishment and Responsibility*, Oxford: Oxford University Press, 1968.

Henckaerts, Jean-Marie, and Louise Doswald-Beck, *Customary International Humanitarian Law, vol. I: Rules*, ICRC, Cambridge University Press, 2005, pp. 482–488.

Hobbes, Thomas. *Leviathan* (1651), edited by *The English Works of Thomas Hobbes*, London: John Bohn; 2nd reprint, Scientia Verlag Aalen, 1966.

Holmes, Robert. *On War and Morality*, Princeton, NJ: Princeton University Press, 1989.

Hume, David. *An Enquiry Concerning the Principles of Morals* (1751), sec. V, part II, para. 24, reprinted in *Hume's Ethical Writings*, edited by Alasdair MacIntyre, Notre Dame, IN: University of Notre Dame Press, 1965.

Hurka, Thomas. "Proportionality in the Morality of War," *Philosophy and Public Affairs*, vol. 33, no. 1 (2005), pp. 34–66.

Hutcheson, Ron. "Bush Uses Sept. 11 to Rally U.S. for War," *St. Louis Post-Dispatch*, June 29, 2005, p. A1.

Hylton v. Hylton (1754), 28 Eng. Rep. 349, 2 Ves Sen 547, at 549.

ICRC Commentary on Geneva Convention IV, published under the general editorship of Jean S. Pictet, Geneva: International Committee for the Red Cross, 1958.

Ignatieff, Michael. *The Lesser Evil: Political Ethics in an Age of Terror*, Princeton, NJ: Princeton University Press, 2004.

Ignatieff, Michael. *The Warrior's Honor: Ethnic War and the Modern Conscience*, New York: Henry Holt, 1997.

Imseis, Ardi. "Critical Reflections on the International Humanitarian Law Aspects of the ICJ Wall Advisory Opinion," *American Journal of International Law*, Vol. 99, no. 1 (2005), pp. 102–118.

International Covenant on Civil and Political Rights, 999 U.N.T.S. 171 (Dec. 9, 1966), Article 7.

Janis, Mark. *An Introduction to International Law*, New York: Aspen Law, 1993.

Kellman, Barry. Book Review and Note on *The Chemical Weapons Taboo*, *American Journal of International Law*, vol. 92, no. 1 (1998), pp. 160–162.

Kingsbury, Benedict. "People and Boundaries: An 'Internationalized Public Law' Approach," in *States, Nations, and Borders*, edited by Allen Buchanan and Margaret Moore, Cambridge: Cambridge University Press, 2003, pp. 298–315.

Kremnitzer, Mordechai, and Re'em Segev. "The Legality of Interrogational Torture: A Question of Proper Authorization or a Substantive Moral Issue," *Israel Law Review*, vol. 34, Fall (2000), pp. 509–559.

Kutz, Christopher. "The Difference Uniforms Make: Collective Violence in Criminal Law and War," *Philosophy and Public Affairs*, vol. 33, no. 2 (2005), pp. 148–180.

Lackey, Douglas P. *The Ethics of War and Peace*, Upper Saddle River, NJ: Prentice-Hall, 1989.

LaFave, Wayne R., and Austin W. Scott, Jr., *Criminal Law*, 2nd ed., St. Paul, MN: West Publishing, 1986.

Landau Commission Report, Report of the Commission of Inquiry in the Matter of Investigation Methods of the General Security Service Regarding Hostile Territory Activity, Israel, 1987.

Lauterpacht, Hersch, "The Grotian Tradition in International Law," *British Year Book on International Law*, vol. 23 (1946), pp. 1–53.

Leiser, Burton M. *Liberty, Justice, and Morals*, 2nd ed., New York: Prentice-Hall, 1979, pp. 375–397.

Lewis, Neil A., and Eric Schmitt, "Lawyers Decide Bans on Torture Didn't Bind Bush," *New York Times*, June 8, 2004, pp. A1 A10.

Lieber Code, Instructions for the Government of Armies of the United States in the Field, General Orders No. 100 (1863), Article 11.

Lippman, Matthew. "Conundrums of Armed Conflict: Criminal Defenses to Violations of the Humanitarian Law of War," *Dickinson Journal of International Law*, Vol. 15, Fall (1996), pp. 59–71.

Luban, David. "A Theory of Crimes Against Humanity," *Yale Journal of International Law*, Vol. 29, no. 1 (2004), pp. 85–140.

Luban, David. "The War on Terrorism and the End of Human Rights," in *War After September 11*, edited by Verna V. Gehring, Lanham, MD: Rowman and Littlefield, 2003, reprinted in *The Morality of War*, edited by Larry May, Eric Rovie, and Steve Viner, Upper Saddle River, NJ: Prentice-Hall, 2006, pp. 413–421.

May, Larry. *Crimes Against Humanity: A Normative Account*, New York: Cambridge University Press, 2005.

May, Larry. "Grotius and Contingent Pacifism," *Studies in the History of Ethics*, February 2006, pp. 1–22.

May, Larry. *Masculinity and Morality*, Ithaca, NY: Cornell University Press, 1998.

May, Larry. *The Morality of Groups*, Notre Dame, IN: University of Notre Dame Press, 1987.

May, Larry. "On Conscience," *American Philosophical Quarterly*, vol. 20, no. 1, 1983, pp. 57–67.

May, Larry. "Professional Action and Liability of Professional Associations: ASME v. Hydrolevel," *Business and Professional Ethics Journal*, vol. 2, no. 1 (1982), pp. 1–14.

May, Larry. *Sharing Responsibility*, Chicago: University of Chicago Press, 1992.

McMahan, Jeff. "The Ethics of Killing in Self-Defense," *Ethics*, vol. 114, no. 4 (2004), pp. 693–733.

McMahan, Jeff. "Realism, Morality, and War," in *The Ethics of War and Peace*, edited by Terry Nardin, Princeton: Princeton University Press, 1996, pp. 88–91.

McMahan, Jeff. "Response to David Rodin's *War and Self-Defense*," *Ethics and International Affairs*, 2004, pp. 75–80.

McMahan, Jeff, and Robert McKim, "The Just War and the Gulf War," *Canadian Journal of Philosophy*, vol. 23, 1993, pp. 501–541.

Meron, Theodor. "The Humanization of Humanitarian Law," *American Journal of International Law*, vol. 94, April 2000, pp. 239–278.

Mill, John Stuart. *On Liberty* (1863), edited by Stefan Colini, Cambridge: Cambridge University Press, 1989.

Model Penal Code, sec. 302, and Comment (1985).

Murphy, Jeffrey. "The Killing of the Innocent," in *War, Morality, and the Military Profession*, edited by Malham Wakin, Boulder, CO: Westview Press, 1979.

Murphy, Mark. *Natural Law and Practical Rationality*, Cambridge: Cambridge University Press, 2001.

Osiel, Mark. "Shared Responsibility for Mass Atrocity: Aligning the Incentives," unpublished manuscript.

Plessy v. Ferguson, 163 U.S. 537 (1896).

Pranger, Carol, editor. *Dilemmas of Reconciliation*, Kingston, Canada: Queens University Press, 2001.

Price, Richard M. *The Chemical Weapons Taboo*, Ithaca, NY: Cornell University Press, 1997.

"The Princeton Principles on Universal Jurisdiction," edited by Stephen Macedo, Princeton, NJ: Program in Law and Public Affairs, 2001.

Prosecutor v. Anto Furundzja, International Criminal Tribunal for Yugoslavia, Trial Chamber Judgment, Case No. IT–95–17/1–T, December 10, 1998.

Prosecutor v. Drazen Erdemovic, International Criminal Tribunal for Yugoslavia, Appeals Chamber Joint Separate Opinion of Judge McDonald and Judge Vohrah, Case No. IT–96–22–A, October 7, 1997.

Prosecutor v. Drazen Erdemovic, International Criminal Tribunal for Yugoslavia, Appeals Chamber Separate and Dissenting Opinion of Judge Cassese, Case No. IT–96–22–A, October 7, 1997.

Prosecutor v. Drazen Erdemovic, International Criminal Tribunal for Yugoslavia, Judgment of the Appeals Chamber, Case No. IT–96–22–A, October 7, 1997

Prosecutor v. Drazen Erdemovic, International Criminal Tribunal for Yugoslavia, Sentencing Judgment of the Trial Chamber, Case No. IT–96–22–T, March 5, 1998.

Prosecutor v. Dusko Tadic, International Criminal Tribunal for Yugoslavia, Judgment of the Appeals Chamber, Case No. IT–94–1–A October 2, 1995.

Prosecutor v. Dusko Tadic, International Criminal Tribunal for Yugoslavia, Judgment of the Trial Chamber, Case No. IT–94–1–T, May 7, 1997.

Prosecutor v. Miroslav Kvocka, et al., International Criminal Tribunal for Yugoslavia, Judgment of the Trial Chamber, Case No. IT–98–30/1–T, November 2, 2001.

Prosecutor v. Miroslav Kvocka, et al., International Criminal Tribunal for Yugoslavia, Sentence of the Trial Chamber, Case No. IT–98–30/1T, November 2, 2001.

Prosecutor v. Mladen Naletilic and Vinko Martinovic, International Criminal Tribunal for Yugoslavia, Judgment of the Trial Chamber, Case No. IT–98–34–T, March 31, 2003.

Prosecutor v. Radislav Krstic, International Criminal Tribunal for Yugoslavia, Trial Chamber Judgment, Case No. IT–98–33–T, August 2, 2001.

Prosecutor v. Tihomir Blaskic, International Criminal Tribunal for Yugoslavia, Judgment of the Appeals Chamber, Case No. IT–95–14–A, July 29, 2004.

Prosecutor v. Tihomir Blaskic, International Criminal Tribunal for Yugoslavia, Judgment of the Trial Chamber of the ICTY, Case No. 95–14–T, March 3, 2000.

Prosecutor v. Zoran Kurpeskic, et al., International Criminal Tribunal for the Former Yugoslavia, Trial Chamber Judgment, Case No. IT–95–16–T, January 14, 2000.

Prosecutor's Report on the NATO Bombing Campaign, The Hague, June 13, 2000.

Protocol Additional to the Geneva Conventions of 12 August 1949, and Relating to the Protection of Victims of Non-International Armed Conflict (Protocol II), 8 June 1977, Article 13.

Public Committee Against Torture in Israel and Others v. Israel and Others (HC 5100/94, 4054/95, 6536/95, 5188/96, 7563/97, 7628/97, and 1043/99), Supreme Court of Israel, 7 BHRC 31, 6 September 1999.

Pufendorf, Samuel, *De Jure Naturae et Gentium* (*On the Law of Nature and Nations*) (1688), translated by C. H. Oldfather and W. A. Oldfather, Oxford: Clarendon Press, 1934.

Raynard, Paul, and David Shugarman, editors. *Cruelty and Deception*, Peterborough, Canada: Broadview Press, 2000.

Restatement of Trusts (3d), sec. 2.

Reydams, Luc. *Universal Jurisdiction*, Oxford: Oxford University Press, 2003.

Roberts, Adam, and Richard Guelff, editors, *Documents on the Laws of War*, 3rd ed., Oxford: Oxford University Press, 2000, p. 563.

Rodin, David. *War and Self-Defense*, Oxford: Oxford University Press, 2002.

Rotberg, Robert I., and Dennis Thompson, editors. *Truth v. Justice*, Princeton: Princeton University Press, 2000.

Schabas, William A. "Commentary" in *Annotated Leading Cases of International Criminal Tribunals*, vol. 3, edited by Andre Klip and Goran Sluiter, Antwerp: Intersentia, 2001.

Schabas, William A. "Mens Rea and the International Criminal Tribunal for the Former Yugoslavia," *New England Law Review*, vol. 37, Summer (2003), pp. 1015–1036.

Schneewind, J. B. *The Invention of Autonomy*, Cambridge: Cambridge University Press, 1998.

Seneca, "On Mercy," in *Seneca: Moral and Political Essays*, edited by John M. Cooper and J. F Procope, Cambridge: Cambridge University Press, 1995, pp. 128–164.

Shattuck, John. Interview with the Center for American Progress about American Exceptionalism, http://www.americanprogress.org/site/pp.asp?c=bijRJ8OVF&b=130841.

Sherman, Nancy. *Stoic Warriors*, Oxford: Oxford University Press, 2006.

Shue, Henry. "Torture," *Philosophy and Public Affairs*, vol. 7, no. 2, (1978), pp. 124–143.

Singer, Peter W. *Corporate Warriors: The Rise of the Privatized Military Industry*, Ithaca, NY: Cornell University Press, 2003.

Sliman, Nidal. "Israeli High Court Decision on Location of West Bank Barrier," *ASIL-Insights*, July 6, 2004, pp. 1–2.

Smith, Holly. "Culpable Ignorance," *Philosophical Review*, vol. 92, October (1983), pp. 543–571.

Statute of the International Court of Justice, T.S. No. 993, 59 Stat. 1055, June 26, 1945.

Statute of the International Criminal Court, Adopted by the U.N. Diplomatic Conference, July 17, 1998.

Statute of the International Criminal Tribunal for the Former Yugoslavia, U.N. S.C. Res. 827 May 3, 1993.

Statute of the Special Court for Sierra Leone, U.N. Doc. S/RES/1315, 2000.

St. Louis Post-Dispatch, May 7, 2004, p. B8.

Suarez, Francisco. "On War," in *Selections from Three Works*, (Disputation XIII, *De Triplici Virtute Theologica: Charitate*) (c. 1610), translated by Gwladys L. Williams, Ammi Brown, and John Waldron, Oxford: Clarendon Press, 1944.

Truman, Harry S, Address to the Nation, August 9, 1945, quoted in R. Tucker, *The Just War*, 1960, pp. 21–22.

Truscott, Lucian K., IV. "Not-So-Long Gray Line," *New York Times*, June 28, 2005, p. A23.

Tuck, Richard. *Natural Rights Theory: Their Origin and Development*, Cambridge: Cambridge University Press, 1979.

Tuck, Richard. *The Rights of War and Peace: Political Thought and the International Order from Grotius to Kant*, Oxford: Oxford University Press, 1999.

U.S. Department of the Air Force, "*International Law – The Conduct of Armed Conflict and Air Operations*," AF Pamphlet 110–31, 1976, p. 6–5.

U.S. v. Wilhelm Von Leeb and Thirteen Others (the German High Command Trial), United States Military Tribunal, Nuremberg, December 30, 1947 – October 28, 1948, quoted in United Nations War Crimes Commission, *Law Reports of Trials of War Criminals*, vol. 12, London: His Majesty's Stationery Office, 1949; reprinted, Buffalo, NY: William S. Hein, 1997.

Valls, Andrew. "Can Terrorism Be Justified?" in *Ethics and International Affairs*, edited by Andrew Valls, Lanham, MD: Rowman and Littlefield, 2000, pp. 65–79; reprinted in *The Morality of War*, edited by Larry May, Eric Rovie, and Steve Viner, Upper Saddle River, NJ: Prentice-Hall, 2006, pp. 316–327.

Villa-Vicencio, Charles, and Wilhelm Verwoerd, editors. *Looking Backward, Reaching Forward: Reflections on the Truth and Reconciliation Commission in South Africa*, Cape Town: University of Cape Town Press, 2000.

Walzer, Michael. *Arguing About War*, New Haven, CT: Yale University Press, 2004.

Walzer, Michael. *Just and Unjust Wars*, New York: Basic Books, 1977, 2000.

Walzer, Michael. "Terrorism: A Critique of Excuses," in *Problems of International Justice*, edited by Stephen Luper-Foy, Boulder, CO: Westview Press, 1988, pp. 237–247; reprinted in *The Morality of War*, edited by Larry May, Eric Rovie, and Steve Viner, Upper Saddle River, NJ: Prentice-Hall, 2006, pp. 297–305.

Watkin, Kenneth. "Controlling the Use of Force: A Role for Human Rights Norms in Contemporary Armed Conflict," *American Journal if International Law*, vol. 98, no. 1 (2004), pp. 1–34.

Wheaton, Henry. *Elements of International Law* (1836), Oxford: Clarendon Press, 1936.

Wight, Martin. *Four Seminal Thinkers in International Theory*, Oxford: Oxford University Press, 2005.

Williams, Bernard. "Making Sense of Humanity," in *Making Sense of Humanity and Other Philosophical Papers*, Cambridge: Cambridge University Press, 1995.

Zohar, Noam. "Collective War and Individualistic Ethics: Against the Conscription of Self-Defense," *Political Theory*, vol. 21, no. 4 (1993), pp. 606–622.

Index